Understanding the Social and Emotional Lives of Gifted Students

Understanding the Social and Emotional Lives of Gifted Students

Thomas P. Hébert, Ph.D.

PRUFROCK PRESS INC.
WACO, TEXAS

To my mother, Madeleine M. Hébert, whose memory
guides me each and every day.

Library of Congress Cataloging-in-Publication Data

Hébert, Thomas Paul.
 Understanding the social and emotional lives of gifted students / Thomas P. Hébert.
    p. cm.
 Includes bibliographical references and index.
 ISBN 978-1-59363-502-2
 1. Gifted children--Psychology--United States. 2. Gifted children--Education--United States. I. Title.
 BF723.G5H43 2011
 305.9'089--dc22
                          2010036453

Edited by Jennifer Robins

Cover and Layout Design by Marjorie Parker

ISBN-13: 978-1-59363-502-2

Printed in the United States of America.

At the time of this book's publication, all facts and figures cited are the most current available. All telephone numbers, addresses, and website URLs are accurate and active. All publications, organizations, websites, and other resources exist as described in the book, and all have been verified. The author and Prufrock Press Inc. make no warranty or guarantee concerning the information and materials given out by organizations or content found at websites, and we are not responsible for any changes that occur after this book's publication. If you find an error, please contact Prufrock Press Inc.

 Prufrock Press Inc.
P.O. Box 8813
Waco, TX 76714-8813
Phone: (800) 998-2208
Fax: (800) 240-0333
http://www.prufrock.com

Contents

Acknowledgements

I would like to thank the reviewers of this text: Kathy Hargrove, Maureen Neihart, and Jean Peterson. Their thoughtful and thorough critiques helped to strengthen this book. I appreciate their significant contributions.

I would like to thank Joel McIntosh and his dedicated staff at Prufrock Press. I especially want to thank Jennifer Robins at Prufrock Press who traveled with me on this journey and kept me laughing throughout the adventure. Her gracious support of my work is most appreciated.

I also want to thank my dear friend Sue Whitlock for her many phone calls to encourage me throughout my writing process.

I am most indebted to my former students who taught me to honor their social and emotional lives.

Introduction

My journey began on a Greyhound bus. My parents waved to me from the bus station in Auburn, ME, as I reached for a thick paperback for the long trip ahead. It was 1977. I had graduated from the University of Southern Maine with a degree in history and secondary education, and I was excited about beginning my professional career. The bus trip lasted 3 days and culminated 1,600 miles later in Douglas, GA, where I was scheduled to interview for a teaching position in the Coffee County Schools. Following a day of meetings with administrators and faculty members at Coffee High School, and enough time to experience sufficient culture shock, I was ready to sign my first teaching contract.

The thought of living in an area of the country that was so different from New England excited me. I saw this opportunity as an adventure. Coffee County, with its tobacco fields, red dirt clay roads, majestic pine trees, and friendly people, was an exotic place to a naïve young man from Maine. I secured the teaching position and returned home to a summer of waiting tables on the Maine coast. With my hard-earned money, I made a down payment on my first car, a trusty Datsun B210, complete with what I would require most: air conditioning!

In early August, I packed my compact car with all of my worldly possessions. As I drove away from 45 Loring Avenue, my parents stood at the end of the driveway and again waved goodbye to their oldest son, this time with tears in their eyes. The driver of that sporty Datsun was also tearful, but determined to make his parents proud. As the first college graduate in my family, I was looking forward to a rewarding career as an educator. I was passionate about teaching history, determined to inspire teenagers, and pleased that my career would begin in Coffee County.

During my first year of teaching at Coffee High School, I met a number of young people who would influence me in significant ways. In my third period Advanced Placement U.S. History class, as I carried on passionately about the administration of Grover Cleveland, a young woman named Meg sat in the first desk of the front row taking copious lecture notes. It was obvious to me that she was as enthusiastic about Grover Cleveland as I was. Meg could not get enough of the knowledge I had to offer that year in U.S. History. She was a conscientious student who had faculty members talking about her in the teachers' lounge every day. "If only they could all be like Meg. Wouldn't life be wonderful?" For the next 2 years, Meg enrolled in other history electives I taught, and I continued to enjoy her enthusiasm and diligence.

On the evening of her high school graduation, Meg handed me a beautifully written note thanking me for having been an inspirational teacher. I appreciated her thoughtful gesture but I was also stunned as I read the note. She highlighted in the message that although she would always remember my passion for my subject, she actually was more grateful for my having been a good listener. She thanked me for spending time with her after school during a difficult period in her senior year when she struggled with her parents' impending divorce. She recalled that I had listened sympathetically and had been patient with her when she submitted several late assignments. For that she would always remember me as a "teacher who really cared."

Meg went on to earn degrees from Harvard, the London School of Economics, and Stanford Law School. Today she practices law in California. I am proud of her accomplishments, and I am grateful to have met Meg early in my career because she taught me such an important lesson. The thank-you letter delivered on that graduation evening both touched and enlightened me. I learned that everything I had done to make history come alive in my classroom may have been important; however, for Meg, my willingness to be authentic and respectful of her as an intelligent young woman with a life beyond my classroom had been far more significant. The important message Meg conveyed has remained with me.

Seated next to Meg in U.S. History was a young man named Beau. The quintessential handsome football player, Beau had a bevy of young women who followed every move he made and suffered serious angst each time he did not look in their direction. For some reason unknown to me, Beau was not quite as passionate about the administration of Grover Cleveland as Meg and I were. Although Beau had been identified as a gifted student in second grade, he was failing my course and his parents were distraught. My university training had not prepared me to understand a student like Beau; the term *gifted underachiever* was not part of my vocabulary at that time. I struggled to figure out what might have been going on in Beau's life that would cause him to put forth only minimal effort in my class.

Although I never succeeded in reaching Beau, another teacher at Coffee High School did. The theatre teacher managed to recruit him into the drama club, and there Beau discovered his passion. Beau eventually managed to pass my history class and graduated from Coffee High. From there he went on to earn a degree in theatre from Valdosta State University. Years later Beau found success in Hollywood, and I joined his family and friends in celebration when he appeared in the popular movie *Driving Miss Daisy*. Today Beau lives in the Atlanta area and continues his involvement in theatre, and I was not surprised to learn that he had handsome children. Although I was not successful in reaching Beau as a student, I often reflected on him as I struggled to understand what might have influenced his lackluster academic performance.

A third student had a major impact on me as a beginning teacher. As I looked out at the students in my Advanced Placement history class each day, I could only wonder what Tremayne was thinking. Tremayne was the only African American student in the class, and I often wondered how he must be feeling as the only culturally diverse student in that setting. Tremayne had a logical and mathematical mind. His penmanship looked like calligraphy, and his artwork won awards. Tremayne led the Coffee High football team to a championship season and was elected student body president. Tremayne was a student with true multipotentiality.

Upon graduation from high school, he pursued an engineering degree from the Georgia Institute of Technology. Today he is an engineer living in Atlanta. As a beginning teacher in 1977, I questioned why there were so few African American students in advanced classes at Coffee High School, and how we had failed to identify and nurture talent in culturally diverse young people. As pleased as I was to have such an outstanding young man in my classroom, I realized that Tremayne needed more from me than simply a passion for studying history. Yet, as a novice teacher, I did not believe I had the skills to support Tremayne emotionally, and I felt frustrated with my inability to do enough for Tremayne and other students like him.

Other gifted students from Coffee High School also stand out in my memories of my first 3 years of teaching. Duncan, another football player, had parents whose high expectations led them to take away the keys to his red Mustang when he earned a B in my course. I remember the wonderful, surprised smile on Valerie's face when she spotted me in the audience the evening she was crowned Miss Black Coffee County. I have often reflected on Drake, a chubby young man in the high school band, who struggled with low self-esteem, yearned to be an athlete, and eventually became a successful university professor.

These young people at Coffee High School taught their teacher more than they realized. Working with them convinced me that I needed to know more about teaching gifted students. After 3 years of teaching in the small rural community in southeast Georgia, I phoned the Georgia Department of Education in Atlanta and spoke with the gifted education consultant. I asked for recommendations for degree programs throughout the country where I might pursue training in gifted education. After I explored the recommendations and read the work of the leaders in the field at that time, I realized that I philosophically agreed with Dr. Joseph Renzulli's broadened conception of giftedness and decided to apply for admission to the University of Connecticut's master's degree program in gifted education. Upon my acceptance to the program, I said goodbye to my friends, students, and colleagues at Coffee High School and returned to New England.

After completing my master's degree, I taught elementary gifted students in an enrichment program in Torrington, CT. The transition from teaching in a secondary classroom to facilitating a K–6 resource room program for gifted students was an enjoyable challenge. Not only were my teaching responsibilities much different, but the concerns of my students had also changed. I remember having to counsel a tearful third grader named Becca when her best friend had called her "buffalo butt" in her new Calvin Klein jeans. As the enrichment teacher, I supported an aspiring fourth-grade inventor as he designed his "Lawn Mower Shoes" and met the challenge of convincing his skeptical peers that his idea would yield lucrative profits. I also came to understand a highly gifted second grader who was fascinated with the life and work of Tchaikovsky and other famous composers, and I worked hard to help him fit in socially with his peers. I grew to appreciate a sensitive 10-year-old girl named Molly. I had organized a trip to visit a beekeeper's farm as part of her research project in the enrichment program. On the way home, Molly's quivering voice begged me to stop the car. She could not bear to keep her newly acquired bees trapped in her jelly jar, so as my car came to a screeching halt, she threw open the door and released her bees.

From Torrington, CT, I moved on to work with gifted high school students who participated in enrichment programming on the campus of Southeastern Massachusetts University. I then spent 3 years as a teacher of the gifted, K–12, in the Department of Defense Dependents' Schools. I had the good fortune to work with children of the military families stationed in Bad Kreuznach, Germany, where I came to deeply appreciate and respect these young people whose transient way of life presented them with many challenges that other children in the U.S. did not encounter. I listened to them yearning for the American shopping malls and video arcades they missed back home. I will always remember the seventh and eighth graders who educated me about the emotional roller-coaster ride of the middle school years. As the itinerant teacher who arrived at the high school to meet them in time for periods 6 and 7 of the school day, I found that occasionally I needed to set aside the curriculum and listen closely to why the earlier part of their day had them feeling emotionally exhausted. As I taught these young people and we traveled the European continent on field trips together, I learned to appreciate the sacrifices they made as their parents served their country and fulfilled their military obligations.

As an educator, I have been blessed with opportunities to teach a variety of student populations, and wherever I am I have always continued to listen. Meg taught me how important it was to try to understand what was happening in young people's lives beyond my classroom. The more I worked with highly intelligent students, the more I realized I was drawn to understanding the social and emotional components of their giftedness. I had gone from being passionate about U.S. history to being passionate about nurturing my students' talents and supporting their psychosocial development. After I left Europe and returned to Connecticut to pursue my doctoral degree, I continued to raise some of the concerns I had as a teacher at Coffee High School. As I reflected on my experiences in public school classrooms, I sought to better understand how the social and emotional development of my students interacted with their cognitive development. More specifically, I wanted to explore how educators could support students' social and emotional development.

In my doctoral studies, I acquired another passion. I discovered that I enjoyed qualitative research, and through my training in qualitative research methods, I was reminded yet again of the importance of listening. In my dissertation research in an urban high school, I had the privilege of listening to 12 gifted young men who shared their life stories with me. Since then, my research agenda in gifted education has been guided by qualitative inquiry. I have spent many hours interviewing and observing gifted young people, seeking to interpret their life stories to better understand their social and emotional development. Through my years of teaching, advanced degree work in gifted education, and training in qualitative research, I have come to understand that comprehending the complexity of students' social and emotional development requires listening closely to what they have to say about growing up gifted. In seeking to grasp the intricacies of gifted students' development, we must come to appreciate and respect their life experiences as gifted young individuals.

I have written this book to honor the social and emotional lives of gifted young people. My intent is to examine theory, research, and practice on gifted youth. Through this book, I hope to illuminate the complexity of gifted students' life experiences in order to assist young scholars as well as educators and counselors of gifted youth. In order to do so, I lay the foundation for the book in Chapter 1 by discussing theories of psychological development. This is followed by a discussion in Chapters 2 and 3 of the social and emotional traits and characteristics of gifted students that educators and counselors must understand and value in order to help these students develop into psychologically healthy adults.

In Chapter 4, I explore environmental influences on the social and emotional development of gifted individuals. Chapter 5 examines the process of identity development in gifted students. Chapter 6 considers the role of family and peer relationships in the lives of gifted children and adolescents. I shift gears a bit in Chapter 7 by paying special attention to underachievement in gifted students and trying to offer some understanding of this complex phenomenon. Chapter 8 examines affective issues that shape the life experiences of gifted students with learning disabilities and attention deficits. In Chapter 9, I discuss social and emotional issues in the lives of culturally diverse gifted students. In the final chapter, I offer a plan for designing psychologically safe classroom environments that foster the social and emotional development of gifted students.

As an educator and researcher, I have listened as many gifted young people have invited me into their lives and have trusted me with their stories. I respectfully share their messages by infusing their voices throughout this book. To support what they have offered, I provide discussion of theory and research. I also incorporate vignettes and quotations from biographies of significant individuals in American society to highlight the importance of the areas addressed. I conclude each chapter by providing a variety of strategies and methods for addressing pertinent issues to help educators and counselors enhance the social and emotional development of their students. To support these efforts, I include several collections of resources in Appendixes A–D, and prompts for further thought and discussion in each chapter. My hope is that scholars and practitioners will consider the questions I raise and reflect further on how to translate theory and research into practice.

Although my bus ride ended years ago, my journey continues. I will continue asking questions of gifted young people. I will continue to listen as I strive to understand, appreciate, and honor their social and emotional lives. I invite my readers to join me on this fascinating journey.

CHAPTER 1

Theories of Psychological Development Guiding Our Understanding of Gifted Students

My goals for this chapter are to:

- Introduce you to theories that guide our understanding of the social and emotional development of gifted individuals.
- Provide you an opportunity to reflect on what each theory explains or does not explain.
- Have you reflect on how the theories may support each other in guiding our understanding of the social and emotional lives of gifted students.
- Serve as a theoretical foundation for chapters that follow.

He who loves practice without theory is like the sailor who boards ship without a rudder and compass and never knows where he may cast.

—Leonardo da Vinci

With the sagacious words of Leonardo da Vinci in mind, I believe it is meaningful to begin this journey with a discussion of theoretical frameworks that may enlighten us. To establish the foundation for much of the discussion of the psychosocial development of gifted students, I have chosen to focus on several theories that can help guide our understanding of their social and emotional lives and also guide decision making regarding what is best for gifted students. An understanding of theory may support teachers and counselors in their efforts to identify students who have high levels of social and emotional intelligence and may need special programming to develop skills in the social and emotional domains or prepare for careers that may require strong social and emotional competence. Theories of social and emotional intelligence or intrapersonal problem solving provide appropriate frameworks for designing educational programs for gifted students. Moreover, an understanding of such theory may support educators in helping gifted students who lack social and emotional intelligence to develop the ability it takes to build strong friendships and work effectively with others as they improve their academic abilities (Moon, 2009).

In addition to the theories presented in this chapter, additional relevant theories are presented in later chapters. My objective for this first chapter is to highlight several overarching theories that are helpful in understanding and appreciating the social and emotional lives of gifted students. I examine the work of Kazimierz Dabrowski on emotional development and consider how it informs our understanding of the social and emotional components of giftedness. Dabrowski's theory of personal development has received considerable attention in the gifted education literature because it captures multiple aspects of the experience of giftedness (Moon, 2009). I continue with a discussion of Howard Gardner's theory of personal intelligences. I explore the contemporary theory of emotional intelligence as proposed by John Mayer and Peter Salovey and popularized by Daniel Goleman to shed further understanding. I examine Robert Sternberg's theory of wisdom as a form of giftedness and conclude with the recent work of Joseph Renzulli examining his Houndstooth theory to explain the development of social capital.

Theories that guide a field of knowledge undergo a series of stages through which they emerge, grow, and transform our thinking and practice. Robert Sternberg (1990) has characterized these stages as initial, early developmental, mature, and postmature:

- ❧ In the *initial* stage people become interested in a phenomenon and begin to study it.
- ❧ In the *early developmental* stage, theorists and researchers present paradigms in their attempt to convince others of the worth of their ideas.
- ❧ The *mature* stage evolves when one or more of the paradigms become prominent while others "wither on the vine."
- ❧ The *postmature* stage emerges when researchers become frustrated with inconsistencies with research findings and a paradigm's inability to answer the questions they raised. (p. ix)

Sternberg (1990) maintained that during the final stage, individuals search for new paradigms. If successful, they reenter the initial stage, which merges indiscernibly with the last stage. If unsuccessful in creating another paradigm, a field risks becoming dormant until other researchers and theorists propose new ideas that may guide our thinking and practice.

The theories I chose to include in this book represent paradigms at various stages of development. Some are more mature than others. They may or may not explain all we want to know about gifted individuals. What one mature theory provides may support or reinforce another in the early developmental stages. My hope is that readers consider the strengths of each theory as well as what each theory does not explain. I also want readers to reflect on how the various theories support each other in helping us make sense of the affective development of gifted students.

To support my readers, I will raise a few questions here to keep in mind as they review the theories presented. Do the personal intelligences described by Gardner reflect similar characteristics represented in Dabrowski's view of overexcitabilities in gifted individuals? Does our understanding of the heightened sensitivities seen in Dabrowski's theory help us to understand emotional intelligence proposed by Mayer and Salovey? If gifted young people are advanced in the development of emotional regulation, is that growth consistent with strong intrapersonal and interpersonal intelligence? Does a child with strong personal intelligence have the natural capacity to develop wisdom proposed by Sternberg? Will that child naturally engage in lessons in wisdom? Will the emotional sensitivities and personal intelligences lead gifted students to become naturally involved in the development of social capital proposed by Renzulli? I ask my readers to reflect on these questions. I chose theories that represent what I believe are critical

Questions that set the purpose.

ideas that are important to understanding social and emotional development in gifted young people. My hope is that readers will also raise questions of each of the paradigms presented in this chapter.

Following the discussion of each of these theories, I pose several questions as I ask my readers to consider how an understanding of them may assist us in appreciating the social and emotional lives of gifted children, and prepare us for our practice of teaching and counseling gifted young people.

Dabrowski's Theory of Emotional Development

Kazimierz Dabrowski (1902–1980), a Polish psychiatrist and psychologist, survived two world wars. As a teenager during World War I, he observed acts of self-sacrifice during a period of horrendous atrocities. He struggled to understand how individuals who were selfless could coexist in the same world as those who were responsible for the incomprehensible inhumanity of that time in history. As a young man, he was "repelled by the cruelty, duplicity, superficiality, and absence of reflection he saw in those around him" (Piechowski, 2006, p. 17). During World War II, as he risked his life, he provided asylum to Jews escaping the Nazi regime. He was imprisoned by the Nazis, tortured, and forbidden to conduct his professional practice. During his internment, he witnessed acts of complete self-sacrifice on the part of others imprisoned with him. His theory evolved from his being confronted by death, suffering, and injustice and wanting to understand the human condition (Nelson, 1989; Silverman, 1993b).

During his early youth, Dabrowski began his quest for universal values and searched for authentic individuals who lived according to them. By examining an untold number of biographies of gifted, creative, and eminent people, he found the values he sought and many of the agonies he too had experienced. He found inspiration in Socrates, Gandhi, and in the great saints (Piechowski, 2006).

Following his release from prison, he returned to his private practice in Warsaw, Poland. His practice attracted gifted individuals, and he was able to continue pursuing the questions he had posed while imprisoned by the Nazis. He noticed early on that his clients displayed an emotional richness similar to what he had seen in his biographical studies and in fellow survivors of imprisonment. He noted that these individuals could not reconcile themselves to a concrete reality; instead, they held on to their personal visions of what ought to be. He found that his clients described how they experienced intense inner conflict, self-criticism, anxiety, and feelings of inferiority while pursuing their ideals. The medical community at that time labeled this conflict *psychoneurotic* and attempted to "cure" individuals who experienced life this way. Dabrowski took a different view of these conflicts and saw these symptoms as a natural part of striving for higher level development. As a result, he attempted to convince the profession that inner conflict was a sign of developmental potential rather than a degenerative sign (Nelson, 1989; Silverman, 1993b).

Through his continued work in biographical analysis and his clinical practice, he came to understand that the intensity of emotions, sensitivity, and tendency toward emotional extremes was a natural part of the psychological and physical makeup of gifted individuals. In their intensified approach to feeling, thinking, imagining, and experiencing life, he recognized tremendous potential for further growth (Dabrowski, 1964, 1972). He recognized internal forces within these individuals that generated overstimulation, conflict, and emotional pain; however, he also saw a search for a way out of the pain and disharmony. He dedicated himself to protecting those individuals "who are tuned in to the pain of the world and who see its dangerous trends, are not heeded, and those who being open to higher realities are poorly adapted to living in this world and thus at risk" (Piechowski, 2002, p. 28).

Through his clinical observations and research, Dabrowski (1964) developed his Theory of Positive Disintegration, in which he proposed that advanced human development requires a breakdown of existing psychological structures in order for an individual to form higher, more evolved structures. The intellectual capacity and emotional makeup of the individual determine the extent of development possible. Moon (2009) explained this succinctly:

> Dabrowski's theory suggests that personality development occurs when the press of internal and environmental forces propels a person to grow through a paradigm shifting mechanism that begins with disintegration of current psychic structures and ends with a higher order reintegration. (p. 22)

Dabrowski maintained that inner conflict generates the tension that impels a person toward higher levels of functioning. *Positive disintegration* is a breaking down of current ways of thinking and dedicating oneself to the service of greater compassion, integrity, and altruism (Dabrowski, 1964). The process of positive disintegration involves serious self-examination that consists of taking an inventory of one's motives and behaviors. This process can be emotionally loaded and may result in moral-self-evaluation and self-loathing. Dabrowski referred to this as "dissatisfaction with oneself," and he noted that this dissatisfaction often is accompanied by feelings of guilt. This guilt is not necessarily associated with any wrongful behavior. Individuals experiencing these feelings of guilt may believe they are simply not living according to their self-determined individual ideals. He posited that inner turmoil—or positive disintegration—enables a person to strive toward personal and spiritual growth (Piechowski, 2006). He proposed that negative disintegration is a breakdown that does not involve a moral or ethical component; it is self-centered, containing none of the qualities that would enable development at a higher level.

Dabrowski's theory incorporates the role of emotions in human development; therefore, since his death it has become known as Dabrowski's theory of emotional development. In this theory, the relationship between cognition and emotion, the evolution of value structures, and the heightened intensity of gifted and creative individuals are addressed. The theory is composed of two parts: levels of development and the overexcitabilities. They are described below.

Dabrowski's Levels of Development

Dabrowski's theory involves five levels of adult development: self-interest, group values, transformative growth, self-actualization, and the attainment of the personality ideal. Dabrowski's five levels represent five stages of human personality or emotional development along a continuum. Mendaglio (2008) explained, "The five levels of development represent a movement from an egocentric mode to an altruistic mode—from behavior being motivated by basic drives and conformity to being motivated by values and autonomy" (p. 35). The levels are in ascending order, with the higher levels representing individuals whose personalities are defined by altruistic values applied to everyday living. In this theory, development does not take place in a lock-step fashion in which an individual reaches the criteria of one level before moving on to the next. Mendaglio (2008) noted, "Individuals may be at one level of development for certain aspects and at a different level with respect to other areas" (p. 34). Moreover, he indicated that there are no age-related criteria associated with each level as young children may exhibit advanced development associated with the higher levels. Table 1 provides a summary of the five levels.

At Level I, individuals have very little concern for others. Their lives revolve around the question, "What's in it for me?" As self-centered beings,

TABLE 1
Dabrowski's Theory of Positive Disintegration

Level I: Primary Integration
At Level I, Primary Integration, egocentrism prevails. A person at this level lacks the capacity for empathy and self-examination. When things go wrong, someone else is always to blame; self-responsibility is not a Level I characteristic.

Level II: Unilevel Disintegration
At Level II, individuals are influenced primarily by their social group and by mainstream values, or they are moral relativists for whom "anything goes," morally speaking. They often exhibit ambivalent feelings and indecisive behavior because they have no clear-cut set of self-determined internal values.

Level III: Spontaneous Multilevel Disintegration
At Level III, multilevelness arises. The person develops a hierarchical sense of values. Inner conflict involves a struggle to bring one's behavior up to higher standards. There is a dissatisfaction with what one is, because of a competing sense of what one could and ought to be (personality ideal). This internal struggle can be accompanied by existential despair, anxiety, depression, and feelings of dissatisfaction with the self.

Level IV: Organized Multilevel Disintegration
Individuals at Level IV are well on the road to self-actualization. They have found a way to reach their own ideals. They show high levels of responsibility, authenticity, reflective judgment, empathy for others, autonomy of thought and action, and self-awareness.

Level V: Secondary Integration
At Level V, inner conflicts regarding the self have been resolved through actualization of the personality ideal. Disintegration has been transcended by the integration of one's values and ideals into one's living. One's life is lived in service to humanity. It is lived according to the highest, most universal principles of loving and compassion for others.

Note. Adapted from Nelson (1989).

they are serious competitors determined to win. As adults, their goals become limited to financial success, power, and glory. These individuals are strongly influenced by the social environment and driven by a high need for approval of others. Others are motivated by gratification of their needs and will use others to reach that end (Silverman, 1993b).

At Level II, individuals are motivated often by what others think of them or fear of punishment. They are ambivalent in many areas of their lives. These people have not established core values that guide their behavior. For this reason, they can be easily swayed. "What will people think of me if I . . . ?" is a question that serves as the basis for much of their decision making. These individuals are more aware and concerned for others than Level I individuals; however, their insecurities do not enable them to establish meaningful, authentic relationships (Silverman, 1993b).

Level III marks the beginning of movement toward advanced development. An individual at this stage has acquired a hierarchical value system. This value system may no longer be aligned with the values of one's peer group. There is a struggle to elevate one's behavior to higher standards. Individuals have begun a search for self-improvement that has enabled them to transcend societal norms. They may feel out of sync with their peers; however, they are relieved to discover that the intense questioning they are experiencing actually leads to personal self-improvement (Silverman, 1993b). Mendaglio (2008) noted that, at this level, individuals develop autonomy and authenticity in their dealings with themselves and others. He explained, "In essence, they have begun creating a hierarchy of values and using it to gauge their mental states, behaviors, and approaches to other people" (Mendaglio, 2008, p. 38). This transformation may be triggered by external events in their lives such as the loss of a loved one or a brush with death.

When individuals reach Level IV, they are experiencing a self-actualizing life aligned with their personal ideals. They have reached a level of self-acceptance and are accepting of others. People at this level are committed to making societal contributions and feel responsible for leaving their world better off as a result of their having lived (Silverman, 1993b). A sense of social justice and connection with others is characteristic of individuals at this level. They have established a set of important values and an authentic sense of integrity. Mendaglio (2008) indicated that, with individuals having reached this level, a hierarchy of values is clearly established and guides their daily behavior.

Level V represents "the attainment of the personality ideal" (Silverman, 1993b, p. 20), or "the apex of human development" (Mendaglio, 2008,

p. 39). At this stage of life, an individual has resolved inner conflicts and is celebrating authenticity, harmony, altruism, and empathy. Individuals experience harmony and live in peace with themselves. Mendaglio (2008) noted, "They conduct their lives by enacting the personality ideal, whereby behavior is directed by their constructed hierarchy of values" (p. 39). They live with no inner conflict and enjoy the highest levels of empathy, autonomy, and authenticity. These individuals have become the gifted givers of society. Several examples of individuals who have been described as having reached this personality ideal are Mother Teresa, Mahatma Gandhi, Dag Hammarskjold, Martin Luther King, Jr., Eleanor Roosevelt, and Albert Schweitzer.

Dabrowski's Overexcitabilities

The overexcitabilities as described by Dabrowski are understood to be innate and are observable in infancy. They represent greater capacities to respond to various stimuli. Dabrowski postulated five overexcitabilities: psychomotor, sensual, imaginational, intellectual, and emotional. Translated from Polish, the term *overexcitability* can be thought of as heightened sensitivity. The overexcitabilities are understood to be an abundance of physical, sensual, creative, intellectual, and emotional energy. The strength of this energy, particularly imaginational, intellectual, and emotional overexcitability, is positively related to advanced emotional development in adulthood.

Much of our understanding of Kazimierz Dabrowski's theory is due to the undying efforts of Michael Piechowski, his scholarly protégé, who dedicated the bulk of his career to transferring Dabrowski's conceptualization into constructs that could be measured. When Dabrowski attained a grant to develop ways of assessing levels of emotional development, Piechowski and others on a research team collected multiple life histories of individuals Dabrowski believed might serve as exemplars of his theory. Piechowski was assigned the task of developing a method to analyze the life histories. In the process of analyzing the autobiographical materials, he found 433 examples of overexcitability and classified them as they appear in Table 2.

Years later, Michael Piechowski served as a research assistant at the Research and Guidance Laboratory for Superior Students at the University of Wisconsin-Madison. The lab was established by John Rothney as a vocational and counseling service for gifted high school students. Students throughout the state of Wisconsin made one-day visits once a year to talk with counselors about their aspirations. Piechowski asked the coun-

TABLE 2
Forms and Expressions of Overexcitability

Psychomotor
- Surplus of energy
  Rapid speech, marked excitation, intense physical activity, pressure for action, marked competitiveness
- Psychomotor expression of emotional tension
  Compulsive talking and chattering, impulsive actions, nervous habits, acting out

Sensual
- Enhanced sensory and aesthetic pleasure
  Seeing, smelling, tasting, touching, hearing; delight in beautiful objects, sounds of words, music, form, color, balance
- Sensual expression of emotional tension
  Overeating, self-pampering, buying sprees, wanting to be in the limelight

Imaginational
- Free play of the imagination
  Frequent use of image and metaphor, facility for invention and fantasy, facility for detailed visualization, poetic and dramatic perception, animistic and magical thinking
- Capacity for living in a world of fantasy
  Predilection for magic and fairy tales, creation of private worlds, imaginary companions, dramatization
- Spontaneous imagery as an expression of emotional tension
  Animistic imagery, mixing truth and fiction, elaborate dreams, illusions
- Low tolerance for boredom
  Need for novelty

Intellectual
- Intensified activity of the mind
  Thirst for knowledge, curiosity, concentration, capacity for sustained intellectual effort, avid reading, keen observation, detailed visual recall, detailed planning
- Penchant for probing questions and problem solving
  Search for truth and understanding, forming new concepts, tenacity in problem solving
- Reflective thought
  Thinking about thinking, love of theory and analysis, preoccupation with logic, moral thinking, introspection, conceptual and intuitive integration, independence of thought

Emotional
- ❧ **Feelings and emotions intensified**
  Positive feelings, negative feelings, extremes of emotions, complex emotions and feelings, identification with others' feelings, awareness of a whole range of feelings
- ❧ **Strong somatic expressions**
  Tense stomach, sinking heart, blushing, flushing, pounding heart, sweaty palms
- ❧ **Strong affective expressions**
  Inhibition, timidity, shyness, enthusiasm, ecstasy, euphoria, pride, strong affective memory, shame, feelings of unreality, fears and anxieties, feelings of guilt, concern with death, depressive and suicidal moods
- ❧ **Capacity for strong attachments, deep relationships**
  Strong emotional ties and attachments to persons, living things, places, and animals; difficulty adjusting to new environments; compassion; responsiveness to others; sensitivity in relationships; loneliness
- ❧ **Well-differentiated feelings toward self**
  Inner dialogue and self-judgment

Note. Adapted from Piechowski (1999).

selors to suggest the names of those students they found most interesting and promising and recruited them for his research. He mailed them a questionnaire designed to tap the expressions of heightened excitability. Eventually, he received 31 completed questionnaires and began to analyze the 1,400 responses within. This questionnaire has since been named the Overexcitability Questionnaire (OEQ). Since this early work in Wisconsin, Piechowski has conducted multiple studies using a revision of the questionnaire and acquired more than 5,000 responses. The total pool of responses served as his database in presenting the most current and comprehensive analysis of Dabrowski's theory (see Piechowski, 2006). Several vivid examples from Piechowski's (2006) work are infused in the discussion that follows.

Psychomotor overexcitability. Individuals with the gift of psychomotor overexcitability are movers and shakers in society. They appear to have an "augmented capacity for being active and energetic" (Piechowski, 1991, p. 287). Children high in psychomotor overexcitability experience extra physical energy. It is evidenced in their rapid speech patterns, animated facial gestures, enthusiasm, nervous habits, and a love of kinesthetic movement. Although they may derive great pleasure from their boundless energy, enthusiasm, and endless activity, others around them may often find them overwhelming. My brother Peter was a highly active toddler who would rock his head back and forth on his pillow until he eventually fell asleep from exhaustion from his action-packed day. As a teenager, during transitions between supper courses, he would drum his fingers on the dining room table, claiming that he was playing one of the Beach Boys' greatest hits. His nonstop energy was evident in all that he did.

Having lived with my younger brother, I appreciated the autobiography of professional skateboarder Tony Hawk. The childhood of this internationally renowned skateboarder was a living testimony to Dabrowski's notion of psychomotor overexcitability. Tony explained that the worst days of his life were those spent in the Christopher Robin Preschool. He described his experience at age 3 when the "absolute worst torture the school inflicted" (Hawk & Mortimer, 2002, p. 8) on him was nap time. He reflected that as a hyper little boy he needed to be constantly running around, tapping his feet, or deeply involved in any activity or else he "went bananas from boredom" (p. 8). Hawk maintains that he still has nightmares about trying to stay still on his preschool sleep mat, squeezing his eyes shut as his teacher walked around the classroom. Eventually preschool became more than the energetic little boy could handle, and the preschool director explained to Tony's parents that he was formally expelled from the program. Tony's memories of the elementary school years were similar:

> The teacher would give a lesson and I'd tap my feet, flip my pencil around on the desk, look out the window—anything to keep myself amused. The weird part was that I got high grades and understood what the teacher was saying, but every day seconds stretched into minutes and minutes seemed like hours. (Hawk & Mortimer, 2002, p. 15)

Concerned about their son's difficulty paying attention in class, Tony's parents arranged for an IQ test and learned he had scored a 144. The school system came to understand that Tony was gifted and learned to appreciate his frustration with his energetic approach to life being out of sync with his school environment. Fortunately, the young boy with psychomotor overexcitability eventually found an appropriate outlet for his energy and went on to revolutionize the world of competitive skateboarding.

Michael Piechowski (2006) reported a vivid description of psychomotor overexcitability provided by the parent of an excitable young boy:

> The movement and the inner rhythm of my own son drove me to distraction when he was in the fourth grade. Upstairs in his room Brendan "studied" vocabulary words while drumming on his books,

tapping his feet on the rungs of his chair, rocking back and forth, and punctuating each beat with hoots and hollers. He sounded like a one-boy percussion band and it felt like a 5.6 on the Richter scale! He consistently got perfect scores on spelling tests and told me that drumming was his method of memorizing. (p. 21)

One of the earliest signs of psychomotor overexcitability is a need for much less sleep in infancy. Silverman and Kearney (1989) presented a parent's experience with his young son: "When other babies were getting 12 hours of sleep, I was lucky if he slept 6 hours. I figured he was smarter than other children his age because he had been awake twice as long" (p. 52). Another mother reported,

Amanda never crawled. She went from sitting to walking. She took her first steps by stacking the stuffed animals in her crib, jumped out, and started out of her bedroom. She never asked for toys because she preferred things she could take apart and build. When she was 5, she wanted a Dust Buster! (K. Denson, personal communication, September 5, 2009)

Restless out of boredom

When not directed, this pent-up psychomotor energy may become evident in restlessness or impulsive behavior. Piechowski (2006) shared a teenage girl's feelings about being forced to cope with boredom from an unchallenging curriculum:

Sometimes in class (it happens quite often) I get bored because I understand what is being taught, and get a lot of energy. This energy is used to goof off, even though I know I shouldn't. The energy just seems to swell up inside of me, then just flows out. Honestly, some classes are boring and I wish those who understand could go ahead and work, then maybe I wouldn't use my energy harmfully. (p. 39)

Children with high psychomotor overexcitability have high potential for being misdiagnosed as having an Attention Deficit/Hyperactivity Disorder (ADHD; Webb et al., 2005). It is important to note that Webb and his colleagues (2005) indicated that "although children or adults with this overexcitability might be riveted to a task mentally, their bodies are likely to fidget and twitch in their excitement in ways that that can resemble hyperactivity" (p. 14). It is also important to understand that psychomotor overexcitability alone does not differentiate between gifted and average development in individuals; it must be integrated with other overexcitabilities before it becomes developmentally significant. Silverman (1993b) reported that many eminent, actualized individuals, such as Mother Teresa and Albert Schweitzer, were known for their unusually high levels of energy and their capacity for working tirelessly for long hours.

Sensual overexcitability. For sensually overexcitable individuals, the sensory experiences of daily living—seeing, smelling, tasting, touching, and hearing—are far more heightened than for others. As children, they look at a sunset and respond much differently to that visual experience than their peers do. The experience of taking in the beauty of a Van Gogh painting may cause a sensually overexcitable teenager to respond emotionally while her friends on the art museum field trip may be simply yearning to get to the museum gift shop. Parents have reported immediate hysterical crying from infants when their diapers are wet (Silverman, 1993b). This same overexcitability may be evidenced in the young child who insists on having tags on the collars of his shirts removed because they are uncomfortable. Wearing certain fabrics may be problematic for these children. Later on they may refuse to part with a favorite chamois shirt that has provided comfort to them for years. Parents have reported toddlers who have refused to wear particular shoes because they did not feel "squishy" enough or others who have not been able to function until the seams in their socks were straight. These may be the same children who insist on carrying a velveteen rag throughout their day or need a particular soft and cuddly stuffed animal in order to fall asleep at night. For these children, the kindergarten teacher can offer a soft and cuddly stuffed animal available for soothing hugs.

Sensually overexcitable young people delight in particular smells. A blueberry scented magic marker in art class may send a child into ecstasy. Another child may respond similarly to the particular perfume or after-shave lotion the teacher is wearing or respond violently to the cleaning fluids used by the custodial staff. The flicker or buzzing in fluorescent lights may bother them and even cause headaches. A busy shopping mall or an amusement park may overwhelm them. Adults have reported that the noise of crowds or loud activity in the work setting bothers them significantly. In addition, the culinary experiences of individuals may be influenced by sensual overexcitability. Children and adults report hating the texture of particular foods: "Lima beans feel too slimy going down my throat." These same individuals are remarkable in their ability to detect different spices in their foods. One person may describe the veal marsala at her favorite Italian restaurant as "ecstasy" while others seated with her at dinner would be content with simple meatloaf. As adults the sensually excitable become gourmet chefs and connoisseurs of fine wines. They are able to differentiate among the merlots, cabernet sauvignons, and chiantis of California and Australia while their friends are content to settle for the house wine. They may cherish the memory of certain foods, whether it is their grandmother's peach cobbler or their favorite shrimp gumbo from New Orleans. Happiness on Valentine's Day may depend on whether the heart-shaped box of chocolates delivered by a loved one is a box of Belgian dark chocolate or a less expensive box of American milk chocolate from Walgreen's.

Imaginational overexcitability. Early signs of imaginational overexcitability include imaginary companions or pets. Parents report statements such as "I didn't color on the bedroom wall, Mom. It was my friend Tickeroo! I told him not to do that. He took my crayons and went wild. He has special powers and when he heard you coming up the stairs, he flew out the window!" My younger brother Peter had a blue dog that followed him around throughout his early years. I remember my father's patience as he pulled the family station wagon to the side of the interstate highway on our way to a family vacation on the coast of Maine. Peter insisted that his blue dog had to get out and "take care of his duty." As I sat in the car complaining, Peter took our family time to supervise the blue dog's "rest stop." My brother was fortunate to have two parents who appreciated his imaginary pet. Having survived my brother's imaginary pet, when I encountered the autobiography of the popular country singer Dolly Parton years later, I could appreciate her description of how her imaginary companions comforted her as a young child in rural Tennessee in a large family of siblings:

> A person might think that a kid growing up with that many others would never be lonely, but often I was. Some kids make up imaginary friends, and I had my own version of that. I called them my angels. I would talk to my angels all the time. I felt safer because they were with me. They understood why I had to sing, why I had such dreams, why I wanted to climb aboard a butterfly and wing my way out of the holler and into a world that I knew lay beyond what I could see. (Parton, 1994, pp. 62–63)

Young people experiencing imaginational overexcitabilities think in images, and they enjoy expressing themselves in metaphorical language. Highly creative, they enjoy dramatic play, rich imaginations, and fantasy and are able to describe their dreams in vivid color. Their daydreaming is active and elaborate. Piechowski (2006) shared how one young boy imagined himself as a college basketball player and visualized his game strategy:

> I imagine what I would do in certain situations playing against some of the best players in the country. I can see everything very clearly, and I do some moves that I know I could do if I were a little taller. Most of my moves end up in slam-dunks, which are very easy to do in my daydreams. I can think through almost a full game. If I really concentrate and get into it, I can even picture the crowd. (p. 76)

Young people high in imaginational overexcitability enjoy poetry and drama. They devour science fiction and fantasy and thrive in any classroom activity that allows them to invent and create. They also are recognized for having a great sense of humor, which might be expressed in writing, dramatizations, or artwork and cartooning.

Intellectual overexcitability. Hallmarks of intellectual overexcitability include curiosity, concentration, a love of learning and problem solving, theoretical thinking, introspection, and a capacity for sustained intellectual effort. Individuals high in intellectual overexcitability engage in gaining knowledge and search for understanding and truth. As children, they are voracious readers and, as adults, they continue to consume books. They also are known for their keen observations. A parent in Fort Worth, TX, described to me that her 3-year-old Jonathan had devoured many books on dinosaurs and when his family visited the Jurassic Park exhibit at the Fort Worth Children's Museum of Science and History, Jonathan called attention to a dinosaur on display that was mislabeled. Upon checking, the museum director discovered Jonathan was correct and had the nameplate changed (S. Taylor, personal communication, July 9, 2008).

Children like Jonathan are intensely curious and bombard their parents and teachers with questions about issues that concern them deeply: "Dad, when do you think the polar icecaps will have completely melted away?" "Dad, what will happen to all those polar bears?" "I don't understand it, Mom. Why is there war?" "Mr. Jackson, where do butterflies go when it rains?" Following a discussion in class, the child asks, "Why do children in Bosnia have to suffer from malnutrition?" In school they appreciate rich curriculum that addresses major concepts and ideas. They are introspective and often focus on moral concerns and issues of justice, and as adolescents they thrive on the school's debate team, where they can argue about important issues and enjoy stimulating conversations about big ideas. They mature into independent thinkers. Striving to reach understanding and obtain truth may be more critical to them than striving for academic achievement and high grades. When I taught in a gifted program in Connecticut, I enjoyed a second grader named Michael Nimchek who had this intellectual excitability.

During my first year of working with him, he began working on a multivolume collection of books on the lives of famous composers. Below is the introduction to Michael's book on Tchaikovsky, in which he posed his overarching research question:

> Some of you may wonder why a second grader would want to write a book about Tchaikovsky. People get interested in different things for different reasons. For example, I got interested in Tchaikovsky because I like his music. I play the piano and I have a whole book of his music. At Christmas I saw the ballet of the Nutcracker Suite. His music can be both cheerful and sad at the same time. I wondered how music could be both happy and sad at the same time, so I decided to learn about Tchaikovsky's life. I wondered if when he was sad he wrote sad music, and if when he was happy he wrote happy music. In this book, you will get to know a little more about Tchaikovsky, how he lived, and about the music he wrote.

I have observed many doctoral students struggle for years in search of the question to drive their dissertation research, and I smile as I reflect on Michael, who at age 7 was ready to ask his.

Emotional overexcitability. The most critical of all of the overexcitabilities is emotional overexcitability—an individual's capacity to experience extreme and complex emotions and intense feelings. Emotionally overexcitable individuals show a heightened concern for and reaction to the environment around them. This overexcitability is evidenced in a person's capacity for emotional depth, intensity, empathy, self-criticism, attachment to people and animals, inhibition, guilt, and anxiety.

This compassion, empathy, and sensitivity can be seen in children at an early age. Virginia Kelly's young son was sent to a small neighborhood grocery store on Thanksgiving morning to pick up some ingredients for the family dinner. Instead of returning with food, Billy came home with another child. When she asked, "Billy, who's your new friend?" he replied, "Johnny. He was at the bus stop and I found out he wasn't gonna' have a real Thanksgiving dinner so I brought him home to have Thanksgiving dinner with us" (Gallen, 1994, p. 25). The child had a bag of potato chips in his hands and Billy asked his mother, "You don't want him to have a bag of chips for his Thanksgiving dinner, do you?" (Gallen, 1994, p. 25). Virginia Kelly explained that she was swept by emotion as she experienced her young son's empathy and caring for others at such an early age. It was this compassion for others that Virginia Kelly believed enabled her son, former President Bill Clinton, to understand the plight of others less fortunate and work to change their conditions.

This empathic quality was also evidenced in Christian Glosser of Phoenix, AZ. When Christian was 8, he learned of children who could not walk due to explosions of land mines and others who suffered from polio. For several days, his mother noticed Christian dragging himself across the floor to try to understand what it would be like for these young victims. The young boy learned about Free Wheelchair Mission, an organization that sends wheelchairs made from patio chairs and bicycle tires to children throughout the world. In planning his eighth birthday party, Christian decided that he did not need any more video games or toys and that there were plenty of children who needed his help. He recruited his best friend Charlie to have joint parties and to ask their friends to bring small donations for wheelchairs instead of birthday presents. The families of the boys' friends were generous, and the result was that Christian and his buddies were able to send a check for more than $600 to Free Wheelchair Mission to purchase 15 wheelchairs for disabled children (Bayless, 2006).

Christian Glosser and his friends would appreciate the efforts of an older teenager whose empathy led her to conduct a similar effort. When Kristel Fritz was a high school junior she was inspired when Miss Kentucky donated her long brown hair to Locks of Love, a national organization that provides children with medical hair loss custom-fitted wigs. Kristel explored the Locks of Love website and became determined to contribute to the cause. When she learned that 2 million children suffer from alopecia areata, a disease that causes hair loss, she conducted a campaign in her San Jose, CA, high school. She explained, "Giving sick kids pride and confidence in themselves was just an awesome, awesome idea" (Rusch, 2002, p. 103). Following months of work organizing and advertising the event, Kristel transformed her high school's center quad into a hair salon and had volunteer stylists from the community prepared to cut the hair of those students volunteering to donate their long locks. She succeeded in delivering 25 long ponytails to Locks of Love. The following year, as a senior, Kristel enlisted the help of many more students, and continued her campaign as she and her friends convinced even more teenagers to make a difference in the lives of young children who were suffering (Rusch, 2002).

When empathic young people like Christian Glosser and Kristel Fritz experience powerful emotions such as sadness over the adversity others face, as well as elation over simple pleasures in life, the behavior can appear extreme and even puzzling to adults. Parents describe their young children as "wearing their hearts on their sleeves" and honest with their feelings. They can be hard on themselves and have difficulty forgiving themselves if they hurt another person's feelings. Emotionally in tune with others, one teenager was recognized by her friends for her strong intuitive abilities: "Beth can walk in the room and know instantly how every other person in that room is feeling. She just has a wonderful way of being able to read people."

Emotionally sensitive and intense young children in elementary classrooms may not be able to function for the remainder of the day after their teacher reads the classic story *The Velveteen Rabbit* or shows a poignant movie such as *E.T.* Because these children are so easily upset by negative events portrayed on the evening news, parents must be cautious about allowing them to watch television. They worry about endangered animals, terrorism, warfare in the Middle East, and the victims of hurricanes. As teenagers, these same students take on the concerns of the homeless in their community and become involved in building homes for Habitat for Humanity. They notice discriminatory practices in their high school and tackle the issue by writing passionate editorials in their school newspaper. As adults, they become involved in environmental organizations and groups engaged in social action. They protest against the evils of war. Throughout life they continue to feel everything more deeply than others do, and this quality at times is both painful and frightening to them.

Research on the Dabrowski Theory

Dabrowski (1972) maintained that when an individual's emotional, imaginational, and intellectual overexcitabilities surpassed the sensual and psychomotor in strength there was greater potential for advancing to the higher levels of personality development. Scholars in gifted education have been interested in research and dialogue on Dabrowski's theory for its appeal as a way to expand conceptions of giftedness by taking into account personality traits related to high ability. In a comprehensive review of the research literature on Dabrowski's overexcitabilities and levels of emotional development, Mendaglio and Tillier (2006) presented a body of research highlighting support for Dabrowski's levels uncovered through adult biographical and case study analyses. They indicated that studies of gifted children and adolescents have focused on measuring overexcitabilities and developmental potential, made possible through the use of Piechowski's original questionnaire as well as a revision that included 21 free responses (Lysy & Piechowski, 1983). Since that time, the Overexcitability Questionnaire II (Falk, Lind, Miller, Piechowski, & Silverman, 1999), a 50-item Likert-type scale instrument, was designed to measure the presence and the strength of the five overexcitabilities.

Using his revised overexcitability questionnaire (OEQ), Piechowski joined with Colangelo (1984) to compare gifted students with gifted and nongifted adults and showed that elevated emotional, intellectual, and imaginational overexcitabilities distinguished participants identified as gifted and those not identified as such. Gallagher (1985) investigated the possibility of significant differences in overexcitabilities when comparing two groups of sixth graders. Her investigation of 12 gifted and 12 randomly selected students examined the relationship between levels of overexcitability and scores on the Torrance Tests of Creative Thinking and the California Achievement Test. When comparing gifted students and students not identified as gifted, she found significant differences between the two groups, with the gifted students scoring higher on the intellectual, imaginational, and emotional overexcitabilities. Breard (1994) found that gifted upper elementary students obtained higher scores than nongifted students across all five forms of overexcitability. Ackerman (1997) found similar results in her comparison of gifted and above-average high school students, with psychomotor, intellectual, and emotional overexcitabilities being the discriminating differences between the groups. Research also has indicated that overexcitabilities are evident in young preschool gifted children (Kitano, 1990; Tucker & Hafenstein, 1997). Bouchard (2004) was interested in exploring the overexcitabilities as a way of identifying gifted students. She developed an instrument to use with elementary school children, the ElemOE, a Likert-scaled checklist. Teacher ratings were obtained on samples of identified gifted children and nonidentified students. Her analyses of the teacher ratings indicated that teachers rated the gifted children higher in the intellectual and psychomotor overexcitabilities. Tieso (2007) conducted a study to examine the underlying construct of overexcitabilities and to identify individual and family level factors that may explain gifted students' patterns of overexcitabilities. Collecting data from a sample of 143 identified gifted students and their parents using the Overexcitability Questionnaire II (Falk et. al., 1999), she found significant differences between gender and age groups and that most of the variance among students on the overexcitabilities was explained by family membership.

Teachers and counselors working with gifted students may find that Dabrowski's theory provides a useful framework for understanding and appreciating the developmental patterns of young people with high ability. Knowledge of this theory may assist all those who work with gifted students. I encourage my readers to reflect on the following questions regarding Dabrowski's theory:

- How might parents and teachers of young people who experience the psychomotor excitability of Tony Hawk channel that high energy in productive ways?
- How does an understanding of psychomotor overexcitability shape our thinking of how we design school curriculum?
- How might an understanding of the sensual excitability in children influence how educators design their classroom environments?
- How should parents and educators support the imaginational excitability of young people?
- What should gifted education programs provide for students like Michael Nimchek who are searching for answers to the important questions they pose?
- What outlets do schools offer gifted students for their emotional excitability?
- How might educators teach young people about the Dabrowski theory? How would an understanding of this theory support them?

Howard Gardner's Theory of Multiple Intelligences

Howard Gardner, the Harvard psychologist who revolutionized contemporary thought on intelligence through his theory of multiple intelligences (MI), has had a profound influence on thinking and practice in education. In his 1983 landmark book *Frames of Mind*, Gardner unveiled a theory of multiple intelligences that rejected the traditional view that aptitude consists strictly of the ability to reason and understand complex ideas. He identified seven separate human capacities: verbal-linguistic, logical-mathematical, visual-spatial, musical, bodily-kinesthetic, interpersonal, and intrapersonal. Years later, he added naturalist to those capacities. He argued that these eight intelligences could not be easily evaluated by IQ tests.

Howard Gardner wrote *Frames of Mind* hoping to stir debate among psychologists about the nature of intelligence; however, such a debate did not occur. Unimpressed with Gardner's view, psychologists of that time looked the other way while educators were enthusiastic. *Frames of Mind* supported what many teachers had known for a long time: students in their classrooms possessed natural aptitude for music, sports, and emotional understanding—strengths that could not be measured with a traditional test. Gardner had provided scholarly support and a "voice" to the experiences of teachers who observed these different intelligences in their students every day. Boston University education professor Scott Seider (2009) described the reaction as a "grassroots uprising" of educators at all levels who embraced MI theory "with a genuine passion" (p. 28). Seider, a former student of Gardner, highlights that MI theory has helped to remind teachers to focus on the strengths and weaknesses of the individual child and has offered conceptual support for educators looking to prevent students from being stigmatized by a low score on any one standardized test. When asked to explain the strong response of educators to his theory, Howard Gardner commented, "One reason for the popularity of the idea of multiple intelligences is that it can be summarized in a sentence. So the idea of a number of relatively independent cognitive capacities is not in itself daunting" (Edwards, 2009, p. 33)

Gardner (1999) defined *intelligence* as a biopsychological potential to process information. He viewed intelligence as the capacity to solve problems or to fashion products that are valued in one or more cultural settings. In *Frames of Mind* (1983), he represented the personal intelligences as separate pieces; however, because of their close association in most cultural settings, he maintained that they are often interwoven. Gardner claimed that the seven intelligences seldom operate independently because they are utilized at the same time and complement each other as individuals develop skills and solve problems. He asked that we consider the metaphor of a musical orchestra: "Just as the sounds of string, woodwind, and percussion instruments combine to create a symphony, the different intelligences intermix within a student to yield meaningful scholastic achievement or other accomplishments" (Moran, Kornhaber, & Gardner, 2008, p. 221). Since Gardner's original conceptualization of the intelligences in 1983, there has been much discussion as to other possible "intelligence candidates" for inclusion. Additional research by Gardner and his colleagues has examined three possibilities: naturalist intelligence, spiritual intelligence, and existential intelligence. Gardner has concluded that the naturalist intelligence merits addition to the original list of seven and continues to research and reflect upon others under consideration.

Sigmund Freud and William James influenced Gardner's conception of the two personal intelligences. Freud was interested in the self and, as a clinician, was fascinated with how an individual develops knowledge of self. James was focused more on the individual's relationship to the community. He thought of one's self-knowledge as evolving from a growing appreciation of how others think of an individual. James saw that the purpose of self-knowledge is to support a smoother functioning of society (Gardner, 1983).

Gardner (1999) examined the development of both of these aspects of personality and maintained that there are two distinct personal intelligences. He defined them succinctly: "Intrapersonal intelligence involves the capacity to understand oneself, to have an effective working model of oneself—including one's own desires, fears, and capacities—and to use such information effectively in regulating one's own life" (p. 43). To explain the second personal intelligence, he proposed that "interpersonal intelligence denotes a person's capacity to understand the intentions, motivations, and desires of other people and, consequently to work effectively with others" (Gardner, 1999, p. 43).

Gardner (1983) indicated that the core capacity of intrapersonal intelligence is an individual's ability to access one's feeling life, the complete range of emotions. He viewed intrapersonal knowledge as "the capacity instantly to effect discriminations among these feelings and, eventually, to label them, to enmesh them in symbolic codes, to draw upon them as a means of understanding and guiding one's behavior" (Gardner, 1983, p. 239). In Gardner's view, such an intelligence involves having the capacity to understand oneself; to have an effective working model of oneself, including one's own desires, goals, fears, and capacities; and to be able to apply this understanding to structure one's life. Gardner and Checkley (1997) explained as follows:

Intrapersonal intelligence refers to having an understanding of yourself, of knowing who you are, what you can do, what you want to do, how you react to things, which things to avoid, and which things to gravitate toward. We are drawn to people who have a good understanding of themselves because those people tend not to screw up. They tend to know what they can do. They tend to know what they can't do. And they tend to know where to go if they need help. (p. 12)

Individuals with strong intrapersonal intelligence have established mental models of themselves and can draw upon that knowledge of self to make decisions. They are able to distinguish their feelings, moods, and intentions and anticipate their reactions to future situations (Baum, Viens, Slatin, & Gardner, 2005). At its most advanced level, intrapersonal knowledge enables an individual to detect and symbolize highly complex and differentiated sets of feelings. Gardner indicated that we see this intelligence in the novelist who writes introspectively about feelings, in the therapy patient who reaches a deep understanding of her feeling life, or the wise elder in a community who draws upon a wealth of internal experiences to provide advice and guidance to others.

The second personal intelligence looks outward to other individuals. Interpersonal intelligence is an individual's capacity to understand the motivations, desires, and needs of other people and, consequently, to work effectively with others. Gardner and Walters (1993) explained that the core capacity of interpersonal intelligence is "the ability to notice distinctions among others; in particular, contrasts in their moods, temperaments, motivations, and intentions" (p. 23). This intelligence enables a person to read the desires of other people even when they remain well hidden and to be able to act upon that information in order to get a group of diverse individuals to collaborate and behave as desired. Gardner and Checkley (1997) elaborated on this view:

> Interpersonal intelligence is understanding other people. It's an ability we all need, but is at a premium if you are a teacher, clinician, salesperson, or politician. Anybody who deals with other people has to be skilled in the interpersonal sphere. (p. 12)

Individuals with strong interpersonal intelligence display sensitivity to the feelings, moods, beliefs, and intentions of others, and they are able to use that understanding to work effectively with them (Baum et al., 2005). Gardner points to examples of highly developed forms of interpersonal intelligence in political and religious leaders, successful parents and teachers, social activists, and individuals involved in the helping professions.

Although personal intelligences are rooted in biology, Gardner (1983) indicated that there are cultural differences in the balance struck between interpersonal and intrapersonal knowledge in understanding and appreciating the self. If we examine the multitude of world cultures, we encounter distinguishable variations in both interpersonal and intrapersonal forms of intelligence and different levels of emphasis on the personal intelligences. In some cultures, much less significance is placed on the individual. For example, among the Maori of New Zealand, a man's identity is determined by his inherited status and his relationship with his group. Outside of his group, he is no one. Cultures also differ in what aspects of the personal intelligences are valued. For example, the Japanese appreciate minimal spoken language and subtle nonverbal cues to provide the essence of one's authentic feelings and motivations, whereas the Navajos place a special premium on a person's ability to be a good listener. Listening is thought of as the key to good decision making and those who listen well are thought to have special gifts.

In summary, regardless of how cultures may differ in their views of personal intelligence, Gardner (1983) asserted that "the fact that one is a unique individual, who still must grow up in a social context—an individual of feelings and striving, which must rely on others to furnish the tasks and to judge one's achievements" (p. 254) is a indisputable aspect of the human condition. Therefore, "every society offers a sense of a person or a self, rooted in the individual's own personal knowledge and feelings" (Gardner, 1983, p. 275).

Gardner's conceptualization of personal intelligences has implications for those involved in the education of gifted students. His theory speaks to what educators may want to consider as they design curriculum and create educational and counseling programs to support the social and emotional skill development of gifted students. I encourage my readers to reflect on Gardner's view of intrapersonal and interpersonal intelligence and consider the following questions:

- How might teachers notice a child with strong intrapersonal intelligence? What would evidence of an advanced understanding of self look like in a child?
- How might educators and counselors support a child or adolescent who has strong intrapersonal intelligence?
- How might teachers notice a child with strong interpersonal intelligence? What would evidence of a child who reads people well and acts accordingly look like?
- How might educators and counselors support a child or adolescent with strong interpersonal intelligence?
- How might educators' understanding of Gardner's personal intelligences shape how they design curriculum for gifted students?
- How might educators view Gardner's notion of cultural differences in both the intrapersonal and interpersonal forms of intelligence? How might extensive experience in working with diverse populations influence these views?

❧ What models of individuals with highly advanced intrapersonal and interpersonal intelligence do educators have in their communities to share with students? How might these individuals be utilized in classrooms?

Emotional Intelligence

An understanding of the social and emotional lives of gifted young people may be enhanced by an examination of a more recent theory of emotional intelligence. Individuals who are emotionally and socially intelligent have the ability to understand and express themselves, to understand and relate well to others, and to cope successfully with the challenges of daily life. Emotionally intelligent people are aware of their own emotions, understand their strengths and weaknesses, and are able to express themselves appropriately. Moreover, they are aware of the feelings and needs of others and are able to establish and maintain healthy relationships and friendships. Ultimately, emotionally intelligent individuals are flexible in managing personal, social, and contextual change as they cope with immediate situations and solve interpersonal problems (Bar-On, 2007).

The theory connecting emotions to intelligence was proposed by Yale University psychologist Peter Salovey and his colleague John Mayer of the University of New Hampshire. In a 1990 landmark article they introduced emotional intelligence to the academic literature, defining emotional intelligence as "the ability to monitor one's own and other's feelings and emotions, to discriminate among them and to use that information to guide one's thinking and actions" (Salovey & Mayer, 1990, p. 189). In a second article that same year, they demonstrated empirically how emotional intelligence could be measured and highlighted how differences in emotional intelligence might predict the emergence of important qualities such as the ability to respond to others empathically. Since their introduction of emotional intelligence to the research literature, multiple definitions and models of emotional intelligence have evolved (Bar-On & Parker, 2000; Brackett & Geher, 2006; Schultze & Roberts, 2006). Most people were first introduced to emotional intelligence through the work of science writer Daniel Goleman (1995), whose popular book *Emotional Intelligence* became one of the best-selling books in psychology. Although multiple definitions and models have emerged, I have chosen to review the model offered by the originators of the construct.

The Mayer and Salovey (1997) theoretical model of emotional intelligence represents an elegant summation of what it means to be intelligent about one's emotional life and relationships. As a theoretical model it has been most influential in the emotional literacy movement, offering researchers and theorists guiding principles for important emotional competencies.

Mayer and Salovey began the conceptual development of emotional intelligence with an astute observation that emotion and intelligence often have been seen as adversaries, with emotions viewed as the intrinsically irrational and disruptive force. These theorists take a different view, suggesting that "extreme emotional reactions promote intelligence by interrupting ongoing processing and directing attention toward what may be important. In this sense they prioritize cognition" (Mayer & Salovery, 1997, p. 9). Mayer and Salovey viewed emotions of all sorts as contributing to thought rather than disorganizing it. With this understanding, they proposed:

> Emotional intelligence involves the ability to perceive accurately, appraise, and express emotion; the ability to access and/or generate feelings when they facilitate thought; the ability to understand emotion and emotional knowledge; and the ability to regulate emotions to promote emotional and intellectual growth. (Mayer & Salovey, 1997, p. 10)

Mayer and Salovey viewed emotional intelligence metaphorically as a trunk with four branches. These branches represent the special abilities included in their definition and are arranged from the more basic psychological processes to the higher, more psychologically integrated processes. Each branch consists of four representative abilities presented developmentally. Individuals high in emotional intelligence are expected to master more of the skills and develop the abilities more rapidly. The following discussion involves a description of the four branches of emotional abilities.

Perception, Appraisal, and Expression of Emotion

The lowest branch of the model involves the accuracy with which individuals can actually identify emotions and emotional content. Infants and young children are able to identify their own emotional states as well as others' and differentiate among them. A mature individual is able to monitor internal feelings. The growing person later is able to evaluate emotion wherever it is expressed, whether in other people, in art, or in poetry. Adults are able to express feelings accurately and express needs surrounding those feelings. Because emotionally intelligent individuals understand the expression and manifestation of emotion, they also are sensitive to the false representations or manipulation of emotion.

Emotional Facilitation of Thinking

Emotional facilitation of thinking is emotion acting upon intelligence. Emotional events help with intellectual processing. Early in life emotions signal important changes in the person and the environment. As a person matures, emotions begin to shape and improve thinking by directing a person's attention to significant changes. For example, a graduate student who is frustrated with an assignment becomes worried about the paper due the next day. With her well-developed thinking, she tackles the assignment before anxiety overwhelms her. Emotions also assist in thinking on demand. When a teacher asks, "How does the character in the story feel?" young people may generate feelings within themselves in such a way that they are able to put themselves in the other person's place. In the growing person, being able to generate feelings can assist with beginning a new year of school, deciding to accept a new professional position, or deciding how to deal with a friend's hurtful remark (Mayer & Salovey, 1997).

Mayer and Salovey (1997) indicated that "there exists 'an emotional theater of the mind' or more technically, a processing arena in which emotions may be generated, felt, manipulated, and examined so as to be better understood" (p. 13). The more realistically the theater operates, the more it can help an individual make appropriate choices. Emotionality also can contribute to multiple perspectives. Consider a pessimistic high school senior who applies to many colleges with low admissions standards. As the student's mood improves, her emotions enable her to consider applying to more rigorous universities. Mayer, Salovey, and Caruso (2000) pointed out that the shifting of an individual's point of view enables one to think more deeply and creatively.

Understanding and Analyzing Emotions; Employing Emotional Knowledge

The ability to understand emotions and use emotional knowledge is represented by the third branch of the model. Shortly after a child recognizes emotions, he is able to label them and understand relationships among them. The child sees similarities and differences between liking and loving, annoyance and anger. With this comes an understanding of what these emotions mean in relationships. Parents teach emotional reasoning by linking emotions to particular situations. The growing person also begins to realize that complex contradictory emotions can occur within a person. We learn that it is possible to feel both love and hate toward the same person. Later, blends or combinations of emotions are acknowledged. Emotionally intelligent individuals go on to reason about sequences of emotion. For example, a person who feels unlovable rejects another's care or concern out of fear of being rejected later. Mayer et al. (2000) maintained that reasoning about the progression of our feelings is central to emotional intelligence. They explained, "The person who is able to understand emotions—their meanings, how they blend together, how they progress over time—is truly blessed with the capacity to understand fundamental truths of human nature and of the interindividual relationships" (Mayer et al., 2000, p. 109).

Reflective Regulation of Emotions to Promote Emotional and Intellectual Growth

The highest branch of the theoretical model represents the conscious regulation of emotions to enhance emotional and intellectual growth. Emotional reactions must be welcomed when they occur regardless of how pleasant or unpleasant they are. There must exist an openness to feelings if individuals are to learn from them. As we develop, we learn to engage and disengage at appropriate times. An emotionally mature person learns to draw back from an emotionally troublesome discussion with cool-headed reasoning. Later, the emotional insights gained from that experience may be applied to other situations. As the individual matures, there evolves an ability to consciously reflect on emotional responses. Experiences of mood take place: "I don't completely understand the way I'm feeling." Such a thought is a conscious reflection on emotional responses rather than a simple perception of feelings. The experience of mood includes two parts: metaevaluation and metaregulation. The evaluations involve how much attention is paid to one's mood, while the regulation concerns whether an individual tries to improve a bad mood, dampen a good one, or disregard the mood. An emotionally intelligent person understands moods without exaggerating or minimizing them (Mayer & Salovey, 1997).

Emotional Intelligence and Emotional Achievement

With academic intelligence, intelligence is the aptitude, and achievement represents what is accomplished. Analogous to this, emotional intelligence represents the core aptitude or ability to reason with emotions. Emotional achievement represents the learning an individual has attained about emotion or emotion-related information. Mayer and Salovey (1997) indicated that emotional intelligence determines one's emotional achievement, and a person must take into account "the family in which one grew up, the lessons about emotions one was taught, the life events one has undergone—all influence how much one has achieved in learning about emotions" (p. 15). These theorists maintained that individuals operate from different emotional starting places that are considered their "emotional knowledge base" (Mayer & Salovey, 1997, p. 19), and the opportunities for learning emotional skills may be dependent on the contexts and culture in which we are raised. Salovey and Mayer suggested that emotional intelligence can be taught and infused in school curriculum.

In summary, Mayer and Salovey (1997) highlighted that the adaptive use of emotion-laden information is an important aspect of intelligence. Using emotions as a basis for thinking and thinking with emotions may both be related to important social competencies and behavior that shape our lives. Therefore, the development of emotional intelligence in intellectually able students should be a goal for educators and counselors of gifted students. The construct of emotional intelligence as conceived by Salovey and Mayer has implications for those educators. I encourage my readers to reflect on this model of emotional intelligence and to consider the following questions:

- How might educators train their students in the four elements of emotional intelligence?
  1. Perception, Appraisal, and Expression of Emotion
  2. Emotional Facilitation of Thinking
  3. Understanding and Analyzing Emotional Information; Employing Emotional Knowledge
  4. Regulation of Emotion

- How might the model serve as a framework for designing affective curriculum for gifted students?
- How might this model support school counselors in their work with gifted students?
- How might the Mayer and Salovey model serve as a framework for supporting parents and families of gifted students?

Robert Sternberg's Balance Theory of Wisdom

Like art, wisdom is difficult to define, but people recognize it when they see it. We encounter it when we reflect on the experiences of Mahatma Gandhi, Mother Teresa, Martin Luther King, Jr., and Nelson Mandela, and conclude that they were highly gifted individuals who were wise. We also conclude that their giftedness went far beyond intelligence measured by a conventional test (Sternberg, 2000). Sternberg (2000) noted, "Human intelligence has, to some extent, brought the world to the brink. It may take wisdom to find our way around it" (p. 253). He proposed a "balance theory of wisdom" in which he maintained that people are wise to the extent that they use their intelligence in seeking the common good. They are able to do so by balancing their personal interests with the interests of other people and of larger entities such as their families, communities, and countries. According to Sternberg (1998, 2000, 2003), people who are wise adapt to new environments, change their environments, or choose new environments to achieve outcomes that transcend their personal self-interest. In order to do so, Sternberg maintained that wise individuals apply tacit as well as explicit knowledge mediated by their values to reach their goals. Sternberg (2003) also posited that wisdom involves creativity in that wise decisions or solutions to problems may be far from obvious. In summary, he proposed that the key to success in life lies in the combination of intelligence, creativity, and wisdom.

The notion of wisdom begins with the construct of tacit knowledge about oneself, others, and the context of a situation. Tacit knowledge involves the lessons of life that are not explicitly taught and often are not even verbalized (Sternberg, Wagner, Williams, & Horvath, 1995). Sternberg (2000) maintained that tacit knowledge is procedural, relevant to the attainment of goals that individuals value, and often is acquired through experience or mentoring. He argued that tacit knowledge plays a far more significant role in wisdom than formal knowledge of a domain. Sternberg (2000) noted that we recognize individuals who are experts in their chosen domains who are not wise. Moreover, some of us know wise individuals who have little formal education. Their education has taken place in the "school of life," where they have acquired tacit or informal knowledge that serves them well.

Sternberg (2000) argued that we need creative abilities to generate ideas, analytical abilities to determine whether they are good ideas, and practical abilities to apply the ideas and persuade others of their value. Moreover, we need wisdom to balance the effects of the ideas on others and on institutions over time. He believes that wisdom is not the same as intelligence and he encourages us to think seriously about developing wisdom in young people:

> We know that IQs have been rising substantially over the past several generations . . . Yet it is difficult for some to discern any increase in the wisdom of the peoples of the world. Levels of conflict in the world show no sign of de-escalating; rather, they have intensified in many parts of the world. So, maybe it is time that psychologists, as a profession, take more seriously the formulation of theories of wisdom. . . . Educators need to take seriously the identification and development of giftedness in wisdom. (Sternberg, 2000, p. 258)

Sternberg proposed that wisdom is a construct that is not only relevant to adults. He believes that we can develop wisdom in children. Teachers can begin to nurture an appreciation of wisdom and what wise people offer to society. He highlighted seven ways that wisdom can be developed in young people:

- Provide students with problems that require wise thinking.
- Help children to think in terms of a common good in solving problems.
- Help students learn how to balance their own interests, the interests of others, and the interests of institutions in solving problems.
- Provide examples of wise thinking from the past and have students analyze them.
- Model wisdom for students by showing personal examples of wise and not-so-wise thinking that taught you important lessons.
- Help students to think dialectically.
- Show students that you value wise thinking.
- Encourage students to transfer what they learn about wisdom outside the classroom so they may change the way they conduct themselves in life. (Sternberg, 2000, pp. 257–258)

Sternberg and his colleagues maintained that for children to become successful citizens of the world they need to develop wisdom-based thinking skills (Sternberg, Jarvin, & Grigorenko, 2009). "In life, we all face difficult everyday problems, and to be successful in life means to be able to solve these difficult and uncertain everyday problems, in which we have to rely on wisdom to make the right decision" (Sternberg et al., 2009, p. 104). Sternberg et al. (2009) proposed that educators provide students with educational contexts in which they are able to reach their understanding of what constitutes wise thinking. They indicated that teaching for wisdom does not involve telling children about wisdom, but rather, letting young people actually experience decision making. In order to prepare them, educators encourage students to engage in thinking reflectively, thinking dialogically, and thinking dialectically.

When students engage in reflective thinking in the classroom, they work on their awareness of their own thoughts and beliefs to increase metacognition. The explicit teaching of metacognitive strategies such as self-questioning and self-monitoring checklists may be helpful. Teachers also can help students practice reflective thinking by designing instructional activities that allow students to explore and determine their own values. An example is included below.

> Students explore Benjamin Franklin's maxims. With a partner they share an example of an experience in their own lives where Franklin's maxim applied. They continue generating their own maxims throughout the year and preserve them in a journal. They then have engaged in reflective thinking and discover that wisdom involves an ability to learn from the past.

When students engage in dialogical thinking in the classroom, they consider different frames of reference and various perspectives to determine the best possible solutions to problems for all parties involved. Classroom activities in which children must consider multiple points of view and different perspectives of an issue are important. Teachers guide their students to understand how optimal solutions to problems are determined from carefully considering alternatives rather than following a prescribed plan of action. An example is included below.

> Students engage in studying literary works by examining the contexts of the time period in which they were written. In 19th-century novels, why are women so often referred to as fragile and delicate beings? How has the perception of gender changed over time?

When students engage in dialectical thinking in the classroom, they work to integrate different points of view. Although dialogical thinking involves considering multiple points of view, the emphasis of dialectical thinking is on the consideration and integration of two opposing perspectives. In essence, students must become their own devil's advocate by first taking on one position and then the opposite point of view. An example is included below.

> A teenager who is strongly opposed to animal cruelty must consider those who argue for the necessary use of animals in medical research. Can this student examine the two points of view and create a synthesis—a reconciliation of the two opposing sides of the issue?

As educators prepare to teach for wisdom, Sternberg et al. (2009, p. 112) offered the following six general guidelines:

- Encourage students to read classic works of literature and philosophy to learn and reflect on the wisdom of the sages.
- Engage students in class discussions, projects, and essays that encourage them to discuss the lessons they have learned from these works and how they can be applied to their own lives and the lives of others. Particular emphasis should be placed on dialogical and dialectical thinking.
- Encourage students to study not only "truth," but values, as developed during their reflective thinking.
- Place an increased emphasis on critical, creative, and practical thinking in the service of the common good.
- Encourage students to think about how almost *any* topic they study might be used for better or for worse ends and about how important that final end is.
- Remember that you, as the teacher, are a role model! To role model wisdom, adopt a Socratic approach to teaching and invite your students to play a more active role in constructing learning—from their own point of view and from that of others.

Sternberg (2003) recognized that this new approach to the teaching of wisdom will be met with challenges. Entrenched structures in schools may be difficult to change. Others may not see the value of such an approach that shows no promise of raising test scores. Sternberg realized that wisdom is far more difficult to develop than the kind of achievement measured by a multiple-choice test. People who have gained influence and power in a society may be reluctant to see a new standard established on which they may not be evaluated favorably. With these challenges considered, Sternberg (2003) reminded us:

Wisdom might bring us a world that would seek to better itself and the conditions of all the people in it. At some level, we as a society have a choice. What do we want to maximize through our schooling? Is it just knowledge? Is it just intelligence? Or is it also wisdom? If it is wisdom, then we need to put our students on a much different course. We need to value not only how they use their outstanding individual abilities to maximize the attainments of others. We need, in short, to value wisdom. (p. 173)

Educators working with gifted students may find that Sternberg's theory is suitable for guiding schools in their efforts to produce citizens who make positive contributions to society. Knowledge of this theory may assist teachers who work with gifted young people who have the potential to become the Mother Teresa, Nelson Mandela, or Martin Luther King, Jr. of their time. I encourage my readers to reflect on the following questions regarding Sternberg's balance theory of wisdom:

- How does the identification and development of wisdom in young people influence their social and emotional lives?
- How might the identification and development of wisdom in students influence our school curriculum?
- Should the teaching of wisdom become a component of K–12 gifted education programs? What might be the challenges in implementing such an approach? What might be the benefits?
- How might educators teach Sternberg's theory to adolescents? How might an understanding of this theory support them?
- In what ways could Sternberg's theory revolutionize our educational system?
- How might the identification and development of wisdom influence school counseling programs for gifted students ?
- How does Sternberg's theory support parents of gifted children in parenting their sons and daughters? What might Robert Sternberg do to further educate parents in nurturing wisdom in children?

Renzulli's Houndstooth Theory of Social Capital

A first grader named Ryan learned from his teacher that some children in Uganda have to walk many miles to gather water for their families, leaving them little time for school. His teacher explained that the water is often unsafe to drink and, as a result, many Ugandan children suffer from serious diseases and die from drinking unclean water. Ryan's teacher explained that $70 is enough to drill a new well to supply water to an entire village in Uganda. Ryan returned home that day and negotiated with his parents that he would do extra chores around the house to raise the funds to build a well. After months of vacuuming, washing windows, and picking up pinecones in his yard, Ryan earned the money he needed. With his parents, he visited the office of WaterCan, an organization building wells in developing countries. Ryan presented his contribution of $75, explaining that the extra $5 was to cover the cost of lunch for the well diggers.

Ryan learned that his teacher was mistaken. It takes $2,000 to drill a well in Africa; the dollar amount his teacher told the class would only cover the cost of a small hand pump that is part of the well. Ryan was undeterred and decided to do more chores. When the local newspaper published Ryan's story, his parents began to receive checks written out to "Ryan's Well." Eventually Ryan's well was drilled next to the Angolo Primary School in northern Uganda. Ryan was invited to a WaterCan meeting during which a speaker explained to the audience that he could drill many more wells in Africa if he had a modern power drill. After hearing this, Ryan announced that he would continue his efforts. As the media highlighted his campaign to raise money for clean water, donations kept pouring in. To date, the Ryan's Wells Foundation has raised millions of dollars to drill wells in Africa, South Asia, and Central America, providing clean water to more than 640,000 people in 16 countries. Ryan was able to see his work in action when he traveled with his parents to Uganda. When he arrived in the town of Angolo, he was amazed that the children of the village were shouting his name (Sundem, 2010)!

Aubyn, an 11-year-old, was appalled when she learned of how many young children living in foster homes were forced to carry their belongings in large garbage bags because they did not have suitcases. In response, Aubyn created Suitcases for Kids, making it her mission to see that all children in foster care have a suitcase of their own. Recruiting support from 4-H groups, Boy and Girl Scouts, churches, civic organizations, and businesses, Aubyn was able to supply more than 17,000 children in foster care with their own suitcases. After 2 years, Aubyn succeeded in getting a chapter of Suitcases for Kids established in all 50 states as well as Canada and the Soviet Union. Aubyn explained:

> I thought it was horrible that children had nothing to carry their things in as they moved so many times. I wanted to make them feel special by giving them something of their own to keep. I tried

to put myself in their place and think how I would feel. (Renzulli, 2009, p. 80)

Michael, a third grader from Malden, MA, was captivated by a guest speaker's presentation on starting a business. Following the presentation, Michael's enrichment teacher spoke to his group about using their talents to do good things for others. That conversation sparked an idea within this young boy.

Michael had observed that many of the recent immigrants to Malden were from Cape Verde Islands (off the coast of Africa) and had never experienced a severe winter. Coming from a tropical climate, the new members of Michael's community did not own mittens or gloves, and he was concerned. He acquired a loan from his school's principal to purchase a button-making machine and started his company. He recruited other children to get involved in his button business as he needed a manufacturing group, an advertising team, and a marketing staff. Michael and his friends sold their buttons for 50 cents each and the profits of the button sales went toward purchasing mittens and gloves for the new immigrants from Cape Verde (J. Renzulli, personal communication, September 14, 2009).

What is it about children like Ryan, Aubyn, and Michael that enables them to notice the suffering of others and want to make a positive difference in people's lives? "What causes some people to mobilize their interpersonal, political, ethical, and moral senses in such ways that they place their human concerns and the common good above materialism, ego enhancement, and self-indulgence?" (Renzulli, Systma, & Schader, 2003, p. 19). Joseph Renzulli has begun to examine these questions and has proposed his Houndstooth theory of social capital. He asks, "Can a better understanding of people who use their gifts for the greater good help us create conditions that expand the number of people who willingly contribute to the growth of both social and economic capital?" (Renzulli et al., 2003, p. 18). He believes that all individuals have a social intelligence and one of the challenges facing the field of gifted education is to devote resources to the development of this type of intelligence. Renzulli (2003) defined social capital as "a set of intangible assets that address the collective needs and problems of other individuals and communities at large" (p. 77). Labonte (1999) referred to it as "the 'gluey stuff' that binds individuals to groups, groups to organizations, citizens to societies" (p. 431). This type of capital enhances the obligations individuals have to one another, builds community life, and strengthens the bedrock of social trust. Reflecting on his early contributions to his field, Renzulli (2003) explained the evolution of his theory:

> In what is now popularly known as the three-ring conception of giftedness (above average but not necessarily superior ability, creativity, and task commitment) I embedded the three rings in a houndstooth background that represents the interactions between personality and environment. These factors aid in the development of three clusters of traits that represent gifted behaviors. What I recognized but did not emphasize at the time was that a scientific examination of a more focused set of background components is necessary in order for us to understand the sources of gifted behaviors and, more importantly, the ways in which people transform their gifted assets into constructive action. (p. 77)

In this theory, the word *houndstooth* refers to the complex background pattern of the interwoven factors that influence gifted behaviors. Just as threads of wool provide strength and pattern in houndstooth fabric, gifted behaviors are interwoven within particular situations. In order to examine the interwoven quality of these behaviors, Renzulli and his colleagues developed a new research project, Operation Houndstooth. The goal of this research is to expand the definition of giftedness to include several traits that characterize individuals who have had a profound impact on the improvement of society. In pursuing this research, Renzulli was influenced by the recent emergence of the positive psychology movement championed by Martin E. P. Seligman (Lopez & Gallagher, 2009; Seligman, 1991; Seligman & Csikszentmihalyi, 2000), which focuses on what is good in life rather than attempting to fix what is maladaptive behavior. Renzulli sees the goal of positive psychology as creating a science of human strengths that enable us to understand how to nurture socially constructive qualities in children. The positive psychology literature combined with Renzulli's interest in components that develop socially constructive giftedness resulted in his research team investigating the personal attributes that form the framework of his Houndstooth theory. The research team conducted a comprehensive review of the literature and a series of Delphi technique classification studies that led to the delineation of 6 components and 13 subcomponents of socially constructive intelligence (Renzulli, 2009, pp. 88–89) described below:

- **Optimism**
    - A quality that incorporates cognitive, emotional, and moti-

vational components and reflects a belief that the future holds promise.

- Subcomponents: hope, positive feelings from hard work

Courage
- The ability to face challenges or danger while overcoming physical, psychological, and/or moral fears.
- Subcomponents: psychological/intellectual independence, moral conviction

Romance With a Topic/Discipline
- When an individual falls in love with a topic or discipline, a true romance evolves. The passion for the big ideas helps to propel the individual in his or her quest for understanding.
- Subcomponents: absorption, passion

Sensitivity to Human Concerns
- The ability to understand another's affective experience and to sensitively communicate understanding through one's action. This sensitivity is characterized by altruism and empathy.
- Subcomponents: insight, empathy

Physical and Mental Energy
- The amount of energy an individual is able to invest toward achieving one's goals.
- Subcomponents: charisma, curiosity

Vision/Sense of Destiny
- This quality may be described as a variety of intercorrelated constructs including internal locus of control, motivation, volition, and self-efficacy. When an individual has a vision or sense of destiny about the future such an image serves to stimulate and direct one's behavior.
- Subcomponents: sense of power to change things, sense of direction, pursuit of goals

The next phase of Renzulli's Operation Houndstooth is a series of experimental studies to determine how school interventions can promote the type of behavior defined within the components of social capital. Renzulli and his colleagues are in the early stages of attempting to understand the complexity of social capital. He points out that promoting social capital as a national goal may take years; however, he believes that time is of the essence. Renzulli (2003) noted that there have been periods in the history of civilization when "the zeitgeist has resulted in elevating a society's values toward social capital" (p. 83), and with the challenges facing society today, the time has come for individuals to place high value on a sense of community and dedication to the greater good. He indicates that the general goal of the next phase of this work is to "infuse the process of schooling experiences related to the components of social capital that will contribute to the development of wisdom and a satisfying lifestyle" (Renzulli, 2003, p. 84). He explained:

> It would be naïve to think that a redirection of educational goals can take place without a commitment at all levels to examine the purposes of education in a democracy. It is also naïve to think that experiences directed toward the production of social capital can, or are even intended to, replace our present day focus on material productivity and intellectual capital. Rather, this work seeks to enhance the development of wisdom and a satisfying lifestyle that are paralleled by concerns for diversity, balance, harmony, and proportion in all of the choices and in the decisions that young people make in the process of growing up. What people think and decide to do drives society's best ideas and achievements. If we want leaders who will promote ideas and achievements that take into consideration the components we have identified in Operation Houndstooth, then giftedness in the new century will have to be re-defined in ways that take these co-cognitive components into account. And the strategies that are used to develop giftedness in our young people will need to give as much attention to the co-cognitive conditions of development as we presently give to cognitive development. (Renzulli, 2003, p. 84)

Robert Sternberg called attention to how an understanding of wisdom might enable us to understand the life experiences of Mother Teresa, Nelson Mandela, and Martin Luther King, Jr. An examination of Joseph Renzulli's theory of social capital may add to our understanding and support us in developing social capital in intellectually able young people. Social capital has implications for schooling, and Renzulli believes the development of socially constructive intelligence should be a goal for educators of gifted students. I encourage my readers to reflect on Renzulli's theory of social capital and to consider the following questions:

  ❧ What do you think enables children like Ryan, Aubyn, and Michael to notice the suffering of others? Have you known children like them? How did you respond to them?

- In proposing his theory, Renzulli (2003) asked, "does anybody really care about the test scores or grade point average of people like . . . Martin Luther King, Jr.?" (p. 83). How does this question influence your thinking on the social and emotional components of giftedness?

- What role does the development of social capital play in the design of services offered to students in gifted education programs?

- How might the development of socially constructive intelligence influence a school's curriculum?

- Should the development of social capital become a component of K–12 gifted education programs? What might be the challenges in implementing such an approach? What might be the benefits?

- Both Robert Sternberg and Joseph Renzulli have recently been influenced by the positive psychology movement. How do you see this movement changing how we think about the social and emotional lives of gifted students?

Having explored the theories of psychological development that guide our understanding of gifted young people and developed an appreciation of their complexity, let us move on to the next two chapters, which consider specifically the social and emotional characteristics and traits of gifted students and examine how they influence their life experiences.

C H A P T E R **2**

Social and Emotional Characteristics and Traits of Gifted Young People: Part I

My goals for this chapter are to:
- ❧ Acquaint you with several of the social and emotional characteristics, traits, and behaviors evidenced in gifted young people.
- ❧ Present strategies to nurture those characteristics, traits, and behaviors.

Recently my neighbor invited me to join him at his 6-year-old son's soccer match. As I sat in the stands and soaked up the sun on a beautiful autumn Saturday morning, I enjoyed watching a teenager negotiate with his younger brother. The little 6-year-old had arrived for the match wearing pants. When he realized all of his teammates were wearing their official soccer shorts, he announced in tears that he was not playing and wanted to return home. His older brother came to his support by reassuring him that playing in his pants would not be a problem. I smiled to myself as I listened in on the conversation between the two brothers. I heard the older brother explain, "Actually, Josh, it's better to have long pants on. You can do skids and you won't wreck your knees. If those other kids had thought about it, they'd be wearing long pants too." As he started to roll up the cuffs of his little brother's pants, he said, "These look so cool. Man, you look like David Beckham!" This supportive pep talk from the older brother apparently made a difference. Josh was convinced that his older brother knew what he was talking about, and he joined his teammates on the field.

I turned to my neighbor seated next to me in the stands and commented on the kindness of the older boy and how sensitive he had been in dealing with his brother's feelings. I did not realize that Josh's mother was within hearing distance of me. Mrs. Warner beamed as she explained to me that those were her two sons. Proud that she was raising sensitive children, she smiled and pointed out that parenting these children included memorable moments as well as challenges. She went on to tell me about her older daughter who years before had been in the same soccer league. With another smile she reflected on one experience when she and her husband were cheering from the sidelines, "Come on, Emma, get the ball! Come on, Emma, take the ball away. Come on, go in there and get the ball!" Four-year-old Emma came running to her parents on the sidelines in tears and announced, "That's not nice. You're supposed to share." Her mother pointed out, "To my daughter, it was all about taking turns. To her, that's what soccer was about. The thought of taking something away from another child was simply unacceptable."

I continued chatting with Mrs. Warner, and she was pleased to share stories of her talented children. She told me about the older son who at age 13 spent time every day processing through the events of his day with a stick. At age 3, Nate had discovered that particular sticks had a special quality about them that enabled him to relax, to think quietly about whatever issues were on his mind, and to think creatively about far-away places and adventures that occurred through his vivid imagination. Gifted with a learning disability, Nate returned every day after school and would walk outdoors for long periods of time processing his thoughts as he waved his stick in different directions. His family kept a stick handy in the family car, and his extensive collection of favorite sticks is under his bed. Both his parents and siblings understand how significant these sticks are to this highly creative boy; however, not everyone has appreciated this about Nate.

Mrs. Warner pointed out that when Nate was 6 he thought intuitively that Steven, his best friend, might understand how he used the stick to support his imagination. He asked Steven, "When you see a stick, what do you pretend it is? What do you think of?" Steven responded, "I just see a stick. I think it's a stick!" That evening, as Mrs. Warner was tucking her son into bed, he was sobbing over his conversation with his best friend. "Mommy, nobody gets me. Nobody else plays with sticks. They all play with toys. What's wrong with me?" Teary-eyed, Mrs. Warner whispered, "It's not always easy being a parent of this type of child."

Later we were joined by other soccer parents in the bleachers, and Mrs. Warner pointed out to her friends that she was chatting with a university professor interested in gifted children. Parents were happy to share stories but several had questions and concerns and wanted advice from me. One father described how Kate, his 7-year-old daughter, was excited about her upcoming birthday party. Her parents had agreed that she could hold her party at the local roller skating rink but she was worried that she would not be the best roller skater at the party. As the birthday girl, Kate could not deal with the thought that she might actually fall. To prevent herself from this potential embarrassment, she insisted that dad take her to the rink for several weeks to practice her roller skating in preparation for the party. As this father described their roller skating practice sessions, he smiled, shook his head, and said, "She is so intense! She stresses over everything."

Another mom shared with us how her 6-year-old daughter Janna commented at dinner, "Mom, several days ago on the playground Chelita said Jennifer was acting like a brat. Mom, I'm nice to her at school, but I really don't like her. She stomps her feet and points her fingers at kids and she's mean to them. I try to be nice to her, but I really don't like her." This mother was intrigued with how Janna had been processing through these school playground "events" for several days and was struggling with how to interpret the recess bully's behavior. She was concerned with how much time her child spent focusing on these issues and wondered if Janna was overly sensitive. She appreciated that her daughter recognized that the schoolyard bully needed friends and attempted to be kind to her. She reassured Janna that she was right and explained, "You can be nice to her at school, but you don't have to be best friends with her." This mother pointed out that she appreciated that her daughter was empathic, yet she wondered just how this quality within her would serve her with other bullies she may encounter in her life.

Much of what these dedicated parents saw in their children are what teachers have described for many years as traits, behaviors, or characteristics related to the social and emotional development of the gifted students in their classrooms. These classroom teachers are joined by researchers and theorists in the gifted education community who maintain that gifted children do exhibit certain social and emotional characteristics and traits that are accompanied by concomitant needs. Others who study the psychology of gifted individuals argue that gifted children do not necessarily have characteristics that are unique; however, the cultural contexts in which gifted children are immersed strongly influence their experiences of growing up gifted. Whether or not gifted learners have unique affective characteristics has been an area of debate for decades, and both lines of thought should be considered.

A comprehensive review of research was conducted by a task force of educators, psychologists, and researchers from the National Association for Gifted Children (NAGC; Neihart, Reis, Robinson, & Moon, 2002). This report revealed a limited research base on which to draw conclusions about whether gifted students have unique social and emotional characteristics and traits. The NAGC task force concluded that there was no evidence that gifted young people were more vulnerable or flawed in their social adjustment. Rather, they noted that many gifted young people have assets that, when supported, may actually augment their ability to overcome adversities and utilize their talents to achieve personal fulfillment. The task force members called for educators to respect the unique and varied characteristics related to giftedness seen in young people.

To continue the dialogue and illuminate our understanding of the role of these characteristics and their interaction with contextual influences, I dedicate three chapters of this book to this discussion as a way of providing a balanced examination of this important issue. In this chapter and the one that follows, I discuss social and emotional characteristics, traits, and behaviors seen as assets within gifted young people. Chapter 4 offers an examination of the contextual influences that may shape how young people experience their giftedness.

My objective for this chapter is to describe these characteristics and explain how they may influence a gifted young person's life. I draw examples from my former gifted students, and I share examples passed on to me by other teachers and parents. I also highlight examples from biographies of gifted individuals. Throughout this discussion, I provide theoretical and research support for what the gifted education community has learned about these positive characteristics, traits, and behaviors. I conclude the chapter by sharing teaching and counseling strategies and methods for nurturing these traits and characteristics and supporting the behaviors.

Several researchers and authors have reviewed the gifted education literature examining the affective development of gifted students and have

TABLE 3

Social and Emotional Traits, Characteristics, and Behaviors Evidenced in Gifted Students

- High expectations of self and others—perfectionism
- Internal motivation and inner locus of control
- Emotional sensitivity, intensity, and depth
- Empathy
- Advanced levels of moral maturity with consistency between values and actions
- Strong need for self-actualization
- Highly developed sense of humor
- Resilience

provided lists of social and emotional traits, characteristics, and behaviors evidenced in gifted learners. I have drawn from the work of Clark (2002); Silverman (1993a); Reis and Sullivan (2009); Ferguson (2009); Davis, Rimm, and Siegle (2011); and VanTassel-Baska (1998) in determining the list shown in Table 3 that guides the discussion of this chapter and the one following. The first four items from the list will be discussed in this chapter, and the rest will be presented in Chapter 3.

Social and Emotional Traits, Characteristics, and Behaviors Evidenced in Gifted Students

High Expectations of Self and Others—Perfectionism

Perfectionism is defined as "a disposition to regard anything short of perfection as unacceptable" (Merriam-Webster, 1998). For many years perfectionism has been a personality characteristic commonly associated with gifted children. Several leaders in gifted education have maintained that perfectionism is one of the most critical issues related to giftedness. Others have indicated that gifted and talented students struggle with perfectionism more than other children do. Psychologists and educators have long been concerned about perfectionism in gifted students because it can be manifested in many forms, some that are valued by society and others that are not (Adderholdt & Goldberg, 1999; Greenspon, 2002; Silverman, 1989; Troxclair, 1999). This issue has received extensive attention by a number of contemporary researchers within the gifted education community (i.e., Nugent, 2000; Parker, 2000; Parker & Adkins, 1995; Parker & Mills, 1996; Schuler, 2000; Siegle & Schuler, 2000; Speirs Neumeister, 2004a, 2004b, 2004c). Moreover, the difference between striving for excellence, labeled *healthy perfectionism*, and the compulsive striving for unrealistic and unattainable goals, labeled *neurotic perfectionism*, became the focus of constructive debate amongst several researchers in a special issue of the *Journal of Secondary Gifted Education* edited by Maureen Neihart and Bonnie Cramond (2000). The debate centered on whether perfectionism is a positive characteristic that should be nurtured within gifted students or a problem that needs to be cured. The discussion also focused on whether or not perfectionism is a one-dimensional or multidimensional construct.

The gifted education community has benefited from the work of psychologists Hewitt and Flett (1991), who proposed a model to explain perfectionism as a three-dimensional interpersonal construct. These researchers saw differences in the ways perfectionists direct their energies. They described self-oriented perfectionists as individuals who establish high personal standards for themselves and measure themselves according to those standards, often highly critical of their efforts and products. Other-oriented perfectionists are individuals who demand very high standards of others in their lives, while socially prescribed perfectionists believe that others in their lives maintain very high standards for them. Clinical psychologists describe individuals from their practice who match these profiles. To illuminate how these differences manifest themselves in young people, consider the following composites from the work of clinical psychologist Monica Ramirez Basco (1999).

Celeste is a self-oriented perfectionist. Mrs. Rushmore, Celeste's seventh-grade teacher, has recognized her artistic talents and her strong interpersonal skills. As a result, Celeste has two important responsibilities related to the seventh-grade historical pageant. She has been assigned the job of designing backdrops for the theatrical production as well as publicizing the event to the local community. Celeste has enjoyed creating beautiful posters advertising the historical play. Many of her parents' friends and teachers at school have commented about the effectiveness of her posters, which are visible throughout the community. Celeste and her team of set designers also are enjoying creating backdrops that will add authenticity to the stage. Mrs. Rushmore has raved about their work and commented to Celeste how proud she is of her efforts. As the seventh graders prepare for the pageant, Celeste also is busy designing handmade invitations to send to important community leaders. She is proud of how historically authentic these individualized invitations appear and is having fun with calligraphy and experimenting with various parchment papers.

All of Celeste's hard work pays off and on the evening of the pageant, Mr. Bearce, the eighth-grade social science teacher turns to Celeste in the lobby of the school auditorium and asks her if Mrs. Huntington, the president of the local historical society has arrived. Mrs. Huntington is a good friend of Mrs. Rushmore and has always been supportive of the many historical projects she has undertaken with her middle school students. Celeste instantly feels sick when she realizes she has forgotten to send Mrs. Huntington an individualized invitation.

"Mr. Bearce, I totally forgot to invite her. How could I be so dumb? What am I going to do? Mrs. Rushmore is going to be so upset with me. Mrs. Huntington is bound to hear about this and she'll be hurt. This could even affect her friendship with Mrs. Rushmore. I'm such a doofus! How can I ever face my teacher again? I may as well forget about my A in history class. Mrs. Rushmore will never trust me again."

Although Mr. Bearce attempts to assuage her feelings, Celeste avoids Mrs. Rushmore and keeps herself hidden backstage. What will she say to her teacher? Feeling miserable, she spends the evening berating herself and thinking of many excuses she could use to explain her faux pas to Mrs. Rushmore.

Celeste is a self-oriented perfectionist who is unable to accept her mistakes. She spends her days worrying about what others will think of her, and her mistakes are constantly blown out of proportion. Her mistakes cause her stress and sleepless nights and she withdraws from other people. She has trouble forgiving herself, for in her mind it is acceptable for others to make mistakes but it is not OK for her to be less than perfect.

Pablo is an other-oriented perfectionist. He acknowledges his talents and feels good about his abilities but his problem is that he often feels completely frustrated with others who let him down. Pablo excels in the classroom and in student leadership. As president of the sophomore class, he appoints his classmates to committees responsible for fund-raising efforts to help support a local homeless shelter. As he arrives home from school one afternoon, his mother sees that he is furious with his friends Sergio, Jessica, and Morgan, who have "dropped the ball again" in not contacting a number of potential sponsors for an upcoming dance marathon to raise funds for their worthy cause. Pablo spends an afternoon in a sullen mood and takes his frustrations out on his younger siblings. When his mother attempts to help, he shuts himself in his bedroom and continues brooding.

Pablo cannot understand why his friends cannot follow his directions. He realizes that his friends' intentions are good, but they simply do not take care of things in time, and again the burden falls on him. He is tired of the daily excuses from Sergio, Jessica, and Morgan. Even when they do contribute, Pablo thinks their work is not up to par and that his friends simply do not care enough. It frustrates him so much that he decides he would rather do the work than deal with their procrastination and "lame excuses."

The other-oriented perfectionism seen in Pablo causes him problems in his relationships. When he attempts to point out his frustration in a polite way to his friends, it invariably causes tension and conflict. Pablo has tried to expect less of others in his life, but continues to struggle.

Heidi is a socially prescribed perfectionist. Several years ago, I was intrigued with a *Sports Illustrated* article featuring the story of Heidi Gillingham, a college basketball player for Vanderbilt University. Anderson (1993) described the college career of this young woman, who had gained the adulation of the Vanderbilt fans and was crowned homecoming queen. At Vanderbilt, Heidi, a 6'10" All American from Floresville, TX, was the tallest woman playing college basketball. As soon as Heidi made her first basketball team in seventh grade, many people in her community expected the squad to win "simply because *that tall girl* was on it" (p. 68). Heidi pointed out that she really never enjoyed playing basketball during high school: "I felt people expected me to be this basketball goddess. I felt like I had to be perfect, but I could never measure up" (Anderson, 1993, p. 69).

Heidi had also struggled with this issue in other areas of her life as a young adolescent. She admitted that as a teenager she had torn up a 4-H sewing project 10 times before being satisfied with her final product. As an honor student, she continually rewrote papers for days until the day they were due. Anderson (1993) reported that even making a phone call to a hair salon to arrange an appointment required meticulous preparation to ensure all would go perfectly. Heidi admitted that before dialing, she wrote out what she planned to say on the phone, followed by all the possible responses from the hairdresser (Anderson, 1993).

When Heidi began playing college ball for Vanderbilt, no matter how much she practiced, there inevitably would be a missed shot that frustrated her tremendously. She also compared herself constantly to another leading player on the team: "Wendy seemed to make every single shot and get every rebound, and I couldn't see any improvement in myself" (Anderson, 1993, p. 70). She explained, "It got to the point where I hated the game. I

realized I had always played because I was tall and society e>
people to play basketball. I really had a bad attitude" (p. 70).

Rather than quit the team, she listened closely to her coac⸱
who succeeded in convincing her that perfection was not expe⸱⸱⸱
sible. He made her understand that Hall of Fame players only make half of
their shots. Heidi reported, "He made me realize that my perfectionism was
actually hurting my game" (Anderson, 1993, p. 70). Eventually, she learned
to be kinder to herself and managed to keep more realistic self-expectations.
She concluded, "I decided that I was going to play basketball because that's
what *I* wanted, not what society wanted" (Anderson, 1993, p. 70).

With Celeste, Pablo, and Heidi, we see perfectionistic behaviors that
may serve them well, as well as other behaviors that are detrimental to their
emotional well-being. Their perfectionism may help them develop high
standards, perseverance, and talents; however, we see evidence that this
trait is not always an asset. Within these three cases are examples of mind
games that perfectionists play, described by Adderholdt and Goldberg
(1999) below:

- *Mood swinging between "highs" and "lows."* A perfectionist sets a
  goal, reaches it, and all is well in the world. When a goal is not
  met perfectly, feelings of low self-esteem set in and the individual
  becomes emotionally drained.
- *The numbers game and all-or-nothing thinking.* A perfectionist may
  never be satisfied with the number of accomplishments achieved.
  All-or-nothing thinking is evidenced in the student who receives a
  report card filled with A's but remains frustrated because of one B.
- *Focus on the future, pine over the past, and telescopic thinking deal with
  goal setting that is not healthy.* The behavior of focusing on the future
  can be detrimental in that the individual does not take time to enjoy
  a successful outcome, but simply directs his energies to reaching
  the next goal. When a perfectionist pines over the past, she cannot
  let go of what might have been, what she could have done better,
  or how a project might have been improved. Telescopic thinkers
  look at goals not met with a magnifying glass and enlarge them. In
  looking at their successes, they use the wrong end of the telescope,
  often minimizing them and treating them as insignificant.
- *Putting your goals first.* An unhealthy game some perfectionists play
  is placing their achievements and goals ahead of family, friends,
  and personal physical and emotional health.
- *"Getting it right."* The game of "practice makes perfect" taken to the
  extreme does not enable an individual to let go of a project.

The challenge for educators and counselors working with students who struggle with perfectionism is to help them understand how it might be channeled so that it enables them to reach their goals as well as enjoy the process. Basco's (1999) perspective may help these individuals understand the double-edged quality of this characteristic:

> The reach for perfection can be painful because it is often driven by a desire to do well and a fear of consequences of not doing well. This is the double-edged sword of perfectionism. On the one hand, it is a good thing to give the best effort, to go the extra mile, and to take pride in one's performance, whether it is keeping a home looking nice, writing a report, repairing a car, or doing brain surgery. It is commendable to attend to details, care about what others will think about your work, and constantly strive to do your best. On the other hand, when despite great efforts you feel as though you keep falling short, never seem to get things just right, never have enough time to do your best, are self-conscious, feel criticized by others, or cannot get others to cooperate in doing the job right the first time, you end up feeling bad. (p. 5)

Rather than view perfectionism as a double-edged sword, researchers in counseling and social psychology, as well as in gifted education, have come to understand perfectionism as a multidimensional trait that influences *adaptive* behaviors such as working hard, striving for achievement, efficacy, conscientiousness, organization, and structured work habits (Frost, Marten, Lahart, & Rosenblate, 1990; Hamachek, 1978; Schuler, 2000; Speirs Neumeister, 2004b, 2004c), as well as *maladaptive* behaviors such as anxiety, underachievement, and the mind games perfectionists play described by Adderholdt and Goldberg (1999).

As a clinical psychologist, Linda Silverman (1989) maintained that perfectionism drives adaptive behaviors and views it as a desirable characteristic. Her perspective, to some educators and counselors, may be refreshing in that she sees perfectionism as a driving force in a gifted individual's personality that propels that person to pursue higher goals. She described it as an energy that must be channeled in positive directions rather than a problem that needs to be fixed. Silverman (1989) added the following:

> The problem, however, may be in our attitudes toward perfectionism, rather than in the characteristic itself. We laud Michelangelo

for his search for perfection and Marie Curie for hers. We are proud of the achievements of our Nobel Laureates, our Olympic champions, our world-class scholars and artists. All of these individuals spend endless hours perfecting their knowledge, working harder than their colleagues, never satisfied with less than their best, pushing themselves beyond their own limitations. They command our respect and admiration. Why, then, do we denigrate this quality in gifted children or in ourselves? . . . The characteristic itself is neither good nor bad, it just is—and it is part of the gifted person's life equipment. If you harness your perfectionism to work for you, rather than letting it control you, you can change the world. (p. 11)

Silverman (1989) maintained that educators need to help young people appreciate the trait rather than be ashamed of this quality. Moreover, teachers can help them to understand that it serves a useful purpose. She argued that gifted young people need to allow themselves to be perfectionistic in activities that really matter to them, rather than in everything all at once. She also believed that gifted young people should maintain high standards for themselves but not impose them on others, focus on their successes, continue striving when their first attempts are not successful, hold on to their ideals, and believe in their ability to reach their goals.

Internal Motivation or Inner Locus of Control

Locus of control is a theoretical construct to explain the degree to which an individual perceives a relationship between his own behavior and the outcome of that behavior (Rotter, 1966). A person who assumes control or responsibility for the events in his life is said to display an internal locus of control. Internal motivation or an inner locus of control has been documented in the gifted education literature. Researchers have seen evidence of this trait in gifted young people (Goldberg & Cornell, 1998; McLaughlin & Saccuzzo, 1997; Yong, 1994). Researchers are interested in exploring this quality because a better understanding of it and how to nurture it within students would enable educators to support gifted underachievers, for example.

In my dissertation research with six gifted high-achieving males in an urban high school, I saw evidence of this quality. An internal motivation enabled them to overcome adversity in their lives and to remain focused on reaching their goals (Hébert, 2000a). One young man named Matteo referred to this drive as an "inner will," an important part of his identity. His explanation of this quality and its significance in his academic achievement in physics is representative of the six males in the study:

> It sounds off the wall, but it's an internal will. For example, if I am curious about something and I want to learn about it, like my science fair topic—cold fusion. I didn't care if the material I needed was radioactive or not. I said to the professor, "Send it to me in a lead bottle UPS. I'll pay the shipping!" Nothing is going to stop me. I am going to do this experiment. If I get this inner drive pointed toward academics, I'll do well. That's basically it. It's like a driving force. If I find some reason to motivate myself to push for something, I'll do it. (Hébert, 2000a, pp. 102–103)

Matteo was an energetic young man who had been recognized for his creativity, curiosity, and sharp intellect in third grade, when he was recommended for a self-contained gifted and talented class. Following an unsuccessful experience in that setting, Matteo's fifth-grade teacher recommended that he be scheduled into a less accelerated program because he was having difficulty with the fast-paced class. Matteo was upset at the time with the school's decision. However, he connected with a sympathetic teacher who helped him with his organizational skills, and he vowed that "he would prove them wrong." He earned grades of A's and B's from that time on and left his middle school with three academic awards, which he proudly received in a school assembly, vindicated on the final day of school.

During his freshman year of high school, he marched himself into his guidance counselor's office and requested to be placed in honors classes again. His request was granted, and Matteo remained there all through high school. Matteo was one of the most active students in his high school. Elected president of his junior class, he campaigned on a platform to eradicate student apathy. Throughout the year, with determination and hard work, he managed to involve his peers in class fund-raising projects and in planning a memorable prom. Besides playing trombone in the school band, playing tennis, and running cross-country, he was elected to the National Honor Society, the Student Council, and a number of executive boards that governed statewide student engineering organizations. In addition, Matteo was involved in a number of specialized summer enrichment programs designed to raise the aspirations of high-ability students from inner city high schools.

After several summers of studying engineering, Matteo decided to pursue a college degree in civil engineering and environmental studies and, because of his family's economic hardships, he decided the most practical way to accomplish his goal was through the U.S. Air Force Academy. Matteo's plans for the Academy consumed him as he prepared for the application process. His daily schedule involved getting up at 5 every morning to run and lift weights to get in better shape. He described the Academy as a "ticket" to his dreams, yet he did not necessarily see himself pursuing a career with the military. He explained his plans in his unique, analogous speaking style:

> The military is the way I will get my goal. The question is whether I will keep the car. I will have been enjoying the joy ride for all it's worth, but I am not sure if I will be staying with the Air Force. That's what will have gotten me the engineering degree. It's kinda' like staying on the bus after New York and deciding whether or not to continue on to Baltimore. I may make a career out of it. I might hate it. I don't know. I'll see down the road. (Hébert, 1993, p. 198)

I found this inner locus of control within a second population of gifted males when conducting a research study of gifted African American males in a predominantly White university. Internal motivation emerged as part of the belief in self that was evident in the participants. Several highlighted an awareness of internal motivation that was naturally incorporated into their views of self. One participant named Caleb was a charismatic young man who typically rushed from one campus meeting to the next scheduled event in his hectic daily calendar. Whether his journey across campus took him to the university's newspaper office, where he worked as an advertising director, to the gym for cheerleading practice, or to a meeting of a competitive team of advertising majors preparing for a regional competition, he was definitely a "man on the move." Caleb had arrived at the university with a Presidential scholarship in hand. Coming from a small industrial city, he had built an impressive high school résumé and was prepared to study engineering. As a sophomore, however, he realized he needed a career in which his creativity could flourish and, therefore, changed his major to advertising. Eventually he was recognized as one of the leading students in his department and went on to win prestigious awards and the respect of his professors and peers. How he saw himself as an achiever reflects an inner drive:

I've always known that I have things to do in life. I've known I have the brains to achieve. I've known that I have something different; it's always been a gut feeling. It's something inside of me that I can't explain. I feel if my hands are idle, there's something wrong. I want to achieve constantly. I don't ever want to "peak." (Hébert, 2002, p. 37)

In an interview with Caleb during his senior year, he described his preparation for his future in the aggressive advertising industry. A strong competitiveness was part of his identity. Again, he noted an internal drive that enabled him to excel:

On Saturday nights, I'm the one going to Barnes and Noble and reading up on advertising books. I'm constantly asking my professors to borrow their books and reading to get ahead. I'm the one who, instead of going to parties, is sitting at the computer for hours learning everything I can learn about new computer software. I'm driven to compete. It's in my nature. (Hébert, 2002, p. 37)

A second participant, John, came to the university from an inner city high school as a scholar-athlete. He arrived on campus with an impressive set of credentials that included involvement in athletics, many extracurricular activities, Advanced Placement coursework, and an internship in a law firm. His high motivation enabled him to pursue dual undergraduate degrees in English and psychology. John's explanation for his success was similar to Caleb's in that he provided evidence of an inner drive that was an important part of his belief in self. His ultimate goal was to earn a doctorate, and he described his strong motivation:

It's an inner drive, an inner motivation that's heightened by the desire to never be poor again. It's something inside of you that says, "Okay, if you quit, this is what happens." I can say, "Okay, I want to quit now because I'm tired. Quit now, and I'll have to get up at 5:00 in the morning, I won't have time to proofread the paper—turn it in—probably get a C. 'Ding!' Don't quit!" . . . I say it's an inner drive, it's an ability to say to yourself, "Okay, you can stop, but here are the consequences of stopping." And somehow that makes you want to keep moving. (Hébert, 2002, p. 37)

John did not stop moving. He went on to earn his master's degree in secondary education and eventually a doctoral degree in higher education. Today, he serves the university in an administrative capacity facilitating leadership programs for talented culturally diverse students. University administrators have expressed no doubts that John helps to foster an internal motivation in the students with whom he works.

Emotional Sensitivity, Intensity, and Depth

The trait of sensitivity is characterized as "a depth of feeling that results in a sense of identification with others" (Lovecky, 1993, p. 38). Sensitivity involves passion and compassion. Lovecky (1993) maintained that passion involves "the depth of feelings that colors all life experiences and brings an intensity and complexity to the emotional life" (p. 38). Within sensitive children, there exists a depth of feelings that influences their daily life experiences as they form strong attachments to people and places in their lives. They cannot bear to see others suffering. They can be easily hurt emotionally and may be acutely aware of the needs and emotions of others. Sensitive children can be hard on themselves, and they do not forgive themselves easily if they happen to hurt another person's feelings. They are often intensely self-analytical and self-critical. Young people who experience life through these sensitivities later join the Peace Corps or become poets, investigative reporters, peace activists, and protectors of wildlife; therefore, educators and counselors need to support and nurture this sensitivity within young people. Silverman (1993a) contended that the expression "too sensitive" must be eliminated from our vocabularies: "In a world that lacks sensitivity, those who are perceived as 'overly' sensitive may have exactly the degree of sensitivity that would be required to find a solution to homelessness or to save the planet from self-destruction" (p. 63). To provide a better understanding of how emotional sensitivity interacts with intensity and emotional depth, I offer an example of a young gifted child named Cameron described here.

Cameron: Living with emotional sensitivity, intensity, and depth. Melinda, a student I once worked with, became intrigued by several of the theories we studied concerning the psychosocial development of gifted children. As part of her coursework, she chose to reflect on parenting experiences with her son Cameron. As she pursued theoretical readings, she maintained a journal in which she connected the theories with many of the challenges and joys she and her husband had experienced as parents.

Melinda realized that she and her husband were in for an interesting journey as parents when Cameron, at 18 months, recognized, out of order, the letters of the alphabet and was able to spell out traffic and store signs. As an infant, he memorized nursery rhymes and would amuse himself during naptime by reciting the rhymes. Melinda discovered that he had taught himself to read when, at age 3, during his first visit to the dentist's office, he read a book he had never seen before to the receptionist and his surprised parent. As a kindergarten student, during his first trip to the school library, Cameron requested a book by Edgar Allan Poe. Much to his dismay, he was allowed to check out a picture book with no words. His fascination with kindergarten soon dissipated, and he announced to his parents that he "wasn't going to be coloring any more big red R's." Instead, he seemed to think it his duty to visit and help other children with their work. Melinda highlighted how his sensitivity, intensity, and advanced moral development were evidenced during this first year in school:

> Coming home from school on the bus presented Cameron a few problems. When older children realized that he could read, they teased him by having him read inappropriate words. Not knowing what these words meant, he obliged them. Cameron was curious as to why other children would do this. Soon, he became friends with these older children, and the situation was resolved. However, Cameron was very upset one day when another child was the object of teasing. As soon as he came into the house, he began to cry. He told us about the teasing and explained that he just couldn't understand how one person could be mean to another.

Cameron's intellectual growth flourished and the intensity of his interests in a wide variety of subjects grew. Occasionally in math, Cameron would complete every third or fourth problem, pointing out that because the problems were essentially the same, he was wasting his time doing all of them. This time, he said, could be spent learning other more important concepts. By sixth grade, Cameron's parents decided to enroll him in the Roeper City and Country School in Bloomfield Hills, MI, an academic environment in which he could flourish. Cameron took the SAT as part of the Midwest Talent Search Project during his first year at Roeper. His combined scores were above 1200. His verbal score was 670. Cameron was one of nine students to score above 630 verbal before the age of 13. For this he was invited to Evanston, IL, to attend an awards ceremony and receive a scholarship to attend Northwestern University's summer program. Although Melinda and her husband were proud of their son's accomplishments, she described how they were at times concerned for their son as a result of his intense approach to many areas of his life:

> Cameron had always loved to learn, and we saw this intensify greatly. This intensity did cause some problems. Cameron began placing a lot of pressure on himself. Much to our dismay, he would overcommit himself. He would take extra classes, become involved in lots of extracurricular activities, and write papers that would reach a minimum of 20 or 30 pages. He just seemed to drive himself. We tried to discuss this with Cameron, and we consistently met with the response that this was what he wanted to do, there was just so much that he was interested in. We did try to see that he had more balance in his life. Unfortunately, I don't think that we were too successful in our efforts. We did convince him to take a summer off and not attend a summer program. He did this; however, the following summer, he asked to enroll in a summer class at a local university. He was 14 at the time. Cameron took a literature class and enjoyed the reading; however, he was most dismayed that class discussions were superficial and other university students were not really serious about the work.

Melinda concluded her journal in my graduate class with a poignant memory of her son as an elementary school child that remains with her. Her description of Cameron underscores one particularly special quality within her son:

> A friend once asked me what of all of Cameron's achievements and awards made me most proud. It really isn't the outward signs of his success. Rather, it was when Cameron was in third grade and a new girl arrived in his class, a child in a wheelchair. The other children did not talk to her. As Cameron told me with tears in his eyes, "I did, Mom." As we continue to deal with the difficult aspects of Cameron's emotional development, I continue to focus on that memory. Yet, I cannot help but find it ironic that what I perceive as Cameron's greatest gift is the one that has the potential to cause him the most difficulty.

In Cameron, we see evidence of sensitivity, intensity, and empathy coming together. However, it is important to realize that sensitivity and empathy are related traits, but they do not necessarily appear together within the same child. For example, some gifted youngsters may be extremely sensitive to criticism, with their feelings becoming easily hurt; however, they may not necessarily be in tune with the feelings of others. Teenagers may be protective of younger children and the elderly, yet they may not be concerned about the feelings of their siblings or peers in school. In each young person varying degrees of these characteristics may interact with other qualities and traits. In the case of Cameron, he lived with three powerful traits that strongly influenced his daily experiences and how he viewed his world. Cameron was fortunate to have two loving parents who supported the development of these characteristics. Melinda and her husband also were lucky to have Cameron in their lives.

Empathy

For several decades, psychological research has examined the question of why people help others, even at considerable costs to themselves. What does this behavior tell us about our capacity to care? Researchers have focused on the claim that empathic emotion evokes altruistic motivation—the motivation to improve another human being's welfare. Empathy is formally defined as "an other-oriented emotional response elicited by and congruent with the perceived welfare of someone else" (Batson, Ahmad, Lishner, & Tsang, 2002, p. 485). If another person is thought to be in need, then empathic emotions such as sympathy, compassion, soft heartedness, and tenderness, and empathic emotions evoke altruistic motivation to help the person.

In examining empathic emotions, Batson and colleagues (2002) have identified seven related concepts from which empathy should be distinguished: knowing another individual's internal state, including thoughts and feelings; assuming the posture of an observed other; coming to feel as another person feels; projecting oneself into another's situation; imagining how another is feeling; imagining how one would think and feel in the other's place; and being upset by another person's suffering (pp. 486–488). Several of these concepts are highlighted in the example of an empathic young boy I describe next.

Several years ago, I taught a graduate course in gifted education in Fort Worth, TX. As part of the course I required a journal of weekly reflections. I asked students to make connections between the theoretical readings in the course and their observations of one particular child in their own classroom. A first-grade teacher named Laura became intrigued with the Dabrowski theory and how it helped her to understand one young boy named Jacob. Early in the semester, Laura submitted a poignant journal entry about her student:

> Jacob's mother shared a new story about her son this week. She mentioned that one day when they were driving down Camp Bowie Boulevard he saw a homeless man with a sign asking for food. He turned to his mother when he saw this and said, "Mom, let's go get him a hamburger and some French fries." His mother told him that they were in too much of a hurry to go out of their way to buy a hamburger for that man. Jacob in turn told his mother, "We are not in so much of a hurry that we can't go through the drive through. That's why they have drive throughs, for busy people who don't have a lot of time!" Sarah said she went directly to McDonald's and bought a hamburger, fries, and a Coke, and Jacob got out of the car himself and delivered the man the food.

Laura reflected on Jacob's compassionate nature and his concern for the well-being of others. She pointed out how he had the insight to know what others might be thinking and feeling. Laura saw it as her job to help Jacob and others like him by giving them an appreciation for their sensitivities and passions. She continued in her journal:

> I believe that Jacob's mother did a great thing by taking him to McDonald's and giving that man a hamburger rather than down-playing his emotions and making him feel silly. I hope that I've given him a sense of good feelings too. His mother told me that he has a list of people that he prays for each night, and at the beginning of the year, I was on the bottom of that list. Sarah pointed out that he always puts his teacher on the list, but she said they rarely make it higher than #10. This week I was told that I had passed God on the list! I have somehow made it to #1. I suppose that I have made a difference in his life. My question now is can I live up to this? This is quite an accomplishment!

Laura continued to enjoy this highly sensitive first grader in her classroom. Each week she had delightful stories to share with our class about her experiences with Jacob. That year Laura announced to her students that she was engaged to be married in June. As a result, she had another story about Jacob to share in her journal:

I will begin this week with the wonderful gift that I received from Jacob. In the morning he brought me a note from his mother, which I did not have time to read at that moment. So like all the other notes, I set it on the table to be read at 9 when the children went out to P.E.

Minutes later Jacob came to me with both hands behind his back. "Miss Laura, I have a surprise for you!" His eyes were beaming. "Close your eyes and hold out your hands!" I did as I was told and when I opened my eyes there was a gold and diamond bracelet in my hands. Costume jewelry, of course. I hugged him and I told him how much I loved it and I put it on immediately. He then told me that it was for my wedding day. He said he had bought it because it was petite like me and would be perfect on my wrist and it could be "my something new." I was astonished to say the least and very touched. I told him, through tears, that I would be sure to wear it.

The children went out to P.E., and I read the note from his mother. Sarah shared with me that he had purchased the bracelet for five dollars at a neighbor's garage sale with his allowance money and he insisted that I had to have it. Just as I finished reading the note, his mother walked through the door of my classroom with a big smile on her face.

The first entry in Laura's journal is a vivid example of empathy within Jacob, and her reflection highlights his emotional sensitivity. Her journal represents the experience of one teacher with one child in Fort Worth, TX. Imagine how many more young children like Jacob there are in our classrooms. Jacob as a first grader was a sensitive child. My guess would be that as a middle school student he continued to respond empathically to the needs of others. By the time he reached high school, I would predict that he would be taking on the causes of those less fortunate. He would become the high school senior who observes discrimination within his school setting and responds by writing passionate editorial commentaries in his school newspaper. By the time he reached college, he would have developed leadership skills he needed to organize others to correct injustices at the university. Children like Jacob become the individuals who follow in the paths of Mother Theresa, Eleanor Roosevelt, and Martin Luther King, Jr.

I once was browsing in an airport newsstand and came upon a magazine for teenagers with a cover story entitled "Twenty Young People Who

Will Change the World." As someone interested in keeping up to date about talented adolescents, I quickly purchased the magazine and made a dash to catch my flight. I was delighted to read that the subjects were all teenagers who were making a difference in their communities by addressing real problems through social action projects. In each case these were young men and women with deep sensitivity and empathy for the plight of others. Allow me to introduce two of them.

Jourdan Urbach of Roslyn, NY, discovered that music can be a powerful healer. He was playing his violin for a group of hospitalized children, and as he was performing, a young girl who had long been unresponsive suddenly began to move, much to the delight of her doctors, who came rushing into Jourdan's bedside concert. The young gifted violinist and student at the prestigious Juilliard School in New York City founded Children Helping Children, a charity that uses music to brighten the lives of children in hospitals and raise funds for medical research. At that time, the young violin virtuoso headlined benefit concerts at Lincoln Center and Carnegie Hall and helped to raise more than $200,000 for hospitals and charities across the country. Jourdan's sensitivity to the plight of others was evident when he was interviewed by a journalist and discussed his efforts: "If a cause touches something inside you, there is no doubt that you'll be successful in making a difference. There is no age requirement for doing something extraordinary" (Mascia, 2006, p. 119).

A second teenager featured in the magazine was Lindsey Williams of St. Joseph, MO. As a sixth grader she read in her local newspaper that the region of the country in which she lived was suffering increased shortages in food due to severe drought. Food pantries were struggling to keep up with the demand. Lindsey explored planting techniques in environmental journals and designed a new irrigation system for small-scale farming that enabled her to produce two and a half times as many vegetables as the more traditional methods. Shortly after, she was harvesting enough vegetables to fill several food banks with fresh produce.

By the time Lindsey was a high school senior, she had donated more than 35,000 pounds of fresh vegetables and provided families throughout her region of Missouri with nutritious meals. This gifted young woman described an experience at a local food bank, "This little boy picked up a tomato, and his eyes got as big and round as that tomato. He looked at me and was like, 'Can I have this?' At that moment, I knew I was making a difference" (Beiles, 2006, p. 117).

Recently, Renzulli, Koehler, and Fogarty (2006) described the work of a fifth grader named Melanie, who noticed that a partially sighted first-grade boy on her school bus was being harassed and teased about his thick eye-glasses. As Melanie came to know Tony better, she learned that although he had access to special textbooks for his school subjects, there were no books in the school library that he could read. First, Melanie, with the support of her enrichment teacher, organized a group of the school's bigger, well-respected boys and girls who met Tony at the school bus in the morning, escorted him to the cafeteria, and talked with him before school started each day. Next, Melanie organized students who served as a team of authors and illustrators in creating a collection of large-print big books focused on Tony's interests in sports and adventure stories. What transpired as a result of Melanie's work was significant. As the project progressed, Tony's attitude toward school changed remarkably. He became a celebrity within his school, and other students began checking out books from Tony's special section of the media center. Melanie's efforts in responding to support this young child resulted in the development of sensitivity to human concerns among a number of children. When interviewed about her work, Melanie explained

simply, "It didn't change the world, but it changed the world of one little boy" (Renzulli ct al., 2006, 16).

Young people like Jacob, Jourdan, Lindsey, and Melanie have helped me to realize that children have changed since I began my work in gifted education in the early 1980s. Other educators and counselors have agreed with me in that they too have seen evidence of changes in children's sensitivity and awareness of societal issues. As an enrichment teacher, I worked with elementary and middle school students as they pursued their passionate interests in ballet, veterinary medicine, sports history, dinosaurs, and the Middle Ages. In my most recent visits to gifted education classrooms, I have observed that gifted students are immersed in pursuing many more projects that address serious societal concerns. Since the events of Columbine High School, the attack upon the World Trade Center, Hurricane Katrina, and problems in the Middle East, young people are asking questions about the larger world and are wanting to make it a little bit better through their contributions to the greater good. Just several years ago a student in my enrichment resource room wondered whether the *Hartford Courant* really had an accurate pulse on the cartoon-page readership by featuring Garfield cartoons rather than Spiderman comics. Although that may have been an intriguing question to some 9-year-olds then, young people today are asking questions about global warming, the energy crisis, and the plight of the underclass in this country.

I celebrate this change. I join Joseph Renzulli and his colleagues (2006) in calling for educators to reflect deeply on how they can support these efforts "to encourage a new generation of students to use their gifts in socially constructive ways and seek ways to improve the lives of others rather than merely using their talents for economic gain, self-indulgence, and the exercise of power without commitment to contribute to the improvement of life and resources on the planet" (Renzulli et al., 2006, p. 23).

Strategies to Nurture the Social and Emotional Characteristics in Gifted Students

Guide Gifted Students to Self-Understanding Through Literature

Having reviewed several of the characteristics, traits, and behaviors that serve as assets to gifted young people in their social and emotional development, I describe below a number of strategies and methods that educators and counselors may find helpful in nurturing and supporting these qualities in their students.

I have long been a proponent of using literature to facilitate discussions with students about their issues or concerns. I believe that authentic interactions with literature contribute to overall affective growth. Such an approach is referred to as bibliotherapy, defined as the use of reading to produce affective change and to promote personality growth and development (Lenkowsky, 1987). Another popular definition is Lundsteen's (1972): "getting the right book to the right child at the right time about the right problem" (p. 505).

I am reluctant to use the term *bibliotherapy* simply because I do not want to raise concerns among parents and administrators that I am doing something I am not qualified to do as a classroom teacher. I am not a therapist; however, as a practitioner, I can facilitate good discussions with young people about good books. In doing so, I can help them draw parallels between their experiences and those of the main characters in the books. I also can help them listen to their classroom peers as they share their feelings about personal experiences related to the focus of the lesson. Such an approach is simply an attempt to help young people understand themselves and cope with problems by providing literature relevant to their personal situations and developmental needs at appropriate times.

I want to emphasize the term *developmental*. My objective is to help guide gifted students to reach self-understanding. In conducting such discussions in classrooms I focus on issues that many gifted students experience—perhaps more intensely and in different ways. Educators or counselors may want to consider using this approach to help students reflect on how or whether the social and emotional characteristics and traits described in this chapter are evident in their own lives. Literature can help young people appreciate their emotional sensitivity and intensity. Good books can help them develop more realistic self-expectations. For others, a book's message regarding the role of resilience in overcoming adversity may be helpful. In addition to supporting these characteristics, other developmental issues such as establishing and maintaining friendships, dealing with parental and teacher expectations, determining healthy self-expectations, and coping with peer pressure are concerns I would feel comfortable dealing with in public school classrooms. More serious concerns, the types I would label "grit your teeth issues," would be reserved for counselors. Teachers of gifted students using this approach believe that reading can influence thinking and behavior, and that guided discussions about selected books can focus on specific needs of students. Such an approach attempts to address concerns of young people before concerns become problems, providing needed information and understanding for facing the challenges of adolescence.

Halsted (2009) proposed that literature can easily engage gifted students emotionally. The therapeutic experience begins when young people pick up a book and discover characters very much like themselves. This interaction is known as identification, and the more gifted students have in common with the people they meet in their books, the closer the identification process. With that identification comes a tension relief, or catharsis, an emotional feeling that lets gifted children know they are not alone in facing their problems. As they enjoy a story, they learn vicariously through the book's characters. They gain new ways of looking at troublesome issues, and insight evolves. With this new insight, changed behavior may occur as they confront real-life situations similar to those experienced by the characters in the books.

McKay and Dudley (1996) proposed that most people have within them the resources to heal themselves. Emotional upheavals experienced by sensitive young people may paralyze their ability to access this valuable resource. Therefore, the use of appropriate literature may be helpful in getting gifted students through their hurt feelings, enabling them to reach down into their personal reservoirs and find answers to troubling questions. In essence, the book, in and of itself, is not therapeutic. The therapeutic effect depends on the response of the readers to that literature as it is facilitated through group discussion, and the change takes place within the student (Hynes & Hynes-Berry, 1986).

In any discussion of a high-quality literature with gifted students, the goal of the discussion is to have participants share their feelings and listen closely to themselves as well as each other. In a group discussion, it is important that the students leave the classroom with an awareness that others have experienced the same feelings. Under the guidance of a knowledgeable and empathic teacher or counselor, a group discussion can bring about the universality of experience—a feeling of "we are in this together."

Teachers and counselors who facilitate such discussions are responding to their need to incorporate meaningful follow-up activities. Such activities might include creative writing, journaling, writing song lyrics, writing raps, designing television commercials, role-playing, creative problem solving, cartooning and other art activities, or self-selected options for students to pursue individually (Hébert & Furner, 1997; Hébert & Kent, 2000).

In conducting the follow-up activities, I have discovered that the more enjoyable they are, the more effective they are. I emphasize enjoyable because I have found that as young people are engaged in something enjoyable they are more apt to continue discussion among themselves about the issues talked about earlier with the group. During this time the students continue to provide each other with supportive feedback. For example, as boys are engaged in an artistic activity, a teacher may overhear comments such as, "John, I didn't know that Butch Mulligan used to pick on you, too, back in second grade. It made me feel better to hear that I wasn't the only kid he bullied."

I have also learned, in conducting these lessons, that effective follow-up activities can be either collaborative or private. Providing students a choice of working in groups or alone addresses their individual learning styles. Moreover, I have discovered that when discussions involve students engaging in serious self-disclosure, private journaling as a follow-up activity provides time to "process" their feelings. I have come to believe that the follow-up activities are as important as the group discussion, and I have found that the more hands-on the follow-up activity, the more boys will talk. Engaging in hands-on activity is critical for young men to feel more comfortable in discussing their feelings. Girls appear to have fewer problems with talking. With these points in mind, guided discussions centered on affective concerns can be enjoyable while providing a time for solid introspection.

In selecting high-quality books to use with this approach, I believe it is important to reflect on Charles Smith's (1986) reminder to educators when using books therapeutically. He points out that children trust their teachers when selecting books, and therefore teachers must remain mindful of their influence. He explains, "Along with this trust comes a responsibility for the teacher to select books of great worth that provide rich metaphors and help children understand themselves and others, books that touch the heart" (Smith, 1986, p. 45). To support educators and counselors in their search for books that "touch the heart," I have included an annotated bibliography of literature appropriate for grades K–12 in Appendix A. The collection includes picture books, chapter books, and young adult novels that can be used to address social and emotional development. In addition, I provide educators and counselors with a sample lesson plan below, featuring a picture book by Mem Fox.

A sample lesson. Fox's (1985) *Wilfrid Gordon McDonald Partridge* touches the heart. This classic picture book presents a poignant story of a young boy named Wilfrid Gordon McDonald Partridge who lives next door to a home for the elderly. Wilfrid becomes a favorite visitor at the home as he develops warm relationships with his neighbors. He grows to have a favorite there, Miss Nancy Alison Delacourt Cooper, because she has four names just as he does. Miss Nancy is 96 years old, and Wilfrid learns from the residents at the nursing home that his friend Miss Nancy has lost her memory. He searches for memories for his beloved friend because she has forgotten hers. He carries a basket of trinkets to Miss Nancy, and as they share the basket together, the simple objects the young child has gathered for the elderly woman bring to her mind many fond memories, which she shares with her little friend. The beauty of the relationship between the young child and the woman is one that is appreciated by children who are sensitive to feelings involved in a special friendship.

Themes/Key Concepts
- Sensitivity and empathy in gifted young people
- The beauty of an important friendship
- Respect for the elderly

Possible Introductory Activities
- Discuss what it means to be sensitive to the feelings of others.

Selected Passage to Be Used in Discussion
- "What a dear, strange child to bring me all these wonderful things," thought Miss Nancy. Then she started to remember.

Menu of Possible Discussion Questions

- What did you like about Wilfrid Gordon McDonald Partridge?
- Why do you think Wilfrid told Miss Nancy Alison Delacourt Cooper all of his secrets?
- What do you think was special about the things that Wilfrid included in his basket for Miss Nancy?
- Why do you think Miss Nancy enjoyed the gifts from Wilfrid so much?
- Has there ever been a time in your life when you had a special friend like Miss Nancy? What did you do for that person? How did that make you feel?
- Why do you think this special friendship was important to Wilfrid and Miss Nancy?
  How have your special friendships been important to you?
- If a sensitive boy like Wilfrid joined us in our classroom, how do you think he would be treated? Why?
- How do you think sensitive qualities help children? Have you had experiences in which your sensitivity has helped you? What happened?

Menu of Possible Follow-Up Activities

- Plan a basket of simple yet special things to share with an important friend.
- Write and illustrate a poem about an important friendship in your life.
- Create a classroom mobile that captures the lesson learned through *Wilfrid Gordon McDonald Partridge*.
- Write a letter to Wilfrid's parents about their special son.
- Design classroom posters celebrating sensitivity in your classmates.
- Use your private journal to write a letter to Wilfrid to let him know how you feel about what he did for Miss Nancy.

Examine Biographies of Gifted Individuals

Along with reading high-quality literature and facilitating discussions that address affective concerns, teachers and counselors should consider examining biographical materials with gifted students. The late Mary Frasier maintained that a carefully selected biography could strongly influence the life of a gifted child (personal communication, September 1998). She pointed out that the person whose life story is being shared through biography may serve as a role model for intelligent young people and assist them in reflecting upon issues that require analysis in a safe environment. In particular, I have found that using biographies with gifted young men is consistent with what they enjoy reading (Hébert, 1995b). Studies of adolescent book selection have indicated that reading preferences of boys change as they grow older, with young men selecting less fiction and more nonfiction in the middle and high school years (Langerman, 1990). The gifted education community has maintained that encounters with biographies or autobiographies can have positive effects on gifted students (Flack, 1993; Hébert, 1995b, 2009; Hébert, Long, & Speirs Neumeister, 2001; Piirto, 1992; Robinson & Butler Schatz, 2002). Flack (1993) noted the critical importance of identification through both biography and autobiography: "Identification occurs when young readers discover that they are not singularly alone in either their dreams and aspirations or their loneliness, frustrations, and disappointments" (p. 2).

Educators who use biographies and autobiographies to support social and emotional development with gifted young people have a variety of options. Counselors may select a biography to read with a student and conduct one-on-one discussion sessions with the child. Some teachers offer classroom collections of biographies, hoping that students might self-select a biographical work, read it, identify with the subject, and discover a quiet reassurance. Others may prefer to organize a discussion group with a plan of sharing passages from a biography and having students consider thought-provoking questions focused on an important issue. Other teachers may incorporate biographical materials in the curriculum and have students share their thoughts and feelings concerning important issues through a reflective journal. Regardless of whether the biographical collection is offered, a discussion group is formed, or a writing experience is suggested, what is most important is that the teacher or counselor be prepared to listen closely to the feeling responses of the students and be prepared to support them emotionally. To support teachers and counselors who want to address affective development using biographies and autobiographies, a bibliography of appropriate biographical materials for use with gifted students is provided in Appendix B.

Connect Gifted Students With Collegiate Role Models and Friends

One of the finest examples of supporting the affective development of gifted students that I have known of was a program designed and facilitated by my colleague and friend Dr. Helen Nevitt. In her role as a faculty member at Southeast Missouri State University in Cape Giradeaux, MO, Helen was assigned to be the faculty advisor to the Governor's Scholars Program. The Governor's Scholars are a group of highly capable students, many of whom were identified as gifted during their K–12 school years and a large number of whom were National Merit Scholars. They represented fewer than 2% of the university student body, a highly selective group entering with a complete 4-year merit-based scholarship.

As coordinator of the Governor's Scholars Program and a professor of gifted education, Dr. Nevitt decided to connect the university scholars with gifted education teachers throughout Cape Giradeaux and the surrounding area. She sent groups of Governor's Scholars into elementary, middle, and high school gifted education classrooms to conduct 90-minute panel discussions focusing on their own experiences growing up gifted. Dr. Nevitt advertised the availability of the students to local gifted education coordinators, and interested teachers contacted the university to request a visit from a group of scholars. Helen organized the Scholar Outreach groups in such a way that each group had various types of giftedness represented. For example, a business administration major who was happy to present himself as the math whiz of the group accompanied an artistic student and perhaps a scholar-athlete. Helen encouraged the university students to focus on the following objectives in their session:

- To present themselves as examples of academically successful gifted students who are comfortable with themselves as gifted individuals.
- To discuss negative influences they have been exposed to in their lives.
- To share strategies for dealing with those negative influences.
- To demonstrate that they have found friends and intellectual peers through participation in a program with other high-ability students.
- To encourage the younger students to enjoy areas of their lives beyond academics.
- To illustrate that maintaining high academic performance can result in significant college scholarships (Nevitt, 1997).

Dr. Nevitt discovered that young gifted students were mesmerized by the college students who visited their classrooms. The university students shared the trials and tribulations of growing up gifted and provided the children and teenagers with helpful advice for addressing affective concerns. Typical themes in the discussions were coping with a peer group that did not appreciate their intellectual orientation, dealing with teacher and parent expectations, pursuing passionate interests, and developing important friendships with like-minded students.

A delightful surprise evolved during one of the first outreach group sessions. The younger students asked to exchange e-mail addresses with the college students, and Dr. Nevitt and the K–12 gifted education teachers watched as the Governor's Scholars became "e-mail pals" with their young gifted friends. Without having planned it, Dr. Nevitt and the teachers had found wonderful mentors for social and emotional development. The messages the university students were delivering to the younger students were the same as those delivered by teachers and parents; however, there appeared to be something magical about getting advice from "an awesome college kid who cares about me." The e-mail exchanges typically lasted for an academic year.

Dr. Nevitt reported that the university students benefited from the experience in that they learned more about themselves and became more comfortable with their giftedness. The younger students also became more comfortable with their giftedness, showed a new willingness to advocate for themselves, improved their classroom performance, and showed more enthusiasm for the gifted education program. Dr. Nevitt also indicated that parents became more supportive of their children and reported an increased understanding of the latter's intensity and emotionality.

Since moving from Missouri, Dr. Nevitt has shared this Scholars Outreach Program model with many other gifted education teachers. By simply making an appropriate connection with the community, she was able to provide many gifted students with important life lessons from an older student and friend.

Facilitate Social Action and Community Service Projects

While I was teaching at the University of Alabama, I had a delightful opportunity to watch a group of sensitive young people address a societal need through creative productivity. I supervised graduate students in gifted education as they taught mini-courses in a summer enrichment program. One group of gifted elementary students were involved in a mini-course in home design and construction. Under the guidance of their dynamic teacher, Berri Byington, these children spent several weeks planning, designing, building, and painting a miniature house, which eventually evolved into a playhouse. They decided to donate their finished product to a local shelter for abused children. Along with putting math and science concepts to work, these gifted students responded to a need in their community.

I also was fortunate to work with Wilma Cook, a fifth-grade teacher at Eastland Elementary School in Fort Worth, TX. Students at Eastland were taught not to touch the empty crack cocaine bags and needles that sometimes littered the school grounds. Wilma's students became concerned when they noticed that gang graffiti covered their school on Monday mornings. Each week they watched school personnel clean it off, but returned to find the building covered again. In response, Wilma's students launched a campaign to get rid of the gang graffiti and to urge students to stay out of gangs. Their efforts included an anti-gang rally. The students asked local grocery chains to supply lunches to be served during the rally. They contacted a local television station as well as the local newspaper. They called upon their favorite radio station to host the rally. They invited speakers from the local police force and the school district's central office. On the day of the rally, students led the student body in anti-gang cheers and performed skits and rap songs. Wilma and her colleagues delighted in the students' response to messages delivered that day. For example, Albert Clark, a fifth grader, rhymed, "My name is Albert and I'm here to say that gang graffiti is not the way!" (Bond, 1994, p. 23A). Following the rally, the fifth graders drew up a petition calling for an end to gang activity in Fort Worth. It was eventually signed by 1,432 students, parents, teachers, and school administrators. The fifth graders appeared before the school board and presented the petition to both the school superintendent and the mayor. Wilma's students also wrote an oath promising never to join a gang and persuaded all 68 fifth graders in the school to sign it, a courageous act in a community dominated by the Crips and Bloods, who some students realized might retaliate for such bold action.

Wilma Cook was an educator who was in tune with the emotional needs of her students. Often listening to their concerns, she was able to channel their energies in a positive direction and guided them to an appropriate outlet to address an important problem. Addressing community problems is an excellent way of supporting the social and emotional characteristics and traits of gifted students. Educators are increasingly asking children and adolescents to address societal issues through their work. Community service projects often are aligned with the required curriculum in a school, and many inspirational educators like Wilma Cook undertake campaigns and causes that bring about positive changes.

One such inspirational teacher is Barbara Lewis, a national award-winning author and educator who teaches young people how to think deeply about the world around them and to solve real problems. Her students at Jackson Elementary School in Salt Lake City, UT, have addressed problems with hazardous waste in their community, initiated several laws in the Utah state legislature, helped to fight crime, and tackled environmental problems in their state. Related to her work in facilitating service projects, Barbara has published some of the best educational resource materials available for teachers interested in helping their students address concerns through social action projects or service learning. The following four books published by Free Spirit are highly recommended: *The Kid's Guide to Social Action* (1998), *Kids With Courage* (1992), *The Kid's Guide to Service Projects* (2009), and *What Do You Stand For?* (1998).

In addition to Lewis's work, Elizabeth Rusch (2002) has authored *Generation Fix: Young Ideas for a Better World*, published by Beyond Words. In this book, teenager Zachary Ebers created a "Breakfast Bonanza" following his visit to a food pantry in St. Louis, MO. When he noticed the shelves of the food pantry were stocked with cans of vegetables, baked beans, and SpaghettiO's™, Zach became concerned that children there were not receiving an adequate breakfast. He organized a large group of friends to be cereal-drive coordinators responsible for helping to publicize the drive, collecting the cereal, and helping to deliver it. He succeeded in involving 18 churches and schools throughout St. Louis. Within the first 2 years of the program, Breakfast Bonanza collected more than 5,000 boxes of cereal for food pantries in St. Louis.

Rusch (2002) also highlighted the efforts of Joshua Marcus of Boca Raton, FL. Joshua learned of the poverty in his community when his mother took him to visit a day-care center in a neighborhood of migrant farm workers. His experience with that visit opened his eyes to the needs of local children. When he learned that they needed school supplies to begin kindergarten, Joshua took action. He began a program he called "Sack It to You," whereby he conducted major fund-raising efforts with local businesses. He bought school supplies with the money raised. After his older brother moved out of the house, the Sack It to You backpacks and school supplies took over his bedroom. Joshua organized parties where his friends, in an assembly-line operation, filled backpacks with supplies and then delivered them to 17 agencies throughout Boca Raton. Over 5 years, Joshua raised more than a quarter of a million dollars to supply backpacks filled with school supplies to children from low-income families.

In Rusch's (2002) book we also meet Shifra Mincer, a sixth grader who spends her afternoons at a soup kitchen in the basement of Hebrew Union College in New York City. While there, she serves as the seamstress for homeless people who stop by for meals. While they are eating, Shifra mends their jackets, shirts, pants, and blouses. Shifra intends to continue work as the soup kitchen's seamstress until she graduates from high school. She explained that volunteering for others less fortunate really makes her feel good, especially if she has had a stressful day at school or received a low grade on a test. "When I'm sewing there, I really can't do anything about school. I really have time to completely forget about any problems. And I see people who have a lot more problems than me" (Rusch, 2002, p. 89). Shifra has realized that her efforts at the soup kitchen have influenced her life in multiple ways. She pointed out, "Volunteering takes a lot of my own time, but you get so much more back. My life is so different from what it used to be. So much fuller . . . Whatever you put in, you get double back" (Rusch, 2002, p. 89).

Encourage Mentorships

Helen Nevitt's approach of connecting gifted collegians with younger students is a realistic model for K–12 schools. Educators have long maintained that mentorships in the classroom can enrich the lives of gifted students at many levels. Mentoring involves a one-on-one relationship between a young person and an older individual who is an expert in a field or has knowledge about a particular topic. In a mentoring relationship, shared passions, common interests, or career interests serve as the foundation of the relationship. Mentors and their young protégés work as partners as they explore a common passion, interest, or career. These explorations have provided differentiated instructional experiences for gifted students, facilitated research projects, and exposed intelligent young people to a variety of career possibilities (Purcell, Renzulli, McCoach, & Spottiswoode, 2001; Roberts & Inman, 2001; Siegle, McCoach, & Wilson, 2009).

In my work with gifted students, I successfully matched them with elderly retirees who had tremendous expertise, much wisdom, and plenty of love, and time to share with my students. I will always be grateful to Mrs. Howard, a delightful woman associated with the Audubon Society who worked with Melissa, a third grader with a passionate interest in robins and cardinals. Under Mrs. Howard's guidance, Melissa developed a board game on birds that other elementary students enjoyed for years. I also was relieved when I found Mr. Bernier, a retired electrical engineer who came to my classroom each week and worked with Stephen on an engineering project I never quite understood; however, I will long remember how much I enjoyed watching them explore electronics together. In my observations of mentor and mentee, I saw much more than an older gentleman sharing his knowledge, expertise, and passion for electronics with a sixth grader who remained fascinated. I saw what Tomlinson (2001) referred to as a "mentor of the spirit—of the heart." She maintained that "powerful mentorships help prepare young people to live with greater purpose, focus, and appreciation at a younger age by drawing not only on the knowledge of the past, but on its wisdom as well" (Tomlinson, 2001, p. 27).

Through this relationship, Stephen had an excellent role model. The relationship certainly boosted his self-esteem as he developed new expertise under the tutelage of a kind, elderly gentleman. With Mr. Bernier, he felt comfortable sharing his intensity and his passion for learning. Moreover, he benefited from a heart-warming friendship that continued through his high school years. With this attentive listener, Stephen could share his hopes, dreams, and aspirations.

Gifted high school students have derived significant benefits from mentoring programs. One excellent example is the Pinnacle Project funded by the American Psychological Foundation (APF), organized by APF's Center for Gifted Education Policy directed by Rena Subotnik. The Pinnacle Summit brings together gifted adolescents who participate in a weeklong mentorship program designed to cultivate their talents. Each student has the opportunity to work with an eminent scholar or practitioner in his or her field of interest. The weeklong Pinnacle Summit is unique in that it brings together established, emerging, and potential talent in intra- and interdisciplinary ways. Each day of the summit provides the students with opportunities to meet, talk about their interests, and develop a plan for the coming year. The week also includes roundtable discussions that facilitate the exchange of ideas among various disciplines. In addition, each of the masters gives a lecture to the entire group and the summit culminates with the students presenting what they learned from their individual team meetings and the projects they have planned for the coming year.

David Sonnenborn, a participant in the Pinnacle Project with an intense interest in political TV journalism, described his experiences at Bard College at Simon's Rock working with journalist Philip Scheffler, executive editor of *60 Minutes*, and Kay Lim, an associate producer of the television show. David explained that his work with Scheffler began every morning with a copy of *The New York Times*, which served as a lifeline for the mentor and his protégé isolated in rural Massachusetts and removed from television sets and the Internet. David noted that the black-and-white newspaper was central to their morning meetings as Mr. Scheffler taught him about journalistic integrity, the Pentagon Papers, the right to a free press, the Vietnam War, and the cracking of the tobacco industry and shared his insights from more than 50 years in journalism. Although his mentor was a giant in his field, David explained, "... he took him under his wing as his student" (Subotnik, 2003, p. 15). Kay Lim joined them as someone who had started in TV journalism more recently and also offered her candid opinions of her field. As a result of his work with his mentors, David returned to his high school and wrote, directed, and edited a news documentary on the topic of character education and teaching ethics in the classroom.

> Today, I am proud of what I accomplished during that period, but much of the expertise and encouragement necessary to make the film I owe to Mr. Scheffler and Kay. Not only did they frequently keep me on task, their constant accessibility and willingness to drop anything to help me was more than comforting—it got me through the project. They helped me focus on the important aspects of the story and guided me through each step involved in writing a script. Despite a lack of time on all of our parts, we finished the documentary, and with it, the entire program suddenly came to fruition. But, even if we never did complete a project, the confidence and excitement that my mentors instilled in me this year would have been reward enough. (Subotnik, 2003, p. 16)

The benefits of mentoring programs on the affective development of gifted students surpass any academic or career focus. Researchers and practitioners have reported increased self-confidence and self-awareness in students (Nash, 2001; Siegle et al., 2009); commitment, empathy, and self-trust (Tomlinson, 2001); increased responsibility and a future-mindedness (Purcell et al., 2001); and positive self-image (Davalos & Haensly, 1997; Goff & Torrance, 1999).

Numerous descriptions of mentoring programs for gifted students are available to educators (see Hébert & Olenchak, 2000; Hébert & Speirs Neumeister, 2000; Purcell et al., 2001; Roberts & Inman, 2001). Each of these reports includes evaluative comments from young participants similar to David Sonnenborn's reflections above. The following statement from a high school student who participated in a summer mentorship program at the University of Connecticut is representative of what many have reported and highlights the benefits of mentoring that are related to the social and emotional development of gifted young people. This message should inspire educators and counselors to consider establishing such programs:

The most important thing my mentor has done for me is to listen, answer my deeply held questions, and share his passion. Living in a dark world where few peers or teachers care about anything deeply takes its toll on the weary traveler. Seeing how active and invigorated my mentor is has given me inspiration to go home, rekindle my goals, and live my life to its fullest. (Purcell et al., 2001, p. 24)

For Further Thought and Discussion

- Imagine that Heidi Gillingham, the collegiate basketball player, visited your high school students in a gifted education seminar. What message would you hope she would deliver to your students? Why?
- What is the significance of the Hewitt and Flett (1991) multidimensional model of perfectionism for educators and counselors working with gifted students? How might an understanding of this model support their practice?
- How might educators and counselors help gifted students develop an internal locus of control?
- What advice do you think Cameron's parents should offer to parents of other gifted boys?
- What can educators, school counselors, and parents do to nurture the empathic qualities of gifted young people?

Resources to Expand Your Thinking and Extend Your Support to Gifted Students

Adelson, J. L., & Wilson, H. E. (2009). *Letting go of perfect: Overcoming perfectionism in kids.* Waco, TX: Prufrock Press.

Adderholdt, M., & Goldberg, J. (1999). *Perfectionism: What's bad about being too good?* Minneapolis, MN: Free Spirit.

Daniels, S., & Piechowski, M. M. (Eds.). (2009). *Living with intensity.* Scottsdale, AZ: Great Potential Press.

Greenspon, T. S. (2007). *What to do when good enough isn't good enough.* Minneapolis, MN: Free Spirit.

Halsted, J. W. (2009). *Some of my best friends are books* (3rd ed.). Scottsdale, AZ: Great Potential Press.

Isaacson, K., & Fisher, T. (2007). *Intelligent life in the classroom: Smart kids and their teachers.* Scottsdale, AZ: Great Potential Press.

Lewis, B. (1998). *The kid's guide to social action* (2nd ed.). Minneapolis, MN: Free Spirit.

Piechowski, M. M. (2006). *"Mellow out," they say. If only I could: Intensities and sensitivities of the young and bright.* Madison, WI: Yunasa Books.

Rusch, E. (2002). *Generation fix: Young ideas for a better world.* Hillsboro, OR: Beyond Words.

CHAPTER **3**

Social and Emotional Characteristics and Traits of Gifted Young People: Part II

My goals for this chapter are to:
- ❧ Acquaint you with several more of the social and emotional characteristics, traits, and behaviors evidenced in gifted young people.
- ❧ Present strategies to nurture those characteristics, traits, and behaviors.

In my work at the University of Georgia, I have had many opportunities to come to know graduate students through reflective writing assignments in my courses. In a class that I teach on underachievement in high-ability students, I asked students to share their personal journeys as K–12 students. I received a reflection from Christopher that beautifully illustrated a number of issues upon which teachers and counselors of gifted students may want to reflect. Christopher's reflection, "A Letter to My Kindergarten Teacher," follows here:

Dear Miss Jan,

I still cannot color inside the lines. No matter how hard I try, the crayon always seems to wander over that thin black line as if of its own accord. I recently found myself sitting Indian style (Do you still use that term?) on the floor next to my daughter's art table, vainly attempting to color in Strawberry Shortcake's little red hat. While my 5-year-old was admonishing me, I suddenly remembered you and that ubiquitous frowny-faced stamp that frequently ended up on my paper.

It seemed fitting that I write to you as I begin the next step in my academic development because it was with you that it all started. I admit to being less than enthusiastic about my first day of kindergarten. If my mother tells the story correctly, I threw up twice that morning, once in the bathroom and once out the car window as we pulled up to the school. My mother insists that it was excitement that tied my stomach in knots, but in truth it was you: your shiny black hair and severe smile that reminded me eerily of the villain from the children's book *Miss Nelson Is Missing*.

From the beginning, I was outmatched. My pictures were always scribbled, my letters invariably were written backwards, and I could never seem to find my place on the carpet before your infernal buzzer went off. I vividly remember being kept in from recess one day because of a picture I drew of my mother. Being a kindergartener, I felt like my portrait captured the very essence of everything I loved about my mother. As recess wore on, I was forced to sit and look at my masterpiece in an attempt to determine what exactly I had done wrong. As the other children returned triumphantly from games of kickball and tag, I realized with a certain clarity what was wrong with my picture. I had forgotten to give my mother hair. It was then that I decided, as much as a 5-year-old can decide anything, I was not cut out for this school business.

First and second grade were a little better. I was terminally messy and unorganized, and my teachers seemed to take that as a sign that I was unfit for any sort of education. First grade presented me the unique challenge of [D'Nealian] pads. Squeezing my as yet unperfected letters into the confines of those little dotted lines seemed impossible. In second grade I was responsible for keeping up with my own lunch card. My mother must have tried hundreds, if not thousands, of ways to ensure that I made it to the lunchroom with that little blue card, but invariably I would reach the lunchroom without it and with no clue as to where it had gone. My teacher even went so far as to drill a hole in the wall behind my desk and insert a hook to hang my card on. Still, I was left to the mercy of the lunch lady three out of five days a week.

Imagine my surprise when, in third grade, I was tested for the gifted program. It must have been the ease with which I mastered third-grade multiplication tables, for that was my sole academic accomplishment in 3 years of schooling. I was taken to the library where an older lady with a perpetually bored expression asked me a series of questions. Three weeks later it was determined that I did not need any special services; or at least not those kind. My mother, however, disagreed, and I was tested again. To this day, I don't think I was placed in the gifted program because of any raw talent or untapped potential. I think they simply got tired of testing me.

My first week in the small group of boys and girls pulled out for special instruction was wonderful. We played games and spent time in the computer lab. I remember you walking by that first week and how I wanted more than anything to shout your name so you would know what had become of me. There was an immediate shift in the way my teacher treated me too. Whereas before I was thought to be unfit to learn, now it seemed as if my teacher thought she might be unfit to teach me. Messy assignments went unremarked. Gold stars started appearing on the top of my papers. It was as if someone had reached down and blessed me in the eyes of the school.

I continued to carry the mysterious blessing of being gifted through fourth grade, and by fifth, I had begun to think I actually belonged, even excelled, at school. Ms. Chapman put an end to all that. She shared your shiny black hair and severe smile. In fact, the two of you were so similar that I remember thinking that perhaps she was your long-lost older sister.

Ms. Chapman taught in themes. The first half of the year we spent studying the Middle Ages, and the second half we immersed ourselves in marine biology. We got to do things I never would have expected at school, like dress up as kings and princes and have a medieval feast, and take a 3-day field trip to the beach. Still, like you, Ms. Chapman loved art and was very particular about the art her students created. Along with every assignment, there was a picture to color. In retrospect, I'm sure Ms. Chapman thought she was being nice by allowing us to color, but for me it was kindergarten all over again. I was sure you and Ms. Chapman were conspiring against me.

In due time, I went to middle school, which was like most middle school experiences, filled with awkwardness and anxiety. The only high point was when I was allowed to take advanced math classes, and because I was awkward and anxious anyway, I ignored my better judgment and became a mathlete. The T-shirts were cool, and I was sure the team's coach, Mr. Weeks, must have been directly related to Einstein. I also joined the band and began to discover that not all art was created in crayon between sharp black lines.

By high school, I realized that while I usually had the answers the teachers were looking for, I could rarely find the piece of paper on which they were written. I was lucky enough, however, to find a number of teachers who placed high value on test scores rather than organization, and I began to excel again in math and English. High school seemed mostly easy, and I was overjoyed to find out that I could choose the classes I was to take. I enrolled in challenging classes in areas I felt were my strength. I also continued to study music, feeling there was something about the symmetry of music that reminded me of math class.

I graduated an honor student and was accepted to all of the universities I applied to. Being a native of Athens, GA, I chose the University of Georgia and began working on a philosophy major the summer after I graduated from high school. That fall I was an English major. By winter I was thinking history, and in the spring the call of South Campus led me to become a mathematics major. Three years and an undisclosed number of majors later, I entered the College of Education. After 4 years of college, I was still 2 years away from any degree, so I left, feeling as though my time of study had been a useless and expensive endeavor. I came to your school shortly after dropping out of college. I stopped by your room and sat in one of the tiny chairs and felt like all those years before: I was not cut out for this school business.

I worked in corporate audit and loss prevention for nearly 4 years where I had the opportunity to supervise a number of high school dropouts. Most of them reminded me of myself during the times when school seemed like a daunting task. It made me realize that the only difference between them and me was a few intermixed years of academic success. I could have easily tired of failing if not for the teachers who had been able to see the ability hidden behind the poor organization. I tutored a number of my employees for their GED and even helped several of them fill out applications for community college.

It was then that I returned to school to become a teacher. I loved my time in teacher education as it provided me with the freedom to pursue topics that I felt were useful to me. I'm currently working on my master's degree and I'm sometimes filled with the anxiety that marked my first day of kindergarten. I imagine getting papers returned stamped with little red frowny faces and being kept in during recess. I try very hard to focus on successful experiences, because I know how much failure can affect my own chance of success as well as how others see me.

I hope that you are well and you've gotten rid of that frowny-faced stamp. When I'm able to color in the lines, I'll send you a sample.

Sincerely,
Christopher Pendley
Kindergarten Class of 1984

I am delighted to report that Christopher is a middle school math teacher who is also pursuing an advanced degree in gifted education. I also want to report that I have never stamped his papers with a frowny-faced red stamp, nor have I kept him in during recess. I celebrate that a teacher with his experiences and sensitivity will soon be working with high-ability students who may be facing the same challenges Chris faced as a student. I share Christopher's letter with my readers, with his permission, because within his message I see evidence of several significant social and emotional characteristics of gifted students that I address in this chapter. Christopher's story highlights the importance of moving toward self-actualization, a highly developed sense of humor, and resilience. These three traits, along with an advanced level of moral maturity, are the focus of this chapter. I begin this discussion with a compelling story of the development of moral maturity in one man's life.

Advanced Levels of Moral Maturity With Consistency Between Values and Actions

John Robbins grew up in affluence. As the son of Irving Robbins, the cofounder of Baskin-Robbins, he grew up in a home where an ice cream freezer had 31 flavors in it. He and his friends enjoyed a swimming pool shaped like an ice cream cone, and he played with his cats named Orange Sherbet and Marshmallow. In 1968, when his uncle (and father's business partner) Burt Baskin died from a heart attack at the age of 51, he struggled to understand how this could happen to such a young man. Robbins remembered his uncle as "a very big man who ate a lot of ice cream" (Levin-Epstein, 2006, p. 66). When John approached his father about the connection between his uncle's ice cream consumption, weight, and heart failure, his father brushed off the issue, explaining, "His ticker just got tired and stopped working" (Levin-Epstein, 2006, p. 66).

As a college student at the University of California at Berkeley in the 1960s, John Robbins realized that he could not sell his family's product if there was a possibility that it adversely affected people's health. He announced to his father that he could not maintain the family's business because he had to live and work according to his personal values. This decision caused a serious rift between father and son, and today he realizes that, although he has reconciled with his father, he does not plan on inheriting any of the family's ice cream fortune.

For the past 20 years, John Robbins has authored several best-selling books on health, vegetarian diets, and the environment. His book, *Diet for a New America,* was nominated for a Pulitzer Prize and sold more than a million copies. As a result of the response to the book, he started EarthSave International, a nonprofit organization with more than 40 chapters throughout the country. This group educates the public about foods that are healthiest for people and best for the environment. A more recent book, *Healthy at 100,* synthesizes the healthy eating practices of the world's longest living people and features citizens from small villages in Ecuador, Pakistan, and Russia. The child who enjoyed a freezer with 31 flavors of ice cream today enjoys a diet of organic fruits and vegetables, whole grains, beans, soy products, and some fish. Robbins maintains that he has more energy than when he was 21 and celebrates his healthy heart (Levin-Epstein, 2006).

This snapshot of John Robbins's experience highlights the role of moral development in the life of a successful individual making important societal contributions and serves as a backdrop for the following discussion of moral maturity as a characteristic of gifted students. Morality has been defined as "a set of internalized principles or ideals that help an individual to distinguish from right and wrong and to act on this distinction" (Shaffer, 2000, p. 353). The major theories of moral development have focused on various components of morality. Psychological theorists have emphasized the affective component, or the significant moral affects. They maintain that young people are motivated to act according to their ethical principles, to experience positive affects such as pride, and to avoid negative moral emotions such as guilt or shame. Cognitive-developmental theorists have focused on the cognitive features of morality, or moral reasoning, and have found that the ways children think about right and wrong changes developmentally. Social learning theorists have considered the behavioral component of morality by examining whether children's actions are consistent with their moral standards when tempted to violate them (Shaffer, 2000; Steinberg, 2005). Implicit in definitions of morality is the understanding that morally mature young people do not follow society's dictates simply because they expect tangible rewards or fear punishment for breaking society's rules. Instead, they internalize moral principles they have learned and conform to those ideals even when adults are not present to enforce them. Internalization, the shift from externally controlled behavior to behavior driven by internal standards and principles, is viewed as a crucial milestone in moving toward mature moral development (Shaffer, 2000).

Evidence of advanced moral maturity in gifted children and teenagers has long been reported in the gifted education and psychology literature (Boehm, 1962; Janos, Robinson, & Lunnenborg, 1989; Kessler, Ibrahim, & Kahn, 1986; Passow, 1988; Vare, 1979). High-level moral thought and evaluation are often observed in gifted adolescents (Piechowski, 1997). Colangelo (1982) found evidence of this in moral dilemmas described by gifted teenagers. Howard-Hamilton (1994) measured moral reasoning using Rest's (1986) Defining Issues Test (DIT), a well-documented measure of moral judgment, based on Kohlberg's theory. Howard-Hamilton found that gifted adolescents received scores on the DIT above the norm for their age range. Narváez (1993) also conducted a study using the DIT and found precocity in moral judgment within a population of high-ability, high-achieving middle school students. Clinicians have described gifted young clients who have exhibited sophisticated moral thinking (Lovecky, 1993; Silverman, 1993a). From these reports we learn of gifted young people who follow their ethical principles when faced with dilemmas and will not follow the crowd if it means compromising their values. They experience a high level of compassion. They transcend societal norms, having internalized their own moral code of ethics.

A powerful example of this was Steven Cozza, a Boy Scout in Petaluma, CA. Although he himself was not gay, Steven became so outraged by the Boy Scouts of America's policy of discrimination that he founded, at the age of twelve, Scouting for All to end discrimination against young gay males (Piechowski, 2003). Steven's behavior was consistent with his value system. His actions were aligned with his beliefs. One of the finest examples I have encountered of this internal consistency between a gifted adolescent's actions and values is the story of Frank Daily in Lewis's (1992) *Kids With Courage*.

On a cold November afternoon in Milwaukee, Frank was traveling home after school on the city bus, feeling rather dejected. Wearing a brand-new pair of Nike sneakers, the high school freshman was pondering what he would do after learning that afternoon that he had not made the junior varsity basketball team. Feeling dejected, he stared out the window of the bus as new passengers climbed aboard.

A pregnant woman dressed in tattered clothing boarded the bus and fell backward into the seat behind the bus driver. Frank immediately noticed that she was in her stocking feet. When the bus driver looked over his shoulder and hollered, "Where are your shoes, lady? It ain't more than 10 degrees out there" (Lewis, 1992, p. 83), the woman explained that she couldn't afford shoes because she had eight children, and she was more concerned about their having shoes. She pointed out to the driver that she believed that the Lord would provide. She made a request to ride the bus awhile so she could keep warm.

When the bus came to the end of the line, Frank waited until everyone else had disembarked. He proceeded down the aisle of the bus with his sneakers in his hands. He approached the pregnant mother and handed her his new basketball shoes, looking down and saying, "Here, lady, you need these more than I do" (Lewis, 1992, p. 84). As he hurried to step down from the bus, he managed to step into a puddle, but he did not mind because he wasn't feeling cold. The woman remained on the bus crying and called out her thanks to Frank. She turned to the driver and exclaimed, "See, I told you the Lord would take care of me" (Lewis, 1992, p. 85). Lewis (1992) reported that the young basketball player never saw the woman again, and on that cold dreary November day in Milwaukee, as he walked home in his stocking feet, he hardly felt the cold street beneath him. On that day the grayness had lifted for him.

Another poignant example of moral maturity is the story of Wade Edwards, a popular fifth grader in an elementary school in North Carolina. Wade came to know a young African American girl named Alyse Tharpe when she was bused to the elementary school from an economically disadvantaged and predominantly African American neighborhood. Alyse had a difficult time finding her place in a school where many other young girls from more privileged situations arrived every day dressed in crisp little smock dresses and wore ribbons in their hair. She felt isolated. Wade noticed that Alyse always ate lunch alone, and this troubled him. He stood up from his own crowded table of popular friends, came over to Alyse, introduced himself, and asked if he could sit with her. During lunch on that first day, he taught her how to play table football, and although he beat her at a game he knew very well, she later returned the favor by teaching him an outdoor game that she enjoyed. This special friendship remained constant all through elementary school (Edwards, 2004).

Wade Edwards had much in common with a fourth grader named Anne. Deidre Lovecky (1992) described a day when Anne's class was planning a Valentine's Day celebration. In preparing for the event, the classroom teacher directed her students not to deliver any valentine cards to Jimmy, the "problem child" of fourth grade. When Valentine's Day arrived, Anne promptly delivered the largest Valentine card she could find to Jimmy's desk. It was the only card he received that day. Anne did not open her cards during the class party because she had a plan. She waited until the she and the teacher were alone in the classroom and then discarded her cards unopened in the teacher's trash can. Lovecky (1992) reported that the young girl and her teacher stared at each other, and the child then left her classroom without saying a word. As a result of this show-down, the teacher changed her attitude toward Jimmy.

The above vignettes of Steven, Frank, Wade, and Anne highlight qualities associated with moral maturity. They are evidence that young people and children are capable of internalizing moral principles they have learned and conforming to those ideals even when adults are not present to guide them. Teachers can support those qualities through school experiences designed to strengthen moral principles.

Strong Need for Self-Actualization

For several decades Abraham Maslow's (1954) work concerning self-actualization has been examined by many and has since become widely accepted. Maslow's developmental theory posits that one's physiological needs, and a need for safety, love, and self-esteem, must be met in a hierarchical order if an individual is to reach self-actualization. Understanding self-actualization, the process by which an individual becomes what he or she is capable of being, is important to fully understanding the developmental needs of gifted individuals.

The research base on the self-actualization of young gifted individuals is growing as researchers continue to experiment with multiple instruments for measuring these traits in various populations of students. Several studies have examined the occurrence of self-actualization in gifted students. Lewis, Karnes, and Knight (1995) found that gifted elementary and middle school students scored higher on measures of self-actualization than did nongifted students. Karnes and D'Illio (1990) also reported a significant relationship between self-esteem and self-actualization with gifted children. More recently, Karnes and McGinnis (1996) found a significant correlation between measures of self-actualization and inner locus of control of gifted middle and high school students. In a study of 140 high school students, Pufal-Struzik (1999) found that gifted students achieved a higher level of self-actualization than the control group did. In addition, the gifted students who had a sense of self-actualization had a higher level of self-acceptance. Moreover, a strong need for intellectual stimulation also characterized the students who had a sense of self-actualization.

These findings are consistent with a qualitative research study a colleague and I conducted. We studied gifted university students involved in an honors program in a small technological university in the Southeast (Hébert & McBee, 2007). The purpose of our investigation was to examine the impact of the honors program on the intellectual, social, and emotional development of the participants. One of the major findings in this study was a strong drive to achieve self-actualization, which we labeled "hunger for growth." All of the participants expressed a desire for self-actualization. This included valuing knowledge and education for its own sake, wanting to bring one's personal behavior into closer alignment with universal ethical principles, and desiring to overcome weaknesses. This drive was often expressed as a fixation with philosophical, religious, or political questions that had great emotional significance rather than being simply intellectualized abstractions. For example, one participant named Dawn expressed this hunger for growth as early as high school. She explained that the first thing she did when she acquired a driver's license was to join the local community singers' group. A classical music lover, she wanted to be part of something that was both challenging and beautiful. When the group performed Vivaldi's *Gloria*, Dawn described feeling "absolutely enthralled" by the experience. Much of Dawn's commentary centered around her concept of "the other world," and she described how she spent most of her life feeling conflicted about this hunger and even tried to cover the resulting behaviors:

> There's a fear of giving yourself to it [the other world] totally, knowing what the interpersonal result of that is going to be, but fear of

not doing it because you know what that would mean for you. Like selling yourself short, or selling out, or even offending the other world somehow by not giving in to it totally. (Hébert & McBee, 2007, p. 145)

Although Dawn's hunger was largely spiritual in nature, Isaac's was intellectual. He read voraciously in his spare time. He enrolled in courses to satisfy his curiosity and paid little attention to his grades. Upon completion of his bachelor's degree in English literature, Isaac contemplated earning another degree in other fields, such as biology or philosophy, so that he could have another intellectual position from which to "triangulate off to figure out what is reasonable and what is not" (Hébert & McBee, 2007, p. 145).

Once given a structure from which to address this need for self-actualization, as well as a teacher to guide the process and an understanding and supportive peer group, many of the students in the honors program participated in a personal development program referred to as "mentor," which required a substantial commitment of time and energy. Under the guidance of the honors program director, 40 to 50 highly motivated students wrote journals on at least a weekly basis, usually focusing on personal events in the students' lives and philosophical, intellectual, political, or spiritual issues. The journals were shared with the honors program director and the other students participating in "mentor" via e-mail. One participant's commitment was reflected in copious journaling and reading: "It was no big deal for me to sit down and write three journals a night. I mean from 1:00 to 4:00 a.m. most every night" (Hébert & McBee, 2007, p. 145). In addition to the journaling, students attended meetings in which groups discussed developmental issues faced by college students. At other times, the meetings might have focused on discussing pieces of literature, art, or poetry; discussing a difficult book; debating current issues; or viewing a provocative film. Fortunately, the gifted collegians in this study found their "oasis" in the university honors program. Their hunger for growth was "nourished" when they arrived on campus and connected with others whose views of becoming self-actualized were consistent with their own.

Highly Developed Sense of Humor

In an interview following his disappointing loss in the 2000 presidential election, former vice-president Al Gore said, "Humor is a healing balm and one of the highest expressions of the human spirit" (Stieg,

2006, p. 96). Educators and counselors concerned about the social and emotional development of gifted young people can appreciate Gore's wisdom, for they realize the role humor may play in the life of a highly intelligent or talented young person. Creativity researchers have consistently found that many gifted students have an advanced sense of humor (Davis, 1998; Gross, 2000; Renzulli et al., 2001; Torrance, 1969). Bleedorn (1982) maintained that the mental processes of humor and creativity are interwoven and inseparable. She proposed that a person's sense of humor was an important part of an individual's personal identity, and that gifted young people were "entitled to the satisfaction of laughing with others who share their style and level of humor" (Bleedorn, 1982, p. 33). Webb, Meckstroth, and Tolan (1982) suggested that gifted children are able to develop a rather sophisticated sense of humor quite early and are able to recognize absurdities in everyday situations. They maintained that a sense of humor helps gifted students handle stress, especially if they are able to develop an ability to laugh at themselves in stressful situations and maintain a sense of perspective. VanTassel-Baska (1998) indicated that a sense of humor and the ability to play with ideas is evidence that gifted children can interpret their world in ways that may reduce threats and defuse painful experiences.

Researchers in gifted education and psychology have reported some important findings regarding giftedness and humor. In a groundbreaking study, Janus (1975) discovered that many professional comedians and comedy writers were highly intelligent, with scores on the Wechsler Adult Intelligence Scale (WAIS) ranging from 115 to 160+ and a median score of 138. Fern (1991) successfully identified 13 child humorists and found that more than half of them scored in the above-average or superior range in their respective group intelligence tests and related achievement subtests. She noted that the children who scored in the upper ranges were producers of humor rather than being exceptional in performing humorously. Shade's (1991) study of verbal humor in gifted elementary and middle school students found that the gifted students performed significantly higher in spontaneous mirth and comprehension of humor than did the general population group in his study. Shade's findings supported the long-held assumption that gifted children have a healthy and sophisticated sense of humor. Ziv and Gadish (1990) also studied a group of gifted adolescent humorists and found that they were more extroverted, more creative, and lower in their needs for social approval than nonhumorous students. The association of this trait with high ability has remained strong throughout decades of research, and many checklists used for identifying giftedness in children include having an advanced or unusual sense of humor.

Teachers who are attuned to these characteristics make a significant difference for many gifted young people when they recognize and nurture these qualities within their students. In examining the lives of popular contemporary humorists, I have discovered that well-known comedians today were recognized for their talents early in their education and received support from their teachers to use their special talents in significant ways. Comedian Jay Leno described his early school experiences as a bright underachiever who was a problem in the classroom until several teachers channeled his comic energies in the right direction. In his autobiography, *Leading With My Chin*, Leno (Leno & Zehme, 1996) reflected on those teachers:

> For some unimaginable reason, a handful of my teachers didn't give up on me as a hopeless moron. Mr. Robicheaud, my history teacher, never doubted that I had a brain that was actually functional. He always made me want to rise to any challenge. Same with Ms. Samara, my homeroom teacher. And my English teacher, Mrs. Hawkes, urged me to take her creative writing class. I figured, "What the hell, sounds easy!" But it wasn't—at first, anyway. One day, after class, she took me aside and said, "You know, I always hear you telling funny stories to your friends in class. You should write down some of those stories and we can make that your homework assignment." Hey, it sounded better than poetry! So I gave it a try and—amazingly—it turned out to be the first time I ever did homework where I wasn't waiting for Ricky Nelson to come on TV. I actually enjoyed it. I'd spend hours writing a story (usually about something stupid that happened at school), reading it to myself, crossing out things that weren't funny. I'd do four or five drafts, then hand it in. Suddenly, it was fun to go to class and stand up to read my funny story—and, best of all, to get some laughs. I was always grateful to Mrs. Hawkes for that. (p. 189)

Another teacher who made a huge impression on Jay Leno was Mr. Walsh, who was often assigned to the library to oversee detention duty. Leno confessed that he spent time there almost daily. This gentleman enjoyed the mischievous Leno and his jokes and Jay therefore spent plenty of time entertaining him. Leno recalled, "Tell him the simplest joke and he'd break up. Everything was *hilarious* to this man" (Leno & Zehme, 1996, pp. 55–56). As a result, Leno came to detention prepared with new material. Eventually, the teacher who was amused by the young comedian suggested that Jay should consider going into show business. Today, Jay Leno remains grateful to Mr. Walsh.

Another comedian and actor well known for his humorous antics is Jim Carrey. His story is filled with adversity and helps us understand what Al Gore meant when he described humor as a "healing balm." The youngest child in his family, Jim Carrey took on the burden of providing comic relief to a troubled family. A native of Canada, he was born into a working-class family that lived a transient lifestyle driven by his father's struggle to stay employed. Carrey learned that he could make his sense of humor work for him in a number of ways. With his humor, he reached out for friendship. As a young child, Carrey was enrolled at the local Catholic school, where, he recalls,

> I was quiet. I didn't have a friend in the world until I started ham-
> ming it up at the back of the class. That was an important lesson. I
> realized that I needed to do something silly and make people laugh,
> and they would want to talk to me. (Knelman, 2000, p. 9)

The young boy also relied on his comic diversions to save his parents from giving into despair. With both parents suffering from chronic depression, Carrey's comedy provided the antidote the family needed. His mother was often bedridden with illnesses real or imagined, and young Jim took on the challenge of amusing her and cheering her up. One of her favorite routines was his imitation of a praying mantis, which he performed in his underwear at her bedside (Knelman, 2000).

Along with entertaining his sickly mother, he loved to entertain himself in front of a mirror and discovered that he had a gift for mimicry. For new material, he turned to his favorite TV shows and movies. He practiced doing impressions of John Wayne and the Riddler, his favorite character from *Batman*. Once he learned to make his face look like someone famous, he discovered that he could imitate voices and could mimic singers. He perfected the art of grinding his pelvis in an Elvis Presley style. He also discovered that he could get his revenge on annoying teachers and relatives by imitating them for the amusement of others. His father encouraged his son's behavior but his mother constantly warned him that he was going to the devil. When she could not tolerate his antics, she sent him to his room, but he didn't mind because he then had a great time in front of his mirror (Knelman, 2000).

He got into the habit of spending long hours alone, either in his bedroom or in a tiny closet he had cleared out to become his sanctuary. It was there he practiced performing impressions, wrote poetry, and enjoyed painting and drawing. For this young boy, creativity and humor became cathartic. In discussing his childhood ritual, he later described it as a trance-like concentration: "I was so lost in it, it was like being in the womb. It was like meditating; I didn't care about anything" (Knelman, 2000, p. 13). A significant event occurred in Carrey's life in third grade. He described a defining moment that strongly influenced his path in life:

> It started out at the back of 3rd grade music class at Blessed Trinity. I was aping this record, and the teacher called me out. "If you're so funny young man, why don't you show all of us?" So I did. The next thing I knew I was starring in the Christmas pageant as Santa doing a song-and-dance routine I'd come up with. And in the middle of the routine I looked down at the principal, Sister Mary John, a very serious person I respected greatly, and she was literally on all fours on the gymnasium floor in her full habit, laughing. After it was over, she got up and said, "Your friend wants to be a performer when he grows up—what do you think of that?" The place went crazy. That's when I said to myself, "Whatever it takes to get this feeling again—and again, and again—I've gotta do." (Costello, 2005, p. 252)

Later in his school experience Carrey's family discovered that he was dyslexic. His teachers and parents realized that he learned to compensate by developing an exceptional memory. Fortunately, when he reached seventh grade at St. Francis School, he had a lucky break. His teacher was Lucy Dervaitis, a woman who viewed teaching as a calling that embraced the challenge of reaching children other teachers viewed as hopeless. Ms. Dervaitis became his soul mate. From day one, she found him to be a delightful little character, and he was so thrilled to win the approval of this important adult authority figure. She recalled, "I never found him a serious behavior problem. I don't even remember giving him detentions. I thought it was great that this funny little guy was showing such talent at a young age" (Knelman, 2000, p. 15).

It became clear that the young comedian craved attention. He loved amusing his classmates with impersonations of some of the teachers at St. Francis. Many teachers would have viewed this behavior as rebelliousness that had to be crushed, but Ms. Dervaitis took a different approach. She invited him to put an act together for the class. Carrey was thrilled, as he would be allowed to share his performance at the end of the school day as long as he did his work and behaved well the rest of the time. This was the breakthrough he needed.

The acts for Ms. Dervaitis's class would typically include an impersonation of Elvis in his late Vegas period or John Wayne. For the class, the comic routine was a break from math worksheets and language arts. Whenever the other students became bored, they would petition Ms. Dervaitis to let Jim deliver his comic routine. His advanced humor was shared in other ways as well when he discovered that he had talent as a cartoonist. A caricature of Ms. Dervaitis losing control of the class and handing out detentions is an example. Today, the cartoon is a cherished item in the teacher's box of memories (Knelman, 2000).

Resilience

Several definitions and descriptions of resilience have been offered in the research literature. Resilience has been described as a protective mechanism that modifies an individual's response to a risk (Rutter, 1981, 1987) or as adjustment despite negative life events. Neihart (2002) defined it as "the ability to achieve emotional health and social competence in spite of a history of adversity or stress" (p. 114). In a comprehensive review of research literature, she reported that studies of resilient children found that they share traits with gifted children: intelligent curiosity (Anthony & Cohler, 1987), self-efficacy (McMillan & Reed, 1994), a positive explanatory style (Dai & Feldhusen, 1996), a healthy sense of humor (Hébert & Beardsley, 2001), and problem-solving ability (Masten & Garmezy, 1990).

Resilience was a significant finding uncovered in a major research study on gifted teenagers. I joined a team of researchers from the National Research Center on the Gifted and Talented who conducted a 3-year study of 35 ethnically diverse high-ability high school students who either achieved or underachieved in their urban setting (Reis, Hébert, Diaz, Maxfield, & Ratley, 1995). Many of the high-achieving participants in our study demonstrated resilience by overcoming problems associated with their families, their school, and their environment. Most of the achievers involved in the study came from homes affected by poverty; family turmoil caused by issues such as alcohol, drugs, and divorce; and other family dysfunction problems. As one participant indicated, "My family story is filled with eyebrow raisers" (Reis, Hébert, et al., 1995, p. 147). Other achievers had relatively calm and peaceful homes. All of the students in the study, however, lived in a city plagued by violence, drugs, poverty, and crime. Jorge described the difficulties experienced by teenagers in his urban high school:

There are people who come to this school every day so they can get a warm meal and a safe place to stay. Some people come from a house where it is twenty degrees inside. They didn't sleep well that night because of the yelling next door. These people come to school every day and they still manage to shine. They work their hardest. So what if they don't wear the latest designer jeans. (Hébert, 1993, p. 274)

Matteo, another participant, eloquently reflected on the resilience of so many of the achieving students and the pain many of them feel despite their ability to achieve in the urban environment:

You can never be prepared for it. When someone kicks you down, it hurts just as bad. I was talking to a friend yesterday who is a diabetic. He said, "You can't tell me that you can learn to deal with pain. I am a diabetic. I have a fear of needles. I take a shot three times a day. That needle hurts just as bad the first time as it does today. It still hurts the same. You just learn how the pain feels and you get accustomed to it. That's why some people lose. They may be stronger people but it still hurts every time they lose. Any time you get kicked down, it still hurts." (Reis, Hébert, et al., 1995, p. 166)

The gifted individuals profiled in the study survived in the city and excelled in their high school. They ignored drug dealers, they turned their backs on gangs, they avoided the crime in their neighborhoods, and they went on to become valedictorians, class presidents, star athletes, and scholars. Some went to Ivy League schools, others attended the most selective colleges in the country, and they all wanted to make a contribution to society. The courage and resilience displayed by these young people seemed remarkable, and yet they simply accepted their circumstances and appreciated the opportunities given to them. One participant, Nicki, came from a family whose problems probably would have overwhelmed some young people. Her family had persistent financial problems, her father battled alcoholism, her parents had divorced, and her mother was bitter. Yet, rather than giving up, she examined her life through her writing and won a $10,000 scholarship in a statewide essay contest sponsored by a large insurance company. Her essay, titled "The Stranger," detailed her troubled relationship with her alcoholic father and her eventual understanding of his love for her. An excerpt follows:

We entered the house like one might enter an unknown country, with silence and apprehension. The stranger isn't there. Upstairs, my mother set foot in my room and stood gaping at my bed. A look of ire and vexation was plastered on her face. That's when I noticed it too. Carved on the wooden head post of my bed were the words, "I love you." The dark surface of the wood was scratched so it looked as if the words were a different color. I kept staring at this message from the stranger. While my mother was distressed, I was glad. Some light spewed into my dark head. One empty question was answered. (Reis, Hébert, et al., 1995, p. 113)

Nicki's career plans were to become an urban educator. She applied to several prestigious New England colleges and was accepted by all of them. She received substantial college scholarships and decided to attend Boston College. As a high school senior, she looked forward to college and starting a new chapter of her life.

Strategies to Nurture the Social and Emotional Characteristics in Gifted Students

Having reviewed several more characteristics, traits, and behaviors that serve as assets to gifted young people in their social and emotional development, I describe below a number of strategies and methods educators and counselors can use to nurture and support these qualities in their students.

Use Guided Viewing of Film

Just as rich literature and enlightening biographies have the potential to nurture the affective development of young people, high-quality movies also can be helpful in guiding gifted students. Using movies to facilitate discussions about social and emotional issues has been referred to as guided viewing of film (Hébert & Hammond, 2006; Hébert & Sergent, 2005; Hébert & Speirs Neumeister, 2001, 2002). Using movies to guide gifted students toward self-understanding has numerous benefits. Movies have the potential to enrich and influence the lives of gifted young people in constructive ways. A good movie can become a meaningful metaphor for the essence of a young person's dilemma (Berg-Cross, Jennings, & Baruch, 1990). When an appropriate movie is combined with discussion and supportive follow-up activities, gifted students may view their situation through a more positive lens, enabling them to appreciate multiple aspects of difficult situations. With movies playing an influential role in contemporary society and functioning as an important part of the culture of children and teenagers, gifted students may be receptive to the notion of discussing sensitive topics through popular movies (Hébert & Hammond, 2006; Hébert & Sergent, 2005).

Teachers and counselors may implement guided viewing of film to address a variety of issues. Supporting gifted students by helping them understand the social and emotional traits and behaviors highlighted in this chapter and the previous chapter is one approach. In addition, films present many developmental affective issues that teachers or counselors may want to address, such as friendship, identity development, peer pressure, and parental and family expectations. Sharing these movies with students can reinforce prosocial messages that are part of the regular curriculum, while simultaneously enabling an educator or counselor to meet curricular or guidance objectives.

Teachers and counselors should also keep in mind the notion of facilitating guided viewing sessions with small groups of students struggling with a specific issue such as perfectionism, giftedness combined with a learning disability, or underachievement. In discussions, they may find more comfort in a setting where there are only students present who have shared similar experiences. There may also be times when it is appropriate to conduct guided viewing sessions with single-sex groups for films that sensitively address gender-specific issues. To support teachers and counselors considering guided viewing, a sample lesson is included below and an annotated bibliography of films for use with gifted students is provided in Appendix D.

An example of guided viewing. The following discussion presents an example of how a teacher or counselor might use *Ellen Foster* (Erman, 2002), a Hallmark movie, in facilitating guided viewing sessions with gifted elementary students. The movie is based on the best-selling novel by Kaye Gibbons and is the story of a gifted, resilient young girl who is left alone following the death of her mother. She draws inner strength from loving memories of her mother when she is forced to move from relative to relative in search of a family to replace her deceased mother and abusive father. Her wealthy and bitter grandmother eventually takes her in; however, Ellen's life in her grandmother's household becomes even more emotionally desolate than before.

Despite the obstacles she faces, Ellen becomes determined to find a new mother. She experiences warm, nurturing families around her and yearns to be part of one. This intelligent young girl takes her situation into her own hands and designs a plan to provide her happiness. In the end, Ellen's strength and determination enable her to free herself of her dysfunctional relatives and the emotionally traumatic events of her childhood. In the process, she discovers that the meaning of family is more than simply being related. It is being loved.

Educators will find that *Ellen Foster* is an appropriate movie to use with gifted students, because it features an emotionally sensitive and intelligent young girl with whom many gifted children can identify. Ellen applies her giftedness to solve her problem and overcome tremendous personal adversity in her life. Her harsh environment may be similar to the home situations of many gifted students from difficult backgrounds. Children from all cultural backgrounds can appreciate Ellen's story and take away lessons that can be applied to their own lives. The film highlights a number of developmental struggles of gifted children and provides educators with material appropriate for classroom discussions that can enlighten all involved. Key issues that emerge in *Ellen Foster* include developing resilience, finding emotional support from people in one's life, applying intelligence to solve life's challenges, and having a strong belief in self.

Break up and discuss

In my work with guided viewing, I have found it helpful to break up a movie and incorporate discussions along the way. A natural break can often be found approximately every 30 minutes. Questions can be infused according to the content of each section. Spacing the film into segments allows students to reflect on elements and thoughts that may be lost by the time the movie ends. Segmenting the film and debriefing segments helps students with shorter attention spans to remain focused, and such an approach allows the discussion to be broken up into a multiple-day plan, rather than requiring a 2–3-hour block of time.

With the key issues for discussion determined and the natural breaks in the movie identified, a menu of discussion questions to pose in facilitating the conversation with children can be prepared. Care should be taken in writing the questions, making sure to include introductory questions that appear nonthreatening to children, followed by more sensitive questions that focus on the problematic situations faced by both the movie characters and the children involved in the discussion. A sensitively crafted menu is needed for a conversation to be cathartic for gifted students. Several sample discussion questions for use with *Ellen Foster* are provided below:

- What challenges does Ellen face in her life? What do you think helps her cope with the difficulties she faces?

- Ellen enjoys her friendship with Starletta Douglas. How do Starletta and her parents support Ellen? Why is their friendship important to Ellen? Who are your important friends? How do they support you?
- During difficult times, Ellen enjoyed cutting out pictures of people from catalogues and creating paper doll families. Why do you think she did this? How might this have helped her? When you are having a difficult time, how do you entertain yourself? How does this help you?
- Although Ellen's grandmother does not treat her kindly, Ellen continues to treat her grandmother with respect and kindness. What does this say about Ellen? Why do you think she treated her grandmother this way? How might that have helped Ellen?
- Ellen is a smart young girl. How do we know this? How does Ellen use her intelligence to solve her problems? How do you use your talents to address the challenges in your life?
- Ellen is a strong girl. Some people would refer to her strength as "resilience." What did you see in the movie that indicated that Ellen was resilient? What lessons about resilience have you learned from Ellen? How might you apply these to your life?

Teachers and counselors should also consider using direct quotations from the movie as meaningful prompts for discussion. Several examples from *Ellen Foster*, accompanied by discussion questions, are provided below.

In an early scene in the movie, Ellen's mother, knowing that she will not live much longer, wraps her arms around Ellen and shares her feelings with her daughter in an attempt to prepare Ellen for life after she is gone. She reminds her daughter of her special qualities that will enable her to survive life's harshness:

You are my favorite person in the whole world. You're smart and you're strong and you can get along, no matter what happens. I absolutely know that. You'll remember I told you that, won't you?

Discussion questions that teachers or counselors might want to pose include:
- Why do you think Ellen's mother delivered this message to her?
- Do you think her mother's message helped Ellen? If so, how?
- Has there been a time in your life when someone you love gave you similar advice? Who gave you the advice? What was the advice?

In a poignant scene in which Ellen visits her mother's grave on the anniversary of her death, she talks with her mother about her supportive art teacher who has taken her into her home. She also spends some time chatting about how she is coping with being forced to live with her bitter grandmother. She attempts to assure her mother that she will survive:

> I think the two of you would have gotten along real good. Maybe you're looking down on me and feeling thoroughly okay about me being her friend, but she ain't nothing like you. She can never be a momma like you, but she'd be my first or second choice, if you know what I mean. But don't you worry about me being with your momma. I'm gonna manage it one way or another. Like you used to say, "Nothing is forever, though it don't seem like it sometimes." I'm doing okay in school. Don't worry, okay.

Discussion questions could follow this prompt:

- ❧ Why do you think Ellen thought her mother would have enjoyed knowing her art teacher? Do you agree?
- ❧ What does Ellen think her mother might be worrying about? How does she try to reassure her mother? Why do you think she does this?
- ❧ Have you ever had an important relationship with an adult outside of your family? How did this person help you? How did your family feel about this person? How did that make you feel?
- ❧ Ellen reminds her mother of having said, "Nothing is forever, though it don't seem like it sometimes." Why does she reflect back on her mother saying this? How do you think this helps Ellen? Do you think this message from Ellen's mother is one you could apply to your life? How?

Later in the movie, Ellen has discovered a woman in her community who operates a foster home. She begins to plan a way to become part of the foster family, and thinking that the woman's name is Foster, she begins signing her school papers with the new name "Ellen Foster." When the school psychologist questions her about this she explains:

> It may not be the name God or my momma gave me, but that's my name now. My old family kinda' wore out the other one and I figured I can start practicing my new name, of my new family, for when they are my family. Foster, it's a clean, fresh name.

To facilitate a discussion, a teacher or counselor might ask these questions:

- Why do you think Ellen changed her name? How do you think she was feeling?
- Has there ever been a time in your life when you also wanted a "clean, fresh" change? Did you do anything about that? If so, what?

The movie concludes with the following:

Every day I try to feel a little bit better about all that went on when I was little. It'll eventually get straightened out in my head. I came a long way to get here. That will always amaze me.

Appropriate questions for concluding the discussion are the following:

- What does Ellen mean when she says, "I came a long way to get here. That will always amaze me." Do you think Ellen is amazing? Why?
- Where do you think Ellen found her strength to cope with the difficulties she faced?
- What lessons have you learned from Ellen that you might apply to your life?

In my work with guided viewing of film, I have found that movies such as *Ellen Foster* elicit emotional responses. Therefore, it is important that facilitators design follow-up activities to allow students to process their feelings. These activities afford time for introspection and discussion of issues explored in the film. Moreover, during follow-up activities, students have time to offer each other emotional support and empathy. The following is a suggested menu of follow-up activities to be used with *Ellen Foster*:

- Pretend that you are Ellen Foster. Write a poem about overcoming difficult obstacles in life.
- The movie *Ellen Foster* has become a Broadway musical. Write the lyrics to a song to be performed in this new theatrical production.
- Pretend that Ellen Foster is being interviewed on a talk show. Design and role-play the interview.
- Write a short sequel to *Ellen Foster*. How will the next chapter of her life read?
- Design and illustrate a road map of Ellen Foster's journey.
- Create a collage of photographs that represent important lessons learned through *Ellen Foster*.
- Select a scene from *Ellen Foster* and adapt it to become a children's picture book.

- Ellen Foster writes a letter to an advice columnist asking for help. How does her letter read? What advice does the columnist provide Ellen? Write both letters.
- Reflect on the following prompt in your journal: What lesson stood out to you in the movie *Ellen Foster*? How might this apply to your own life?
- Ellen Foster has become an inspirational speaker to young people throughout the country. Write a speech that Ellen will present to your elementary school.

Nurture Resilience Through Extracurricular Activities Involving Social Action

In my dissertation research in an urban high school, I met Jorge, who spent many hours after school tutoring elementary school students struggling to learn English. Following his high school graduation, and with the support of his parents, Jorge pursued a degree in bilingual education to continue to help young children in his community. His dedication to them evolved from his ability to understand and appreciate their struggles. He explained, "I remember how I felt when I first came to this country from the islands, and I found myself feeling so alone in my new school. I was overwhelmed." He elaborated, "I decided to work with bilingual students because I knew I could relate to the problems they were facing." Today Jorge teaches young children; however, he collaborates with a high school teacher in his community in facilitating an afterschool club in which high school students tutor younger bilingual children. The high school students have reported that they benefit from this program more than they give.

Orlando was a friend of Jorge's and was another research participant who helped me to see the value of gifted teenagers becoming involved in community service. Linda Silverman (1993a) maintained that service is a need of gifted young people and I came to understand this as I watched students like Jorge, Orlando, and their friends. I saw that they experienced a deep sense of fulfillment once they discovered their paths of service. Orlando's schedule of classes may have ended at 3 p.m.; however, that was just the beginning of an action-packed afternoon. The remainder of his day was dedicated to serving others through a variety of student organizations. A deeply empathic young man, Orlando directed his talents and energy to philanthropy projects throughout his urban community. Through youth groups he was associated with, he visited convalescent homes and organized students to volunteer at drug rehabilitation centers and soup kitchens.

He also did volunteer work for the Salvation Army and worked as a tutor. He dedicated his weekends and summer breaks to Habitat for Humanity, helping to build modest homes for economically disadvantaged families.

Orlando's close friend Tania, an African American female, served as president of a student leadership group known as Common Ground. She described the group as an organization of teenagers from urban and suburban high schools who came together to discuss stereotypes and combat racism. She explained, "We're all about finding a common ground. This group teaches people about the ways they are all alike." Tania pointed out that through this group she felt she could make a difference for others because she had experienced racism as an urban teenager.

Students like Jorge, Orlando, and Tania remind educators of the value of extracurricular activities involving community service. As a teacher or counselor works with gifted students and observes social and emotional characteristics such as moral maturity, sensitivity, and empathy, a rather natural approach to supporting those qualities is to encourage these young people to engage in extracurricular activities associated with causes about which they are passionate. Such groups serve as outlets for their moral maturity, sensitivity, and empathy. For gifted students, involvement in organizations that focus on service and social outreach addresses their strong need for consistency between their values and their actions. Through these efforts, they can apply their idealism and their strong ability to conceptualize and address societal, social, and environmental problems. Researchers exploring the impact of social-action projects and service-learning on moral development have reported positive results (Hart, Matsuba, & Atkins, 2008). Involvement in community service contributes to moral development by generating an interest in addressing authentic community problems and becoming effective voices for change (Hart, Atkins, & Donnelly, 2006).

In addition, it is important to understand that involvement in extracurricular activities producing tangible products or performances, such as building homes with Habitat for Humanity or the creation of a youth group such as Common Ground, builds a sense of accomplishment and success. Pro-social activities provide students evidence that something can be gained by persevering. Products also demonstrate that choices matter, effort does make a difference, and some adults value what young people do with their talents (Heath & McLaughlin, 1993). Urban educators and researchers have consistently found that involvement in extracurricular programs in urban areas offers structure and predictability that might be missing in other areas of life (Halpern, 1992; Heath & McLaughlin, 1993; Hébert, 2000a).

When students become involved in meaningful extracurricular activities, they develop relationships with adults who influence how they see themselves. Heath and McLaughlin (1993) noted that the most important contribution urban youth groups provide is an adult who sees them as young adults, cares for them as individuals, and serves as mentor, critic, or advocate. Resilience researchers also found that relationships with adults outside the family provided psychosocial support and served as a protective factor in stressful environments (Garmezy, 1985; Hébert & Reis, 1999; Jones, Bibbins, & Henderson, 1993; Rhodes, 1994; Torrance, Goff, & Satterfield, 1998; Werner & Smith, 1982).

Facilitate Moral Discussions

Educators concerned with the development of moral maturity in their students have a long tradition of teaching morals, values, and character. Discussions of social and moral dilemmas, real-life and hypothetical, are effective ways to help young people take the perspectives of others and contribute to their moral maturity (Hilderbrandt & Zan, 2008). Max Malikow's (2007) *Profiles in Character* is a book for teachers addressing the affective domain through serious class discussions centered on moral development. He recognizes the power of stories for promoting thoughtful discussions of the complex everyday dilemmas that real people face. Malikow presented a collection of 26 short stories designed to teach 17 universally admired virtues: adaptability, altruism, authenticity, compassion, courage, empathy, endurance, forgiveness, happiness, honesty, humility, integrity, loyalty, perseverance, responsibility, thoughtfulness, and wisdom. Each story can be read in 5 minutes and is accompanied by thought-provoking discussion questions and follow-up activities. Malikow believed that "Students need to talk and be heard" (p. xi) and by sharing and learning how others have arrived at certain perspectives in life, discussions centered on such serious topics can change how teenagers view important decisions they must make if they are to live lives of such integrity. Such teaching should serve as the foundation of any educational program for gifted teenagers.

Educators may also want to explore the work of Robert Coles to develop strategies and curriculum for supporting the development of moral maturity in gifted children. Robert Coles is a research psychiatrist for Harvard University and the author of *The Moral Intelligence of Children* (1997), through which he shared how he used a powerful short story by Leo Tolstoy to teach the Golden Rule—the essence of empathy, so critical to any discussion of morality and of being a good person. He maintained that *The Old Grandfather and the Grandson* can be taught to anyone at any level, from elementary school to postgraduate school. Below is Tolstoy's story:

> The grandfather had become very old. His legs wouldn't go, his eyes didn't see, his ears didn't hear, he had no teeth. And when he ate, the food dripped from his mouth.
>
> The son and daughter-in-law stopped setting a place for him at the table and gave him supper in back of the stove. Once they brought dinner down to him in a cup. The old man wanted to move the cup and dropped it and broke it. The daughter-in-law began to grumble at the old man for spoiling everything in the house and breaking cups and said that she would now give him dinner in a dishpan. The old man only sighed and said nothing.
>
> Once the husband and wife were staying at home and watching their small son playing on the floor with some wooden planks: he was building something. The father asked, "What is that you are doing, Misha?" And Misha said, "Dear Father, I am making a dishpan. So that when you and Mother become old, you may be fed from this dishpan."
>
> The husband and wife looked at one another and began to weep. They became ashamed of offending the old man, and from then on seated him at the table and waited on him. (Coles, 1997, pp. 10–11)

Coles (1997) asked that we consider sharing such stories and that we ask young people for their interpretations. He encouraged educators to follow his example, sharing with children times in his life when he was so preoccupied with his own responsibilities and interests that he failed to respond to the people closest to him. When adults offer a forthright sharing of their experiences, students are more able to offer reflections of their own. Coles suggested that students write an essay about the Tolstoy story, about its personal meaning to them, and how they might imagine using it with their own children one day.

For Further Thought and Discussion

- Consider Christopher Pendley's letter to his kindergarten teacher. What evidence do you see in his story of the social and emotional characteristics highlighted in this chapter?
- What role does moral education have in gifted programs?
- How might the university students from the Hébert and McBee (2007) study inspire other gifted young people?
- How do the experiences of Jay Leno and Jim Carrey speak to gifted students today?
- How might educators and counselors support the development of resilience within gifted young people?

Resources to Expand Your Thinking and Extend Your Support to Gifted Students

Canfield, J., & Switzer, J. (2005). *The success principles: How to get from where you are to where you want to be.* New York, NY: HarperCollins.

Coles, R. (1997). *The moral intelligence of children.* New York, NY: Random House.

Lewis, B. A. (1992). *Kids with courage: True stories about young people making a difference.* Minneapolis, MN: Free Spirit.

Purkey, W. W. (2006). *Teaching class clowns: And what they can teach us.* Thousand Oaks, CA: Corwin Press.

CHAPTER 4

Contextual Influences on the Social and Emotional Development of Gifted Students

My goals for this chapter are to:
- Explain Bronfenbrenner's Ecological Systems Theory to understand the role of contextual influences on development.
- Provide you with an understanding of how contextual influences shape the social and emotional lives of gifted students.
- Examine four qualitative research studies of gifted young people through Bronfenbrenner's theoretical lens to highlight the significant role played by contextual influences.
- Have you reflect on how Bronfenbrenner's theory may be applied to your work with gifted students.

Bette Midler, the woman known to her fans throughout the world as "The Ultimate Diva," and "The Divine Miss M," is a brilliant performer, singer, and actress. Her life's narrative is one of determination, resilience, creativity, and survival. Bette Midler's early years are especially intriguing in that her childhood was a story of stark contrasts and the events of her adolescence played a significant role in shaping the professional woman. Born December 1, 1945, she was the youngest daughter of Fred Midler, a house painter, and his wife Ruth.

Fred Midler was employed by the U.S. Navy and moved his family from Passaic, NJ, to Honolulu, HI. For a short period of time, the Midlers lived in modest but pleasant military housing, but eventually the government moved all nonmilitary personnel without much concern for keeping families in comfortable conditions. As a result, Bette's family was sent to "Halauu housing—poor people's housing" (Spada, 1984, p. 2). This move was difficult for the family. Their lack of money combined with the fact that they were the only Caucasian family in a community of Fillipinos, Samoans, Japanese, and Chinese, made life challenging for them. Bette grew up as the only White girl in her class. She reflected, "It wasn't easy being the only Jewish kid in a Samoan neighborhood" (Bego, 2002, p. 6). Feeling like a misfit, she let others think she was Portuguese, an ethnic group that comprised another large segment of her neighborhood. She explained, "The Portuguese used to work in the fields, and the 'hacles'— white people—were the overseers. I wasn't Portuguese, but I let them think it (Bego, 2002, p. 15). She indicated, "It was easier than anything else. Portuguese people were accepted. Jews were not. I was an alien, a foreigner—even though I was born there" (Spada, 1984, p. 3).

Life in the Midler home was often tense. Bette described her father as a man who thrived on screaming. "My father was a bellower. To get a word in, you had to bellow back. He loved a good argument, he loved the adrenaline rush" (Bego, 2002, p. 13). She saw her mother as a woman who was unfulfilled. "I saw this misery, this incredible misery that she could not force her way out of, this loneliness and bitterness" (Bego, 2002, p. 13). However, Bette reflected on her mother's life sympathetically, for she adored her as a beautiful woman who had personal dreams that were never actualized.

Life for Bette and her two sisters became more complex when their younger brother Daniel was born. As a result of a postnatal illness, Danny was left mentally handicapped. This became a source of constant frustration for Fred Midler as he could do nothing to change his son's condition. The public health authorities wanted to have the child institutionalized, but the Midlers would not hear of it. Fred Midler would return from a long day of work, sit with his son at the family's kitchen table, and attempt to teach him to talk, read, and write. Bette recalled that these sessions often ended up with Mr. Midler "screaming at the top of his lungs out of frustration, and Daniel would be crying" (Bego, 2002, p. 14). Eventually Daniel did learn. Bette appreciated the challenges her parents faced and reflected years later, "My brother was mentally handicapped and they raised him at home. That was a real struggle. They succeeded, but they sacrificed their entire life for it" (p. 14).

With such difficult challenges at home and in her neighborhood Bette often felt like a pariah. There were also personal qualities that contributed to her feeling different from others. As a child she enjoyed a rich fantasy life. She recalled, "I believed in the things in fairy tales. I lived in a cloud. I was afraid of people . . . I always worried what they thought of me. I was very shy, lived very much in my head, in my daydreams" (Spada, 1984, p. 3). Fortunately, Bette's mother encouraged her fantasy life and supported her daughter's daydreams. Living under the dark cloud of her tyrannical father, Bette adored her mother. A woman with unfulfilled aspirations, Ruth Midler was completely preoccupied with Hollywood, and Bette became fascinated with her mother's collection of movie magazines. Bette soon developed a passion for several of the Hollywood starlets of the day and imagined herself as the sultry heroines of theatrical productions she created with her vivid imagination. Her cinematic dreams were enriched as she spent hours watching MGM's most famous movie stars and their glamorous musical numbers. Bette reflected, "You felt like you were in paradise when you saw those pictures" (Bego, 2002, p. 15).

Her fascination with the colorful life beyond her modest neighborhood became stronger when a local librarian became enamored with the strange little Jewish girl and provided her a ticket to her first live theater performance. She reflected, "Mrs. Seto. I'll never forget her. She believed in fairies" (Spada, 1984, p. 4). The theatrical play served as an authentic revelation to Bette. "I looked up at the stage and there were all those shining people. They were dancing and singing, looking so happy" (Spada, 1984, p. 4). Inspired by this experience, she reflected, "It was the most wonderful thing I'd ever seen, and I just thought—I want to do that. I want to *be* one of those rosy, rosy people" (Spada, 1984, pp. 4–5).

Regardless of how glamorous these productions were for this lonely young girl, reality would eventually erase Bette Midler's fantasy world. She remained the unattractive, chubby little Jewish girl with problems who tried to be like the other kids; however, her efforts did not change her social situation. As she grew older she felt even more isolated. "I was miserable—I guess it was because I looked like I do" (Spada, 1984, p. 4). She was poor, white, Jewish, homely, and as she struggled the treatment she received from the kids in school grew worse. In that tough neighborhood, her classmates mocked and taunted her, threatened to beat her up and chased her home in tears.

In fifth grade she enjoyed a brief respite when she teamed up with a classmate and presented a skit in front of her class. She recalled, "Me and this girl Barbara Nagy—I remember *everybody*—we decided to put on a skit for the class. She was the man, I was the woman: Herman and Oysterbee" (Bego, 2002, p. 17). Both girls forgot their lines and ended up improvising the dialogue. When their classmates roared with laughter, Bette realized an entirely new kind of love when showered with laughter and applause. The following year she entered a school talent show and won first prize for her rendition of "Lullaby of Broadway." She recalled, "All the class voted, and I got the first $2 prize! I will never forget that flush of happiness" (Spada, 1984, p. 4). It was then that she became convinced that becoming an actress was her destiny. "As I grew older, all the best times in my life were when I was standing in front of an audience performing. I learned that I could be popular by making people laugh" (Bego, 2002, p. 17). She went on to admit, "I became a clown to win people's acceptance, and I think that's when I decided I wanted to be in show business" (Bego, 2002, p. 17).

As a high school student, Bette's struggles were exacerbated when she developed a prematurely ample bosom, and her tormentors now had even more reason to single her out for her differentness. She kept trying to be like everyone else but nothing seemed to work. Of her years at Radford High, Bette recalled, "The school I went to was just like any high school anywhere . . . We had rock & roll, sock hops, *American Bandstand*" (Bego, 2002, p. 17). She explained, "The only thing different was that all the kids were Japanese, Chinese, Filipino, Samoan, and all the girls hated me because I had such big boobs" (Bego, 2002, p. 17). Of these painful teenage years, she reflected, "I had to go to phys ed class with all these Oriental girls who had brassieres that were holding up nothing. It was horrible. They teased me incessantly because I would, like, bobble on my way home" (Bego, 2002, p. 18).

Unhappy with her home life and her lack of social life, Bette found it easy to immerse herself in her textbooks: "I got buried in studying. I was always best in English. I had to be the best, because it was all I had" (Bego, 2002, p. 19). In her sophomore year, Bette was accepted into the Regents, an exclusive academic girls' club, and was voted its president the following year. Also elected into the National Honor Society, the shy, intimidated teenager with the sandy blonde hair that frizzled in the Honolulu humidity and the Harlequin-shaped eyeglasses began her transformation. That same year, Bette became best friends with a girl named Beth Ellen Chambers, whom she remembered as "hysterically loud and loved a good time" (Bego, 2002, p. 18). This friendship was significant to Bette: "She was the most adorable thing. She made me feel okay to be who I was, enjoyable, good to have around. My family never made me feel this way. She drew me out of myself" (Bego, 2002, pp. 18–19). As more students from military families enrolled in her high school, Bette found herself enjoying a different peer group, as these teenagers were more academically oriented. However, she maintained that she still never really fit in socially even though she was elected senior class president. She explained her election: "I won that by default: You should have see the other candidate!" (Bego, 2002, p. 19).

In high school, Bette's theatrical experience included the senior class production of Cornelia Otis Skinner's *When Our Hearts Were Young and Gay*. Her experience as the leading lady only reinforced in her that she had found her calling. By her senior year she was determined to become an actress and became involved in speech festivals throughout the state. By the end of high school, Bette's academic efforts paid off and she was declared class valedictorian; however, that honor did not mean as much to her as her prospects for pursuing a theatrical life did. When Bette graduated from high school in 1963, the school newspaper's graduation edition summarized her high school experience and predicted success, "Bette Midler, who is considered to be one of Radford's greatest dramatists, is the president. Her ambition is to join the Peace Corps and, perhaps, someday become another Bette Davis" (Bego, 2002, p. 19). The following fall, she entered the University of Hawaii to study drama, but she was more eager to do something in the theater than to remain a student.

In 1965, Bette's big break arrived. She learned that several sequences of the film version of James Michener's novel *Hawaii* were being filmed on location and that several extras from the local community would be hired. She jumped at the opportunity, landed a part, and played the role of a missionary's wife aboard the ship sailing from New England. When the production company was finished filming on location in Hawaii, several of the local actors and actresses were flown to Los Angeles to complete some of the scenes. Bette was delighted to join that group. As far as she was concerned, the trip to Hollywood was her big break because the earnings from her role in *Hawaii* meant an airline ticket to New York City to begin her life in the theater. Following tearful good-byes to her family, the determined young Bette Midler said aloha to Hawaii, departed for New York, and began the journey that would take her to stardom.

Why is Bette Midler's story important to educators of gifted students?

Like many individuals who struggle through lonely, unhappy childhoods and difficult teenage years, Bette Midler developed the determination to make something of herself. Although Midler's story is inspirational, her story is important to educators attempting to understand adolescent development. Bette Midler's life experiences provide an example of how a person is embedded within environmental systems that interact with each other and influence how that person develops. Moreover, Midler's experience helps us to understand the role that context plays in a young person's social and emotional growth.

To understand the significance of contextual influences on development, I next examine a theoretical framework provided by Urie Bronfenbrenner that illuminates how environment interacts with personality over time and shapes an individual's life. I apply the Bronfenbrenner framework to Midler's life story and following that discussion, I present the findings of several studies I conducted with colleagues regarding contextual influences in the development of gifted individuals. The chapter concludes with a discussion of the implications of this theory and research.

Bronfenbrenner's Ecological Systems Theory

For many years, social scientists interested in human development conducted studies of children and adolescents in one setting at a time. They examined family or peer relations. They considered school settings, home environments, or communities. More recently, they have acknowledged the linkage among the various contexts of development, and they are beginning to pose questions about the nature of the connections. Rather than examining how home environments affect adolescents, researchers are asking questions about how events in the home might influence events in the peer group. This change in research orientation represents an increasing awareness of and respect for a perspective referred to as the ecology of human development (Steinberg, 2005). Through this approach, a researcher does not focus only on the developing individual but also on the interrelationships between the individual and his or her contexts and also on the interconnections among the contexts themselves.

The most significant proponent of this view was psychologist Urie Bronfenbrenner (1979, 1989, 1993), who provided a thorough explanation of the environmental influences that shape an individual's development. Because this theory also indicates that a person's biologically influenced characteristics interact with environmental forces to shape development, his perspective may be described more accurately as a bioecological theory (Bronfenbrenner & Ceci, 1994).

Bronfenbrenner (1979) first proposed that natural environments are the chief source of influence on human beings as they develop. He maintained that environmental influences were often overlooked or simply ignored by researchers who chose to study human development in artificial laboratory settings. He defined development as "the person's evolving conception of the ecological environment, and his relation to it, as well as the growing person's capacity to discover, sustain, or alter its properties" (Bronfenbrenner, 1979, p. 9). Bronfenbrenner (1970) defined *environments* or *natural ecology* as a "set of nested structures, each inside the next, like a set of Russian dolls" (p. 3). The developing person is situated at the center of and embedded in a series of environmental systems that interact with one another and with the individual to influence development in significant ways. Figure 1 provides a graphic representation of Bronfenbrenner's theory, and Table 4 offers Bronfenbrenner's original definitions for each of the environmental systems. Bronfenbrenner (1989) proposed the following as the cornerstone of his theoretical framework:

> The ecology of human development is the scientific study of the progressive, mutual accommodation, throughout the life course, between an active, growing human being, and the changing properties of the immediate settings in which the developing person lives, as this process is affected by the relations between these settings, and by the larger contexts in which these settings are embedded. (p. 188)

Bronfenbrenner's Contexts for Development

The Microsystem

The innermost environmental layer in Bronfenbrenner's theoretical model is referred to as the microsystem. This system involves the activities and interactions that occur within the individual's most immediate surroundings. For example, with infants, the microsystem may be strictly the family. The infant's natural environment gradually becomes more complex as the child is exposed to other microsystems, such as day care, preschool classes, Cub Scouts, and friends in the neighborhood. Children are influenced by the people in their microsystems while their own biologically and

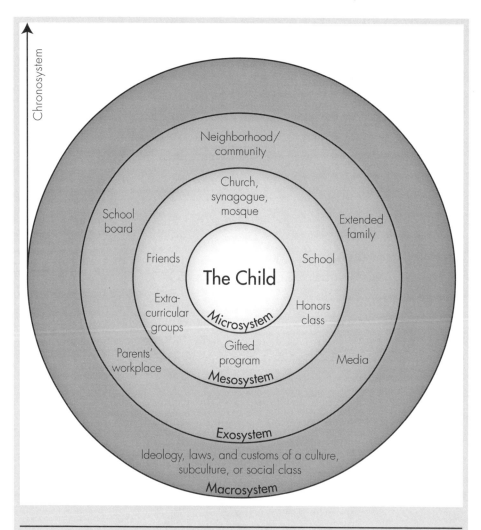

Figure 1. Bronfenbrenner's Ecological Systems Theory.

socially influenced characteristics (i.e., temperaments, physical characteristics, and talents) influence the behavior of their friends simultaneously. For example, an extremely emotional and perfectionistic gifted child may create marital friction between parents who have differing views of how to cope with the child's concerns. Bronfenbrenner (1979, 1989, 1993) also indicated that interactions between any two individuals in a microsystem are affected by a third person. For instance, fathers play an important role in mother-child interactions. If mother is happily married and emotionally supported by her husband, she will tend to interact more patiently and sensitively with her children. A mother experiencing marital tension may feel as though she is raising her children alone, and her interactions with them may not always be positive.

TABLE 4

Original Definitions of Terms Incorporated in Bronfenbrenner's Ecological Systems Theory

The Ecology of Human Development

The ecology of human development involves the scientific study of the progressive, mutual accommodation between the active, growing human being and the changing properties of the immediate settings in which the developing person lives, as this process is affected by relations between these settings, and by the larger contexts in which the settings are embedded. (Bronfenbrenner, 1979, p. 21)

The Microsystem

A microsystem is a pattern of activities, roles, and interpersonal relations experienced by the developing person in a given face-to face setting with particular physical and material features, and containing other persons with distinctive characteristics of temperament, personality, and systems of belief. (Bronfenbrenner, 1989, p. 227)

The Mesosystem

A mesosystem comprises the interrelations among two or more settings in which the developing person actively participates (such as, for a child, the relations among home, school, and neighborhood peer group; for an adult, among family, work, and social life). A mesosystem is thus a system of microsystems. (Bronfenbrenner, 1979, p. 25)

The Exosystem

The exosystem encompasses the linkages and processes taking place between two or more settings, at least one of which does not ordinarily contain the developing person, but in which events occur that influence processes within the immediate setting that does contain that person. (Bronfenbrenner, 1989, p. 227)

The Macrosystem

The macrosystem consists of the overarching pattern of micro-, meso-, and exosystems characteristic of a given culture, subculture, or other broader social context, with particular reference to the developmentally-instigative belief systems, resources, hazards, life styles, opportunity structures, life course options, and patterns of social interchange that are embedded in each of these systems. The macrosystem may be thought of as a societal blueprint for a particular culture, subcultures, or other broader social context. (Bronfenbrenner, 1989, p. 228)

The Mesosystem

The mesosystem, the second environmental layer in Bronfenbrenner's theory, refers to the interrelationships among microsystems such as home, school, and peer groups. Bronfenbrenner maintained that optimal development is more likely to occur with strong, supportive links between microsystems. For example, gifted children with secure and loving relationships with their parents are more likely to have an easy time establishing secure and meaningful friendships with their peers throughout childhood and adolescence (Gavin & Furman, 1996; Kerns, Klepec, & Cole, 1996). For these same children, success in school will be more likely to occur if parents value education and consult and cooperate with their children's teachers (Luster & McAdoo, 1996). Conversely, if nonsupportive links between microsystems exist, children's experiences may be troublesome. For example, when adolescent peer groups determine that it is not cool to be involved in the gifted program, they often undermine a gifted teenager's academic performance, regardless of how much parents, teachers, and school counselors encourage academic achievement and involvement in the gifted program (Ford, 1996; Steinberg, Dornbusch, & Brown, 1992).

The Exosystem

Bronfenbrenner's third environmental layer, the exosystem, consists of contexts that children and adolescents are not necessarily a part of, but do indeed influence their development. Examples of such contextual influences may be their parents' work environment, the popular media, and the school board overseeing their school district. Whether or not parents are enjoying their professional lives may influence their emotional relationships at home. How the popular media depicts intellectually oriented children and adolescents may also shape how they feel about themselves. A school board's decisions regarding the gifted and talented program may also have an impact on intellectual, motivational, and emotional development.

The Macrosystem

According to Bronfenbrenner, development also occurs within a macrosystem. The macrosystem is the broad overarching ideology, laws, and customs of a culture, subculture, or social class. This ideology dictates within a culture how children should be treated and educated. This value system varies from one culture to another, across subcultures as well as social classes, and greatly influences the lives of young people in their homes, schools, communities and all other contexts that affect them. Consider the following: Would the number of young women involved in athletics after school (a mesosystem experience) be greater in those cultures (or macrosystems) that view the passions and interests of children as something other than gender-specific? Would a young boy from a working class neighborhood in an industrial community find it difficult to pursue ballet?

Bronfenbrenner's Temporal Dimension: The Chronosystem

Bronfenbrenner (1989) maintained that the "characteristics of a person at a given time in his or her life are a joint function of the characteristics of the person and of the environment over the course of a person's life up to that time" (p. 190). With this understanding, Bronfenbrenner's theory included the chronosystem, a temporal dimension that highlights that changes in the child or in any of the ecological contexts of development can affect the direction development will take. For example, cognitive and physiological changes that take place during puberty often contribute to increased conflict between adolescents and their parents (Steinberg, 2005). The impact of environmental changes will also be influenced by the age of the child. For instance, although a divorce wreaks havoc in the lives of children of all ages, older adolescents are less likely than their much younger siblings are to assume guilt for their parents breaking up (Hetherington, Bridges, & Insabella, 1998).

In reviewing the life experiences of Bette Midler, we understand the powerful role played by the greater culture, the macrosystem. In American society at the time Bette Midler was growing up in Hawaii, young women believed that being petite and attractive was highly valued and that being attractive and popular enabled a young woman to enjoy adolescence and remain respected by her peers. The exosystem, which includes the role played by the mass media, reinforces the notion that femininity in American society is closely associated with one's physical appearance. Within Bette Midler's mesosystem, the school setting, her situation was challenging. Being the only Caucasian female in her class, being tormented by school bullies, and not being appreciated by students who measured social worth with rigid rules and who did not understand or appreciate her cultural background was difficult for this young woman. Bette's interaction with Beth Ellen, the teenager who befriended her in high school and from whom she learned to appreciate her many positive qualities, was critical to the development of Bette's self-understanding, but Midler's experience within her microsystem was most influential in her development. Her early family history was not positive; however, the loving relationship with her supportive and inspirational mother appears to have played a major role in the evolution of her strong belief in self. Woven throughout the layers of environmental influences were Bette Midler's personality characteristics. Her creativity, sense of humor, determination, and resilience interacted with the significant individuals in her life, counteracted the negative forces she encountered, and enabled her to attain success.

A Review of Research Studies in Which Contextual Influences Were Significant in Shaping the Social and Emotional Development of Gifted Young People

Several research studies I conducted with gifted young people are discussed here. These studies were carried out in four entirely different contexts: an urban high school swim team, a Greek social fraternity in a large university setting, an undergraduate honors program in a technological university, and an isolated, impoverished rural community. Although the studies are vastly different in context, they highlight how significant contextual influences shape the social and emotional lives of the gifted young people featured in each of the studies.

Coach Brogan and the South Central High School Swim Team

In a study of high-ability males in an urban school setting, I uncovered a subculture within the culture of South Central High School (SCHS; Hébert, 1995a). South Central, situated in a community in the Northeast, had a diverse student body of 1,676 students. The school's population was 67% Hispanic and 20% African American, and the remaining students were from a variety of ethnic backgrounds. Like many urban high schools, SCHS suffered from gangs, drug traffic, and a disenchanted student body. Within this setting, I found a group of gifted young men whose experience at SCHS was quite different from the majority of the student body. I discovered that the SCHS swim team led by Coach Brogan had a significant influence on the social and emotional well-being and achievement orientation of the gifted male student athletes. Within this context, the gifted young men found a family, a place to belong, and counseling support.

The high achievers on the SCHS swim team continually referred to important relationships in describing their swim-team experience. The swim team was a family, and a sense of brotherhood existed amongst the athletes. One swimmer reported, "We're very close. We do everything together. We're hard workers. We know when it's time to work and when it's time to play. We're unique in this school" (Hébert, 1995a, pp. 314–315). Another swimmer said, "With the swim team, we do everything together—movies, slam dancing, guitar, hanging out and sleeping over" (Hébert, 1995a, p. 315). A third athlete explained, "It's just one big family down by the pool. We help each other out in many ways" (Hébert, 1995a, p. 315). A younger team member explained how significant this familial experience was to him as a newcomer:

I knew how the swim team were winners, so when I was a fresh-man meeting the older guys was cool. I looked up to these guys. They took me under their wing. They're my best friends now. We're a group that always hangs out together before and after school. There is real team unity. (Hébert, 1995a, p. 315)

The swimmers spent as much time as they could by the swimming pool. They requested passes to the pool from study hall monitors in order to avoid the disruptive atmosphere of the study halls, and they spent their time with Coach Brogan by helping him maintain the Olympic-size swimming pool. Others were often seen sitting by the side of the pool chatting with each other or with members of the women's swim team. Some swimmers spent their study hall time working out by the pool, and others were seen studying, reading quietly, or tutoring a fellow teammate nearby. The environment created by Coach Brogan and his swimmers served as a friendly place where student-athletes felt removed from the nonproductive behaviors of other students and the gang problems experienced by the large inner-city high school. By the swimming pool the gifted males felt socially accepted and apparently used the pool as a place to connect with good friends. As one young man expressed, "South Central is too big to have one 'in crowd' so you have to find a place here. I just found where I belong" (Hébert, 1995a, p. 319).

Within the swim team was an established emotional support system. Some swimmers described the coach as a father figure or a big brother; others apparently saw him as a friend, a man with whom they could talk about anything. One athlete described, "He is a father figure to a lot of us. If something goes wrong, he talks to us about a lot of things, like the gang stuff that's going on around here." He elaborated, "He doesn't want us making major mistakes. He takes the time to listen and he tries to understand" (Hébert, 1995a, p. 319). Regardless of what they labeled him, Coach Brogan was a caring adult who supported them emotionally and motivated them academically. He provided emotional support by counseling his athletes either individually or in-group sessions as a team. One swimmer explained as follows:

> If there is an individual problem, say like my problems with my stepfather, he'll talk with me personally. With things in general that are going on around school, he'll usually have a session where we all sit together and he goes over progress on the team and any issues that are affecting the team. (Hébert, 1995a, p. 320)

The students described how they felt comfortable talking to Coach Brogan privately about personal issues. One senior described how he had addressed his jealousy when other swimmers on the team surpassed him. He worried that he might express his feelings outwardly and cause team problems. He shared his concerns privately with Coach Brogan and received sound advice for dealing with his feelings.

Along with the familial relationships formed in this supportive subculture, all of the swimmers thought the team experience had played a major role in building their self-confidence and molding them as young adult males. One athlete described the impact of his 4-year swim team experience:

> If we took my four years at South Central High minus the swim team experience, I'd be a totally different person. Socially, I'd be hanging out with different people. Swimming has given me everything. It has provided me friends, a job working at the pool with physically challenged students, and women. Yes, even the girls I date are swimmers. (Hébert, 1995a, p. 316)

Coach Brogan reinforced academic achievement but also made a positive difference in the lives of gifted young men. Through their high-quality experience with this coach, they benefited socially and emotionally. Along with physical fitness, they learned the value of having a passion, the rewards of cooperative teamwork, the importance of working toward excellence, the joy of reaching a goal, and the importance of a caring mentor.

The supportive environment Coach Brogan created was a place where hard work in athletics and academics was valued and talent development evolved naturally. A star swimmer could excel in physics class, and a computer geek could feel comfortable participating in a team sport with others who appreciated his intellectual abilities. In that inner-city high school filled with teenagers disenchanted with the system, there existed this significant subculture for gifted males. A parent explained, with tears in her eyes, why families encouraged their sons to become involved with Coach Brogan's program as a means of surviving the inner-city school experience:

> He really cares about the kids. There's love there and it works both ways. There needs to be a place for these gifted kids. His swimmers know where they can find him. With Coach Brogan, they can always find him by the pool. The relationship is so important to these kids, especially in a big city high school like this one. Otherwise, they get lost. (Hébert, 1995a, p. 315)

In the context of the SCHS swim team, the young men came from microsystems in which their immediate families were challenged by difficult economic situations and the hardships of raising families in an urban environment. Given these difficulties, the role of the swim team as a mesosystem became even more important. The camaraderie and familial support within the team enabled these young men to enjoy their high school experience. This athletic brotherhood was more than just bright teenage males enjoying their involvement in a team sport. Coach Brogan had been successful in creating an environment where the psychosocial development of each adolescent male was nurtured appropriately. For these teenagers, this mesosystem was especially remarkable when one considers the exosystem in which the swim team was situated. The exosystem, a large urban school district plagued with financial problems, had been forced to cut back on gifted education programs, Advanced Placement courses, and school counselors. This problematic situation was embedded within the larger context—the macrosystem of a large urban community plagued by drugs, gangs, and violence. In this setting, it is easy to understand why Coach Brogan and the swim team were so significant to the social and emotional development of these students.

In this group of gifted young men there were important personality characteristics that interacted within the systems in place that also shaped their experiences. Strong intellectual abilities combined with sensitivity, multicultural awareness and appreciation, and strong resilience in overcoming the adversity within the urban environment were most notable.

Gifted University Males in a Greek Fraternity

In a second study examining the experience of gifted males, I discovered a culture of achievement in a Greek fraternity at a large university in the Southeast. At a time when the positive features of the Greek university experience were frequently overshadowed in the national media by incidents of hazing and excessive consumption of alcohol, my finding a group of gifted high-achieving males is noteworthy. The group I described as the Alpha Tau Iota fraternity (Hébert, 2006) provided gifted young men with significant talent development opportunities beyond the college classroom. In addition to benefiting from a fraternal culture that valued high achievement, the fraternity brothers enjoyed experiences through which they developed mature interpersonal relationships, learned leadership skills, became involved in community service, benefited from healthy psychosocial development, and enjoyed a sense of fraternal camaraderie.

The participants in this study provided evidence that the success of Alpha Tau Iota was due to an achievement orientation that was valued from the beginning. The gifted males realized they were recruited to the chapter because of their potential for contributing to the group, and their contributions helped to shape the culture of the fraternity. The brothers were achievement-oriented young men who were successful in various domains, maintained a healthy balance academically and socially, and continually focused on self-improvement.

The fraternity brothers were proud to be associated with such a high-powered group of intelligent young men, and they highlighted how they were the most well-rounded fraternity on their university campus. They saw well-roundedness as the healthy balance among academics, social life, and involvement on campus. A participant named Leighton reflected on his first year at the university, when he was considering which fraternity to join: "I heard that the ATI's are made fun of for being so serious about grades, but at the same rate, those are the guys that ended up being the doctors, the lawyers, and the successful businessmen" (Hébert, 2006, p. 36). He asked others on campus for their views of who the achievers were within the Greek community, and students responded with, "Those are the ATIs. That's what Alpha Tau Iota brothers do" (Hébert, 2006, p. 36). With that information gathered, he made his decision: "I wanted to join a well-rounded group of guys. ATI is just so well-rounded. We have a good time. We know how to kick back and relax and have a good time, but we still have our heads on our shoulders" (Hébert, 2006, p. 36).

Casey described the culture of Alpha Tau Iota by explaining, "It's not just study, study, study, and don't do anything else. It's make sure you have that taken care of but don't neglect the other aspects of your college experience. You're also here to have a good time" (Hébert, 2006, p. 36). Rob commented about balance: "We tie it all together—academics, community service, and a good social atmosphere." He smiled and said proudly, "There isn't another fraternity that compares." Leighton noted, "ATI has the whole package. You've got some brilliant guys from whom you can learn so much. You've got the strong spiritual influence that you can soak up. You've got some of the greatest guys as your closest friends" (Hébert, 2006, p. 36).

Within their descriptions of the "whole package"—the achievement orientation and the well-roundedness of their brothers—the gifted fraternity members consistently delivered a message that incorporated strong respect for intelligent males who were serious scholars. The respect for excellence in scholarship was evident in the chapter's receiving national ATI awards for the highest grade point average of any ATI chapter in the country. Being an excellent student was an important component of the culture of this ATI chapter.

The culture of ATI also addressed social and emotional development. Alpha Tau Iota respected young men who were dedicated to self-improvement in several aspects of their lives. ATI brothers designed discussion groups for reflecting on becoming better men. The fraternity members described sessions that were held on Monday evenings following dinner together, with as many as 25 brothers in attendance. Those who chose to participate in the weekly sessions came prepared to discuss a book the group had agreed to read. Jock enthusiastically described his experiences with the group's discussions of *Wild at Heart* by John Eldredge: "It examines how men's hearts are pretty wild, the way they act as boys and how society shapes us as men. Eldredge discusses how our fathers and the women in our lives have influenced ways we see ourselves as men." Jock labeled it "an awesome book" and seemed proud that his fraternity brothers were comfortable in serious discussion of contemporary masculinity: "We're all about becoming better men" (Hébert, 2006, p. 37).

It is helpful to analyze these findings through Bronfenbrenner's theoretical lens. The young men in the fraternity study came to the university from a microsystem that had been supportive of their development as young children. They came from middle-class families with parents who had worked hard to provide their sons with comfortable, supportive homes and positive school experiences. Their mesosystem on campus was the Greek fraternity that provided them great opportunities for developing into accomplished campus leaders and serious scholars before moving on to advanced degree programs and early career opportunities. The supportive environment with Alpha Tau Iota enabled them to develop the well-roundedness that was highly valued. The exosystem in this case was the larger university context, which had undergone years of controversial experiences with various fraternity chapters on campus. However, the university administrators were positive in their assessment of the ATI chapter and the culture of achievement evident in this group. The macrosystem influencing these young men is evidenced in societal perceptions of Greek fraternities and their value in shaping character development in adolescent males. It is interesting to note the personality characteristics within these students that enabled them to benefit from the ATI chapter. The intelligence of the young men, combined with their high motivation and their desire to constantly be working on self-improvement, was the right combination for them to create a fraternity culture of achievement that supported both intellectual and psychosocial development.

Gifted Students in a University Honors Program

As mentioned in Chapter 3, I conducted a study with Matthew McBee (Hébert & McBee, 2007) in which we examined the experiences of seven gifted university students in an undergraduate honors program. This program was situated in a technological university in the rural Southeast. Located in a conservative community of 30,000, the campus culture of Southeast Technological University reflected the values of the surrounding area. The student body of 8,500 included both undergraduate and graduate students, with the majority pursuing bachelor's degrees in engineering, business administration, and education.

The findings indicated the gifted students as adolescents experienced a sense of isolation, resulting from the differences among their abilities, interests, life goals, religious value systems, and the communities in which they lived. At the university, the seven gifted young people discovered in the honors program an intellectual and social network with other gifted individuals. Together they recognized their strong drive for self-actualization. In advanced-level courses, they found intellectual stimulation and academic challenge. Through several components of the honors program they developed significant psychosocial growth.

The participants in the study described a feeling of being at home in a real community once they connected to other gifted students in the honors program. For example, Kim highlighted how her friendships with others in the program quickly became the focal point of her university experience:

> I was learning new things. I was with a group of people who were similar to me. I felt like I was home. I had found a niche. All through high school I had been feeling out of place even though I had friends. In honors [at Tech] I was in a place where I was comfortable. I could be myself. I was happy. (Hébert & McBee, 2007, p. 144)

The sense of community within the program supported the gifted students intellectually, socially, and emotionally. Marcus highlighted how the discussion groups within the program allowed him to "open up and build tight friendships." Mike described a period during which he was struggling with the death of his grandmother and the ending of a romantic relationship. He found support among his colleagues:

> I remember being incredibly broken up about that and Kevin and Jacob just listening and being very compassionate about it. My freshman year, there was a group of five guys and we just talked about life, the universe, anything that we needed to discuss. That was a really powerful experience, to listen to these guys talk about values, life, important issues. I became very attached to that group. (Hébert & McBee, 2007, p. 144)

The participants in the honors program also benefited from an organized system of online journaling with peers in the discussion groups. Entries in journals reflected a high level of trust within the group, freedom to disagree with the honors program director, hard work in identity development, and discussions of vocational and philosophical issues. The journals were outlets for examining the process of learning about self. The following entry from Kim is representative:

> "Waking up" was knowing that I have problems with control. I have to know things. I don't have to do anything with the knowledge, but I want to know things. I hoard it miserly and I glory in it. I want more of this knowledge. I know this is one of my faults. I realize that I have bad points, and I am not a perfect person, nor am I a good person. I am merely a person. I can see my faults and try to fix them, or deal with them as best as I can, but if I can't fix them, then I live with them. Big revelation: I'm human, and I'm

not perfect. I'm also not always right, though I try to be and I want to be all the time. (Hébert & McBee, 2007, p. 146)

The interaction of the various environmental levels is important to note here. The nuclear families of the students were their microsystems before leaving home. The mesosystems that impacted their development included the peer group in their local communities, which did not always appreciate their intellectual giftedness. The more positive mesosystem was the honors program, a subculture within the larger university that supported their intellectual and psychosocial development. Fortunately, the exosystem, the larger university, supported the efforts of the honors program director, enabling her to deliver a program that addressed the needs of gifted undergraduates. In this situation, the students were supported at the macrosystem level with legislation and funding for honors programs. As in previous studies described here, the mesosystem shaped social and emotional development. In this study, the personal variables that interacted within the ecological systems were the giftedness of the students, their need for independence, and their ability to engage in deep personal reflection.

Jermaine: A Gifted Black Child Living in Rural Poverty

During ethnographic case study research, I collaborated with Teresa Beardsley, a public school teacher, to examine the life experiences of Jermaine, a gifted Black child living in an impoverished rural environment (Hébert & Beardsley, 2001). Teresa and I described Jermaine's creativity, his resilience, his struggle to find a place for himself in his community, and significant factors that influenced the early formation of his strong identity.

In this case, context played a significant role in shaping Jermaine's experiences. The study was conducted in Milledge County, AL, in a community Teresa and I called Pine Grove. Historically significant events had taken place fewer than 30 miles away in Selma, AL. On March 7, 1965, more than 600 civil rights marchers were stopped at the Edmund Pettus Bridge in Selma, where state and local lawmen attacked them with billy clubs and tear gas and drove them back. Two days later, Martin Luther King, Jr. led another symbolic march to the bridge. Later that month, more than 3,000 marchers walked from Selma to the state capital in Montgomery. Shortly after, President Johnson signed the Voting Rights Act of 1965. The memories of those events remained for residents of Pine Grove. Several community members had been with Dr. King and expressed their hope that children in Alabama appreciated "the gas they had to breathe" during those horrendous times in America's history.

Noted as the poorest county in Alabama, the per capita income reported at that time was $10,759, with 45.2% of the county's population falling below the poverty level (Alabama Department of Archives and History, 1998). The majority of people in Milledge County survived on public assistance. A manufacturer of corrugated cardboard was the only industry in the county, employing only several Pine Grove community members. Residents of this rural community commuted more than 30 miles beyond the county lines to work in catfish-processing plants. Others were employed in the fast food restaurants in Selma.

Teresa and I reported that Jermaine struggled to find a place in Pine Grove as a child. Initially, he was not understood or appreciated. His immediate family members were important to him, as were extended family members living outside of Alabama. Jermaine found extrafamilial support from Teresa and other community members. He also found support for his creativity and vivid imagination, and, with emotional support from significant mentors, his identity emerged in positive ways.

As a young child growing up in Pine Grove, Jermaine initially faced real difficulties. According to Teresa and other residents, the rural community of Pine Grove determined a ranking for its members. As in many small towns, families in Pine Grove had roles according to their perceived place in the community. Jermaine's family fell into the lowest rank; they were considered outcasts and largely ignored. They were often spoken of in derogatory terms and used as examples of how not to be. The reason given by most residents interviewed was the "crazy factor." The whole family was marked as being inclined to odd or "crazy" behavior. The main generalizations that anyone could provide for this attitude was the presence of multiple family members with mental or physical handicaps. Another reason mentioned was the cemetery near the family property because "no one in their right mind" would live near a cemetery. Jermaine's family did not maintain church affiliation, and community members expressed disgust with this as well. The general view was that Jermaine and his family were outside the normal population of the community.

A portfolio of creative writing maintained by Teresa provided many fine examples of Jermaine's creativity. His love of language and creative expression was evident throughout his work. As a first grader, he chose to write an autobiography, with the following paragraph as the introduction:

I was tumbling through my mother's stomach—BOOM . . . BOOM . . . BOOM. I came out crying. Everybody comes out crying. Someone was holding me, and I wanted my momma. I was named Jermaine after my granddaddy. He didn't have a nickname or a middle name, so I don't either. He was my momma's daddy. (Hébert & Beardsley, 2001, p. 93)

Also included in the portfolio was a book entitled *Jermaine's World*. The book provided readers with a glimpse of Jermaine's view of himself. In this story, he was a hero who used his calculating mind to solve problems. A first-grade story entitled *How the Sun Got Hot* had colorful, vivid illustrations that were expressive, detailed, and depicted the emotions of the characters.

Jermaine's creativity was inspired by satellite television programs, his voracious reading, his extended family members' tradition of family storytelling, and the rural countryside surrounding him. He explained that the quiet of the countryside inspired his ideas, and daydreaming fostered his creative thinking process. Along with being inspired by the chirping of crickets and daydreaming about what a day in the life of a cricket would be like, he pointed out that his daydreams took place at night as he pondered a sunset or watched the glow of fireflies. He also indicated that daydreaming was an important part of every school day and may have served as a strategy for surviving the boredom he often experienced in school:

Most of my day I spend daydreaming. In class, I daydream all the time. I think about my future plans for all the movie scripts I'm going to write when I become a movie producer. I just can't get over daydreaming. I read a book that explained it was normal for a kid my age to daydream a lot. At night, when I'm not daydreaming, I like to go out and stare at the dark and think. I call it my "thinking in the dark time." It's my nighttime inspiration. I like to think about some of the movies I've watched and think of ideas for movies I want to write someday. (Hébert & Beardsley, 2001, p. 94)

Jermaine had support from members of his extended family and from people beyond his family. A school lunchroom worker took a special interest in the young writer and encouraged him daily, often sneaking extra food on his lunch tray. Sister Sophia, a teacher's aide whose son was in Jermaine's class, saw Jermaine as "a lost child." She invited Jermaine to spend weekends with her children, and Jermaine celebrated Thanksgiving day with the family so that "he could get a good meal like everybody ought to have" (Hébert & Beardsley, 2001, p. 95).

Jermaine also found support within Teresa's family. He visited her home and joined her son for afternoons of games on the family computer and bowls of ice cream. He also enjoyed sharing his creative writing with her daughter. Teresa served as an advocate for Jermaine throughout his elementary school years, working during his primary grade years to get other teachers to understand his behavior and appreciate his special abilities.

Another significant source of extrafamilial support evolved when Mr. Cooper, a gentleman from Michigan, returned to Pine Grove to retire. Upon arrival, he decided he needed something to occupy his time, and he therefore formed athletic teams for the children. He also organized a Boy Scout troop. Jermaine became involved with a number of sports and scouting. Mr. Cooper played an important role for Jermaine in recognizing Jermaine's intelligence and selecting him to be the quarterback for the new football team. As a result, Jermaine explained, "Because I'm the quarterback, I'm getting new respect. A lot of kids who didn't used to like me now wave to me in school and say, 'What's up?'" (Hébert & Beardsley, 2001, p. 95).

Jermaine eventually found a small group of students who appreciated his creativity and could compete with him academically. With the exception of a B in math, he had achieved straight A's in fifth grade. The appreciation for his creativity and the community respect for his new role as quarterback helped redefine his identity. As a 10-year-old, he was constructing a new sense of self, with a new confidence that was apparent in a number of ways.

Jermaine explained that problems typically associated with urban communities had begun to creep into Pine Grove. According to him, gangs were beginning to form in the county's middle and high schools, and he appeared worried. He commented, "There's a lot goin' on in the country nowadays. There are gangbangers and kids doin' smoke. There are kids in the middle school with blades. Even here in Pine Grove, young brothers need to get off the streets and get jobs" (Hébert & Beardsley, 2001, p. 96). Jermaine assured the adults in his life that he wanted nothing to do with gang culture. He saw himself as perfectly comfortable being a fifth grader. He saw no need to rush the process of becoming more worldly and sophisticated. He described an experience at a birthday party in which several youngsters were talking about having boyfriends and girlfriends and became involved in kissing games that Jermaine felt were too serious. He explained that he wanted to simply "talk to girls like friends."

Jermaine appeared happy being 10. He saw himself as a good person with special talents and was feeling positive about his abilities that had become valued by his peers. His emerging identity and the positive view of himself was also evident in a story he wrote as part of a writing contest sponsored by the county teachers' association. The guidelines for students were to write a creative essay about themselves tackling problems of crime and misguided youth in Milledge County. In his essay, he addressed a community problem by transforming himself into a superhero named Turbo Man. He described himself as living two lives: that of Courtney Davis, a well-respected lawyer, and as Turbo Man, a hero who helps people in trouble. In this manuscript, Turbo Man's adventure concluded with Jermaine's character capturing a kidnapper and returning his community to safety.

Teresa reflected on a favorite memory of Jermaine during an afterschool meeting in her classroom. She described how he opened one conversation with her: "You know what the real meaning of life is? It is to care about each other" (Hébert & Beardsley, 2001, p. 96). Teresa explained that, after this profound statement, he decided to read by himself. His only follow-up comment was that he "did not hear it on TV" (Hébert & Beardsley, 2001, p. 96).

Besides having empathy, Jermaine had a strong sense of ethics. He described an incident at school in which a jar of pennies being collected by students for a fund-raising project was stolen. He found this upsetting and could not understand how children could steal from one another. He shook his head and expressed his concern for his community. This young man, troubled by the school crime, dreamed of becoming a lawyer one day, but explained that his legal career would serve as his second profession. He intended to first spend several years working as a Hollywood film producer.

When applying the Bronfenbrenner theory to Jermaine's experiences, it is evident that contextual influences shaped how he felt about himself as an intelligent, highly creative child. Although most members of the Pine Grove community saw his family as dysfunctional, he had a loving connection to his mother and older sister. His mesosystem became a small circle of friends who approached his level of intellectual ability and were involved in school projects with him. In Jermaine's case, the exosystem, his impoverished rural community, certainly influenced his well-being. Fortunately, he received support from extended family living beyond Pine Grove. The macrosystem, the cultural laws that drive the discrimination and inequities in this country that allowed an entire community to suffer from poverty for generations, shaped the quality of his school system, his community, and his lack of exposure to a world beyond Pine Grove.

Implications of Bronfenbrenner's Ecological Systems Theory

In reviewing Bronfenbrenner's theoretical framework for explaining psychological development, we can examine the situations described in this chapter and ponder how life might have been quite different for the gifted young people we have met. We may wonder how the adolescent experiences of Bette Midler would have been different had she grown up in a community with a Jewish population. If she had been a teenager in New York City, would her experiences of adolescent emotional development have been different? We might also hypothesize how the experiences of the gifted young men swimming for Coach Brogan would have been different in an affluent suburban high school setting. Would a swim coach in a more affluent setting have had the same level of influence that Coach Brogan had? We may wonder if collegiate males in the Greek fraternity would have had similar benefits in another extracurricular university group. Would they have found the same experience in the university marching band? In addition, we might consider whether the students in the undergraduate honors program would have had a much different experience in another college setting. Finally, how would Jermaine's childhood have been different had he been living in urban poverty? Would mentors be equally influential?

We cannot answer those questions definitively. We can only wonder about the possibilities. This theory offered by Urie Bronfenbrenner helps us realize that in the psychological development of a gifted child, there is not much within our control. Influenced by the work of Urie Bronfenbrenner, Cross (2004) called attention to the complexity of contextual influences on development by highlighting chance factors. He categorized these factors into psychobiological influences, cultural influences, sociohistorical influences, and family variables in context. Examples were the genetic makeup of the child's parents, the time period in history during which a child is born, the location of a child's birth and upbringing, and the socioeconomic status of the child's parents. According to Cross (2004), the responsibility of educators is simply to identify the influences that are to the advantage of the gifted student and provide educational services accordingly.

Educators could not change the fact that Bette Midler grew up in a community with limited exposure to the arts. However, supportive adults could play a role in helping the young woman find others with the same passion for singing and theatre. Educators cannot be responsible for the impoverished economic conditions that Jermaine experienced as a child. However, finding other children with an interest in creative writing and connecting him with them and mentors like Coach Cooper both fall within the realm of caring educators. The difficult environmental conditions facing urban teenagers outside of the walls of South Central High School cannot be controlled by educators; however, teachers and counselors help gifted students make connections with others within that high school setting. Appropriate athletic teams and activities and caring coaches can be found. Educators and parents preparing their gifted sons and daughters for college certainly cannot control a university's environment; however, helping gifted teenagers make informed decisions about extracurricular involvement on campus may make a difference. The young men who joined the Alpha Tau Iota fraternity helped to create a culture of achievement and provided each other with the emotional support they needed. The same was true for the students at Southeast Tech, who found compatible peers within the context of the honors program. In the studies described in this chapter, gifted students found social and emotional support from others similar to themselves in their immediate environments.

These studies highlight the importance of the mesosystem's influence. They underscore that we cannot change the microsystem into which these gifted individuals are born. We also have little control over the exosystem, the cultural blueprint that guides the society in which they live. We may not be able to change the exosystem, but we may be able to alter the mesosystem for them. We can indeed find a mentor for a child. We can help a student make a connection with an appropriate extracurricular activity that will support her passion. We can make sure a college student enrolls in a challenging educational program and connects with other intellectually oriented young people. All of these interventions can shape Bronfenbrenner's mesosystem in that young person's life and such changes can affect the psychological development of gifted students considerably.

For Further Thought and Discussion

- Imagine you are a graduate research assistant of Dr. Urie Bronfenbrenner. You have been asked to examine cases of gifted young people in your community and analyze their psychosocial development through the lens of his ecological systems theory. Select a gifted individual you know and highlight how this theory helps us to understand and appreciate his or her life story.

❧ You have the opportunity to interview Bette Midler while on a concert tour. Consider the role of the chronosystem in Bronfenbrenner's theory and discuss how that might influence the questions you pose to Midler. What questions will you ask? Why?

❧ How are the studies conducted by Hébert and his colleagues highlighted in this chapter similar and different in relation to Bronfenbrenner's theory? How have these studies shed light on your understanding of the theory's application to social and emotional development in gifted young people?

❧ How does Bronfenbrenner's ecological systems theory complement other theories of human development? Why is this theory especially significant in understanding the psychosocial development of highly intelligent individuals?

❧ Design a plan for training teachers of gifted students and school counselors about Bronfenbrenner's ecological systems theory. What practical applications of this theory would you want to suggest?

CHAPTER 5

Identity Development in Gifted Students

> My goals for this chapter are to:
> ❧ Introduce you to several theories of identity development.
> ❧ Examine how these theories help us to understand identity development in gifted students.
> ❧ Provide you with strategies to support identity development in gifted young people.

Like many teachers, I have saved a photograph collection of former students along with each school yearbook from the numerous schools in which I taught. Occasionally I take out those photographs, reflect on my experiences as a teacher, and wonder about what became of many of the wonderful young people who were such an important part of my life. As I browse through the yearbooks and savor the memories that these snapshots evoke, I reflect on a number of students who stand out in my mind and reminisce about my experiences working with them, and I am reminded of the reasons why I became involved in gifted education.

One of my earliest memories of my first year of teaching was working with Meg Anderson, a young woman in my history class at Coffee High School in Douglas, GA. I introduced her to my readers in the early pages of this book. Having moved from Maine to teach in this small rural community in southeast Georgia, I was enjoying my immersion in a culture that was so different from my New England background and learning so much from gifted students like Meg. Meg was an incredibly conscientious student who absorbed everything I had to offer her in U.S. history. As a beginning teacher, my challenge was to develop a curriculum that addressed this young woman's intellectual needs. Meg graduated from Coffee High School, left her small community of 13,000, and moved on to study at Harvard University. Years later she earned a degree from the London School of Economics and a law degree from Stanford Law School.

I have kept in touch with Meg over the years and have celebrated her success. I am proud of Meg's many accomplishments; however, I have often wondered just what it was about Meg that enabled a teenage girl from the Deep South to feel confident and secure enough in herself to leave her family and small community to pursue an Ivy League education in a region of the country so different from her own.

As Meg left for Harvard, I also left Coffee High School to begin graduate school. After completing my master's degree in gifted education, I became an enrichment teacher in an elementary gifted education program at East School in Torrington, CT. There, I worked with a student named Robert Branford. Even as a young boy, Robert appeared to know just who he was. A popular young man who was well respected by his friends and teachers, Robert excelled academically, was a dedicated older brother, enjoyed great success in athletics, and earned a fine reputation as a computer expert. Robert's elementary school years were filled with good times with two other gifted boys who were friends from first through eighth grade.

When Robert arrived in high school, his buddies found a different group of friends, pursued drinking and partying, underachieved academically, and developed interests that concerned their parents. In contrast, Robert maintained a solid achievement orientation throughout high school, kept busy with sports and extracurricular activities, and became involved in local government, working as a volunteer for several political candidates in his community. In his senior year, Robert was elected class president.

He graduated as the valedictorian of his class, and received an appointment to West Point Academy.

Following my years working with elementary gifted students, I entered a doctoral program in which I had the opportunity to pursue dissertation research in the most culturally diverse urban high school in Connecticut. While collecting data, I spent months reviewing academic records, conducting observations of students, and interviewing some of the brightest and most interesting teenagers I have ever met. I developed important relationships with the participants in my study of gifted urban youth. One such student, Wallace Jamison, was an African American scholar-athlete who I grew to respect. In a conversation with Wallace, he described how some of his peers disparaged his academic regimentation. His friends complained that he was "hitting the books too much" and were often after him to go out with them at night. Wallace maintained his status as a student-athlete and eventually his friends stopped nagging him. He explained, "I'm not an egghead jock who's only worried about playing ball, and I'm not a nerd. Wallace the student and Wallace the athlete balance each other out."

I remained in touch with Wallace following my dissertation research. Upon graduation, Wallace was awarded a 4-year academic scholarship to Bates College in Lewiston, ME, where he pursued a degree in political science. As a freshman, he was recruited to play football for the Bates College team. The following year Wallace became concerned about challenge of maintaining a heavy academic course load while playing a varsity sport. Determined to leave Bates with his undergraduate degree, he chose not to play football and instead to concentrate all of his energy on academics. The decision for Wallace was not difficult; he knew that he had to focus on academics to maintain his scholarship. He realized that his family could not afford to provide him the high-quality college education he was receiving, and according to Wallace, his eventual completion of law school would enable him to provide economic security for his parents.

I have always wondered what it was about Meg, Robert, and Wallace that enabled them to remain so solid in their identities at such an early age. As a teenager growing up in the rural South, Meg knew she wanted an Ivy League education and was determined to achieve it. As a young boy, Robert chose not to follow the crowd and remained focused on his goals while his friends wandered down another path. As a college student, Wallace saw himself as a scholar rather than an athlete. In each case, the identity formation of these gifted young people was strong; they had determined who they were and where they wanted to go in life.

As a result of working with many intelligent young people like Meg,

Robert, and Wallace, I have become intrigued with the complex phenomenon of identity development in gifted students. I have come to believe that is one of the most critical elements in our understanding of the social and emotional development of gifted individuals. With this understanding, my goal in this chapter is to review the work of the leading theorists in identity development and examine research on identity development in gifted adolescents. Following this discussion, I will highlight implications of the theoretical and research literature for practice and present strategies to assist teachers and counselors in supporting the identity development process of gifted children and adolescents.

Theories of Identity Development

Erikson's Stages of Psychosocial Development

Erik Erikson's (1968) theory of psychosocial development identified eight developmental stages during which human beings confront major crises in the course of a lifetime. Erikson maintained that these crises were not problematic catastrophes, but rather significant turning points in life that made individuals more vulnerable than usual, and therefore presented them with opportunities for enhancing their potential (Santrock, 2003). Shaffer (2000) delineated Erikson's stages succinctly as follows:

- *Trust Versus Mistrust*—The infant establishes feelings of physical comfort and experiences minimal fear or apprehension about the future.
- *Autonomy Versus Shame*—Toddlers learn to be autonomous, discovering that their behavior is their own as they begin to claim a sense of independence.
- *Initiative Versus Guilt*—Preschool children try to act grown up and attempt to take on responsibilities that are beyond their capabilities. They undertake activities that conflict with the expectations of their parents and these conflicts may cause them to feel guilty.
- *Industry Versus Inferiority*—Children from age 6 to puberty master important social and intellectual skills. They are enthusiastic about learning; however, they judge their competence by comparing themselves with their peers and may therefore develop a sense of inferiority.
- *Identity Versus Identity Confusion*—Adolescents are forced to grap-

ple with questions such as: Who am I?, What am I all about?, and Where am I going in life? During this period they must craft their identity or they will remain confused about the roles they will play as adults.

- *Intimacy Versus Isolation*—Individuals develop strong friendships to achieve a sense of love or companionship, a shared identity with another person.
- *Generativity Versus Stagnation*—In mid-adulthood, individuals meet the challenge of becoming professionally productive and responsible for the needs of others.
- *Integrity Versus Despair*—In older adulthood, adults look back and evaluate their lives. A retrospective view of a life well lived results in integrity. If earlier life stages have not been resolved positively, despair occurs.

Erikson's Theory of Identity Development

Much of our current understanding of adolescence evolved from Erikson's theory of psychosocial development. With the end of World War II, Erikson examined the struggles faced by many veterans as they made the transition back to civilian life. Through his clinical work he came to believe that the psychological difficulties some veterans confronted in transitioning from the role of soldier to that of civilian were similar to those faced by some adolescents as they left childhood and moved through adolescence to adulthood (Erikson, 1968).

From Erikson's clinical work and research evolved a psychology of adolescent identity formation. He drew from his psychoanalytical thinking on ego development to offer a definition of identity. Erikson proposed that the ego structured a coherent personality to maintain the sameness and continuity of an individual's existence and that this personality was consistently recognized by others. Erikson (1968) explained:

> Ego identity then, in its subjective aspect, is the awareness of the fact that there is a self-sameness and continuity to the ego's synthesizing methods, the *style of one's individuality*, and that this style coincides with the sameness and continuity of one's *meaning for significant others* in the immediate community. (p. 50)

According to Erikson, individuals who had established an identity had a firm and coherent sense of who they were, understood where they were headed in life, and were comfortable with where they fit into society. The process for arriving at this established identity began in adolescence, and Erikson noted that multiple factors influenced its formation. Acknowledging that cultural variations existed in different societies' views of adolescence, Erikson (1968) nevertheless maintained that all societies offered a "psychosocial moratorium" during which a young person was expected to make "commitments for life" and to establish a firm self-definition. This moratorium was accompanied by a sense of crisis. Erikson defined *crisis* as a normative life event that designated "a necessary turning point, a crucial moment, when development must move one way or another, marshaling resources of growth, recovery, and further differentiation" (p. 16).

The identity crisis of adolescence forced a young person to struggle with some important choices. Adolescents had to consider questions such as: Who am I as a man or a woman? What religious or moral values do I hold? Which career is the best match for my talents? Where do I fit into society? Realizing that these questions were daunting for adolescents, Erikson used the term *identity crisis* to represent the confusion and anxiety they experienced as they struggled to find answers (Shaffer, 2000). According to Erikson (1968), identity formation was the most essential challenge of adolescence because it was necessary to resolve these questions to prepare for adulthood. During this period, teenagers had to make sense of their life experiences, their unique personality characteristics, and the beliefs they had maintained throughout adolescence, and combine them to form a cohesive self.

Meg, Robert, and Wallace are examples of adolescents who successfully met this challenge. Their life experiences, their unique personality characteristics, and the beliefs they held combined to shape their identities. Meg had decided she was ready to meet the challenges of a Harvard University experience. Robert was secure in his decisions regarding where he was going in life and was not deterred by his peers who chose to pursue another path. Wallace had determined that he wanted to be academically as well as athletically successful and eventually made difficult decisions in order to pursue his goal of becoming a lawyer.

Meg, Robert, and Wallace made some rather difficult decisions as adolescents. These decisions led to the formation of a cohesive self and required them to engage in hard psychological work and self-reflection. Santrock (2003) noted that identity formation involves a long, messy process. He observed that "at bare minimum, it involves a commitment to a vocational direction, an ideological stance, and a sexual orientation" (Santrock, 2003,

p. 302). He captured the essence of this complex adolescent process poignantly as he explained:

> Identity development gets done in bits and pieces. Decisions are not made once and for all, but have to be made again and again. And the decisions might seem trivial at the time: whom to date, whether or not to break up, whether or not to have intercourse, whether or not to take drugs, whether or not to go to college or finish high school and get a job, which major, whether to study or to play, whether or not to be politically active, and so on. Over the years of adolescence, the decisions begin to form a core of what the individual is all about as a human being—what is called her or his identity. (Santrock, 2003, p. 302)

Meg, Robert, and Wallace made the difficult decisions required in adolescence and appeared comfortable with them. Their experiences may lead educators to consider whether the process of identity development among gifted students is more intense or accelerated than it is for other students. It is evident that intelligent adolescents have the potential to take charge of shaping their identities. Yet others, like Robert's friends, do not successfully confront the challenge in high school. Other highly successful high school students sometimes "lose themselves" in later adolescence and veer off course in college. With this understanding, gifted students may benefit from examining the concept of identity development and reflecting on how it plays out in their lives. Moreover, by sharing multiple theories of identity development with gifted students, teachers may help facilitate their successful resolution of this developmental stage.

Marcia's Theory of Identity Formation

Inspired by the work of Erik Erikson, James Marcia (1980), a clinical psychologist and psychotherapist, theorized that individuals establish identities through four distinct approaches that could be categorized into one of four identity statuses: foreclosure, moratorium, achievement, and diffusion. An individual's status could be determined on whether he had explored various alternatives and made firm commitments to a vocational or occupational choice, religious and political ideologies, and interpersonal values such as sex role attitudes and sexuality.

Marcia (1993) used identity status interviews to determine individuals' degree of exploration and commitment with respect to identity development. Through these interviews, he assessed the extent to which individuals had genuinely examined and experimented with alternative life directions and beliefs. According to Marcia's (1993, 1994) theory, *foreclosure* was an identity status characterized by commitment in the absence of exploration. Individuals classified as foreclosed had committed to an identity without considering or exploring other possibilities. They preferred to be told what to do by an authority figure rather than choosing their own direction in life. They were often conformists who set high goals for themselves, adopted the values taught by their families, and lacked emotional depth in their relationships. Such individuals often developed friendships with others who were much like themselves.

Individuals categorized in the *moratorium* status were involved in an identity crisis, posing serious questions about life commitments and searching for answers. They often wavered between rebellion and conformity and their family relationships fluctuated with this vacillation. Relationships with others were often intense and brief. They valued intimacy; however, because they were often in motion, they had difficulty maintaining committed relationships (Marcia, 1993, 1994).

Identity *achievement* was the status used to describe individuals who had undergone an exploratory process and had subsequently determined occupational and ideological commitments. They were solid in their beliefs, having made life decisions based on self-constructed values. Identity achievers were at peace with their families, had resolved their identity issues, had solid self-esteem, dealt well with stress, and were high in moral development (Marcia, 1993, 1994).

The status of *identity diffusion* included those people who had done some searching but remained uncommitted. They had not mapped out a direction in life. Some were apathetic and socially isolated while others sought contact almost compulsively. They were shallow in their interpersonal relationships. They struggled with stress and self-esteem, and exhibited the lowest levels of moral development among the four statuses (Marcia, 1993, 1994).

Marcia's theory offers gifted students an opportunity to reflect on where they are in the process of identity formation. Gifted teenagers enjoy determining whether they are foreclosed, in moratorium, achieved, or diffused. Rich discussions with students center on whether young people today break away from their family value systems and determine their own direction in life. Some gifted students may see themselves in the moratorium stage in which they struggle between rebellion and conformity as they search for answers as to who they are. Some may claim to be identity achieved, brush off the discussion, and proudly announce that they are diffused in their search and proud to be there. Regardless of where students see themselves on Marcia's continuum, intelligent adolescents will benefit from exposure to this identity development model.

Identity Formation in Females

In light of Meg's story in the introduction to this chapter, we are reminded that identity development theories may apply differently to different populations. For example, Erik Erikson's theory, based upon his research with primarily White, middle-class males, has been criticized by a number of researchers for not being representative of women's experiences (Gilligan, 1982; Josselson, 1987). In the case of a gifted young woman like Meg who was determined to earn her Ivy League degree and remain focused on her career path, other theories of identity development better help us understand her experience. For this reason, educators need to consider specific theories that illuminate identity formation in females in order to support gifted young women in their classrooms.

One of the first theorists to address identity development in women was Carol Gilligan. In her groundbreaking work, *In a Different Voice*, Gilligan (1982) maintained that women defined their identities differently from men. She began her work by asking the question: "How is it that men in speaking of themselves and their lives, or speaking more generally about human nature, often speak as if they were not living in connection with women, as if they did not have a voice or did not experience desire?" (Gilligan, 1982, p. xiii). A central assumption guiding Gilligan's work was that the way people talked about their lives, and the language they used to describe their experiences, revealed a great deal about their development. Through extensive interviews that focused on experiences involving conflict and choice, Gilligan examined individuals' conceptions of self and morality.

Gilligan (1982) noted that the men she interviewed often spoke of their lives using a "language of achievement," devoid of emotion and characterized by their measures of success and failure. Gilligan (1982) observed, "individual achievement rivets the male imagination, and great ideas or distinctive activity defines the standard of self-assessment and success" (p. 163). She explained further that, "Power and separation secure the man an identity achieved through work, but they leave him at a distance from others, who seem in some sense out of his sight" (Gilligan, 1982, p. 163).

Gilligan's interviews with women, in contrast, led her to conclude that women saw their social reality differently than men and that these differences centered on experiences of attachment and separation, important transitions that shaped their lives. When asked to describe themselves, all of the women she interviewed described a "relationship depicting their identity *in* the connection of future mother, present wife, adopted child, or past lover" (Gilligan, 1982, p. 159). Gilligan (1982) noted that in describing themselves even highly successful and high-achieving women did not discuss their academic or professional accomplishments. Instead, they viewed their professional work as jeopardizing their sense of self, and the conflict they experienced in choosing between achievement and relationships often left them feeling distressed.

In all of the women's descriptions of self, identity was defined in a context of relationship and judged by standards of responsibility and care. Gilligan (1982) observed that "women's sense of integrity appears to be entwined with an ethic of care, so that to see themselves as women is to see themselves in a relationship of connection" (p. 170). She concluded:

> We have come more recently to notice not only the silence of women but the difficulty of hearing what they say when they speak. Yet in the different voice of women lies the truth of an ethic of care, the tie between relationship and responsibility, and the origins of aggression in the failure of connection. The failure to see the different reality of women's lives and to hear the differences in their voices stems in part from the assumption that there is a single mode of social experience and interpretation. By positing instead two different modes, we arrive at a more complex rendition of human experience which sees the truth of separation and attachment in the lives of women and men and recognizes how these truths are carried by different modes of language and thought. (Gilligan, 1982, p. 174)

In the two decades since Gilligan wrote *In a Different Voice*, her scholarship has inspired multiple feminist researchers and has galvanized policy makers. Her work has become popularly acclaimed. However, when a scholar is inducted into the popular culture, other scholars feel compelled to criticize. Gilligan's work has been closely scrutinized and challenged by a number of researchers (see Greeno & Macoby, 1986; Luria, 1986; Tavris, 1992). Her critics have accused her of incorporating unorthodox interview methods, depending on small research samples, lacking control groups, and failing to publish her data in peer-reviewed journals (Eakin, 2002). Gilligan (1993) responded to these challenges in her preface of the second edition of *In a Different Voice*. Regardless of the controversy, her work is considered groundbreaking and continues to shape psychological theory on women's development.

After reading Carol Gilligan's work on identity formation in women, I wished I had access to it when Meg Anderson was my student. Although Meg was recognized as the most intelligent young woman in her school, most teenagers in her rural community valued other characteristics or traits in young women. When Meg was one of 10 young women from her senior class nominated for homecoming queen, she struggled with two issues. Not only had she been nominated for this honor by the high school faculty, something that was considered "nerdy" by the cultural dictates of high school teenagers, but she also faced the challenge of finding an escort for the evening. As a member of the homecoming court, Meg would be presented to the high school community at halftime of the homecoming football game walking down the 50-yard line on the arm of a young man. Not having a steady boyfriend, Meg spent a great deal of time worrying about this issue. For an intellectually gifted young woman like Meg, the world of homecoming queens and steady boyfriends seemed foreign; however, the cultural expectations of her community placed her in a difficult situation. Meg recruited an escort, survived the homecoming festivities, and enjoyed the remainder of her senior year. It may be safe to assume that she let out a sigh of relief as her family drove away from Douglas, GA, on their way to deliver Meg to her new adventure at Harvard University.

As teenage girls grapple with issues regarding friendships, dating, and romantic relationships, there is no better time for them to be exposed to Carol Gilligan's thinking on female identity formation. The secondary school experience is a period in which peer relationships play a significant role in shaping the identity of students. Thus, it is important to provide gifted young women with the means to reflect on the role that relationships play in their lives and the influence they may have on their life goals and career aspirations. Early exposure to Gilligan's theory in a middle or high school classroom may influence girls' lives in important ways. Moreover, it is important that males in secondary classrooms receive the same exposure to Gilligan's work as they consider relationships with the females in their lives and define their expectations for life partnerships in the future.

Ruthellen Josselson's (1987) theory of identity formation in women also focused on the importance women place on relationships. Through a longitudinal investigation of college women, Josselson attempted to describe the journey of identity formation in females. She saw this journey as a process that evolved gradually and incrementally through the entire life cycle. Josselson maintained that identity became a means through which women organized and understood their experiences and shared their understanding of life with others. According to Josselson (1996), a woman formed her sense of self and defined her values and beliefs through connections with people in her life, both within her family, and in her professional setting. She explained, "Identity in women is more rooted in 'being' than in 'doing,' and a woman's life story is often centered on how she experiences herself, or wishes to experience herself, with others" (Josselson, 1996, p. 32).

In her work with college women, Josselson (1987, 1996) used Marcia's interview methods to determine what paths the women took in forming their identities. She posed questions about four areas—occupation, religion, politics, and sexual standards—that she identified as central to the understanding of identity. Josselson examined whether the women had undergone a period of exploration in determining their values and goals and whether they had made distinct choices. After interviewing late adolescent females about their decision making with regard to these four areas, she categorized her participants into four distinct groups that situated them in one stage or another on the path to identity formation: Guardians, Pathmakers, Searchers, and Drifters.

According to Josselson (1996), Guardians determined their identity commitments without making a conscious choice, by following life plans mapped out in childhood or designed by parents. Guardians were likely to feel that "This is how I am because it's how I was raised or how I've always been" (Josselson, 1996, p. 35). These women knew where they were going in life without ever having considered alternatives. They had absorbed the values of their families and held onto them. "Reluctant to 'leave home' emotionally, they wanted their adult lives, as much as possible, to be a continuation of the warmth and comfort of childhood in their families" (Josselson, 1996, p. 37).

Pathmakers were women who had undergone a period of exploration or crisis and subsequently determined identity commitments on their own terms. Their view was, "I've tried out some things, and this is what makes sense for me" (Josselson, 1996, p. 35). These independent women had undergone identity crises and were now self-confident. They had considered options, tried out alternative ways of experiencing themselves, "charted their own course" (Josselson, 1996, p. 37), and designed lives that enabled them to balance work, personal interests, and significant relationships.

Searchers were women who were still involved in a period of struggle or exploration, trying to make commitments, but not yet succeeding. They expressed their situation in these terms: "I'm not sure about who I am or want to be, but I'm trying to figure it out" (Josselson, 1996, p. 35). Josselson found that these women were still in the midst of crisis and remained unsure about which path to follow in life. They were still exploring and experimenting; they often felt guilty about breaking away from the values of their childhoods, and were fearful that they would not make the appropriate life commitments.

Drifters were without commitments and did not attempt to make them. These women either felt lost or simply followed the impulses of the day. As one woman noted, "I don't know what I will do or believe, but it doesn't matter too much right now" (Josselson, 1996, p. 35). These women were neither in crisis nor had they made commitments. Josselson (1996) observed: "They were like leaves blown by the wind, living each day, sometimes happily, sometimes despairingly, but they tried to ignore the approach of the future" (p. 38).

Josselson (1996) described the four groups as representing various "gateways to adulthood," noting that where a young woman was on the path to identity formation indicated how she would approach her adult years, and eventually how she would craft her life story. She explained, "The pathway she was following at the end of college served as a portal to the future, a way of entering adulthood, with conviction and direction, with openness and flexibility, or with confusion and tentativeness" (Josselson, 1996, p. 39).

Reflecting on Meg's determination to pursue an Ivy League education, we might speculate as to why she was so secure in her plans to pursue this path. Although she was quite young to have undergone a lengthy period of exploration and experimentation with identity, she was ready to chart her own course. What was it about her that enabled her to do so? She appeared to be an example of an early Pathmaker. Gifted students like Meg may benefit from reflecting upon whether they will be Guardians, Pathmakers, Searchers, or Drifters in life. Classroom discussions and writing activities based on Josselson's theory would allow gifted students the opportunity to think seriously about how they will approach their "portals to the future."

Mindful of Meg's experience as a gifted female in a rural environment, educators need to consider theories that address multilayered conceptions of identity. Since the pioneering work of Gilligan and Josselson in women's identity development, other researchers and theorists have proposed models. Jones (1997) and Jones and McEwen (2000) indicated that previous identity development models for women failed to address how an individual may simultaneously hold multiple identities. In their grounded theory research with female college students, they uncovered "intersecting social identities" (Jones & McEwen, 2000, p. 405) that included racial, ethnic, sexual, gender, social class, religious, geographic or regional, and professional identities.

Jones and McEwen (2000) provided a conceptual model that encompasses multiple dimensions of women's personal identity. These researchers proposed that at the center of a woman's identity was a core sense of self. The core identity was experienced as a "personal identity" incorporating "valued personal attributes and characteristics" (Jones, 1997, p. 383). Surrounding the core identity and integrally connected to this core were the "social identities"—what women experienced as externally defined dimensions such as gender, class, race, culture, sexual orientation, and religion. These researchers indicated that contextual influences such as family background and life experiences also played important roles in shaping women's multidimensional identities. Moreover, sociocultural conditions such as sexism and racism interacted with facets of identity and resulted in women developing more understanding of particular dimensions of their identity. Jones and McEwen's (2000) findings illuminated how identity in women can be understood and experienced differently under differing circumstances and at different times in a woman's life.

Identity in Culturally Diverse Populations

Wallace Jamison's story in the introduction to this chapter reminds educators that the identity formation experience of culturally diverse young people may be more complex. Along with identity issues that all young people confront, ethnically diverse adolescents must also establish an ethnic identity—a personal identification with an ethnic group and the value system and traditions maintained by the group (Phinney, 1996). For some young people of color, this task may be difficult. Researchers who examine ethnic identity issues indicate that a commitment to an ethnic identity is an important component of the self-concept of culturally diverse teenagers and helps to prepare them for success in a multicultural society (Phinney, 1996).

General models of racial/ethnic identity development have been proposed (see Atkinson, Morten, & Sue, 1993; Phinney, Lochner, & Murphy, 1990) as well as culture-specific models of racial/ethnic identity (see Arce, 1981; Cross, 1995; Kim, 1981). Ponterotto and Pederson (1993) examined these five models and identified commonalities across the various theories. They noted that in each of the models the cultural group underwent several stages in the process of determining a racial identity. Although Ponterotto and Pederson noted that the models differed with respect to the number of stages, they succeeded in collapsing stages drawn from the five identity models and identifying four themes that were consistent across all five theories. With these four themes, they proposed an integrative model that included the following stages:

- Identification With the White Majority,
- Awareness, Encounter, and Search,
- Identification and Immersion, and
- Integration and Internalization.

Ponterotto and Pederson (1993) labeled the first stage Identification With the White Majority. Individuals at this stage either did not see the relevance of ethnic identity to their lives or preferred to live by the norms and values of the dominant White culture. In the second stage of the model, Awareness, Encounter, and Search, individuals questioned their previously held beliefs, began to question their status as minorities in a racist society, and engaged in a search for their own racial identity. In the third stage, Identification and Immersion, individuals were ready to commit to and immerse themselves in their own cultural values and traditions. They wholly endorsed the norms, values, and customs of their own group while simultaneously rejecting the values and norms of the White majority culture. In the final stage, Integration and Internalization, a reappraisal occurred and a bicultural or multicultural identity was eventually established. According to Ponterotto and Pederson, the emotions associated with the previous stage—condemnation of the dominant culture and admiration for one's own group—became rechanneled into the development of a secure racial/ethic identity combined with an appreciation of other cultures. In this final stage, individuals developed a strong affiliation with and sense of belonging to their group and a determination to contribute to its overall well-being.

Exposure to racial identity development models like Ponterotto and Pederson's (1993) helps teachers and students think deeply about the life experiences that have shaped their views of themselves as gifted young people of color. Educators benefit from an understanding of these models and appreciate that their gifted students may move through these stages at a faster pace than other adolescents. Teachers must understand that stage models are fluid, and gifted culturally diverse youngsters may fluctuate between stages in unpredictable ways. In light of research findings indicating a heightened sensitivity among intelligent adolescents (Piechowski,

1997), gifted culturally diverse teenagers may respond more emotionally to and be more deeply affected by events that trigger movement from one stage of racial identity to another, and teachers and counselors need to provide them emotional support.

Identity Development in Gifted Adolescents

Researchers and theorists of gifted education have explored identity development in adolescents and have proposed that gifted teenagers, like all adolescents, struggle with the formation of an identity (Coleman & Cross, 2001; Coleman & Sanders, 1993; Hébert & Kelly, 2006). Several research studies have shed light on this issue. In assessing the ego-identity formation of gifted high school students, Howard-Hamilton and Franks (1995) found that gifted adolescents scored at the adult level of identity development on the Rasmussen Ego Identity Scale (Rasmussen, 1964). This study indicated that the students had successfully negotiated the psychosocial tasks Erikson identified as critical to the formation of a stable identity and were equipped with the tools they needed to develop a healthy identity. These findings led researchers to speculate that identity formation may occur more rapidly in gifted adolescents than in more typical students.

In an analysis of interview data from Lewis Terman's (1925) sample of more than 1,500 gifted children, Zuo and Tao (2001) contributed to our understanding of identity development in gifted individuals. In their examination of Terman's data, these researchers looked retrospectively for evidence of identity exploration and commitment and classified the sample into Marcia's (1980) four identity statuses. They reported that conformity was seen most often in the identity foreclosure group. Subjects categorized as identity diffused displayed higher levels of inferiority and lower levels of self-confidence, persistence, and sense of purpose. Continuing this line of inquiry, Zuo and Cramond's (2001) analysis of the Terman data indicated that the highest achieving subgroup of participants consisted primarily of identity achievers, while lowest achieving participants were mostly classified as identity diffused. These findings may help to explain one of the most important distinctions between gifted achievers and underachievers. If an intelligent young person is able to resolve the question of "Who am I?" then it seems logical that the student will also be able to resolve the question of "Where do I want to go in life?" With identity in place, a gifted adolescent will more readily adopt an achievement orientation.

Coleman and Cross (2001) considered the tools behind identity formation and examined how gifted students managed their identity. They maintained that gifted youngsters faced more internal conflict in their lives than other young people because their advanced development and specific talents placed them beyond societal expectations. In addition to facing the usual identity development tasks of adolescents, gifted teenagers had a role to play as the gifted student that other youngsters did not have to manage, making it more challenging for them to reach a clear understanding of who they were.

Calling attention to the role that social context played in adolescent development, Coleman and Cross (2001) noted that the problem became one of "fashioning an emerging identity in the midst of conflicting social demands" (p. 187). These demands involved mixed societal messages that gifted young people had to interpret. Gifted children received the societal message that they were different, and "being different is problematic in that differentness prevents, or at least interferes with, full social acceptance and personal development" (Coleman & Cross, 2001, p. 187). They also received the message that their difference led to being praised and criticized for their strengths. The student who was so smart was expected to be humble.

A third societal message was that the young person's special gifts or talents required outstanding performance at all times. Coleman and Cross (2001) indicated that this particular message could be misinterpreted in a way that led to anxiety and stress. A fourth message was that gifted students were expected to be constant achievers. Even gifted adolescents may struggle to master a difficult skill or concept, but others may not understand how the particular task could pose a challenge for the gifted teenager. For example, able learners may encounter surprise or disbelief from others when they earn a low grade on a class assignment.

Finally, Coleman and Cross (2001) called attention to another challenge adolescents faced: the experience of being known for one's achievements rather than one's self. Gifted teenagers complained that others saw the label "gifted student" but did not see them as individuals. When they finally succeeded in getting others to look beyond the labels, they heard messages such as, "Hey! You are really are a cool kid after all!" Confronted by these complex and confusing messages, gifted students' middle and high school years involved a far more challenging array of conflicting messages and identity development tasks than they had faced earlier in childhood. Coleman and Cross (2001) explained, "At this stage in life, the developmental tasks become sharply focused, the range of acceptable behaviors from peers becomes narrower, and the implications of one's ability and differentness can be grasped" (p. 191).

In another research study, Coleman and Cross (1988) explored how adolescents experience being gifted in high school. Through qualitative interviews with 15 teenagers attending a special summer science program, these researchers uncovered strong evidence supporting the hypothesis "that many (not all) gifted students do experience giftedness as a social handicap" (Coleman & Cross, 1988, p. 55). As a result, they maintained that "gifted students do feel stigmatized and consequently employ techniques to try to camouflage their differences" (Coleman & Cross, 1988, p. 55) in order to minimize their visibility as gifted students. Coleman and Cross (1988) also noted that their data suggested the past experiences of these teenagers and their school context played important roles in how the students experienced giftedness.

At the beginning of this chapter I introduced Wallace Jamison, a participant in my study of gifted urban teenagers. In this study of six high-ability, high-achieving males in a multiethnic urban high school (Hébert, 2000a), I identified a strong belief in self as the most important factor influencing the success of the young men. These gifted young men had constructed a solid identity that provided them with the energy, drive, and tools they needed to face life's challenges in an urban environment. Within this belief in self, the young men had clearly defined aspirations that were aligned with their personal qualities, strengths, and talents. They saw their aspirations as attainable because they realized they had the motivation and drive to succeed.

In addition to being motivated and having high aspirations, several qualities merged in these young men that assisted them in constructing their identities: sensitivity, multicultural appreciation, and an inner will. Through my data analysis, I identified factors that influenced such a strong belief in self. I found that relationships with supportive adults who respected the gifted males as young adults were influential. In addition, involvement in talent development opportunities such as extracurricular activities, sports, special programs, and summer school experiences appeared to reinforce their belief in self. I also found that the young men's secure sense of identity was reinforced by strong emotional support from their families.

In a second study of gifted males (Hébert, 2000b), I also uncovered a strong sense of personal identity within a group of gifted university males pursuing elementary education careers. As part of their belief in self, the gifted young men displayed empathic qualities and comfort with their psychological androgyny. These gifted males recognized characteristics traditionally viewed as feminine within their personalities and they celebrated those traits. Their identity included a sincere caring quality that they believed allowed them to be better men and more successful professionals. In addition, their empathy incorporated an appreciation for the developmental struggles faced by young children in elementary classrooms.

Speirs Neumeister (2002) explored identity formation in gifted females by examining factors influencing the professional achievements of three newly married, gifted young women. She found that her participants attributed a significant part of their identity to their status as high-achieving females. She identified three factors that were instrumental in shaping and directing the high-achieving components of their identities: foundational influences, including formative educational experiences, consistent high-achieving peer groups, and supportive family members and adults; personality characteristics; and the view of marriage as a partnership.

The gifted education literature includes only one study on identity development in gifted students with learning disabilities. Dole's (2001) groundbreaking work in this area investigated how dual exceptionalities affected the identity formation of four gifted college students with learning disabilities. Through qualitative narrative inquiry, Dole uncovered both contextual and personal influences that shaped identities. Within the contextual influences, she found two themes that were integral to the students' identity formation: support systems involving family, teachers, mentors, and friends; and involvement in extracurricular activities, volunteer work, and jobs. Within the personal influences, she uncovered three themes in identity formation: self-knowledge, self-acceptance, and self-advocacy.

Dole (2001) viewed identity formation within the gifted college students with learning disabilities as an ongoing, circular process. "Like a spiral that is advancing or receding, yet continuously developing, it began with self-knowledge—not only of their learning disabilities, but also of their learning abilities, talents, and strengths" (Dole, 2001, p. 122). Within these young people, she found that "Knowledge of self was ongoing and led to self-acceptance and self-advocacy, not necessarily in that order" (Dole, 2001, p. 122). She also noted that the students' self-acceptance and self-advocacy led them to self-determination or the setting of realistic career goals. With this self-determination, the students tapped into their strengths and interests and developed the persistence to accomplish their goals.

Contemporary researchers who study identity formation stand on the shoulders of giants such as Erikson, Marcia, Gilligan, and Josselson. From that vantage point, it becomes evident that further exploration in the area is needed. This review of literature on identity development within gifted individuals has uncovered limited research. The gifted education community is just beginning to explore this important phenomenon. Moreover, the majority of research in this area consists of qualitative studies utilizing small samples of participants, limiting the generalizability of their findings. These studies have opened the door to exploring the complexity of identity formation; however, more questions need to be raised. Researchers in gifted education must pursue more comparative research on identity development in gifted versus nongifted students. Longitudinal studies of identity development across the lifespan of gifted individuals would also help to enlighten us, for the answer may lie in uncovering information about the long-term challenges in identity development that confront gifted individuals beyond adolescence into adulthood and old age.

Implications for Teachers and School Counselors

Erik Erikson maintained that the formation of identity was the most important challenge of adolescence because it was necessary preparation for adulthood. Gifted young people like Meg, Robert, and Wallace, were, as adolescents, well on their way to adulthood with a strong sense of personal identity. Their experiences highlight the significance of Erikson's message. The review of theoretical and research literature conveys the complexity of identity as a psychological construct. In addition, this literature suggests that identity formation within gifted individuals may be even more complicated.

Educators should consider a number of important questions as they work with gifted adolescents. For example, if identity development is crucial preparation for adulthood, and gifted youngsters are intellectually advanced, can we assume that their identity development may also be advanced? Reflecting on Meg's determination to pursue an Ivy League experience, Robert's self-understanding and determination to remain focused on his goals, and Wallace's view of himself as a serious scholar-athlete, we might speculate that the intelligence of these gifted young people influenced the development of their strong belief in self.

Another key question is whether identity development is a more intense process for gifted students than for other young people. Will the search for personal identity within a gifted student take many different directions? Experienced teachers working with gifted adolescents reflect on former students who experimented with a variety of identities within a short period of time. They speak of students who arrive in high school presenting themselves as young conservative-looking intellectuals, who shift within a year to clothing and hairstyles driven by popular trends and immerse themselves in new interests and activities that reflect their identity search. The middle school science and math wizard becomes a songwriter and poet! As teachers and parents of gifted students observe these changes, researchers must consider whether the multipotentiality seen in gifted students leads to their "trying on many more hats" in their search for an identity.

The literature reviewed in this chapter suggests that context may play an important role in shaping identity. Several researchers noted that extracurricular activities and out-of-class experiences made a difference in shaping students' identities. Networks of high-achieving peers and supportive adults and the availability of role models also made a difference for some.

Secondary educators who observe students gravitating to involvement in the high school band or orchestra are also going to note whether such involvement is respected or valued by the peer group. What is valued in one context may not be valued in another. In high school environments where intellectual achievements are celebrated equally with athletic achievements, will the culture of the school influence how gifted young people feel about who they are within that culture? Consider Meg Anderson's challenges as a gifted female in a rural high school culture that valued athletics and homecoming queens. Consider how the context of Bates College may have influenced how Wallace Jamison saw himself as a scholar rather than an athlete. As young people experiment with identities, teachers of gifted students can help them in becoming aware of the role that their school context plays in influencing decisions regarding who they want to be.

The work of theorists such as Erikson, Marcia, Gilligan, and Josselson has provided a strong theoretical foundation for understanding identity development within gifted young people. Cross (2004) reminded us of the challenge presented by applying this work to such a complex population. Cross (2004) highlighted the significance of Erikson's work in understanding identity development in gifted students, maintaining that individual gifted children may be affected by psychosocial crises at earlier ages than Erikson posited. Cross (2004) argued that some gifted children are able to understand the world at a more intellectually advanced level than their same-age peers while remaining at the same level of emotional development as their peers. He explained, "To take advantage of the explanatory power of Erikson's theory, one needs to interpret an individual gifted child's behaviors in light of the theory and the child's idiosyncratic development and personal characteristics" (Cross, 2004, p. 29). This recommendation may be applied to all of the theories reviewed in this chapter. Educators must take into account individual differences among gifted teenagers when considering how the models proposed by Erikson, Marcia, Gilligan, Josselson and others may be applied to individuals.

Strategies to Support Identity Development in Gifted Students

The examples of Meg Anderson, Robert Branford, and Wallace Jamison clearly illustrate the importance of identity development among gifted students. For educators, the challenge becomes determining what can be done in our K–12 classrooms to support that development. I offer the following strategies for teachers and counselors to consider. Several may appeal primarily to educators working with elementary students while others are more appropriate for those working with middle or high school students.

Encourage Involvement in Extracurricular Activities

From the review of research on identity development in gifted students, we understand that extracurricular activities play an important role in shaping identity. Educators can encourage their gifted students to become involved in activities beyond the classroom. Gifted education scholars have found that gifted students participate actively in extracurricular activities that are both academic and athletic (Bucknavage & Worrell, 2005; Olszewski-Kubilius & Lee, 2004). Teachers and counselors may encourage students to experiment with various outlets for their gifts and talents. Involvement in clubs, teams, or campaigns provides opportunities for intelligent young people to build a sense of self-efficacy and success (Calvert & Cleveland, 2006; Hébert & Reis, 1999). A strong sense of self evolves from being a member of a group noted for accomplishment. These group experiences enable teenagers to construct a positive sense of self and raise their aspirations for the future. When teachers encourage their students to become involved in extracurricular activities, they let these young people know that their individuality is valued and their emerging identity is celebrated.

As a teacher working with gifted students, I often reached for the work of Canfield and Wells (1994) entitled *100 Ways to Enhance Self-Concept in the Classroom.* In their anthology of practical, field-tested exercises that can be integrated into the elementary or secondary curriculum, Canfield and Wells incorporated several exercises designed to help young children and teenagers take inventory of who they are, who they want to be, and just what they want to accomplish in life. The following activity entitled "If I were . . ." presents teachers and school counselors with an effective framework for getting children to reflect on their identities:

If I were . . . Canfield and Wells (1994) suggested that teachers have students work in groups of three. Children share what they would be if they suddenly turned into an animal, a bird, a car, a food, a flower, a musical instrument, or a building. In this enjoyable exercise in synectics, it is important that students think of the best representations of their current personality and share reasons for the particular choices they made. For example:

- If I were a building, I'd be small hut on a deserted island. I guess I feel that lonely sometimes.
- If I were a fruit, I'd be a pineapple because pineapples have a hard tough surface, but inside they are soft and sweet.
- If I were a bird, I'd be a canary because I like to sing a lot.

After sharing these, students may want to try "I would rather be . . ." statements. For example, the student who saw himself as a small hut may add: "But I'd rather be a church so people could find peace in me." Canfield and Wells indicated that I would rather be . . ." statements often highlight needs or strengths that young people would like to see actualized in themselves.

Canfield and Wells (1994) provided another helpful activity for young children that they named "If I could be . . ." In this exercise, students clarify who they are, what they want to be, and what they want to do. Following their responses to a number of thought-provoking prompts, they work in pairs and discuss their written responses to items such as: "If I could be any animal (e.g., bird, flower, food), I'd be a(n) _____ because _____." When the dyad sharing is completed, students form larger groups to share their choices and reasons. Several prompts that Canfield and Wells suggested are presented below:

- If I could be any animal, I'd be a(n) _____ because _____.
- If I could be a car, I'd be a(n) _____ because _____.
- If I could be a foreign country, I'd be a(n) _____ because _____.
- If I could be a game, I'd be a(n) _____ because _____.
- If I could be any color, I'd be a(n) _____ because _____.

Teachers or counselors working with gifted elementary students enjoy infusing prompts such as these in creativity training sessions, creative writing activities, or as healthy openers for class discussions.

Facilitate Discussion Groups

Along with the work of Canfield and Wells (1994), Jean Peterson's (2008) work in facilitating discussion groups with young people has provided gifted education teachers and school counselors with another invaluable resource. As a middle and high school English teacher, Jean Peterson tuned into the social and emotional worlds of adolescents. When her students responded to literature in their journals or when they interacted with their teacher outside of class, they told her about themselves. She learned that gifted teens shared a wide array of concerns that may not necessarily be apparent to others.

Peterson (2008) explained that her students wanted "*to be known*—to be recognized for their individual worth and uniqueness, not just for their intellect or talent" (p. 2). She realized that adolescents crave acknowledgement and nonjudgmental listening. When she became involved in gifted education, Peterson realized that discussion groups facilitated outside of the regular classroom would help high school students in the gifted program cope with stress, and she developed and facilitated a series of sessions. As a result, Peterson (2008) authored a helpful resource entitled *The Essential Guide to Talking With Gifted Teens*. In her work, she provides educators and counselors user-friendly discussion plans focusing on personal and social development issues that are important to teenagers. Session topics encourage young people to engage in self-reflection on identity, feelings, and peer, family, and community relationships, acknowledging that giftedness may influence these areas. A significant number of sessions address issues related to identity development. One such session is entitled "Façade, Image, and Stereotype." Peterson (2008) provided educators and counselors a wonderful opportunity to discuss with students how image and stereotypes affect gifted teens. In this session, she wanted to help young people understand that gifted teenagers, like all others, may become trapped by image. She explained:

> Regardless of whether he or she is perceived accurately, a teen who's seen as a rebel, risk-taker, joker, or member of the popular crowd may feel stuck in that hole. A bubbly, energetic student may feel constrained from expressing sadness. A nice guy may be tired of being nice. The class comedian may yearn to be taken seriously. A bad reputation can be difficult to escape. The "brainy" student may not feel able to ask a "stupid" question. It's possible to be a prisoner of image. (Peterson, 2008, p. 39)

In order to help teenagers address this challenge, she focused on three objectives in this discussion session. First, teachers and counselors facilitating this conversation will want to have gifted teens explore the idea of a "social face." Second, participants consider how they may or may not fit stereotypes that are applied to them. Third, students learn that when they share their doubts and authentic feelings, the level of trust is enhanced within the group.

In this session, the facilitator begins by having the students discuss what is meant by a façade or social face. They also consider what social purposes a façade may serve. Students are asked to reflect on their personal social faces at that moment. The discussion is directed to having students consider where they feel comfortable enough not to have to wear a social face. They are then asked to discuss the role of image in teenagers' lives and whether or not they believe they have to live up to particular images. The conversation is extended to having them define stereotype and considering stereotypes of gifted teenagers. The following are sample discussion prompts or questions that Peterson (2008) suggested using:

- What is your social façade? Do you have more than one—for various places? What purpose does it serve?
- Where can you take off your façade? What are you like when it's off?
- How might the facades of adults and teenagers differ?
- Have you ever had an image that you thought you had to live up to?
- What might be the cost of always living up to an image? What might be the benefit?
- How do you define stereotype? What is the stereotype of a gifted student? How do you fit that stereotype? How not?
- What do you wish your classmates understood about you? Your teachers? Your parents? (pp. 40–41)

Teachers and counselors who want to have meaningful discussions with bright adolescents greatly appreciate Peterson's (2008) guide. Each session is self-contained, presented in a linear fashion, and accompanied by reproducible handouts. I encourage my readers to explore this excellent resource in their work with gifted teenagers.

Use Reflections and Journal Prompts

Gifted education teachers have advocated the use of journals in writing classes. In the high-tech environments of contemporary classrooms, educators are experimenting with online journaling. Others prefer to provide opportunities for journaling in traditional writing assignments related to the curriculum. Regardless of whether students are reflecting on a laptop or a traditional composition notebook, having young people engage in personal reflection in journal formats may be helpful for students and their identity development process. Phipps (2005) maintains that "personal reflection encourages students to examine their motives related to their worldview, ethical behaviors, and basic beliefs about who they are and what they want to become" (p. 62). The following is an example of personal reflection by Kerrie Dimeler (1995), a then-13-year-old from Seavile, NJ. Kerrie's work serves as reminder to teachers and counselors who may be hesitant to dedicate precious time in a fast-paced curriculum to opportunities for personal reflection.

Learning to Be Me

When I was younger, I suffered the consequences of being me. People didn't like me, and I didn't know why. I spent a lot of time trying to come up with a plan to get people to understand me and to be my friend.

Success, as I see it, was getting used to who I am. Again and again I had tried to be like everyone else, but that was a mistake. Instead of giving up, I found in myself a resourceful and powerful person. I set aside the rest of the world and worked on who I was and who I wanted to be.

Rather than care about what was "in," I did exercises to expand my horizons; I even went so far as to study human behavior. Finally, I realized how great it was to be a separate person, different in so many ways.

Really being satisfied with who I am and where I stand, and establishing my place with others and in society was the biggest achievement I have ever made. (Dimeler, 1995, p. 5)

Employ Photo Elicitation

In pursuing qualitative research studies, I have conducted numerous interviews with gifted college students. In facilitating interviews on identity development with these young people, I have enjoyed incorporating a technique referred to as *photo elicitation*. I provide the participants in my study with a digital camera and ask them to respond to the following simple prompt: "Using this camera, shoot 12–15 pictures that represent your identity as a gifted individual." I provide them as much time as they need to reflect on how they will respond and the necessary time to shoot the pictures. Once they return the camera to me, I have the film developed into snapshots or together we transfer them to a computer. With the collection of photographs, I have the participant discuss how each picture represents what he sees as his identity. I have discovered that as a researcher I can learn a great deal from these conversations that I may not have uncovered in a more traditional research interview. I share three examples of this work below.

Aaron had struggled with underachievement in high school, and included in his collection of photographs several that called attention to issues that were troubling him. The photos were clearly representative of his identity formation. He included a photograph of a shelf in his dormitory bedroom. On the shelf were books and figures made from LEGOs. He explained, "I took a picture of my poetry books and my LEGO figures to represent my creativity." In a second snapshot of a bicycle parked outside a classroom building, Aaron explained, "If you look closely, you'll notice that the bicycle has a flat tire. That's my learning disability. It really hasn't allowed me to travel as fast as I would like to travel." He shot a picture of a construction site on the university campus because he felt this represented who he was as he explained, "I see myself as a work still under construction. I'm working at not becoming a slacker, but I've still got a long way to go."

Kip, a highly creative student, produced a collection of photographs that disclosed several facets of his identity. He shared a snapshot of himself wearing a hat that covered his face and attached to the hat was a large sketch of Wile E. Coyote, the well-known cartoon figure. As he presented this photo to me, he explained, "Wile E. Coyote is important to me because he represents the ideas that travel so fast through my head, my hyperactivity, and my creativity applied to my life." To let me know that he saw himself as a creative student who learned through a hands-on approach, he took a picture of a baking soda and vinegar volcano model to which he had added Hershey's chocolate powder. He pointed out, "The chocolate volcano represents my love of exploration, my curiosity, my deep need to research everything extensively, as well as all of my creative investigations." When he discussed a snapshot of an intersection of two paths in the woods where he jogged every morning, he commented, "This is the path where I jog every day. It symbolizes the choices I've made in my life. I've often taken the road less traveled."

Susan was pursuing training in dance and music. At the time of the interview, she had injured her leg and was wearing a cast. She included a photograph that incorporated a calendar, a microphone, a scale, and a handicapped parking tag. She explained the items in the snapshot: "The calendar points to my being 21 and that's old for one to be starting out in the arts. The scale represents that I'm not the ideal body type, and my handicap sticker says that I just happen to have a foot injury. But I don't doubt that I can reach my goals in dance and music. The microphone represents my passion for performing." With her snapshot of a hand grasping a large lighted flashlight Susan indicated, "I just love being in the spotlight."

Susan also included a photo of a tall ladder pointing toward a high ceiling and explained, "I took a picture of a ladder because I'm very hard on myself. I want to go very far and high. This photo is of the bottom of the ladder. I feel that you can always strive to climb higher." A favorite photo of Susan's was that of the trunk of her car, which was jam-packed. She indicated: "This picture of the trunk of my car represents just how much I pack into each and every day." Another photo included a collection of certificates, awards, trophies, and blue ribbons. She explained, "I am driven. I am a very competitive woman, and I love to be number one in everything that I do."

In sharing photo elicitation with educators at gifted education workshops and conferences, I have discovered that teachers and counselors are enthusiastic about the curricular and counseling possibilities in using this approach. Teachers have shared with me how they have infused the photo elicitation technique into creative writing as well as crafting autobiographies with their students. Others see many different ways to infuse this strategy into instructional units that focus on celebrating individual differences, talents, diversity, and even career development. Some comment on how much rich information they acquire about their students through this technique, enabling them to develop more supportive relationships. Counselors also note the value of this technique as they work individually with gifted students on personal development issues.

Strategies to Support Racial Identity Development

Educators also want to develop strategies designed specifically to support the racial identity development of their culturally diverse gifted students. Ford and Harris (1999) maintained that creative outlets incorporated into the curriculum are effective for engaging gifted culturally diverse students. They indicated that poetry can be used to promote identity development and highlighted works by Langston Hughes, Zora Neale Hurston, Maya Angelou, Nikki Giovanni, and Pleasant DeSpain that focus on themes of achievement, self-determination, hope, identity, and family. Discussions, personal journaling, and writing assignments associated with the poetry may also help to support identity formation in young people of color.

I have enjoyed exploring such poetry and have discovered numerous poems that would appeal to young people and focus on celebrating the beauty of ethnicity and the pride in one's cultural heritage. For example, Willie Perdomo (2002) offered a wonderful glimpse into the life of Langston Hughes through the eyes of a young African American girl in his poem entitled "Visiting Langston." As a young child growing up in Harlem, she sees herself as a budding poet writing jazz-like poems. Gifted African American children may also appreciate poetry celebrating the beauty of Black children in works by Joyce Carol Thomas (1993) entitled, "Cherish Me," and "Brown Honey in Broomwheat Tea." In each of these poems, young African American children reflect on the beauty of their ethnic physical features. Juan Filepe Herrera (1998) shared delightful reflections of his Mexican life in a poem entitled "If I Was Picasso I Would Paint a Crab." Teachers and counselors discover that a trip to the public library enables them to locate rich collections of multicultural poetry to share with students. Following exposure to such poetry, students may want to craft their own poems in which they celebrate their cultural heritage and ethnic identity. Below is a powerful example of such poetry. The poem is entitled "Black," and is written by then-12-year-old poet Landyn Waldrup (2006), an African American gentleman from Lafayette, LA, who published his work in *Creative Kids*, a national magazine for children.

Black

When I think of black, I think of my strong African American culture.
Black are the words "I have a dream," flowing from Martin Luther King's mouth.
Black is the color of the slave's hands after picking cotton.
Black are the letters on a reward poster for finding runaway slaves.
Black are the shackles that tightly clenched many innocent African American legs.
Black is ALIVE!
Black is the seat that Rosa Parks didn't give up.

Black are the sharp notes coming from the horn of the great Louis
Armstrong.
Black is the tunnel that Harriet Tubman once followed.
Black is the color of "The Road to Freedom" that many African
Americans once traveled.
Black is ALIVE!
Black should never be forgotten because Black is history. (p. 19)

Incorporate "This I Believe"

As a secondary English teacher, Christian Ehret worked with gifted
students at Monsignor Donovan Catholic High School in Athens, GA.
He recently shared one of his class projects with me that I am delighted to
pass on to my readers. Christian had long been intrigued with the notion
of addressing identity development through writing assignments he provided his Advanced Placement students. He discovered This I Believe, an
international project that engages people in discussing and writing the core
values that guide their daily lives. The project is based on the popular 1950s
radio series of the same name hosted by Edward R. Murrow. During the
1950s broadcasts, Americans of all walks of life read 5-minute essays about
their personal philosophy of life, sharing insights regarding the values that
influenced their daily living. The project has returned with people sharing their short statements of belief on the This I Believe website (http://
thisibelieve.org) and in regular broadcasts on National Public Radio (NPR).

Teachers of gifted high school students will be delighted to visit to
the This I Believe website, where visitors discover educational curricula
designed to assist students in the writing of a This I Believe essay, a personal essay that combines elements of both a personal narrative and memoir. The website also features excellent examples of essays published by
teenagers from across the country.

Christian Ehret maintained a website of his high school English courses.
He chose to have his students in his Advanced Placement Language and
Composition class write a This I Believe essay and create podcasts of themselves reading their personal essays. Christian began by having his students
discuss the definition of a belief, how an individual holds on to a belief,
how a person's beliefs may change, and finally how their own beliefs had
changed in their lives. Following reflection on this discussion, he shared
the This I Believe website with his students, and they enjoyed listening to
the recorded examples of personal essays. Christian's students were then
ready to write about their personal beliefs. They were asked to model their

personal essays on those they had enjoyed. Christian discovered that the introductory discussion forced his students to think seriously about their worldviews and, in doing so, they realized they were examining the development of their identities. He noted that as they looked back on their personal journey of shaping a belief system, they discovered where they were as young adults and this appeared to be a cathartic experience. Christian also indicated that his students enjoyed the peer review process as their podcasts were posted and appreciated having an opportunity to express themselves creatively. He pointed out that that rather than share their work on NPR, they disseminated their products through Donovan Public Radio (DPR). These teenagers from Donovan High appreciated that their teacher was tapping into the tech-savvy culture of contemporary adolescents and were proud to share their finished products with this audience. High school teachers may want to consider Christian's approach to addressing social and emotional development through reflective writing assignments. These teachers will appreciate the curriculum materials available for free from This I Believe and should find them helpful in supporting their students.

Address Identity Development Through an Integrated Curriculum

In her discussion of how educators must naturally play the role of counselors of gifted students, VanTassel-Baska (1991, 2006) asserted that strategies for nurturing social and emotional development should not be presented as isolated activities but rather incorporated into the curriculum for gifted students. She maintained that teachers must integrate affective issues into cognitive strategies in order to have the greatest impact on young people. She argued that "gifted students respond better to stimuli that are offered in an intellectual framework that provides a context and a system for understanding rather than a piecemeal approach frequently typified by one-to-one counseling experiences in school" (VanTassel-Baska, 1991, p. 51). Consistent with VanTassel-Baska's philosophical approach to supporting the affective components of giftedness, Rogers (2002) maintained that an affective curriculum should incorporate knowledge and skills in the areas of social relations, personal adjustment, motivation, emotional expression, humanistic values, and moral reasoning" (p. 307).

Several other influential leaders in gifted education have collaborated on a curriculum model for use in both regular and gifted education classrooms, a model that includes a component supporting the development of affective knowledge and skills. Carol Ann Tomlinson and colleagues

(2008) coauthored *The Parallel Curriculum: A Design to Develop Learner Potential and Challenge Advanced Learners* (2nd ed.). The parallel curriculum model offers four parallel approaches to curriculum development to ensure rich curricula for all learners while also offering ascending intellectual demand as a means of extending the intensity of challenge for gifted students. The term *parallel* indicates several formats through which educators can approach curriculum design in the same subject or discipline. The four parallels are the Core Curriculum, the Curriculum of Connections, the Curriculum of Practice, and the Curriculum of Identity.

Teachers and counselors who seek to support identity development in gifted students by infusing affective instruction into curriculum may want to consider the Curriculum of Identity. Tomlinson and her colleagues (2008) indicated that the curriculum of identity is:

> designed to help students see themselves in relation to the discipline both now and with possibilities for the future; understand the discipline more fully by connecting it with their lives and experiences; increase awareness of their preferences, strengths, interests, and need for growth; and think about themselves as stewards of the discipline who may contribute to it and/or through it. The Curriculum of Identity uses curriculum as a catalyst for self-definition and self-understanding, with the belief that by looking outward to the discipline, students can find a means of looking inward. (p. 37)

Since the initial conception of *The Parallel Curriculum*, practitioners throughout the country have been field-testing the model and designing instructional units based on this approach. The work of dedicated teachers collaborating with leaders in gifted education resulted in the publication of several exemplary instructional units based on the model entitled *The Parallel Curriculum in the Classroom: Units for Application Across the Content Areas, K–12* (Tomlinson et al., 2006). I highlight two examples of instructional material presented through the Parallel of Identity featured in this work. These exemplars should serve to inspire other teachers interested in developing curricula that support identity development in young people. The examples selected include a social science instructional unit for middle and high school students designed by Cindy Strickland and a language arts unit on the study of biography and autobiography with secondary students designed by Jann Leppien and Curt Bobbitt.

Strickland's exemplary 6-week unit entitled "With Liberty and Justice for All" explores the ideals associated with the founding of the United

States, examines the framework and function of the government, and provides an in-depth investigation of the justice system with respect to the Supreme Court. Strickland (2006) explained how identity issues may be incorporated into this unit: "Students learn how studying the ideals and working habits of the founding fathers as well as the current guardians of the Constitution can help them begin an examination of their own ideals and ways of working" (p. 249). One example of infusing work in identity development into her instructional unit is evidenced in Strickland's use of what she referred to as "complex instruction journal prompts." In facilitating the unit, she incorporated a journal in which she asked students to maintain their research notes while completing projects associated with the unit. In addition, she required that students set aside time each day to respond to particular journal prompts. The following are a sampling of the prompts regarding the study of the Supreme Court that Strickland incorporated to address identity development:

- What do Supreme Court justices think about? How do they work? To what degree are these things familiar, surprising, and/or intriguing to me?

- What are the problems and issues on which Supreme Court justices spend their lives? How do Supreme Court justices handle these and other problems associated with their position? How do I handle problems and issues in my life? Give specific examples. What are my strengths and weaknesses in this area?

- How does it happen that the Supreme Court has reversed itself numerous times? What are the implications of this? Should this be allowed? What happens when I change my opinion about something concerning my ideals and/or beliefs or those of my family? Give an example.

- What kind of a person appeals a case to the Supreme Court? Am I that kind of person? Explain.

- What makes a good Supreme Court justice? Could I be that kind of person?

- How does learning about the Supreme Court help me understand the ideals America was founded upon? How does learning about the Supreme Court help me understand myself better? (p. 287)

A second example from the Parallel Curriculum Model is a unit developed by Leppien and Bobbitt (2006) for use with high school students studying biography and autobiography. The unit requires that high school students learn to read biographies and understand how they are constructed.

Students are asked to identify recurring traits, characteristics, and patterns of behavior to determine whether a set of universals can be applied to the lives of the individuals featured in the biographies. In the final phase of the unit, students reflect on what they have learned about the lives they have read about to uncover what they have learned about themselves.

Leppien and Bobbitt (2006) included several project options for students to "explore their own conception of the life they have lived by sharing their triumphs and tragedies, to develop action plans that explore personal challenges, to profile someone meaningful in their lives, or to conduct actions to solve a problem" (pp. 293–294). The semester-long project options are referred to as "Personal Commitment to a Creative Action." The structure for this project-based approach has been purposefully designed to give teenagers an opportunity to explore how their lives can impact others and how actions can be taken to overcome personal obstacles and challenges. The projects require that students identify the key ideas that the biographies or autobiographies revealed and explore how these important ideas apply to their own lives.

In pursuing the project tasks, teachers ask that young people identify a problem that they feel strongly about and design a course of action they will take to address the issue. Understanding that they must tap into their personal strengths, courage, and motivation, they are then required to take action and develop a product or provide a service that addresses the problem or concern. As they conduct their work, they reflect on how their work parallels the lives of the individuals they have read about in their biographies. Upon completion of their product, they are required to write a personal reflection explaining what their project work revealed to them about their personal strengths, interests, and any need for growth in their field of study. Students have multiple options to select from in completing such a project. The following menu provides several examples that Leppien and Bobbitt (2006) have students consider:

- Students create autobiographical self-portraits, memoirs, or autobiographies that highlight a personal struggle that they faced in life. They are asked to discuss the factors that shaped how they took on their challenges and design a plan to face the future.
- Using the methodologies of the biographer, students write a biographical sketch of a contemporary local individual who demonstrates some of the traits and characteristics found in the biographies they have read.
- Students locate a problem that needs to be solved. The problem should be of a serious nature that requires them to leave their com-

fort zone and take complete responsibility for resolving the problem. The problem should be one that involves a serious personal interest and the resulting authentic product should reflect the students' preferred style of expression.

Some educators may be comfortable facilitating activities in their classrooms that directly address identity development. Others may prefer to infuse such instruction into the broader curriculum. Regardless of the approach a teacher or counselor chooses, gifted students are bound to benefit from these experiences. Young people like Meg, Robert, and Wallace deserve educators who are willing to incorporate such strategies. I encourage you to try.

For Further Thought and Discussion

- Craft an imaginary conversation between you and Erik Erikson regarding identity development in gifted individuals. What would you say to him? How might he respond?
- Select one identity development theory presented in this chapter. Generate a menu of questions you would pose to gifted students regarding how they see themselves in relation to the theory. Predict how you think they would respond.
- Consider the areas of context that may have influenced the identity development of Meg Anderson, Robert Branford, and Wallace Jamison. How might their experiences be different in other settings?
- Discuss your position on the following statements:
  - Identity development is more accelerated for gifted individuals because of their advanced cognitive abilities.
  - Identity development within gifted individuals is more intense and involves more time as a result of the individual's multipotentiality.

- Ponterotto and Pederson (1993) proposed a four-stage integrative model to explain the racial identity development of racially diverse individuals. Using this model, describe how the stages may reflect the experiences of a gifted person of color. Do you believe that Ponterotto and Pederson did justice to racially diverse populations in their model? Why or why not?
- As a result of reading this chapter, you have become interested

in designing a research study examining identity development in gifted students. Describe your proposed study.

❧ Consider how you would incorporate this chapter's suggested strategies for supporting identity development into your classroom. What effects would you hope they might have?

Resources to Expand Your Thinking and Extend Your Support to Gifted Students

Canfield, J., & Wells, H. C. (1994). *100 ways to enhance self-concept in the classroom.* Boston, MA: Allyn & Bacon.

Peterson, J. S. (2008). *The essential guide to talking with gifted teens: Ready-to-use discussions about identity, stress, relationships, and more.* Minneapolis, MN: Free Spirit.

Peterson, J. S. (2009). *Gifted at risk: Poetic portraits.* Scottsdale, AZ: Great Potential Press.

CHAPTER 6

Friends and Family: Significant Relationships That Influence Social and Emotional Development

My goals for this chapter are to:
- Introduce you to literature highlighting the benefits of friendship for children and adolescents.
- Examine how friendships evolve and change during childhood and adolescence.
- Examine the gendered nature of friendship.
- Discuss family influences on friendships.
- Examine research on friendships within the lives of gifted young people.
- Share my insights on friendships gleamed from my work with gifted students.
- Share my insights on friendships from my research and work with graduate students.
- Present strategies to assist you in supporting gifted students in forming and maintaining friendships.

Recipe for the Perfect Friendship

From the Kitchen of Lisa Gisselbrecht

1	gallon of cooperation juice
1	teaspoon of promise sauce
2	cups of caring cubes
3	tablespoons of trusting powder
1	pinch of loving salt

Mix cooperation juice and promise sauce gently in a big bowl. Blend in the trusting powder slowly. In a pan on low heat, slowly melt the caring cubes and gently mix in the loving salt with the other ingredients in the bowl. Mix lightly and serve tenderly because friendship takes a long time to prepare. Serves 10 Friends. (Gisselbrecht, 1985, p. 22)

Lisa Gisselbrecht (1985) wrote her recipe for the perfect friendship as a student in my classroom quite a few years ago; however, the ingredients she chose to include in her dish would remain true today if she were to return to her kitchen to prepare her delicacy again. Lisa, as a fourth grader, was clever in her response to my creative writing activity but, more importantly, she beautifully captured the essence of friendships for children in her simple recipe that would serve as a real treat to many children today. Lisa's recipe helps us to reflect on our own innocent childhood friendships and reminds us of the importance of those friendships and the role they played in shaping who we are as individuals today.

Friendships influence all of us on many levels and have significant value in shaping a life well lived. In this chapter, I examine children's friendships. I explore how friendships change from childhood to adolescence. I also examine the gendered nature of friendships. Moreover, I highlight the significant family influence on friendships. Following this discussion, I examine what all of this means for the social and emotional development of gifted children and adolescents. The voices of gifted young people who participated in research studies in which friendships emerged as important findings are presented. I conclude the chapter with a discussion of strategies that educators and counselors may consider using to help gifted students develop and maintain important friendships in their lives.

The Benefits of Friendship for Children and Adolescents

Merriam Webster's (1998) collegiate dictionary defines a friend as "one attached to another by affection or esteem." The term *friend* is one that we all use frequently; however, few of us spend time reflecting on the important influence friends play in our lives. In a comprehensive review of literature on friendship research, Sherman, DeVries, and Lansford (2000) noted that friends play significant roles in the social, psychological, and physical health of individuals across the lifespan. The value of a friendship can influence a person's well-being by enhancing happiness and self-esteem, and by providing emotional support and companionship throughout a lifetime (Rowe & Kahn, 1998).

High-quality relationships with friends are strongly related to children's well being (van Aken & Asendorpf, 1997). Friendships provide security and social support, they help children develop social problem-solving skills, and they serve as preparation for positive adult adjustment (Shaffer, 2000). For children, having one supportive friend can make a significant difference in reducing the loneliness and victimization that unpopular children experience when they are excluded from a larger peer group (Hodges, Boivin, Vitaro, & Bukowski, 1999).

A close relationship with another child may provide a sense of security that helps children deal with new challenges, or an emotional safety net that allows them to deal with the stressors in their lives such as a family divorce or problems with a sibling. Supportive friendships also play an important role in promoting self-esteem in children from noncohesive families (Shaffer, 2000). Through successful friendships, they learn important social concepts and rules, and develop personal growth.

The experiences of amicably resolving conflicts with friends are another important benefit of friendships. By middle childhood, youngsters learn to follow rules and not cheat while playing competitive games and to respect the opinions and needs of their partners while resolving conflicts. Such experiences of peacefully resolving disagreements with friends are important contributors to developing mature social problem-solving skills (Fonzi, Schneider, Tani, & Tomada, 1997). Having a close friend with whom they can share their thoughts and emotional feelings helps children progress developmentally, from being egocentric to being able to understand other people's perspectives.

Friendships also shape a young person's identity. Feedback that children receive from their peer relationships helps them understand how they are perceived outside their families, an important step to developing self-knowledge and shaping identity (Shaffer, 2000; Sheely, 1998). Most children receive nurturing comments at home and can assume that they are valued by their families. However, to earn trust and mutual respect from their peers helps to validate the child's individual self-worth. Gaining such trust and peer respect only strengthens positive self-esteem as a child matures.

Friendships also serve as preparation for developing healthy adult relationships. In childhood and adolescence, increasing intimacy and mutuality between friends may be necessary for individuals to develop the interpersonal sensitivity and commitment observed in adult romantic relationships. Researchers have found that close reciprocal bonds formed by friends during this period provide the foundation for developing a positive sense of self-worth and the growth of compassionate qualities that a person needs to form and maintain intimate relationships later in life (Bagwell, Newcomb, & Bukowski, 1998).

Changes in Friendship Patterns From Childhood to Adolescence

Because friendships play such a significant role in preparing children for relationships later in their adult lives, it is important to understand how changes in friendship patterns occur from childhood to adolescence. A young poet from Ramsey, NJ, named Jackie Scheid helps us to appreciate these changes through her poem in *Creative Kids* magazine presented below entitled "My Type."

My Type

The tears swell in my eyes
as sorrow surfaces within me.
I can't stand it any longer,
so I let the tears trickle down my face
like raindrops.
As each one falls,
I feel as though I'm losing my friends
over and over again.
No one notices me.

No one notices my tears.
No one feels my pain.
I am alone and wilting.

I remember that horrible day.
She sauntered down the hallway,
followed by her posse.
There they were—
Giddy, gossiping, secretive, and superficial
with their cell phones and mini-skirts,
acting as if they owned the place.
Though, in some ways, they did.
As I glanced their way,
she looked at me and rolled her eyes,
giving me a look that said,
"You're not my type."
Then, without a trace of remorse,
she skipped off with other friends,
leaving me stunned and hurt.
She had decided that I was not *her* type.

I sit in a crowded hallway,
my tear-stained face beneath my hands
to shield me from the pain.
Not a single person approaches,
not a stranger, nor a friend,
nobody.

What have I done wrong?

I realize that it is not what I have done,
it is what she lacked:
trust, loyalty, compassion.
I feel courage take root.
And then, like a flower beginning to grow,
I feel strength within me.
I hold my head up high with confidence,
For I have realized,
She just isn't *my* type. (p. 32)

Through her poetry, Jackie has poignantly captured an emotionally upsetting event that many young people face in early adolescence. Jackie reminds us in her poem that as we leave an elementary school playground and move into a middle or high school environment, we will easily notice that for adolescents the peer groups change in structure, as well as in the significant roles they play in the lives of teenagers. Many young people see their friends changing from the kind, tenderhearted playground pals of their elementary school settings to the powerful leaders of posses. Children often discover painfully that friends wander apart from each other, shift in their interests, and discover new groups of friends with similar interests, value systems, and ways of interpreting their adolescent worlds.

Adolescent Peer Groups, Cliques, and Crowds

In order to understand this period of changing friendships in children's lives, Steinberg (2005) has delineated four specific adolescent developments that stand out during this important time of transition. The first development he highlighted was the significant increase in the amount of time young people spend with their peers. During this period, more than half of a typical adolescent's waking hours are spent with peers. Secondly, because teenagers are provided more independence during adolescence, the peer group functions more often without adult supervision. In addition, during adolescence, an increasing proportion of a teenager's significant others are opposite-sex peers. Finally, the emergence of larger groups of peers or crowds evolves during this developmental period.

Adolescents will still maintain close friendships; however, a visit to a middle school cafeteria allows us to scan the room and note the various crowds that are scattered throughout the lunchroom: the "preps," " brains," and "druggies." These crowds or "subcultures" may be so pronounced that they might include particular ways of talking, fashion styles, and behavior patterns. Researchers have indicated that during this period in development, young people are easily able to list the various groups that characterize their schools and describe the stereotypes that differentiate one crowd from another (Kinney, 1993).

Devin Friedman, a freelance journalist, courageously returned to his high school in suburban Cleveland 16 years following his high school graduation to investigate the changes in high school culture. Friedman's (2006) report of his visit to his high school cafeteria vividly captures what researchers indicate remains true from one generation to the next. The names of the groups may change, but the important role the subcultures play in schools has not. Friedman described:

> In class, it's hard to suss out social status just by eyeballing a kid.
> . . . But in the cafeteria, I can see who's waving what flag. Some
> types I've seen before: the punks with their Sex Pistols T-shirts
> and bad skin; the Hacky Sack-throwing hippies who wear hemp
> and lack political referent; the thug-lites in their white Air Force
> 1s; the preps with their popped collars; the hyperinvolved instru-
> ment-playing union-organizing antitobacco-lobbying Darfur-pro-
> testing kids who already have their applications in to Wesleyan;
> the extreme misfits, who appear physically stricken, faces frozen
> in fearful smiles and arms wrapped around themselves like they've
> just dropped naked from the sky into northern Mongolia. (p. 317)

Friedman reflected on the how these subcultures serve as a support structure for adolescents as they undergo their search for identity. He posited
that it was important for teenagers to have secured some sense of identity
to protect them from being too personally evaluated by their peers. The
subcultures in high school simply served as one way to acquire that protective identity.

The important changes that take place in peer relations are rooted in
the biological, cognitive, and social development of adolescence (Steinberg,
2005). Puberty stimulates adolescent interest in relationships with the
opposite sex and detaches adolescents from their parents and other adults
in their lives. The cognitive changes that occur during this time provide
young people with more sophisticated understanding of social relationships, which may explain the abstract categorization that encourages them
to group individuals into crowds. As young people determine these new
social definitions, changes in peer relations and friendships emerge.

What Jackie Scheid (2006) earlier portrayed in her poem of an adolescent female suddenly categorizing a person into a new social category is an
authentic experience that occurs often. These changes in social definitions
may cause changes in friendships and such changes in peer relationships
may be thought of as an adaptive response. For example, the larger, more
impersonal environment of a high school may force a teenager to look for
new friends in other teenagers who they see as having common interests
and similar values in order to design once again the more intimate groups
of friends that were such an important part of childhood (Kinney, 1993).
Rather than feeling lost and alone in a large high school for 4 years, the

teenager who belongs to the "preps," "jocks," or "drama club geeks" may feel more comfortable heading for that particular table of friends in the high school cafeteria every day.

In order to appreciate the powerful role that peer relations play during adolescence, it is important to understand the difference between two different yet related structures within adolescent peer groups: cliques and crowds (Shaffer, 2000; Steinberg, 2005). Steinberg (2005) indicated that cliques are small groups, between 2 and 12 individuals, generally of the same sex and age that may be defined by common activities (e.g., the drama group) or simply by friendship (e.g., a group of boys who have known each other for a long time). The clique serves as the social setting in which adolescents come to know each other well, form friendships, and "hang out." Steinberg (2005) pointed out that adolescent cliques are quite different from crowds in their structure and purpose. Brown (1990) defined crowds as "large, reputation-based collectives of similarly stereotyped individuals who may or may not spend much time together (p. 177). The labels for these crowds vary from one American high school to another; however, typical crowds are popular youth, athletes, loners, drug-using or rebellion-oriented groups, and academically focused students (Brown, 2004; Shaffer, 2000).

Although membership in a clique depends on shared activity and friendship, membership in a crowd is driven by reputation and stereotype, rather than actual friendship. Steinberg (2005) described this in concrete terms and called attention to a problem involving this issue: An adolescent does not have to actually have "brains" as friends, or to hang around with "brainy" students, to be a member of the "brain" crowd (p. 177). He elaborated, "If he dresses as a 'brain,' acts as a ' brain,' and takes honors courses, then he is a 'brain,' as far as his crowd membership goes" (Steinberg, 2005, p. 177). He also indicated that because crowd membership is based on reputation and stereotype, this issue may be a difficult problem for some teenagers, who, if they do not change their reputations early on in high school, may find themselves, in the eyes of their peers, labeled as a member of a crowd that they do not actually belong to. These stereotypes are often based on false assumptions, inaccurate representations of the adolescent, longstanding in the minds of the peer group, and emotionally troubling to a sensitive young person.

Consider what high school stereotyping may do to an emotionally sensitive gifted teenager. The literature on high school culture includes a classic work that may help us to appreciate this difficult issue. In his examination of the high school experience entitled *Is There Life After High School?*, Ralph Keyes (1976) interviewed hundreds of adults regarding their recollections of their high school experience and drew a serious conclusion: There are many people for whom high school is the peak, the zenith of their success and achievement. For them, life after high school was filled with disappointment and a lack of fulfillment. For others who struggled for status in high school and never achieved it, life following high school was that of self-actualization. Keyes included many admired American cultural icons and celebrities from a variety of domains in his research. Below are direct quotes from interviews with several of these well-known individuals who suffered from stereotyping and the rigid social caste systems of their high schools. In each case, we hear painful memories and detect anger regarding how they were treated as teenagers in high school:

"Cause I was the Jewish girl growing up in a Samoan neighborhood . . . I left . . . and, you know, the old story about 'I'll show *them*' . . . I really felt that way and I had a lot of anger built up from all those years."—Bette Midler (p. 109)

"If they don't like me, some day they'll learn to respect me."—Betty Friedan (p. 109)

"Thank God for the athletes and their rejection. Without them there would have been no emotional need and . . . I'd be a crackerjack salesman in the garment district."—Mel Brooks (p. 110)

"If I had been a really good-looking kid, I would have been popular with my classmates, I would have been smooth with the girls, I would have started scoring at about age fourteen, I would have been a big fraternity guy in college, and I would have ended up selling Oldsmobiles. For sure I wouldn't have had the bitterness and fierce ambition I've needed in order to become a successful freelance writer."—Dan Greenburg (p. 110)

These talented individuals overcame their difficulties in high school and became successful adults. There is evidence of emotional struggle imbedded in their poignant quotes, and they remind us of the powerful influence the adolescent peer group has on psychosocial development. Many intelligent teenagers who struggle to follow the rigid peer group rules of high school culture may find it refreshing to learn that these celebrities also experienced difficulties in school.

Regardless of the structure of the particular school setting or the

norms of a particular adolescent clique or crowd, peers play a very important role in shaping how teenagers feel about themselves. Problematic peer
relationships have been associated with a variety of psychological problems.
Those who are unpopular or who suffer from poor peer relationships during adolescence are more likely than their popular peers to be low academic achievers, display delinquent behavior, drop out of high school, and
struggle with a variety of emotional problems later in life (Steinberg, 2005).

Peers promote normal psychosocial development by providing different
models and feedback that adolescents do not receive from adults. Within
the peer group, young people can experiment with various roles and personalities and field-test different identities with more ease than they can
within the family. In addition, the peer group provides a context for developing autonomy as adolescents experiment with decision-making skills in
an arena free of adults who monitor or control their choices (Brown, 2004).
The adolescent peer group also plays the central role in socializing teenagers in developing their capacity for intimate friendships and appropriate romantic relationships (Buhrmester, 1996). It is a significant influence
on adolescents' daily school behaviors and attitudes, including whether or
not they value school and how much effort they dedicate to academics, as
well as their performance in class (Altermatt & Pomerantz, 2005; Barry
& Wentzel, 2006; Crosnoe, Cavanaugh, & Elder, 2003). Researchers have
noted this peer influence is especially significant for ethnically diverse
teenagers and students from economically disadvantaged environments
(Crosnoe et al., 2003; Steinberg et al., 1992).

The Gendered Nature of Friendship

I ask my readers to spend some time in a local park and watch a group
of adolescent males play basketball. I encourage you to observe closely and
listen in on the conversations that are held during that game. I guarantee you
that throughout that game you will hear young men expressing warmth for
each other in indirect ways and with lots of good-natured teasing. Through
their animated conversation, you will hear unspoken masculine rules that
govern boyhood. You will learn about their views of the girls in their schools.
You may also get a glimpse into the dreams and aspirations of these boys as
they enjoy their game. Casually observing and listening to adolescent males
enjoying the company of their buddies teaches us that friendships for males
may be quite different than friendships for females and the significant roles
friends play in shaping who we are as men and women.

There are gender differences and similarities in friendship across the lifespan (Sherman et al, 2000). As early as preschool, the social networks of young children become increasingly segregated by gender, and by elementary school children rarely play with others of the opposite gender (Golombok & Fivush, 1994).

Theorists and researchers have speculated that boys and girls grow up in social worlds that provide very different socialization experiences (e.g., Maccoby, 1990), and have described numerous gender differences in the friendships of children and adolescents. In same-sex friendships, beginning in middle childhood, girls show more responsive and supportive behavior and more self-disclosure than boys do (Brendgen, Markiewicz, Doyle, & Bukowski, 2001; Kuttler, La Greca, & Prinstein, 1999). As these relationships become more intimate during adolescence for both boys and girls, the relationships between young women are more focused on intimacy, loyalty, and commitment, and boys' friendships are more oriented on doing things together (Buhrmester, 1996; Camarena, Sarigiani, & Petersen, 1990; Maccoby, 1990; McNelles & Connolly, 1999; Reed & Brown, 2000; Thomas & Daubman, 2001). Girls tend to self-disclose more and provide each other with greater emotional support than boys (Brown & Gilligan, 1992; Johnson, 2004). Whereas girls enjoy intimacy in their friendships, boys' interactions with friends are characterized by frequent rough and tumble play, aggressive interaction, and establishing hierarchies of dominance (Pellegrini, 1995; Pollack, 1998; Reed & Brown, 2000). Female friendships involve face-to-face emphasis in conversation, and male friendships are characterized by a side-by-side orientation focused on doing things together (Aukett, Ritchie, & Mill, 1988; Buhrmester, 1996). These shared activities for males often involve achievement, recognition, and power-oriented pursuits such as competitive games and sports. When male friends do talk, their conversations often focus on the accomplishments of admired sports figures or their evaluation of the prowess of their peers in sports or school (Buhrmester, 1996; Pollack, 1998).

The same-sex friendships that are so important to children early on play a major role in actively shaping girls' needs for community and boys' needs for active involvement. The heavy exposure to such childhood practices contributes to that expectation later in adolescence. Young girls get rewarded for acting like ladies and young boys receive gratification for their active involvement in competitive play. Buhrmester (1996) described this phenomenon by drawing an analogy to adults developing an "acquired taste" for coffee by drinking multiple cups a day. The same can be said for children and their gender-specific ways of behaving with same-sex friends.

If young boys hang out with their best buddies engaging in power-oriented competitive play, then it remains likely that they will continue this behavior in adolescence and adulthood. In general, our culture seems to reward boys who are motivated to be manly. We value and reward a young man's pursuit of individual achievement, identity and purpose, and interpersonal influence over others. Therefore, the competitiveness, the status-related bantering, and the focus on engaging in games with complex rules for winning play an important role in how we socialize boys to become successful men (Kindlon & Thompson, 1999; Pollack, 1998).

The norms and cultural expectations that govern boys' and girls' friendships may actually lead to overtly discouraging the pursuit of some needs and encouraging the pursuit of others. Several researchers (Brown & Gilligan, 1992; Maccoby, 1990; Tannen, 1990) maintained that norms for girls appear to actively reward intimate self-disclosure and providing others with emotional support, while discouraging open competition. In contrast, Maccoby (1990) indicated that what society celebrates in active young boys' friendships often goes against building intimate connections. There is evidence to support the notion that male-male friendships actively discourage males from expressing a need for communication and emotional support (Bank & Hansford, 2000; Buhrmester, 1996; Reisman, 1990). Cultural norms dictate to males that mushy sentimentality and the open expression of affection for a male friend are not allowed (Buhrmester, 1996; Kindlon & Thompson, 1999). Researchers have indicated that emotional restraint and homophobia toward gay males provided the strongest explanation for gender differences in intimacy and support in best friendships (Bank & Hansford, 2000).

The cultural norms that direct the emotional lives of boys were closely examined in the 1990s when a number of books about boys were published by well-respected counseling psychologists (e.g., Gurian, 1996; Kindlon & Thompson, 1999; Pollack, 1998). These publications were a response to the media's coverage of extreme cases of violence by boys that began healthy conversation regarding how we were teaching and parenting boys. In addition, an increased emphasis in schools on special programs to nurture talents in girls also prompted many educators to look for ways in which boys could overcome gender stereotypes restricting their choices. Moreover, many psychologists experienced in helping adult males became more interested in exploring whether or not boyhood served as an incubation period for many of the problems faced by men.

Because of the dialogue created by these psychologists, the discourse on cultural norms shaping the lives of boys is being heard, and attitudes are changing. These clinicians indicated that adolescent males are crying out for changes in how we conceptualize masculinity. This changing attitude on the part of younger men in this country is evidenced in how they view their masculinity and its influence on their friendships with other males. Pollack and Shuster (2000) conducted a comprehensive study that examined masculinity in contemporary society. In their work entitled *Real Boys' Voices*, we meet Graham, a suburban teenager whose voice may be representative of the many young men calling for these changes. Graham described what he sees needs to happen for him in a meaningful friendship with another young man:

> Most guys find it hard to talk about their feelings. I have a big group of friends and we're all pretty comfortable with one another, we all like each other. But we never talk about our feelings unless something is *really* up. . . . We would live in a better society if guys could share their feelings more easily. But guys still hear mixed messages from our society. On the one hand they hear that it's OK now to talk about their feelings, but on the other hand they still hear that they have to be tough and that only girls get emotional... Some of my friends are like me and, and believe guys should talk about their pain and that sharing doesn't make anyone less of a man. But we get mixed messages on this from our parents, our friends, and from society in general. (Pollack & Shuster, 2000, pp. 271–272)

Graham has described the essence of what so many males experience in childhood and adolescence. He and other boys like him need to be heard by adults who deliver mixed messages to young men, in order to generate healthier approaches to parenting and educating boys.

Family Influence on Friendships

Recently I was listening to my favorite Atlanta radio station and the commentator shared a story that reminded me of just how significant a close-knit family can be in shaping the life of an emotionally sensitive child. The commentator shared how her daughter had been involved in her first Girl Scout slumber party the night before. After the child left home for the sleepover, her parents discovered a note on the kitchen table that read, "Even though I may not be here tonight, you are still in my heart."

The young girl had decorated the note to her family with her drawing of a large pink heart. During the course of the sleepover, she called home three times. In the first phone conversation, she called to check in on her family and find out how her three younger sisters were doing without her. The second phone call involved her curiosity. She wanted to know whether or not her family had found her note on the kitchen table. Her final phone call was simply to say goodnight. Her parents reported that when she returned home the next day, as her mother was cleaning out her overnight bag, she discovered that her daughter had packed several snapshots of her family. I was moved by this tender story of the young girl's love for her parents and her siblings. I stopped by the side of the road, grabbed a pen and some paper, and jotted down short notes to myself in order to remember the details of the story and share it in this chapter. I did so because I believe it captures what we would like to think is the ideal family, and we might hope that many gifted children have such a family experience.

Along with being moved by a recent story on the morning radio, I was also struck by a *TIME* magazine feature article that caught my attention. The cover of the magazine read, "How your siblings make you who you are." In his thought-provoking article, Kluger (2006) discussed the important socializing effects that siblings have on one another. He examined a number of psychological studies conducted on sibling relationships and called our attention to the influential roles that brothers and sisters play in shaping other relationships in our lives. He explained:

> From the time they are born, our brothers and sisters are our collaborators and co-conspirators, our role models and cautionary tales. They are our scolds, protectors, goads, tormentors, playmates, counselors, sources of envy, objects of pride. They teach us how to resolve conflicts and how not to; how to conduct friendships and when to walk away from them. Sisters teach brothers about the mysteries of girls; brothers teach sisters about the puzzle of boys. Our spouses arrive comparatively late in our lives; our parents eventually leave us. Our siblings may be the only people we'll ever know who truly qualify as partners for life. (Kluger, 2006, pp. 47–48)

The story shared on the Atlanta radio station, as well as Kluger's message, provides us with rich food for thought regarding the importance of family. To better understand how relationships affect children's lives beyond the home, it is critical to consider relationships within the home and how they may shape how young people discover and maintain friendships.

Literature on the family and its influence on adolescent development is extensive. Research studies have examined families from different ethnic and cultural backgrounds, socioeconomic levels, household compositions, and parenting styles. Throughout this body of research, the one factor that appears to influence adolescent adjustment the most is the quality of their relationships at home (Garnefski, 2000). In a comprehensive study of the lives, behavior, and health of 90,000 teenagers, Blum and Rinehart (2000) determined: "What emerges most consistently as protective is the teenager's feeling of connectedness with parents and family. Feeling loved and cared for by parents matters in a big way" (p. 31). Researchers have consistently found that young people who believe that their parents or guardians are there for them are more competent, healthier, and happier, regardless of how competence, health, or happiness are measured. This conclusion remains true regardless of the child's ethnicity, social class, or age, and across all types of family structures, whether married or divorced, single or multiple parent, wealthy or poor (Dornbusch, Erickson, Laird, & Wong, 2001). Steinberg (2005) summarized the issue succinctly:

> Despite the tremendous growth and psychological development that takes place as individuals leave childhood on the road toward adulthood, despite society's pressures on young people to grow up fast, despite all the technological and social innovation that has transformed family life . . . the fact of the matter remains that adolescents continue to need the love, support, and guidance of adults who genuinely care about their development and well-being. (p. 163)

This consistency in findings regarding the family is refreshing. Moreover, one of the most consistent findings reported across studies that have examined adolescents' peer and family relationships simultaneously is that the quality of these relationships are closely linked (Doyle & Markiewicz, 1996; Paley, Conger, & Harold 2000; Steinberg, 2005). The positive characteristics that are evident in nurturing families carry over into positive peer relationships and friendships for young people. The quality of relationships between parents and their children influences the relationships among brothers and sisters, which in turn influences relationships with peers for children and adolescents (Brody, Stoneman, & McCoy, 1994; Paley et al., 2000; Reese-Weber, 2000). For example, how parents authentically express emotional warmth, deal with conflict, and tolerate independence in their children has positive effects for adolescent friendships. In other words, the features of adolescent relationships with their parents are reflected in their relationships with friends and romantic partners (Allès-Jardel, Fourdrinier, Roux, & Schneider, 2002; Taradash, Connolly, Pepler, Craig, & Costa, 2001). Supportive sibling relationships have also been found to influence the peer relationships and friendships of young people (Updergraff, McHale, & Crouter, 2000). This connection between the quality of family relationships and peer relationships has been found across ethnic groups (Way & Chen, 2000). These research studies suggest that the important lessons we learn from parents and siblings at home serve as a template for the close relationships we develop with others.

Scholarly literature on families of gifted children is limited, with the majority of researchers and theorists focusing on the role of the family in supporting talent development, giftedness as a family organizer, and the interactions between family dynamics and the labeling of a gifted child (e.g., Bloom, 1985; Cornell, 1984; Cornell & Grossberg, 1987; Jenkins-Friedman, 1992). Moon and Hall (1998) conducted a comprehensive review in family counseling and therapy literature focusing on families of gifted children. These researchers highlighted that parents of gifted children face stressors and concerns that are different from others families because of issues resulting from the unique cognitive and personality characteristics of gifted children. They also indicated that, within these families, parenting styles tend to be child-centered and parents of gifted children tend to also have high expectations for achievement. Moon and Hall pointed out that the literature indicated that although some families of gifted children have been found to generally have close relationships, others experience stress, disorganization, and dysfunction. They also highlighted difficulties some families face when a child is initially labeled gifted. The new label may cause siblings to question their abilities and their role in the family. The dynamics of sibling relationships may be affected by competition and less cooperation on the part of nonlabeled siblings. Colangelo and Assouline (2000) indicated that over time the negative effects of labeling dissipate as counselors assist families in dealing with the strain by communicating openly about the gifted label. They also noted that families alerted to the possible changes in sibling dynamics are more likely to adjust to this situation.

In the literature on the family's role in talent development, Subotnik and Olszewski-Kubilius (1997) discussed an important issue that influences friendships for gifted students. They maintained that parents model their values and the personality dispositions that are essential to talent development such as taking risks, coping with setbacks and failures, and locating support systems. They indicated that parents support their children by helping their talented sons and daughters build social networks that provide them emotional support as they develop their special abilities. Social networks consist of the interconnected individuals within a young person's life. Olszewski-Kubilius (2002a) explained the significance of these relationships in the talent development process:

> Size, memberships, and the degree of interconnectedness among members affect the extent to which social networks are psychologically and physically supportive of an individual. The social world of the child begins with the family, but over time, as higher levels of talent development are achieved, it expands to include teachers, coaches, mentors, and a wider scope of peers. Participation in special activities, such as competitions or afterschool and summer programs, can augment and populate social networks with peers who provide emotional support for achievement in the talent domain. Friends and companions who are involved in the talent field can be essential to sustaining commitment during critical times. (p. 206)

Friendships in the Social and Emotional Lives of Gifted Children and Adolescents

Early Research: Terman and Hollingworth

I have situated the issues of childhood and adolescent friendships in psychological literature. The discussion that follows focuses on literature that examines friendship issues specific to gifted young people. No discussion of the social relationships in the lives of gifted children would be complete without an introduction to the pioneering work of Lewis Terman and Leta Hollingworth. In the 19th and early 20th centuries, the belief was that brilliant children were doomed to lives of social isolation and alienation (Silverman, 1992). Lewis Terman and his colleagues worked diligently to counter this myth. In his initial landmark longitudinal study of 1,528 children above 140 IQ, Terman (1925) analyzed the subjects' family composition, early development and physical health, special talents and abilities, educational history, reading interests, hobbies, and personality traits. From his initial examination, he established that gifted children were above average in many respects, including emotional stability, social adjustment, and moral development. For many years, Terman's ground-breaking work remained unquestioned and helped to establish the belief that gifted young people were without problems.

It is important to bear in mind that within Terman's (1925) report were data on children of IQs greater than 170. In his follow-up studies, Terman reported that teachers and parents described these highly gifted students as solitary or "poor mixers." Terman indicated that this did not mean that these young people were disliked or even unappreciated by their classmates. Several of these young people had even been elected as class officers. Terman maintained that the gifted students with IQs of 170–180 were not socially rejected—they were loners by personal preference (Gross, 2004).

Concerns about Terman's (1925) work were reported by critics related to methodological problems in the selection of his subjects. Critics called attention to a lack of ethnic and economic diversity in the sample. Moreover, a substantial number of the students had been academically accelerated. Terman's subjects were, in other words, a group of intellectually gifted students fortunate enough to be identified by their schools. The generally positive academic and social adjustment reported for these children may not have been characteristic of children of similar ability levels whose talents were not spotted by their teachers and selected for the study (Gross, 2004). Regardless of the flaws in research methods, Lewis Terman and his colleagues put to rest many stereotypes of gifted children as physically stunted, socially awkward, and emotionally unstable. In doing so, Terman left us with the notion of the gifted child being happy, healthy, popular, and destined to accomplish great things in life.

During this same time period, Leta Hollingworth (1926, 1942) contributed significantly to our understanding of the social and emotional development of gifted children, as she was the first psychologist to systematically examine peer relationships of children at differing ranges of intellectual giftedness. Hollingworth's pioneering scholarship on gifted children was that of an educator who conducted research in the naturalistic settings of public school classrooms. In 1922, she designed and carried out two special advocacy opportunity classes at New York City's Public School 165: one for students with IQs of 150 and above and the second for children with IQs ranging between 134 and 154. In 1936, Public School 500, the Speyer School, opened with classes for intellectually gifted children. Hollingworth designed the Speyer curriculum with the intention of providing the children with academically and psychologically appropriate learning experiences while also addressing the students' social, emotional, and ethical development (Passow, 1990). A woman ahead of her times, with her training as a clinical psychologist, she developed innovative case study methodology to assist her in systemizing her daily classroom observations. Through her work as a clinician, researcher, and teacher, she was able to enter the world of gifted children and learn from them.

Hollingworth was intrigued by the differences she discovered in the cognitive and affective development of moderately and highly gifted children. She defined the IQ range of 125–155 as "socially optimal intelligence" (Hollingworth, 1926). She indicated that children within this range were well-adjusted, self-confident, outgoing young people who easily found and maintained friendships of age peers. She noted, however, that above the 160 IQ level the difference between the exceptionally gifted children and their age peers was so drastic that it led to problems of social isolation. The findings of Terman and Hollingworth regarding highly gifted children were congruent.

In examining the legacy of Leta Hollingworth, Silverman (1990) conducted a comprehensive review of the special problems facing gifted children that Hollingworth observed and wrote about in her work with the children in her classroom. Silverman (1990) reported that Hollingworth collectively addressed the following 11 specific concerns:

- finding enough hard and interesting work at school,
- adjusting to classmates,
- being able to play with other children,
- not becoming hermits,
- developing leadership abilities,
- not becoming negativistic toward authority,
- learning to "suffer fools gladly,"
- avoiding the formation of habits of extreme chicanery,
- conforming to rules and expectations,
- understanding their origin and destiny from an early age, and
- dealing with special problems of being a gifted girl (p. 172).

It is interesting to note that most of Hollingworth's concerns are closely related to issues of developing healthy social relationships and friendships. Within her classroom, she identified eight highly gifted children with IQs above 180 and consistently found that these children required additional individualization in their instruction and counseling. The difficulties that the highly gifted Speyer School children faced in forming friendships stemmed from the lack of other children who were like-minded. The more intelligent the child, regardless of age, the less often he or she was able to find a true companion. Many of the highly gifted children with IQs of 180 or above had developed their personal habits of solitary play. She noted that they were not unfriendly, they simply did not share the same interests as other children. Moreover, she found that these children displayed rather unconventional interests in play whereas the children in the 130–145 range tended to share the interests of other children. She noted that the moderately gifted children often gravitated to older children socially. They sought their intellectual peers, other children with whom they could share their deeper levels of thinking and be respected and valued for it. When they discovered the right connections with others like them, social adjustment naturally fell into place. Rather than chronological age peers, they simply needed to be with mental age peers (Silverman, 1990).

With the highly gifted population, Hollingworth saw that they tended to be more socially isolated. They enjoyed entertaining themselves by constructing imaginary communities, entertaining imaginary companions, and immersing themselves in private design and construction activities. They also absorbed themselves in reading, which further isolated them. Adding to the problems of this highly gifted group was the fact that many of them were only children or from families with siblings who were much older or younger. Coming from such families, they had little social experience at home (Silverman, 1990).

Silverman (1990) called attention to Hollingworth's notion of teaching gifted children to "suffer fools gladly." Rather than offend people who might interpret her message negatively with an emphasis on "fools," she wanted the children to understand her emphasis was on "gladly." Hollingworth believed that teachers needed to help gifted children by teaching them tolerance and how to handle the apparent foolishness of others with patience and kindness: "The highly intelligent must learn to suffer fools gladly—not sneeringly, not angrily, not despairingly, not weepingly—but gladly, if personal development is to proceed successfully in the world as it is" (Hollingworth, 1939, p. 586). She saw this as an important component of affective education for intelligent young people.

Hollingworth found that facilitating a discussion in a classroom with a group of highly intelligent children was challenging. She found that her students often had trouble remaining silent when they had ideas they wanted to share, with the result being a classroom of children all talking at once. She saw that she needed to train them in listening respectfully and speaking with some semblance of order. With time and practice, the children gradually learned self-control in social situations. Moreover, she noted another characteristic within this population was an argumentative quality. They demanded that others have their facts straight and insisted on precision in all of their mental activity. She found that they enjoyed finding the loopholes in other children's statements or arguments. Discovering this, she included in the Speyer School curriculum training in forensics, logic and the psychology of thinking, debate, and etiquette and the art of polite disagreement (Silverman, 1990).

Although some may have been concerned that a special program for highly gifted children was elitist, Hollingworth reported that the Speyer School helped to decrease elitist attitudes among children. These children who, for so long had been accustomed to being at the very top of their classes without effort, learned humility in coming to the Speyer program. Arrogance disappeared when they discovered other children were just as smart as they were. Ironically, Hollingworth reported that several parents had more difficulty accepting the fact that their child was no longer at the top of the class (Silverman, 1990). Overall, Hollingworth emphasized that when highly gifted children who were not accepted socially by their age peers were removed from an inappropriate grade placement and permitted to work and play with their intellectual peers, their loneliness and social isolation disappeared and the children were seen as valued classmates and friends (Gross, 2004).

More Recent Research

Since the work of Terman and Hollingworth, research has consistently confirmed earlier findings. Studies of elementary aged gifted students conducted during the Sputnik era compared social adjustment of moderately gifted students to students with extremely high IQs and found that social acceptance was a greater challenge for highly gifted students who were not radically accelerated. Gallagher (1958) compared the friendship patterns of gifted children with IQs above 165 to those below, and noted that the highly gifted had more problems of social acceptance than did children scoring between 150 and 164. DeHaan and Havinghurst (1961) conducted a similar study and consistently concluded that the moderately gifted students were intelligent enough to overcome minor social problems that most children experience, and achieved good social adjustment because they were not different enough to have the same problems encountered by the more highly gifted.

An important contribution to the research on highly gifted students and friendships was reported by Paul Janos (1983). In a comparison of highly gifted students with IQs above 164, and moderately gifted students, he reported that the highly gifted children were socially isolated from their age peers, had more problems with social development, and appeared to lack motivation to develop their talents. Janos concluded that the social isolation was not related to clinical emotional disturbance, but instead caused by the lack of a suitable peer group with whom highly gifted children could relate. Janos, Marwood, and Robinson (1985) later conducted a study in which they compared the responses of very high IQ and moderately high IQ children and their parents on a set of questions concerning friendships. Both boys and girls preferred same-sex friendships. More of the high IQ students reported that their friends were older, they did not have enough friends, and that being highly intelligent made it more challenging to develop friendships.

In more recent studies, when gifted children were compared with average students, the overall picture is favorable. Robinson and Noble (1991) conducted a comprehensive review of studies incorporating assessments of social and emotional adjustment of preadolescent gifted children and reported:

> as a group, gifted children were seen as trustworthy, honest, socially competent, assured and comfortable with self, courteous, cooperative, stable, and humorous, while they were also seen as showing diminished tendencies to boast, to engage in delinquent activity, to aggress or withdraw, to be domineering, and so on. (p. 62)

In addition, Field and her colleagues (1998) conducted a study to examine differences between the self-perceptions of gifted and nongifted high school freshmen and indicated that the gifted students reported feeling the same as or better than their peers about the academic and social skills. The gifted students saw themselves as enjoying more intimacy in their friendships and more confident in risk-taking.

Longitudinal Research by Miraca Gross

The work of Miraca Gross (1992, 1993, 2002b, 2004) and her colleagues (Gross & van Vliet, 2005) have added a great deal to our understanding of friendships in gifted children. Gross examined the long-term effects of acceleration and found significant social and emotional benefits. She conducted a longitudinal study of 60 Australian children with an IQ of 160 or higher who were radically accelerated and compared them to those who were not. Of the 17 participants in her study who were radically accelerated, she found no evidence of any social or emotional harm or damage. Moreover, the children who were retained with their age peers "experienced significant and lasting difficulties in forming or maintaining friendships" (Gross & van Vliet, 2005, p. 159), demonstrating that failure to accelerate gifted students was associated with adjustment problems. Gross (2004) explained:

> Where the gifted child's gravitation towards intellectual peers in older age groups is not facilitated by the school, or where it is actively thwarted through the school['s] insistence that the child remain full time with chronological peers, there is a strong tendency for exceptionally gifted children to become social isolates, preferring the intellectual stimulation of their own thoughts and play to the tedium imposed by continual interaction with children whose intellectual and social development, ideas, interests and enthusiasms are still at a level which they themselves outgrew several years previously. (p. 134)

Expanding upon her longitudinal research, Gross also examined friendships with highly gifted children. She conducted a study with 700 children, aged 5–12, to investigate whether children's conceptions of, and expectations of, friendships are influenced by chronological age or mental age. Through a standardized questionnaire, she surveyed conceptions of friendship held by three groups: children of average intellectual ability, moderately gifted children, and exceptionally gifted children. Her findings indicated that children's views of friendship undergo a developmental hierarchy of age-related stages, with expectations of friendship and beliefs about friendship becoming more sophisticated and complex as children mature. Gross (2004) delineated five specific linear stages described below:

- *Play partner*—In the earliest stage, the friend is seen as someone who engages in play and permits other children to use or borrow playthings.
- *People to chat to*—In this stage, the sharing of interests becomes an important component of the friendship.
- *Help and encouragement*—A friend is now seen as someone who offers help, support, and encouragement. At this stage, the benefits of friendship are seen as flowing in one direction. The child does not see support being reciprocal.
- *Intimacy/empathy*—The need and obligation to offer support and encouragement is now seen as flowing in two directions: Giving

and receiving affection becomes important and emotional sharing and bonding occurs.

🕊 *The sure shelter*—Friendship is seen as a deep and lasting relationship of trust, loyalty, and unconditional acceptance (p. 136).

The essence of "the sure shelter" was captured by Gross (2004) in an interview with an exceptionally gifted 12-year-old boy who poignantly described what he saw in a real friend:

> A real friend is a place you go when you need to take off the masks. You can say what you want to your friend because you know that your friend will really listen and even if he doesn't like what you say, he will still like you. You can take off your camouflage with a real friend and still feel safe. (p. 136)

In addition to highlighting the developmental stage of children's conceptions of friendship, the study found that what children look for in a friend is driven not so much by chronological age as by mental age. Gross (2002a) found a strong positive relationship between the intellectual ability of children and their views on friendship. The more intellectually gifted children were further advanced in their conception of friendship stages than the children of average ability. Gifted children were in search of developing friendships involving trusting relationships and emotional bonding when their age peers of average ability were looking for play partners. Gross (2002a) also found that children with IQs higher than 160 began their search for "the sure shelter"—friendships involving complete trust and honesty—4 or 5 years earlier than their age peers. The majority of the exceptionally gifted children aged 6 and 7 presented conceptions of friendship that did not develop in children of average ability until the age of 11 or 12. The differences in the gifted students in this study and their age peers were more pronounced in the earlier years of school than during adolescence. This supports Hollingworth's finding that loneliness and social isolation experienced by many exceptionally gifted children is most intense before the age of 10 (Gross, 2002b). During this period of schooling, gifted children are most likely going to have challenges in finding other children who have similar expectations of friendships; however, Gross (2002b) assured us that "with increasing age and changes in life circumstances, the field of friendship choices widens" (p. 23).

Gross (2004) also noted substantial gender differences. At all levels of intellectual ability, girls were significantly higher on the developmental scale of friendships than boys. She indicated that exceptionally gifted boys who went in search of intimacy associated with "the sure shelter" at an unusually early age might be at great risk of social isolation from other boys.

In summary, it remains evident that social adjustment and the ability to seek out and enjoy important relationships with other young people will depend on just how superior intellectually one child is over another. The research evidence indicates that differences exist between highly gifted students and their age peers. Children with IQs in the moderately gifted range may experience some social challenges; however, with development and maturation, these children learn social adjustment and are certainly capable of celebrating important friendships.

It is important to note that this research by Gross and her colleagues is consistent with other researchers who have examined the experiences of gifted students who have been accelerated and have found that no significant negative social or emotional consequences have been reported (Colangelo, Assouline, & Gross, 2004; Olszewski-Kubilius, 2002b; Rinn, 2008).

Insights on Friendships Gleamed From My Work With Gifted Students

With this research base as a backdrop and my years of classroom experience working with gifted students, I have come to believe that the most important way in which educators and parents can help a gifted child is to assist the child in finding one soul mate—a special friend who appreciates that child's intensity, celebrates his passionate interests, and values his sensitivity. While teaching gifted children, I was influenced by the classic work entitled *Guiding the Gifted Child*, in which Webb et al. (1982) helped me to appreciate just how important these special friendships were to gifted children. They explained, "This special friend provides a haven where the child's uniqueness is appreciated, a haven which helps the child tolerate the pressures, slights, and insults he may receive from others" (Webb et al., 1982, p. 150). They elaborated, "The conversations with this special friend allow the child to develop a different perspective on the situations with which he will be confronted, to give and receive affection, and to receive validation of his own worth" (Webb et al., 1982, p. 150). When considering what is important in friendship formation for gifted young people, educators, counselors, and parents need to realize that bringing together intelligent children who share the same interests will enable them to develop relationships with others who appreciate their passions.

In Chapter 1, I introduced my readers to Michael Nimchek, a student who had developed a fascination for the life of Tchaikovsky and other famous musical composers. I met Michael during my first year as a teacher of gifted students in Torrington, CT. A second-grade boy with a serious research question on Tchaikovsky! Needless to say, there were not too many other elementary students in this working-class industrial community who shared a fascination for musical composers. However, Michael also had phenomenal ability in mathematics. He arrived in kindergarten multiplying double-digit figures in his head. As a result, he was accelerated in mathematics and enjoyed friendships with older students in his math classes as well as members of the school's competitive Math Olympiad team. Michael's parents also worked hard to get him involved in a number of different afterschool activities to meet other students.

What made a significant difference for Michael was his involvement in the resource room enrichment program where he connected with others who were passionate about their research topics. One of Michael's best friends in second grade was another gifted student named Derrick Burritt, a young man with a fascination for plantar warts. Although the young musician and the wart aficionado did not share interests in a common topic, they appreciated each other's intellectual abilities and the passion they maintained for learning all they could in their chosen areas. As a new teacher of the gifted, I learned from students like Michael and Derrick how important time spent with true intellectual peers was for these children. In the gifted program at East School, Michael, Derrick, and others like them found their true peers and developed solid friendships that lasted through high school. Silverman (1992) highlighted this issue:

> With true peers, gifted children can be themselves, laugh at the same jokes, play games at the same level, share the depth of their sensitivity, and develop more complex values. In relationships there is more opportunity for equal give and take. And through interaction with others with similar capabilities they quickly learn that they cannot be the best at everything or always have their own way. Boys and girls alike are happier and better adjusted when they have opportunities to relate to other gifted children. (p. 308)

From these two young boys I also learned that some gifted children like to have different types of friends. Michael had friends in musical groups, while Derrick found friends on soccer teams. Both boys enjoyed important friendships through Cub Scouts. My experiences with Michael and Derrick are similar to those of Annette Sheely, a counselor at the Gifted

Development Center in Denver, CO. Sheely (1998) described a young man who had established this approach to appreciating a variety of friendships:

> Ten-year-old Ben has what he calls "football friends" and "debate friends." His football friends are boys his age, about his size, in his neighborhood, with whom he can play all the rough-and-tumble sports and games he loves. But he doesn't expect these boys to provide everything he needs in his friends, and he satisfies his intellectual needs with friends of all sizes and ages. He can debate with these others who are, as he describes them, "people who stretch his mind." (p. 6)

Insights on Friendships From My Research and Work With Graduate Students

Following my career in K–12 gifted education programs, I conducted a doctoral dissertation study that examined a population of gifted male teenagers in an urban high school (Hébert, 1993). This research involved examining the factors that influenced achievement and underachievement in the lives of the 12 participants. While conducting my research, I soon discovered that many gifted young men who had achieved academically in this particular setting were involved in the high school's swim team. As I interviewed and observed the gifted achieving young men in my study, I saw that several of them were swimmers for a man named Coach Brogan. As I noted in Chapter 4, for many intelligent young men in this high school the swim team was the focal point of their high school experience and the relationship with Coach Brogan was something that they valued.

Throughout my conversations with Vaughn and Lucio, two participants in my study, and many of their friends on the team, there were constant references made to a "family" down by the high school's swimming pool. The friendships that were formed amongst the athletes on this team were very close. The swimmers reported that their best friends were all members of the team and they claimed they were inseparable. Along with practicing every day after school, they were seen hanging out by the pool during their study hall periods and even volunteering to help physically handicapped students in the high school by providing them with swimming lessons. They reported that their social lives centered on parties at each others' homes as well as taking in local nightclubs where grunge music was popular. The supportive relationships with an inspirational coach as well as with each other had significant influences on these gifted young men motivationally, academically, and emotionally (Hébert, 1995a). My findings within the swim team were substantiated by many students in this high school. The close friendships seen within this group of athletes were something that most of the students at South Central High School were aware of. Faculty members also acknowledged the special quality of these important relationships. Coach Brogan had created a context within this urban high school where gifted teenagers could be comfortable developing such supportive relationships (see Chapter 4 for further discussion of the contextual influences). When I asked Coach Brogan how others in the building perceived the team, he seemed pleased to highlight just how secure these gifted young men were with themselves and their friends on the team:

> Other teams regard our kids as a bit weird. I think at lot of it is jealousy. We are the only ones who have maintained a winning record all these years, and the kids who swim truly become uninhibited. For instance, they are very, very secure as high school kids go, about their own sexuality. They are not afraid to touch each other. They are not afraid to hug each other, and I think other kids who are not as secure look at this as strange. The swimmers are just not concerned about that sort of thing. They know who they are. (Hébert, 1993, p. 219)

One of my graduate students at the University of Georgia conducted her master's thesis research on bibliotherapy and the reading interests of gifted high school females. As part of her research, Elizabeth Romey (2000) conducted interviews with gifted young women in a rural school district in southern Alabama. One of the major findings in this research was that these young women developed new friendships as a result of their connection through literature. A theme of a common bond through shared reading interests was most clearly represented in the tight friendship shared by Louisa, Mara, and Eponine, three young women who were all new to their school, having moved from the North. Louisa described this important friendship that evolved from a love of reading:

> In the gifted program there's a group of us who are all new here, from the North, and we all read the books together, like a group. Mostly *Les Mis*, *Phantom*, and *Star of the Guardians*. Those are the main ones that we talk about. We met in the gifted class, and we started hanging out. It's weird, outside of the gifted class, we're so different, we don't hang out with the same people. In [the gifted

class] and on weekends, when we get together, though, we just click. . . . There's actually a card game, *Star of the Guardians* . . . and we play it, or we just talk, and like sing songs from *Les Mis* or *Phantom* . . . and we'll talk about stuff, what we see in the characters. . . . Having this group has really helped me settle in here. . . . We like the same things, the books, the music, and we actually talk about that stuff. (Romey, 2000, pp. 63–64)

In my work with doctoral students, I am fortunate to have the opportunity to supervise students in their internship experiences in gifted education. Matthew McBee, one of my former students, served as an instructor in the summer Duke University Talent Identification Program (TIP) working with highly able middle school students. I asked Matt to maintain a reflective journal throughout his work with TIP. One of the earliest entries in his journal describes his early impressions of the other highly accomplished graduate students working as instructors or counselors in the summer program. Matt's journal reflections on this group provide evidence of the importance of finding true intellectual peers:

My general observation of the other instructors in this program is that, for the most part, they are ridiculously brilliant. These people are highly literate, thoughtful, and observant. They catch obscure references to such things as postmodernism, the New Deal, deconstruction, the 70's sci-fi movie *Logan's Run* (including the scene with the crazy guy who quotes T. S. Eliot), Supreme Court cases, including who dissented and why, Buddhist philosophy and mythology. It's amazing! Often someone will say something and two or three of us will respond with the same reference at the same time, which is really odd considering that we've just known each other for a few days. For instance, when we watched *Oh Brother, Where Art Thou?* there were only two people in the room who had not read *The Odyssey*. They make me realize that my knowledge and understanding of things is woefully inadequate and I consider this a good thing. Things that I thought only I knew or cared about, they know, and usually better than I do. I fit in though. This place feels like home.

Danny Hammond, another former graduate student, worked as a resident's assistant in the Georgia Governor's Honors Program (GHP). In this program, some of the most talented high school students in the state spend

6 weeks in the summer in a university setting immersed in intellectually challenging and enriching courses. Danny's reflective journal describing his work with gifted high school males also provides evidence of the importance of gifted students needing time to spend with their intellectual peers and the need to develop important relationships and friendships. Danny reflected on the first week's discussion session with the young men he supervised in the dormitory that summer:

> I surveyed the guys tonight at the hall meeting, curious about what their favorite part of GHP has been, what they dislike so far, and if anything has been particularly surprising. The answers that I got were thoughtful. The biggest dislike, not surprisingly, was the cafeteria food, with waking up early and the summer heat coming in second and third. As for their favorites, there was definitely a variety. Dylan and Josh, my two chemistry majors, said that they really enjoyed being around an entire population of people who they felt were "on their level." They really enjoyed being able to have intellectual debates without having to worry about being teased, ridiculed, or embarrassed. Jon, one of my Jazz majors, kiddingly said, "the girls," then reconsidered and said, "no, seriously, the girls. I can actually talk to the girls here and not have to worry about being the nerd or the introvert guy. I really like that." I thought this was also a very telling statement about the magic of this program. Many of the kids will have their first loves this summer, and hopefully it's something from which they can learn a great deal before they return home. Finally, when I asked the guys about the most surprising thing that they had experienced this first week, I got a couple of answers which I think are really indicative of the culture here. Bryan, a social science major, said that things were not nearly as competitive as he thought they might be. He said that being surrounded by some of the best students in Georgia, he feared that people might be unfriendly or looking to get to the top. This wasn't the case at all. Bryan found that he enjoyed working with students from around the state who shared a similar passion for learning, especially in his area of interest. David, a young African American male, spoke of how surprised he was that everyone was getting along without any kind of reservation. He said there was some anxiety at the very beginning as far as kids from different races hanging out, but it had melted away almost immediately as the kids spent time in and out of class together.

The experiences Matt and Danny described in the summer enrichment programs for gifted students are consistent with the gifted education literature. Researchers have found that gifted students enrolled in special programs experience multiple benefits including enhanced self-esteem because of the opportunities these special classes provide for social interaction with true intellectual peers (Coleman & Fults, 1982; Feldhusen, Sayler, Nielsen, & Kolloff, 1990). The positive outcomes of summer programs for the gifted have been well documented (Kolloff & Moore, 1989; Olszewski-Kubilius, 1989, 2003; Olszewski-Kubilius & Limburg-Weber, 1999) and have highlighted the significance of the friendships that evolve as an added benefit from such programs. Sheely (1998) poignantly described the significance of these summer program relationships:

> For some of these children and teenagers, attending one of these programs may be the first time they'll meet a peer who shares their interests, sees the world in a similar way or who shares their emotional intensity. Even if their future relationship may need to be conducted cross-county via e-mail or letters or be limited to summer visits, they no longer feel like aliens, knowing there are friends out there who understand them. For some gifted children, this makes all the difference in the world. (p. 7)

Sheely's (1998) thoughts on the importance of summer program relationships for gifted adolescents is reinforced by the experiences of Kate Brown and Sarah Greer, two successful medical doctors. These two women met each other as seventh graders involved in the Summer Program for Verbally and Mathematically Precocious Youth (VAMPY) at Western Kentucky University in Bowling Green, KY. The friendship formed during the 3-week summer enrichment experience continued for three consecutive summers as they returned to VAMPY and it continues today. Brown and Greer (2007) reported on the significance of their lifelong friendship that was born through the opportunity to spend time with intellectual peers who were also age peers. Sarah shared her thoughts on this important friendship:

> So 16 years after we met at VAMPY, we are both dermatology residents. . . . In junior high, we shared VAMPY, now we commiserate over learning skin pathology and studying for our board exams. No matter what is going on in my life, I can always talk to Kate about it, because chances are good she has gone or is going

through the same thing. When you have so many things in common, you would expect there might be a greater chance for competition, but instead, we have always encouraged each other. I know that in addition to my family, Kate is always behind me. Plus she makes me laugh. That would sum up our friendship: "Laughing together for 15 years." (Brown & Greer, 2007, p. 3)

Kate had this to offer:

Thinking about it now, I'm sure we influenced each other more than we realized to go into medicine and consider our specialty choices. But we've supported each other through every phase of growing up, it seems, from prom dresses to boyfriends, to picking colleges, and deciding what kinds of women we want to be. (Brown & Greer, 2007, p. 2)

Insights on Friendships From Research Studies on Gifted University Students

As I noted in Chapters 3 and 4, I had the opportunity to conduct a research study with Matthew McBee (Hébert & McBee, 2007) in which we examined the experiences of gifted college students involved in a university honors program at a midsize technological university in the Southeast. In conducting this study, we discovered that the friendships that resulted from this honors program remained solidified for many years following their college graduations. Alumni of the program continue to come together annually during the winter holidays for reunions and maintain correspondence with each other through a computer listserv.

Dawn, a participant in this study, shared her experiences of searching for friends in her new college environment. When she arrived at the university, she went in search of a group of new friends who would appreciate her creativity, her intellectualism, and her passion for learning. She described walking down the hall in her dormitory noticing the difference between how she decorated the door of her room and what other students chose to put on their doors: "I had *Far Side* cartoons and quotes and pictures. I was walking down the hall seeing all of these frilly sorority banners and the fru-fru girly stuff, and I thought: 'Where are the people who are going to put *Far Side* cartoons on their door?'" (Hébert & McBee, 2007, p. 144). Wondering how she might connect with other students with similar interests, Dawn explained, "I was looking for a place to belong, looking for a social network where people were going to be like me somehow" (p. 144). Soon she became president of the science fiction club on campus, which had a membership roster of seven students. On the day that campus organizations recruited new members, Dawn set up a table in the student union where she displayed science fiction books and installed a video monitor to play science fiction movies. Within a short amount of time, she had a roster of 75 names and through this newly energized club she became connected to Dr. Holt, the advisor to the science fiction club and the director the university's honors program. Enrolling in Dr. Holt's literature class, she then became connected to a group of students in the honors program. It was there that Dawn found her intellectual peers and established her social network. She celebrated when she made the connection with the group, describing the students as "the kind of people I had been looking for all of my student life—a group of people who loved what they were doing and weren't afraid to openly love it, and to challenge each other" (Hébert & McBee, 2007, p. 144). She explained that within the program she discovered others like herself who were intellectually alive:

> There were all kinds of geeks there and I loved hanging out with them all because what makes a geek a geek? Total dedication and love for what you're doing, in whatever way it expresses itself. Whether it's expressed in pocket protectors, or Birkenstocks or long flowing skirts. Geeks of all trades! I love being around people who are passionate about what they do. I needed to be around people who loved it, because it felt good. It felt safe. (Hébert & McBee, 2007, p. 144)

Dawn went on to describe the honors program as a safe environment where she was comfortable being herself amongst her friends who influenced her motivation and achievement:

> One of the most powerful components of the Honors Program was the safe environment it offered. It was an environment where, to use the Army slogan, you can be all that you can be. I should say, where you can be all that you have the potential to become. It was a place where you could work on that, where you could experiment, where you could test, where you could excel and not be afraid to excel. You were around people who were going to challenge you to excel, and could provide models for what it looks like to excel and the kind of dedication it takes to excel. It was a place where

you could be exposed to people who are 10 steps down the developmental pathway ahead of you, and where you could soak up by osmosis without even realizing that you were doing that. (Interview Transcript, February 7, 2005)

Dawn's experiences in her university years were consistent with what Oswald and Clark (2003) reported regarding the importance of a strong supportive network of friends in transitioning to collegiate life. With her story in mind, I pursued another research study with a group of gifted collegians—high-achieving gifted young men involved in a Greek fraternity (Hébert, 2006; see Chapter 4 for more information). The five gifted university males in the study had enjoyed academic success throughout their K–12 school years. With reputations as student-athletes, they were recruited to the Alpha Tau Iota fraternity as intelligent young men who could become significant contributors. As brothers in ATI, they became associated with older gifted males in the fraternity who were establishing themselves as student leaders. Following the advice of older fraternity brothers, they became involved in a multitude of extracurricular activities and programs associated with the fraternity and other campus groups involved in philanthropic campaigns, campus leadership, and student government. These experiences served as outlets for talent development. Through the fraternity their talents were nurtured within a culture of intelligent, well-rounded young men who respected academic achievement and continued self-improvement in multiple ways.

The following are representative quotes from interviews with the participants that provide evidence of the many benefits of the high-quality relationships celebrated by the gifted young men (Hébert, 2006). Woven throughout their comments are indications of the significance of these important friendships:

When we look for guys in rush, we look for the three a's – academics, athletics, activities. We're looking for well roundedness. You take that kind of raw potential coming out of high school and you're placed among a bunch of guys with those attributes and it's amazing how much you're able to grow in your talents. (p. 34)

There was a brother from Eastport who was really an influential person in my making a decision to pledge ATI. His name is Mike Johnson. He's been a great friend. He's in law school now, one of those awesome guys you really respect when you come here as a freshman. I thought of him as the kind of person I wanted to become—a good student, a very smart guy, very athletic, a gentleman, someone who didn't forget church when he came to college, just a great guy. (p. 34)

I could see if you came to school every day and didn't have anything to go back to, like a fraternity or some campus organization, a school of over 30,000 students would become overwhelming. A fraternity makes this university so much smaller and that's important. It's a BIG university. You can make it as big as you want or you can cut it down in size by getting involved and meeting as many people as you can. I've had my closest friends in ATI, but at the same time, I've made a lot of other friends through my campus involvement and that's been important to me too. (p. 35)

ATI was not a bunch of rednecks or stereotypical partying frat boys . . . We have guys from south Georgia who hunt and fish, and we have other guys who've never held a gun in their lives. There are guys from Atlanta listening to Widespread Panic and other guys who listen to country. We have one guy who is actually a skateboarder guy! . . . What's great is that they are all good guys, well-rounded guys. I think we're the most well rounded fraternity on this campus. (p. 36)

ATI has the whole package. You've got some brilliant guys from whom you can learn so much. You've got the strong spiritual influence that you can soak up. You've got some of the greatest guys as your closest friends. (p. 36)

As I reflect on Lisa Gisselbrecht's recipe for friendship, the animated conversations between Michael Nimchek and Derrick Burritt in my classroom, and my observations of the camaraderie of the ATI fraternity brothers in college, I realize that friends are important all through life.

Lisa's poem reminds of the importance of friendship formation in childhood. From Jackie Sheid's poem entitled "My Type," we understand the importance of painful transitions in friendships, and through the scholarly literature on adolescence, we realize that friendships change significantly during this important developmental stage. We realize that families play an important role in preparing children for peer relationships. By examining research literature in gifted education, we understand how important it is for gifted young people to find soul mates as well as discover and maintain a variety of friendships. With this understanding comes the realization that educators and counselors have important work to do in helping gifted students find and keep good friends. Below I describe several strategies to support those efforts.

Strategies to Support Gifted Students in Forming and Maintaining Friendships

Encourage Students to Make Friends

Early in my teaching career, I discovered a helpful resource that enabled me to continually infuse class activities designed to encourage students. The work of Canfield and Wells (1994) entitled *100 Ways to Enhance Self-Concept in the Classroom* is one of the most worn books in my professional library. I reached for my copy any time I noticed my students needed to be reminded of their personal strengths.

Canfield and Wells (1994) offered a strategy for teachers and counselors to assist children in forming new friendships. They were inspired by the work of a Pitirim Sorokin, a Harvard University sociologist who directed the Center in Creative Altruism. Sorokin asked his Harvard students to name their worst enemies and then directed them to determine something they could do for those enemies. Sorokin discovered that in more than 75% of the situations, conducting a simple act of unselfishness for an enemy changed the enemy into a new friend. In this activity entitled "Making Friends," Canfield and Wells suggested that educators and counselors should share this information with their students before conducting the following:

- Ask students to write down in private the name of a person whom they would like to have as a friend. This person must be an individual in their lives and not a movie or rock star.
- Brainstorm with the class a variety of acts of kindness and unselfishness they might do for others that would be sincere and appreciated. Emphasize that this is not an attempt to buy a friend. It should represent the essence of friendship.
- Share with the class how you will be following up the next day and again on a regular basis to check on their progress. In follow-

up sessions, support them through the rough spots in the process, particularly the issue of what they can do for their selected friend.

ᴄᴇ Following 2 weeks of this effort, ask the students to explain what they have learned about relationships as well as about themselves.

Implement The Car Wash

Canfield and Wells (1994) described an enjoyable classroom activity they inherited from one of their college students. This activity, entitled The Car Wash consists of the teacher or counselor lining up the class or group into two parallel lines quite close together. One student is then sent through the wash, between the lines, and everyone touches the student and provides words of praise or encouragement. The pats on the back, high fives, and verbal support help to produce a "shiny new happy car" at the end of the car wash. Canfield and Wells suggest that educators run one or two students through the car wash each day rather than one class-size clean-up. This practice helps to ensure that the responses of the car washers remain fresh, personalized, and authentic. They also indicate there may be times when a group has been through an emotionally intense experience together and the teacher or counselor would want to send every member of the group through the car wash as a significant way of concluding a session. In planning to infuse this strategy in a classroom, educators need to think about the children who consider themselves unpopular. In being "scrubbed" in the car wash and bombarded by compliments from every student in the class, one could assume that these young people are bound to feel more positive about being members of this classroom community. As they return home at the end of the school day, they will have time to process through all of the delivered compliments. As a result of this ego-boosting experience, they should be more open to reaching out to their classmates for friendship.

Find Friends Through Extracurricular Activities

One of the best ways that educators, counselors, and parents can support gifted students is to help them find others like them through their interests and passions. Whether through the school or beyond its environment, involvement in extracurricular activities help young people to value their special talents and construct positive self-concepts and identities. With students who are new to the community or struggling to find friends, teachers or counselors need to brainstorm with these students all possible outlets for getting involved in their areas of interest. Have the students consider debate teams, science clubs, math leagues, youth symphony orchestras, dance schools, special summer and Saturday programs, creative writing clubs, photography clubs, theatre groups, literary groups, athletic clubs and teams, computer clubs and technology groups, art classes, political campaigns, humanitarian organizations, and social action groups. Continue brainstorming until all possibilities have been generated. The children should discuss how their talents are aligned with the objectives of the groups that may appeal to them. Have them understand that one of the best ways to find new friends is to search for others with similar interests and, through their extracurricular activities, they may be able to connect with other students who appreciate their passions.

Consider a Big Brother–Big Sister Program

Experienced teachers of gifted students who have been teaching in the same school district for a number of years may want to consider having their former students who are in high school visit their classrooms and share their experiences with growing up gifted. Teachers who have experimented with this approach have typically found that younger gifted students will listen far more attentively to what an 18-year-old has to offer them for advice than they listen to parents or teachers. These sessions may be regularly scheduled and serve as a Big Brother–Big Sister program in which gifted teenagers serve as mentors in social and emotional development. During their visits with younger students, the high school students can share their friendship experiences from elementary and middle school and provide the children with sound advice on how to find and maintain good friends. Gifted high school students should feel comfortable describing how they connected with their true friends and share stories of great times they have shared with friends. Meaningful conversations will evolve without teacher facilitation.

Following these visits from their Big Brother or Big Sister, students will probably want to continue the dialogue with their new high school mentors. In this age of technology, e-mail correspondence between the high school students and the younger children will evolve and both the younger and older students will benefit from these important friendships. In addition, teachers of middle and high school students may want to reach out to former students who are home on vacation from college, as university students may continue to serve as helpful e-mail friends.

Journal

Educators and counselors may want to infuse journaling in helping gifted students resolve friendship issues. Flack (2003) indicated that "journals are the notebooks of the mind" (p. 15) and with gifted students they can serve as places for reflecting, problem solving, and communing with one's self. Journaling with young people is a very personal experience that helps them reflect on who they really are. By articulating their thoughts and feelings in a meaningful way, students may develop self-understanding as they reflect on the important relationships in their lives (DeSalvo, 1999). Moreover, this strategy is one that teachers and counselors should consider emphasizing with gifted males. Journaling has long been associated with girls and their teenage diaries; however, Heydt (2004) indicated that a journal could serve as an important outlet for a young man to express his feelings because so many boys often struggle to find such outlets for their feelings (Pollack, 1998).

In a classroom setting, the use of dialogue journals may be most appropriate and effective in helping a gifted student come to terms with friendship issues. Dialogue journal writing is essentially the use of a journal to conduct ongoing written conversations between two individuals (Staton, 1988). In facilitating dialogue journaling, a teacher or counselor provides a child with a channel for self-expression, builds a strong sense of trust between the child, and enables the adult to provide the younger person with important information (Armstrong, 1994). Through this approach, an empathic teacher or counselor can provide guidance and emotional support with the feedback he or she offers students in responding to what gifted students share in their journals. In dialogue journals with students, a teacher or counselor can pose questions for young people to consider. Several examples of nonthreatening questions are provided below:

- How have your friendships changed over the years?
- What do you look for in a friend?
- What do you value in friendships? What do your friends value in you?
- Do you have different kinds of friends?
- What have you learned through friendships?
- How are friendships important in your life?

The reflection on self through journaling can be an effective way of expressing emotions and addressing problems with friendships. The infusion of journaling can be helpful in the classroom as well as prepare a gifted young person with a strategy that will carry over into adulthood.

Analyze Poetry and Popular Music

Our bookstores and libraries offer rich collections of children and young adult poetry that celebrates friendship. Teachers may want to explore these resources and lead discussions centered on these poems. Rich conversations regarding the content of each poem will lead to drawing parallels to the lives of the students. Below are several anthologies of poetry written for children and teenagers that offer many enjoyable and meaningful poems that address important issues of friendship.

- Grimes, N. (1994). *Meet Danitra Brown.* New York, NY: Lothrop, Lee and Shepard Books.
- Grimes, N. (1997). *It's raining laughter.* New York, NY: Dial Books for Young Readers.
- Rylant, C. (2001). *Waiting to waltz: A childhood.* Scarsdale, NY: Atheneum.
- Soto, G. (2005). *Worlds apart: Traveling with Fernie and Me.* New York, NY: Putnam.
- Woodson, J. (2003). *Locomotion.* New York, NY: G. P. Putnam's Sons.

In addition to examining poetry, teachers might have gifted students analyze the lyrics of contemporary popular music they enjoy. Students can search through their music inventories at home and share their favorite examples of songs that celebrate friendships. They may discover interesting or thought-provoking themes throughout their collections of music. Analysis of popular music is also easy to combine with poetry analysis and the following strategy described below.

Facilitate Discussions on Friendships Through Good Books and Movies

Another classroom strategy for helping gifted students establish and maintain friendships is to facilitate classroom discussions and enriched learning activities centered on high-quality literature or films. Appendix A provides a rich collection of literature, and Appendix D offers a menu of films appropriate for classroom use. Many of the books and movies suggested focus on issues pertaining to friendships with gifted students.

TABLE 5

Relationship Bank Account Deposits and Withdrawals

RBA Deposits	RBA Withdrawals
Keep promises	Break promises
Do small acts of kindness	Keep to yourself
Be loyal	Gossip and break confidences
Listen	Don't listen
Say you're sorry	Be arrogant
Set clear expectations	Set false expectations

Teachers or counselors should consider the sample lesson plans offered in Chapters 2 and 3.

Discuss Students' Relationship Bank Account

Sean Covey (1998) authored a national best-seller entitled *The 7 Habits of Highly Effective Teens*, a guide to help teenagers improve their self-image, build friendships, resist peer pressure, reach their goals, enjoy their parents, and much more. Covey engaged teens with practical strategies and infused stories offered by American teenagers to emphasize the important advice he offers adolescents. One chapter of his work focuses on establishing and maintaining a relationship bank account (RBA). To teenagers, the relationship bank account represents the amount of trust and confidence they have in each of their relationships. Covey explained:

> The RBA is very much like a checking account at a bank. You can make deposits and improve the relationship, or take withdrawals and weaken it. A strong and healthy relationship is always the result of steady deposits made over a long period. (p. 132)

Covey helps teenagers understand how they can build rich relationships in their lives one deposit at a time and provides six specific relationship deposits that he maintains are effective. He also calls attention to the fact that with every deposit, there is an opposite withdrawal that young people need to avoid making. Table 5 shares his specific suggestions.

Covey helps teenagers understand that keeping small commitments and promises to friends and family members is vital to building trust. He emphasizes that if an individual cannot keep a commitment, then he or she should let the other person know why. Sean Covey encourages teenagers to conduct small acts of kindness and generosity, and he provides some good examples of how other teens have done so either individually or in groups. He discusses how loyalty serves such an important role in maintaining a friendship and helps teenagers understand that people who are loyal keep secrets, avoid gossip, and stick up for others. Covey helps young people see that learning to apologize when friends squabble, overreact, or make stupid mistakes can quickly restore an overdrawn relationship bank account. Finally, the RBA involves maintaining trust by not sending vague messages or implying something that is not likely to happen. He helps teenagers see that building trust happens through voicing clear expectations right up front. Teachers and counselors may want to investigate Sean Covey's material and infuse it into their daily interactions with gifted students as they work with them in building rich and satisfying relationships in their lives.

Summary

The above strategies are enjoyable, easy to facilitate, and should be appreciated by gifted students. Through implementation of these strategies, educators are supporting the social and emotional development of gifted students and addressing one of the most important experiences of life—having friends. With this in mind, I conclude with *To Have a Friend*, a poem by Stephanie Lael (1995), a then-12-year-old poet from Branson, MO.

> To have a friend
> Is like having a sailboat
> That sails into the skies;
> To have a friend
> Is like having a cookie
> That never crumbles apart;
> But to be a friend
> Takes something more special,
> Something that comes from your heart. (p. 26)

For Further Thought and Discussion

- ❧ Reflect on the significant friendships in your life. How have your friendship patterns been consistent with the theory offered in developmental psychology literature?
- ❧ If you could invite Bette Midler, Betty Friedan, Mel Brooks, and Dan Greenburg to speak to a large audience of adolescents, what message would you think they would share with the students? What message would you hope they would deliver? Why?
- ❧ Consider the quote from Graham who was included in *Real Boys' Voices* by Pollack and Shuster (2000). Do you think his feelings about same-sex friendships for adolescent males are typical of most young men today? Why? Why not?
- ❧ What role do you believe siblings play in shaping peer relationships for gifted students?
- ❧ Leta Hollingworth wrote collectively about specific concerns for the social and emotional development of gifted students. Many of them were related to friendships. Do these concerns still apply to gifted youth today?
- ❧ What advice would you offer for helping a gifted student find a soul mate?
- ❧ Consider the quality of the relationships found in the TIP summer program, the Georgia Governor's Honors Program, the honors program students in the Hébert and McBee (2007) research, and the ATI fraternity. How could secondary educators design similar environments for gifted students to discover and build significant friendships?

Resources to Expand Your Thinking and Extend Your Support to Gifted Students

Abrahams, G., & Ahlbrand, S. (2002). *Boy v. girl? How gender shapes who we are, what we want, and how we get along.* Minneapolis, MN: Free Spirit.

Covey, S. (1998). *The 7 habits of highly effective teens.* New York, NY: Simon & Schuster.

Galbraith, J., & Delisle, J. (1996). *The gifted kids' survival guide: A teen handbook.* Minneapolis, MN: Free Spirit.

Keel, P. (2004). *All about me—teenage edition: The story of your life.* New York: Random House/Broadway.

Kranz, L. (1998). *Through my eyes: A journal for teens.* Flagstaff, AZ: Rising Moon.

Lorig, S., & Jacobs, J. (2005). *Chill and spill: A place to put it down and work it out.* Seattle, WA: Art With Heart Press.

CHAPTER 7

Teachers and Counselors Supporting Gifted Underachieving Students

My goals for this chapter are to:

- Introduce you to the school experiences of three prominent Americans to highlight issues related to underachievement in gifted students.
- Present literature examining the influential factors that shape underachievement.
- Acquaint you with the phenomenon of selective achievement and have you compare it to underachievement.
- Have you analyze a case study of a gifted underachieving student.
- Present strategies and methods for addressing underachievement.

If a child is to keep alive his inborn sense of wonder, he needs the companionship of at least one adult who can share in rediscovering with him the joy, excitement, and mystery of the world we live in.

—Rachel Carson

In this chapter, I offer an examination of one of the most complex issues in the field of gifted education. Understanding and appreciating the complexity of underachievement in high ability students is a significant challenge for all who work with bright young people. To begin, I explore the school experience of three prominent Americans to highlight several important issues that must be understood if teachers, counselors and parents are going to change the achievement patterns of gifted students who are not academically challenged in school.

"Making the Walk" in the South Bronx: Colin Powell

Many Americans have watched in awe as the career of Colin Powell has unfolded on the stage of American military and political life. The former Secretary of State has served his country in a number of important roles and has had a significant influence in shaping world affairs. Although Colin Powell has achieved eminence in American politics and international affairs, perhaps what endears many Americans to him are his humble beginnings in the South Bronx. The celebrated high achievements of his adult life are indeed remarkable; however, many people may be surprised to hear that young Colin Powell did not begin his journey in life with a strong achievement orientation.

As a teenager growing up in New York, Powell had the opportunity to seek admission to a number of high schools. In his autobiography, *My American Journey*, Powell (1995) described his rather lackluster academic and athletic high school record. In 1950, he entered Morris High School. His older sister had gone to the elite Walton High School. With the prompting of his parents, he attempted to get into Stuyvesant High, another prestigious school. He explained: "I still have the report card with the guidance counselor's decision: 'We advise against it.' Morris High, on the other hand, was like Robert Frost's definition of home, the place where, when you show up, they have to let you in" (Powell, 1995, p. 17).

Powell described himself as "directionless," a young man who was "not fired up by anything." He explained, "My pleasures were hanging out with the guys, 'making the walk' from Kelly Street, up 163rd Street around Southern Boulevard to Westchester Avenue, and back home" (Powell, 1995, p. 17). His Saturday morning routine with his buddies was to take in a double feature of cowboy movies at the Tiffany Theater. As an athlete, Powell did not excel. He explained, "I did well enough at Morris to win a letter for track, but after a while I found slogging cross-country through Van Cortlandt Park boring, and so I quit. I switched to the 440-yard dash, because I could get it over with faster, but I dropped out after one season" (Powell, 1995, p. 20). He elaborated: "We had a church basketball team at St. Margaret's. I was tall, fairly fast, and the coach was inclined to give me a chance. I spent most of my time riding the bench, so I quit the team, to the relief of the coach" (Powell, 1995, p. 20).

The directionless teenager understood that his parents were concerned: "My inability to stick to anything became a source of concern to my parents, unspoken, but I knew it was there" (Powell, 1995, p. 20). During that period in his life, Colin's older sister continued to set the Powell standard in education. She had been an honor student all through high school and excelled at Buffalo State University. This high standard within the family shaped young Colin's experience: "in spite of my final high school average of 78.3, I started to look at colleges because of my sister's example and because my parents expected it of me" (Powell, 1995, p. 21).

Colin Powell's pattern of academic underachievement continued into his college experience. He attended City College of New York (CCNY), where during his freshman year he became intrigued with a group he noticed upon arrival—young men on campus in military uniforms. Shortly after he inquired about the Reserve Officers Training Corps (ROTC), he enrolled. This event had a lasting effect on the college student without goals and direction. He described the significance of that day in his life: "As soon as I got home, I put the uniform on and looked in the mirror. I liked what I saw. At this point, not a single Kelly Street friend of mine was going to college. I was seventeen. I felt cut off and lonely" (Powell, 1995, p. 26). He explained further: "The uniform gave me a sense of belonging, and something I had never experienced all the while I was growing up; I felt distinctive" (Powell, 1995, p. 26).

Academically at CCNY, Powell (1995) noted that he "stumbled through math, fumbled through physics, and did reasonably well in, and enjoyed, geology" (p. 26). However, he explained that all he ever really looked forward to was ROTC. With his success with the military group on campus, he was courted by a campus military society known as the Pershing Rifles (PRs). It was within this group that he felt at home. Powell (1995) reflected, "My experience in high school, on the basketball and track teams, and briefly in Boy Scouting had never produced a sense of belonging or many permanent friendships. The Pershing Rifles did. For the first time in my life I was a member of a brotherhood" (p. 28). Moreover, Powell discovered within that group a way of life that was right for him: "The discipline, the structure, the camaraderie, the sense of belonging were what I craved. I became a leader almost immediately" (Powell, 1995, p. 28). The selflessness within the ranks of the young men reminded him of the caring atmosphere within his family. He explained, "Race, color, background, income meant nothing. The PRs would go the limit for each other and for the group. If this was what soldiering was all about, then maybe I wanted to be a soldier" (p. 28). The teenager from the Bronx determined that military life would provide him the direction he needed. As a student at CCNY Powell continued doing just enough to get by academically, with his mediocre grade point average salvaged by straight A's in ROTC. In his autobiography he humbly admitted that he was no scholar: "I have joked over the years that the CCNY faculty handed me a diploma, uttering a sigh of relief, and were happy to pass me along to the military" (Powell, 1995, p. 37).

Stuck Out in the Middle of Virginia: Christine Todd Whitman

In a world far removed from the city streets of New York, Christine Todd Whitman experienced her adolescence in a culture of affluence and power. The young woman who would capture the nation's attention when she was elected the first female governor of New Jersey and later appointed by President George Bush as the director of the Environmental Protection Agency struggled with her direction as a student in school. Christine Todd was raised in an affluent family and trained in politics by her parents and grandparents, who were powerful Republican fundraisers and party leaders. Beard (1996) described the difficult adolescent years of this young woman in *Growing Up Republican: Christie Whitman: The Politics of Character.*

As the daughter of prominent Republican party leaders, she was educated in private schools and found herself removed from the family she needed. A young tomboy who lived in the shadow of her academically overpowering older brother, Christine found her passion in horseback riding. In 1960, she graduated from the eighth grade at the Far Hills Country Day School, where her mother Eleanor was chairman of the Board of Trustees. She received only a conditional diploma because she had not passed Latin.

From there she attended the Foxcroft School, a girl's boarding school in Middleburg, VA. Students in that setting either loved or hated Foxcroft. Beard (1996) described the culture of the school:

> Many started by hating it, then they came to love it—some would say the way prisoners learn to love their captors. . . . The routine, the discipline, and the camaraderie of this combination convent and military school could be reassuring. (p. 80)

In such a sheltered and structured environment, "a girl could stretch out her childhood a little longer, and in some ways, keep adolescence at bay. But Christie was miserable from the first, and stayed miserable" (Beard, 1996, p. 80). Whitman described herself as lacking confidence and compensating by being aggressive except when it came to academics. She explained, "If I didn't think I was going to do well, I turned off, because then my excuse was that I hadn't tried. I could have done better if I had applied myself" (Beard, 1996, p. 81).

As a teenager, Christine Todd believed that the convent-like environment was not right for her. She longed to be home with her parents and the world of politics. Instead, she found herself required to attend frivolous parties in the home of the school's headmistress. She reflected, "Here it was a presidential election year and I was stuck out in the middle of Virginia with people who didn't even care that we were sending rockets to the moon" (Beard, 1996, p. 82). Surrounded by young women with no interest in current affairs and removed from politics, Christine was more frustrated that she could not become involved in what really mattered to her.

After a miserable year at Foxcroft, with incomplete grades for her freshman year, she begged her parents to allow her to leave Foxcroft. The Todds faced a dilemma, because only a school that understood that her scholastic problems were the result of an unfortunate academic mismatch, rather than lack of ability or application, would accept her. The headmistress of The Chapin School, a girl's day school in Manhattan, which Christine's mother had attended, was willing to give Christie a chance. She agreed to admit Christie as a sophomore, and if she earned a C+ average, Chapin would also grant her credit for her freshman year. Christie was delighted because she could spend the weekends at home in New Jersey, where she could do the two things she loved most: ride her horse and "politick" with her mother as they conducted door-to-door canvassing together.

Her years at Chapin remained academically lackluster. By her senior year, her grade point average and College Board scores were good enough to get her into Wheaton, then an all-women's college near Boston. Considered less academically rigorous than the "Seven Sisters"—Barnard, Bryn Mawr, Mt. Holyoke, Radcliffe, Smith, Vassar, and Wellesley (Beard, 1996), Wheaton students were perceived as hard-working students rather than brilliant young women. Whitman's biographer summarized her high school years: "Christie was smart, but she was a late bloomer; it wasn't really until college that she was ready to learn" (Beard, 1996, p. 93).

A Young Man Without Direction: Tom Brokaw

While Christine Todd Whitman was struggling academically as an adolescent, another gifted teenager in South Dakota was also not performing up to his potential. The renowned television journalist Tom Brokaw (2002) reported his experiences as a student in his autobiography, *A Long Way From Home: Growing up in the American Heartland*. Through his autobiography, we learn that Brokaw also underwent a period of serious academic floundering.

By the second semester of his senior year in high school, Brokaw was experiencing great success in school. An alumnus of Harvard University was encouraging him to apply for admission. He was earning medals and ribbons as a member of the high school forensics club. The scholar athlete was a starting guard on the varsity basketball team and president of the student council. He had been elected governor of Boys State the preceding spring. The actual governor of South Dakota, Joe Foss, often summoned Tom to the state capitol to preside over events for teenagers; however, Brokaw admitted in his biography that he had been spending more weekends on the fraternity party circuit at the nearby University of South Dakota.

In his senior year Tom auditioned for and landed the leading role in the all-school play. On the night of the dress rehearsal, he ditched his responsibilities to enjoy a party with older, hard-drinking friends at the University of South Dakota. Furious with him, Tom's father insisted that his son be dropped from the dramatic production and demanded that he apologize to the faculty sponsor and the entire cast.

After high school graduation he enrolled at The University of Iowa, a Big Ten school with a reputation for academic excellence. Coming from the small town of Yankton, SD, the number of students on campus outnumbered the population of his hometown. He suddenly felt like a very small fish in a much larger pond. Moreover, many of the students were from Chicago or its affluent suburbs, and they carried a self-assurance that Tom Brokaw had rarely encountered in Yankton. Reflecting on his adolescence, Brokaw indicated that he really did not know what to expect in college. His small high school had no college counselors, no one in his family had experienced the world of higher education, and his only experience on a university campus had been at drunken fraternity parties or an occasional speech tournament. He saw life at Iowa as simply an extension of high school in a larger, more glamorous setting and admitted that his one year there was embarrassing. He described his approach to life on campus:

> Instead of hitting the books with dedication, I cruised the student union, bedazzled by the rich population of fetching coeds, especially those from the moneyed suburbs of north Chicago. I also tucked myself into a corner of a gathering place for the small population of black students, to watch them dance and listen to the coolest music on campus. I drank beer and played pool and seldom studied for an exam until the night before, if then. I sold blood at the student infirmary to finance dinner dates and I never missed a football or basketball game. I joined a fraternity and failed to make the grades required for full membership. (Brokaw, 2002, pp. 215–216)

Following this experience, he transferred to the University of South Dakota; however, his situation there did not improve. He reported, "Too many mornings, I awoke with a blinding hangover, having slept through one class and unprepared for the next. I'd look into the mirror and resolve to straighten out immediately" (Brokaw, 2002, p. 217). Unfortunately, Brokaw's resolve would last only until an invitation to another party arrived. Halfway through his second semester as a sophomore, Tom received a private dinner invitation at the home of W. O. "Bill" Farber, a legendary political science professor with a history of mentoring many of the state's leading politicians and statesmen. Brokaw (2002) reflected on the significance of that evening with Dr. Farber:

> After an agreeable dinner, Bill turned to me and cheerfully began a conversation that saved my life. He said, "Tom, I've been thinking about you." "You have?" I was secretly delighted at being on Farber's agenda. But then he went on, "Yes," he said, "I think you should drop out of school. Get all of this wine, women, and song

out of your system and come back when you'll do yourself some good, your parents, and this school." (p. 218)

Should Parents and Educators Be Concerned?

To educators and parents struggling to understand underachievement in gifted young people, the three scenarios just presented provide a glimpse into the complexity of this phenomenon. They also raise questions regarding the social and emotional needs of intelligent adolescents. Was Colin Powell struggling to find his identity as his older sister overshadowed him academically? Was he simply searching for acceptance by his peer group? Was young Christine Todd Whitman's frustration with her boarding school lifestyle a call to her family for help? Did Tom Brokaw one day decide to rebel because he could no longer meet the expectations of his community and play the role of well-rounded high achiever?

The scenarios of Powell, Whitman, and Brokaw may provide a sense of relief to educators and parents concerned about gifted youngsters who are underachieving academically. It may be reassuring to read that three prominent individuals were at one time a source of concern to their teachers and parents. However, although it may be cathartic to learn that these three highly accomplished adults faced adolescent challenges like so many teenagers today, there is still reason to be concerned about gifted students who are not performing up to their potential. The adolescent experiences of Powell, Whitman, and Brokaw highlight the importance of addressing underachievement if we expect our most capable students to make significant contributions in their chosen domains.

The issue of underachievement is recognized as one of the most serious issues in education. In 2003, Rimm maintained that this problem had reached national epidemic proportions. Underachievement in gifted students is a perplexing phenomenon and the literature describing the problem dates back to Conklin (1940), who described gifted students who were failing school. In spite of six decades of research, underachievement among high-ability students remains a critical problem (Reis & McCoach, 2000). In this chapter, I examine this phenomenon by reviewing the literature on factors that influence underachievement. I raise several serious questions concerning underachievement and call attention to the phenomenon of selective achievement, describing how it differs from underachievement. Following this review, I present one case of a student whose performance falls short of potential. Justin Kerry's story is a composite of several young people included in research studies I conducted to examine underachievement in gifted students. Following Justin's case, I pose several questions related to his situation. The chapter concludes with a discussion of strategies, highlighted in the scholarly literature, for addressing underachievement.

Related Literature: Influential Factors That Shape Underachievement

In a comprehensive review, Reis and McCoach (2000) scanned the literature for definitions of underachievement in gifted students. They found no universally agreed-upon definition and noted that the literature was replete with both operational and conceptual definitions proposed by researchers. From their review, the authors found three general themes that emerged from the various operational and conceptual definitions. The first theme represented underachievement as a discrepancy between potential (or ability) and performance (or achievement). A second theme defined underachievement as a discrepancy between predicted achievement and actual achievement. The third theme portrayed underachievement as a failure to develop or use latent potential without reference to a measure of potential; underachievers were seen as individuals who fail to self-actualize. In their analysis of three decades of research, Reis and McCoach (2000) noted that definitions of gifted underachievement as a discrepancy between potential and performance were by far the most common. They reviewed the problems inherent in defining and identifying underachieving gifted students and delineated "an imperfect, yet workable operational definition" (Reis & McCoach, 2000, p. 157) for defining and identifying underachievers in general, as well as gifted underachievers.

Reis and McCoach (2000) proposed the following:

> Underachievers are students who exhibit a severe discrepancy between expected achievement (as measured by standardized achievement test scores or cognitive or intellectual ability assessments) and actual achievement (as measured by class grades and teacher evaluations). To be classified as an underachiever, the discrepancy between expected and actual achievement must not be the direct result of a diagnosed learning disability and must persist over an extended period of time. Gifted underachievers are underachievers who exhibit superior scores on measures of expected

achievement (i.e., standardized achievement test scores or cognitive or intellectual ability assessments). (p. 157)

In offering this definition, Reis and McCoach (2000) called attention to the need for researchers to standardize both the predictor and criterion variables and identify underachievers as students whose actual achievement is at least one standard deviation below their expected level. These researchers also highlighted the reality that standardizing classroom grades is neither feasible nor meaningful.

In addition to defining underachievement in gifted students, researchers have investigated the origins of this complex phenomenon and have uncovered personality, family, social, cultural, and environmental or school-related influences as contributors to underachievement. Below is a discussion of the various influences on underachievement. To introduce discussion of each of the influential factors, the voices of participants in various research studies I have conducted are presented.

The Influence of Personality

I know if I went across the street to the pharmacy and bought a new notebook, I would start fresh again. If I had a new notebook, I know things would change. There is something about a new notebook that gets me all psyched. I get all psyched up when it's the start of a new school year. I even write neater when the notebook is new. It might sound crazy, but it's the little things like that that make a difference for me. (Hébert, 2001, p. 183)

Those words were spoken by a teenager named Skip, a participant in my research study on gifted underachieving males in an urban high school. This statement from Skip is a rather vivid example of a bright young man lacking an internal locus of control. He represents much of what is highlighted in the literature on the influence of personality in shaping underachievement.

Several researchers have noted a number of personality differences between achieving and underachieving gifted students. Gonzalez and Hayes (1988) cited studies describing underachieving students as more aggressive and judgmental and less persistent than achieving students. Underachievers have also exhibited an external locus of control (Hébert, 2001; Laffoon, Jenkins-Friedman, & Tollefson, 1989; Reis & McCoach, 2002). In addition, specific mental health problems, such as anxiety or depression (Ford, 1996; Whitmore, 1980, 1986) may be associated with underachievement, and inappropriate coping strategies, such as avoidance, procrastination, and defensiveness, may accompany anxiety (Mandel & Marcus, 1995). A lack of academic and school survival skills may also contribute to the problem of underachievement (McCoach & Siegle, 2003; Reis & McCoach, 2002). For example, bright underachievers often have poor organizational skills (Rimm, 1995) and little motivation to play the conventional school game (Seeley, 1993). Gifted students may face challenges with undiagnosed learning disabilities or attention deficits of various types that affect or cause underachievement (Baum, Olenchak, & Owen, 1998; Olenchak, 1995).

The Influence of Family

> I come here and nobody knows me as Morgan, they know me as Margaret's brother and that's hard. It's always been like that. In elementary and middle school, it was the same way. So here [at South Central High School] it will be nice when she leaves [laughs nervously], but they're still going to know me as Margaret's brother. (Hébert, 2001, p. 184)

Morgan, another young man involved in my research on gifted underachieving males, felt overshadowed by his high-achieving sister. Morgan's case represents how a family issue such as sibling rivalry may contribute to a young person's losing motivation for school. This issue is simply one of many conditions within a family that may impact a young person's achievement orientation. When families face difficult challenges, children are affected academically. For example, researchers have examined the effect of the death of a family member on children and have found that bereavement is prolonged for some children and has a significant effect on underachievement (Abdelnoor & Hollins, 2004). Similarly, parents' marital relationships have serious effects on family interactions. Parents who are otherwise disengaged with each other may join forces and attack the underachieving behaviors of a child (Perosa, Perosa, & Tam, 1996), and young people at times serve as buffers between parents struggling with tensions in their marriage (Akhtar & Kramer, 1997; Rimm, 1995). When such conditions exist in a family, young people often underachieve in school.

Research on family characteristics of underachieving gifted students suggests that type of home environment may influence the achievement patterns of students. The emotional climate of the home has also been studied, and researchers have indicated that underachievement may be influenced by a family's lack of appropriate support for the student. Bright underachievers often come from homes that do not provide structure and guidelines about school behavior and academic performance (Baker, Bridger, & Evans, 1998; Hébert, 2001; Peterson, 2001). In such homes, parent-child relations may be oppositional and conflicted (Reis, Hébert, et al., 1995; Reis & McCoach, 2002). Rimm (1995) proposed that under-achievement could be a form of suppressed aggression in which young people engage in power struggles with adults closest to them. Families of gifted underachievers have also been described as delivering mixed messages regarding the value of achievement by emphasizing an achievement ideology but failing to model it. Parents of underachieving gifted children may verbalize the value of achievement; however, children may actually observe their parents living lives characterized by frustration and lack of fulfillment (Reis & McCoach, 2000).

The Influence of Community and School Environment

> It's the dumbest thing I've ever heard of in my life. If you get outside suspension, you get to go home and watch *The Price Is Right*. It's just like if I was in prison and started a fight, they'd send me home for a week's vacation. It makes just as much sense. In inhouse suspension, you sit in a room all day and there is no teaching. It just doesn't make sense. They have you with other kids just like you cutting up all day. No homework is done. The monitor is a lady who tries to control the place. So what do you do? You start a little rumble and you get a little vacation. (Hébert, 2001, p. 187)

Skip is speaking here again and shares how the contextual influences in his urban high school setting are playing a role in how students view their environment and how those perceptions have an effect on how hard they work in school. Skip's experience in his urban high school is consistent with what researchers have found regarding the role of community and school environment.

Environmental factors may play a role in the underachievement of gifted students. Some students may not perform academically for reasons associated with difficult home environments. Although definitions of *at risk* may vary, a consensus exists that many students do not receive support from home or community to succeed in school. Differences in learning outcomes may result from the interaction between students and their adverse environments (Ford, 1996)

Features of the school environment or school experience may also influence underachievement in gifted students. In a comprehensive study examining school records, Peterson and Colangelo (1996) concluded that the school experiences of bright underachievers appear bleak when compared to those of achievers on variables such as school absences and participation in extracurricular activities. These researchers called attention to the need to be alert to attendance and tardiness patterns in identifying underachievement and potentially recognizing student needs. They suggested that school may be a contextually different experience for achievers and underachievers. Low teacher expectations for culturally diverse students are often an unfortunate reality in public schools. Ford (1996) found that many of the gifted African American students she surveyed reported that, although teachers perceived them as working to their potential, the students believed they could achieve higher than their grades reflected. Ford's (1996) findings highlighted that underachievers did not perceive classrooms as environments where their talents were supported, reported less positive relationships with teachers, and wanted more time to understand material in class. Diaz (1998) examined factors influencing underachievement among gifted students of Puerto Rican descent, and found that the most critical factor was the absence of early, appropriate academic experiences, which thwarted possibilities of developing talent later in life.

The Influence of Inappropriate Curricular Experiences

> Yesterday, I took a quiz in geometry. I thought I failed it miserably. Lately, I've been too tired in class. This is period 8. It's hard to pay attention by that time. I took the quiz, and I didn't know what I was doing. I guessed. She gave me my paper back and she said, "You got the highest grade in the class. Obviously, you have been misplaced. You should be in an honors class." Everyone in there is failing, and I have a B average. Everyone is paying attention and taking notes, and I never do. It's actually 12:20 by the time class starts. I sit in the back of the room and nod off. (Hébert, 1998, pp. 404–405)

The above scenario was presented by John, another research participant who described a situation that frustrates many educators and counselors working with bright underachievers. His comments highlight the critical role that appropriate curriculum and opportunities for acceleration play in the experiences of gifted students. Unfortunately, what John described is also consistent with the literature. Researchers have paid attention to inappropriate academic programming and have noted that a mismatch between instructional approaches and the learning styles of gifted students exacerbates underachievement if students are not provided with encouragement or viable ways of expressing their talents (Baum, Renzulli, & Hébert, 1994; Hébert, 2001; Montgomery, 2000). Gohm, Humphreys, and Yao (1998) found that students gifted in spatial ability who were not allowed to fully utilize their capabilities and interests became less interested in school and underachieved. Inflexible curricular requirements and lack of acceleration opportunities have also been described (Fehrenbach, 1993) as inhibiting intelligent youngsters from becoming involved in meaningful school experiences.

The Influence of Peers

> Think of seafood dealers. They never have to put a lid on their seafood tanks because the crabs always keep each other in. Every time a crab tries to climb out of the tank, other crabs clutch it and bring it back. So the dealer never has to use a lid on the tank. I don't want to say that misery loves company, but with some brothers it's an understood solidarity. It's understood that you're not supposed to be different. The nail that sticks out gets hammered back in. (Olenchak & Hébert, 2002, p. 206)

Those are Andre's words. That poignant message was presented in a study Rick Olenchak and I conducted on underachievement in culturally diverse gifted university students. As a gifted Black male, Andre believed that the stream of subtle remarks directed to him by other African American students regarding his placement in advanced classes kept him questioning whether it was worth the risk to achieve academically. Apparently, Andre's peer group was powerful in shaping his achievement orientation. Andre's situation is representative of the social factors occurring in adolescence that influence how young people perform academically.

A gifted student's social environment includes peers who may influence achievement status. Although being perceived as intelligent is often a social asset in elementary school, social pressures in middle and high school may influence gifted students to underachieve in order to camouflage their giftedness (Brown & Steinberg, 1990; Clinkenbeard, 1991;

Wolfle, 1991). When gifted teenagers underachieve, peer relationships may be far more important than school, and these students' poor performance may be reinforced negatively by friends (Rimm, 1995). In addition, gifted minority students may face cultural peer group expectations that impede their success. For example, in a classic study, Fordham (1988) found that the fear of being accused of "acting White" created a social and psychological situation that diminished the academic efforts of African American students and led to underachievement.

The Influence of Culture

Culture plays an important role in shaping school experiences. Moore, Ford and Milner (2005b) defined culture as "a set of beliefs, values, dispositions, traditions, customs, and habits that are specific to a group" (p. 169) and indicated that these served as lenses through which culturally diverse students see themselves and others. Understanding how an individual's culture operates and its influence on a student's behavior may help educators understand how culturally diverse students interpret academic achievement. Research and theory suggest that educators and counselors who understand and address the needs and cultural styles of culturally diverse students into the curriculum promote and enhance achievement among these students (Ford & Harris, 1999; Ladson-Billings, 2002).

Culturally or linguistically diverse students appear to be at greater risk of academic challenges than students from the dominant culture (Gándara, 2005), and these students tend to be underrepresented in gifted education programs (Castellano, 2002; Diaz, 2002; Tomlinson, Callahan, & Lelli, 1997).

Several issues present potential problems for understanding the complexity of underachievement within culturally diverse populations. Psychometric or standardized tests used to screen for gifted underachievement may not be valid or reliable measures of students from culturally diverse backgrounds (Castellano, 2002; Kitano & Espinosa, 1995). Researchers have also suggested that minority language background may adversely affect the achievement of culturally diverse students (Castellano, 2002; Granada, 2002). Cultural relativism is another factor that must be considered. Reis and McCoach (2000) noted that "What is prized in one culture may not be valued in another, and it is difficult to impose one belief system on a culture that may define achievement and underachievement differently" (p. 163). They elaborated, "Researchers and educators may need to adjust their views of both giftedness and underachievement when attempting to identify and address this complex phenomenon within culturally diverse student populations" (Reis & McCoach, 2000, p. 163).

Underachievement Versus Selective Achievement: A Question of Conflicting Value Systems?

In recent literature on underachievement, several scholars have raised issues that should be considered before teachers, counselors, or parents label a child an underachiever. In pursuing research studies on gifted underachieving university students, Kristie Speirs Neumeister and I (2003) were fortunate to work with Sam, a university student. He had been nominated as a participant for our study because he demonstrated behaviors typical of underachievers. For example, Sam did not purchase all of his college textbooks, his class attendance was minimal, and he was known for sleeping through lectures. During high school, Sam had established a pattern of similar behaviors, such as beginning major research projects the evening before the assignment was due, negotiating with an older sister to complete his homework in exchange for favors, and refusing to work for certain teachers. Sam's teachers throughout middle and high school, as well as his family members, were quick to label him an underachiever as a result of observing these behaviors. As we analyzed the early data, it became apparent that Sam's internal characteristics simply were not consistent with those associated with underachievement, such as low self-esteem, poor self-regulation, or inadequate coping skills (Reis & McCoach, 2002). What we discovered was that Sam's self-regulation skills were strong, and he was very goal-directed. Therefore, we questioned whether Sam should be included in a study on underachievement. Instead, we chose to closely examine him as a single case to try to understand how he interpreted his school experiences and his inconsistent achievement-related behaviors (Speirs Neumeister and Hébert, 2003).

An overarching theme in Sam's case was his self-reflection and self-awareness, which led to his formation of a value system that placed respect and service to others highest. As a university student, much of Sam's time was spent doing service work, such as building homes for Habitat for Humanity and taking care of lawn work for elderly residents within his university community. In addition, he sponsored a child from Honduras. His dedication to service often resulted in less time for academics, which led people to consider him an underachiever. Sam argued:

> Maybe I'm not slacking off in what's really important . . . A lot of people take the view that academics have got to be the most important. But, if you take a more worldly view, I don't [think they are]. When, for instance, there are people dying of starvation, how important is it that I get a little grade? (Speirs Neumeister & Hébert, 2003, p. 226)

Because he placed academics at a lower priority than serving and working with others, Sam may have underachieved in school because of the lack of time he dedicated to this part of his life; however, his devotion to serving others led him to be a high achiever in a domain he considered more important.

As a result of self-reflection, Sam developed a strong sense of his own abilities, learning style, and preferred method of instruction. He had an accurate gauge of his ability level and awareness of his learning style. He explained to us his preferences for independent learning and believed he could master the content of a course on his own when he immersed himself in the material for long, uninterrupted periods of time. To learn best, Sam also indicated that he needed to be actively engaged and he did not resonate with the lecture method of instruction.

At times Sam's strong metacognitive awareness worked against him in the culture of academics. Sam was not willing to conform to a structured system that involved lectures, attendance policies, and insignificant class assignments, which he believed did not contribute to his understanding of course material. He preferred efficient methods of learning, and his resistance to the traditional methods of the classroom often caused others to think of Sam as an underachiever.

Because Sam had a clear sense of his own abilities, he was frustrated when others told him he was not capable of accomplishing something quickly. He felt he knew himself better than they did. His response was to take such comments as a challenge and prove to himself and others that he could accomplish what they said he could not. He enjoyed sharing his experiences with a physics course, where he proved he could achieve without conforming to expected behavior. The course had a reputation for being difficult, designed for engineers with the intention of weeding out weak students. He explained as follows:

> When I come to a class [like Physics] that everyone is complaining about, it's almost a challenge to me. [I say to myself] "I'm going to do the worst thing that I can do in this class by not going to it and

seeing how I do." That's what I love. (Speirs Neumeister & Hébert, 2003, p. 232)

Sam never attended the physics class, choosing instead to learn the material in his preferred learning style, by independently working through the problems. Although it appeared that Sam was underachieving because he attended only the laboratory experiments, he actually mastered the material, earning an A, because of his strong self-regulation of learning. Rather than view Sam as an underachiever, we coined the term *selective achiever* for it more accurately reflected what we saw in Sam.

Having been involved in the ROTC program at his university, Sam completed his education degree and fulfilled his commitment to the military in the U.S. Navy. His strong intelligence and leadership abilities were recognized early, and he was selected to be trained as a submarine pilot. He later became a Navy lieutenant stationed in undisclosed locations throughout the world.

Since working with Sam, I have been introduced to several other gifted young men like him. Catherine Schreiber and I (Hébert & Schreiber, 2010) have continued this line of research on selective achievers and have examined this phenomenon with two additional university students, Greg and Shannon. Just as we saw in Sam's case, these two students provided evidence that strong intrinsic motivation, combined with independence and resistance to conformity, played important roles in shaping who they were as gifted selective achievers. We also found that they demanded serious intellectual challenges associated with acquiring practical knowledge. To them, learning had to be challenging, practical, and applicable to their personal goals. For example, Shannon believed that practical application made learning meaningful:

> With everything I do with computers, there's information that I have to use. It's all practical application. I remember things that I need and use. If I have no practical application for a piece of data, it doesn't stay in my head. That's why I don't do well with multiple-choice tests but I rock at essays. I can remember things that I need and use them in developing my arguments. . . . With biology, I said, "Screw this!" Give me an essay test on the theory of evolution and I'll ace your class. Don't have me reiterate the steps to mitosis and mycoses. That's pointless. I'm not learning anything. (Hébert & Schreiber, 2010, p. 586)

In addition, for Greg, Shannon, and Sam, an educator's personality and teaching style were critical to whether they would put forth effort in a course. Greg highlighted a number of engineering professors whom he admired; however, those who had the greatest impact on his motivation to achieve were instructors who were experts in their field, passionate about passing on their knowledge to students. They taught for understanding. Greg described one of his favorite professors:

> We can walk down the corridors of Brown Hall and hear him out in the hall. He's very loud. He's as country good ole' boy as they come, but he knows thermal sciences up, down, left, and right. He's a very strong proponent of "Understand this stuff!" He knows it well enough that he can ask you the same question 15 or 25 different ways, and depending on which way he asks the question determines if you really understand the concept. He has a great fervor for what he's teaching, and his point at the end of the day is "Do you understand thermal dynamics? I really do love this stuff and I want you to understand it." (Hébert & Schreiber, 2010, p. 595)

Shannon also appreciated teachers who were passionate about their work, and he admitted that he worked harder for them than for others. A significant high school English teacher had a positive influence on him: "She just really enjoyed what she did. You could tell. She was really into it" (Hébert & Schreiber, 2010, p. 590). He highlighted how this teacher's passion for her work affected him. "When I'm around somebody who's really fired up about what they're doing, then I'm into it too because I feed off of intensity. When somebody's just really intense about something, I'm like "Man, I'm right there with you!" (Hébert & Schreiber, 2010, p. 590).

Along with appreciating teachers who were passionate about their work, Shannon also felt strongly about educators who allowed students to learn according to their preferred learning style. He described his philosophy succinctly: "I will give what you're looking for teacher if you will let me travel the way I want to. Show me where you want to go, and I'll get there running my own way" (Hébert & Schreiber, 2010, p. 591). Shannon shared stories of several teachers during his K–12 school experience who allowed him to "travel his way." He described a journalism teacher's flexible approach to nurturing his talents and indicated how hard he was willing to work for this teacher:

Mr. Chandler never tried to confine what I was doing. As long as I had my editorials and my pictures in and I helped out with layout, it was done. As long as the paper was published on time, I could do my work whenever. I was like, "You rock, dude! You're the best teacher, Mr. Chandler." He didn't try to put me on a leash. He didn't try to confine me. If I had something to contribute to the paper, he would let me find it, and he would nurture that. He would say, "this is the place where you chose to be, so let's roll with something, give me a little artwork here. "Okay, man, I'm all over this. Boom!" And I would not leave my desk until it was done. (Hébert & Schreiber, 2010, p. 591)

Shannon earned his master's degree in educational technology and later served as a middle school coordinator of educational technology in metropolitan Atlanta. Greg earned his degree in mechanical engineering and was later employed by an engineering firm in Knoxville, TN. The insights of Sam, Greg, and Shannon, three successful young professionals, should force teachers, counselors, and parents to reconsider how they view achievement in gifted youth. A closer examination of students like these three bright young men reveals a picture quite different from common underachiever stereotypes. Through our case study research, my colleagues and I have described examples of developmentally advanced, self-directed achievers. Sam, Greg, and Shannon reflected the belief systems of the participants in Kanevsky and Keighley's (2003) study of underachieving gifted high school students who sought five interdependent features—"5 Cs"—in their learning: control, choice, challenge, complexity, and caring. These students helped teachers, parents, and counselors understand how adolescents may interpret achievement and learning differently from the adults in their lives.

The findings of Kanevsky and Keighley (2003) were similar to those found in a landmark study by Linda Emerick (1992). She investigated factors that had influenced the reversal of underachievement in 10 gifted students, aged 14 to 20, who had moved from chronic underachievement to academic success. The participants all had long-standing out-of-school interests and activities that served as an escape from less than favorable school situations and a provided them a sense of self-worth and success. Involvement in these activities also helped to maintain a love of learning and the skills to become independent learners. The parents of these students supported the out-of-school interests, maintained a positive attitude toward them, and remained calm during the period of underachievement.

The participants all identified particular intellectually challenging classes that contributed to the reversal of their underachievement. These classes incorporated student discussions, authentic assignments that were relevant to their lives, a focus on process as well as product, and opportunities for independent study in their areas of interest. The students also believed that they had developed goals that personally motivated them and were directly related to academic success. The students in this study all indicated that a specific teacher was the single most influential factor in the reversal of their underachievement. They respected these educators who sincerely enjoyed their students as individuals, communicated with them as peers, were enthusiastic and in love with the subjects they taught, incorporated varied teaching methods, and held high but realistic expectations for the under-achieving students. The final influential factor was a significant change in the student's concept of self, which included more self-confidence, a new view of academic achievement as a source of personal pride, and an ability to reflect on and understand the factors that might have contributed to underachievement.

Through my work with students like Sam, Greg, and Shannon I have learned that there is an important difference between *underachievement* and *selective achievement*. The insights provided by these young men as well as the participants in both Kanevsky and Keighley's (2003) and Emerick's (1992) studies highlight the need for educators and parents to consider whether academic achievement is driven by a student's values. Reis and McCoach (2000) raised this issue:

> Labeling a student an underachiever requires making a value judg-ment about the worthiness of certain accomplishments. A teacher may believe that reading *Huckleberry Finn* is more worthwhile than mastering a new video game, but a child may not. This behavior illustrates a values conflict between adult and child. (p. 156)

Educators must acknowledge this challenge each time they examine an individual student's situation. Louise Porter (2005), a child psychologist, addressed this issue eloquently:

> These selective learners tend to be self-confident people who realize that there is more to life than intellectual pursuits, so they balance their academic striving with other demands and interests. If they feel personally fulfilled by their choices, others should not criticize

them for failing to reach the expected heights of academic output. (p. 192)

As we explore the complexity of underachievement, we must reflect on what Reis, McCoach, and Porter have asked us to consider. To help us develop more understanding of this challenge, the following case study of Justin Kerry is provided.

The Case of Justin Kerry[1]

Justin Kerry stepped off the city bus and began walking slowly down one of the busiest streets in Portland, ME. As he maneuvered his way along the crowded sidewalk, he appeared to carry the weight of the world on his shoulders. The red-headed, freckled-faced fifth grader stopped to browse through every magazine stand along Congress Street, surveyed the latest comic books, and checked out the most recent edition of *Sports Illustrated*. Justin realized he was just killing time. He really didn't care that he would be late for soccer practice, and he knew that the conversation he would soon be having with Coach Fitzgerald was not going to be smooth. He could envision his coach's face turning crimson, and he could hear the dreaded yelling; however, Justin was determined to stick with his plan. As he approached Patriot Park, he checked his duffel bag once more. Inside the bag was the soccer uniform he planned to turn in to his coach. He checked to be sure he hadn't forgotten anything. Arriving at the field, he heard Coach Fitzgerald's gruff voice call out, "Well, it's about time you got here, Kerry! You're late. That's gonna be an extra 15 laps around the park for you today. You know the rules, Kerry. When am I ever gonna get that through your thick head? Huh? Tell me, big guy!"

"Hey, Coach, I need to talk with you about something."

"I haven't got time to listen to your problems today, Kerry. I've got a team to run. Some of these guys really want to play soccer, remember? So get out on that field, and let me see you work on your volley kick! Hurry! Get out there!"

Justin took a deep breath, and with all the courage he could summon, he blurted, "Coach, you don't understand. I'm quitting the team. I'm here today to turn in my uniform. I don't want to play any more."

"What do you mean? You don't want to play? You're my star forward.

---

1   This case report is a revised and updated version of a case previously published. See Hébert (2004).

What do you expect me to do without a forward? You know Carmichael can't fill your shoes. Now get out there and practice!"

As Justin reached into his duffel bag and pulled out his uniform, the expression on the coach's face changed. He realized that his star player meant what he said. He really was there to quit the team.

Justin walked over to the back of the coach's SUV and left his uniform on the back seat. His coach stood there, shaking his head. As Justin attempted to say goodbye, Coach Fitzgerald cut him off, muttering, "You're gonna regret this one day, Kerry. Trust me, you're gonna be sorry."

Justin Kerry was not feeling sorry. He knew he did not want to continue playing soccer. He had practiced his speech over and over in his head for weeks. Although he figured he would feel relieved when it was over, Justin didn't feel that way at all. Instead, he felt another wave of dread. He now had to figure out what he was going to say to his parents when Coach Fitzgerald called his father. He could hear his dad carry on about his never sticking to a commitment. He still had a couple of hours before his family expected him home for dinner, so he planned to walk home in a roundabout way. He passed Longfellow Square and decided to spend some time in his favorite museum. Miss Winstead, his art teacher, had mentioned on Tuesday that the museum was featuring a special exhibit on cartooning. She seemed really excited about the work that was being displayed, and she encouraged the students to ask their parents to take them to see the new show. Justin decided the museum would be a great way to kill some more time before he had to face the "I'm so disappointed in you" speech from his dad.

***

It was a quiet Friday afternoon, the perfect ending to a hectic week at Mahoney Elementary School. Carolyn Clark was seated at her desk grading her fifth graders' papers when Beth Winstead came rushing into her classroom holding a small canvas. The art teacher was obviously excited as she waved Justin Kerry's work and placed it on the desk before her.

"Carolyn, will you look at this? This kid is amazing! Justin constantly astounds me with his talent. I've been teaching art for 12 years, and I've never met a student with such a natural gift. I introduced our fifth graders to Salvador Dali this month, and for the past 3 weeks Justin has been working on surrealism. Look at the imagery in this painting. It's incredible."

As Carolyn admired the painting, she too was impressed with Justin's artistic ability. She smiled as Beth carried on about Justin's artistic talent and his ability to "see the world through the eyes of an artist." Beth explained that she was struggling with a dilemma. She wanted to recommend Justin for the school district's magnet program in the fine arts for next year, but this would mean that Justin would no longer be involved in her art program. Having talented youngsters like Justin Kerry kept Beth Winstead professionally invigorated: "It's kids like Justin who keep me believing that I can make a difference."

Beth decided to share Justin's painting with the staff in the front office and therefore grabbed the painting from the desk and dashed out of the room, leaving Carolyn Clark with her thoughts. Carolyn was pleased to see Justin's painting; however, she had mixed feelings that afternoon. She had been worried about Justin for a while. She wondered why he would immerse himself in surrealism so intensely. She reflected on the article she had read recently about troubled adolescent boys hiding from their personal problems through their artwork, and she remembered how the author had indicated that Dali's surrealism was often seen as an escape for many youngsters. This seemed to be consistent with what she had noticed lately about Justin.

As she reviewed her grade roster, Carolyn thought about Justin's recent lack of progress in her fifth-grade class. She also thought about the conversation she had earlier in the week with the school's enrichment teacher, Susan Curtis, who had shared her concerns about Justin's lack of motivation in the gifted program. Susan had been working with Justin since he was identified for the program in first grade, with an IQ score of 140, creativity test scores in the 98th percentiles, and strong teacher recommendations. She pointed out that this was the first year Justin had not chosen to pursue an independent study project during research time in the resource room. In the past, Justin had been enthusiastic about his individual research projects on endangered animals, the Vietnam War, and the cartoon art of Charles Schultz, and he had always been a competitor on the elementary school's Quiz Bowl team. This year was different, and Susan was puzzled. She mentioned to Carolyn that she had decided that Justin was simply experiencing nothing more than a late "fourth-grade slump."

Carolyn Clark was not convinced that Justin's behavior was merely a slump. She thought back to her lunchroom duty several days ago when she had watched Justin eating his lunch in a corner of the school cafeteria. In the mob of boisterous students, he had appeared more detached than ever. As Carolyn supervised the lunchroom, she had noticed Justin closely watching a group of guys clowning around at the next table. The students enjoying this rowdy conversation had a reputation at Mahoney for their disruptive behavior. Teachers in the faculty room had commented on the likelihood that these boys would someday become a high school gang. Carolyn worried that Justin was becoming intrigued with the behavior of the disreputable students. Now as Carolyn studied her class grade roster, she felt guilty. She had intended to call Justin's parents to talk about his plummeting grades and the recent change in his behavior, but she dreaded making that phone call and had been putting it off for several weeks.

Margaret and Mike Kerry had been Carolyn's good friends during their years together at Bowdoin College. Margaret and Carolyn had both majored in English. Carolyn knew that Margaret was teaching in a parochial school in the city, and Mike was employed in the city planner's office. Carolyn thought back to their college days during the late 1960s and smiled to herself. She reflected on her own idealism at that time and the passion she, Margaret, and Mike had had for a number of causes. Margaret and Mike had been significant personalities at Bowdoin College, taking on a heavy load of extracurricular activities and providing leadership on a number of important campaigns involving students' rights. Now these two well-established professionals continued their involvement in important causes and were well known as social activists. Carolyn had taught their daughter Maureen a number of years ago and had marveled at how wonderful a student she was. Having excelled academically, socially, and athletically, Maureen had a magical way of turning everything she touched into gold. In fact, Carolyn had just read in the *Portland Press Herald* that Maureen had been awarded a Jeffersonian Fellowship and would be studying at the University of Virginia in the fall. As she read the article she wondered how Justin had coped with having such a tough act to follow.

Although she dreaded making that phone call to her old friends, she knew she had to do it. As she reviewed Justin's grades, she noted that his language arts average had dropped from an A to a C. He had not turned in any social studies homework for 2 weeks and had failed his most recent test. His grades in science were also dropping. She thought back to a conversation with Mr. McGowan, Justin's math teacher, who had referred to Justin as a "kid with an attitude." Apparently, his progress in math might also be a problem. She wondered if any of Justin's other teachers had contacted his parents. She decided to include Susan Curtis, Justin's enrichment teacher, in her plan. She would call the Kerrys and arrange a parent-teacher conference. Having Susan at the meeting might help Carolyn deliver the troublesome message.

***

Carolyn poured coffee for Margaret and Mike as they waited for Susan to arrive. Margaret initiated the conversation with her concern for her son.

"I'm so grateful to you for calling us, Carolyn. We've been noticing a number of changes in Justin at home lately and wondered if the same was true in school. Mike has been upset with him for quitting the soccer team."

Mike interrupted, "He seems to have so few interests these days. All he does after school is lie on his bed and listen to his iPod all afternoon. We can't get him outside. This is the same kid who was the star forward on his team. The kid is a natural athlete, and now we don't hear anything about sports or the guys he used to hang out with. We don't know who his friends are these days. We ask him about it, but he just shrugs his shoulders. We don't know what to think."

Margaret became teary-eyed as she spoke, "He's so different from his sister Maureen. We've always been able to communicate openly with our daughter. She's always been so easygoing. I guess boys are different. He seems so moody all the time."

Susan Curtis arrived in the classroom and apologized for being late. The Kerrys were happy to see her again. She had been working with Justin since first grade, and they felt assured that she had his best interests at heart. Susan shared with Margaret and Mike that Justin had not begun an independent study project, and she was wondering if they might have an explanation. Both parents assured Susan that the enrichment program she facilitated had been the highlight of Justin's elementary school experiences for years. They were puzzled, but Mike said, "That's consistent with what we're seeing. He doesn't have any interests these days and he's simply not making a commitment to anything."

Margaret became more emotional as she described what Justin had been like as a younger child: "Justin has always been such a sensitive child. I'll always remember the night we stayed up until wee hours of the morning trying to comfort him after he watched the movie *E.T.* He was such an emotional mess after that movie. We thought he'd never fall asleep."

Mike interjected, "Yes, this little guy wouldn't be able to fall asleep because he was worrying about bald eagles becoming extinct! After a while we hesitated about allowing him to watch *National Geographic* specials on television. We never knew what might happen as a result."

With more emotion in Margaret's voice, she commented, "And when his first-grade teacher had the class involved in a project raising money for a soup kitchen, we dealt with night after night of assurances that his efforts would definitely make a difference for the homeless people in Portland. He was convinced we could deliver pillows and blankets to all of them throughout the city! Even though he has this deep sensitivity and intelligence, he simply doesn't seem to care about anything these days. I just don't understand."

Carolyn hesitated before she said, "I need to let you know where Justin stands academically in a number of his subjects. First of all, I want you to know that Beth Winstead, the art teacher, thinks the world of Justin. She was in here a few days ago so excited about a painting Justin had finished in her art room. She thinks he's one of the most gifted artists she's ever seen. I did check with Rick McGowan and I know there are problems in math. Rick couldn't be here this afternoon, but he left Justin's math test grades with me. Rick claims that Justin hasn't turned in any math homework lately, and he failed his most recent test."

Carolyn could tell this news was not what Margaret and Mike Kerry wanted to hear, but she continued, "I'm not seeing any social studies homework from Justin, and his grades in language arts and science are also spiraling downward. Right now he has a C average in language arts and a D in social studies and science."

"This is totally out of control!" Mike Kerry blurted. "Wait until I get home. This kid is in deep trouble!"

Carolyn remained calm as she spoke, "Now Mike, keep in mind, lots of kids go through stages like this. Justin may be trying to tell us something. We have to listen closely. Yesterday in language arts class I asked the students to work on writing simple cinquain poems, and I was surprised with the response I got from Justin. I found his poem rather troubling. Here. I want the two of you to take a look at this."

Carolyn placed the poem on the table before them. She read:

> Fifth grade
> A place to vegetate
> Boring, frustrating, wasting
> Free my spirit—send me away
> Failure

When they were finished reading the poem, Susan spoke softly, "I've changed my mind. What I saw as a slump is more serious than I thought. Poor little guy. I've known Justin for years, and I hate to see this happening to him. Margaret, Mike, do you think we should have Justin talk with our school counselor? John DiBiaggio has a great way of working with our kids. The students here really gravitate to him. He's like a big burly teddy bear, but we've seen him make a difference for a lot of kids. Maybe Justin would let us know what's troubling him through a little work with John. What do you think?"

Margaret Kerry sighed and leaned back in her chair. Her worried look registered her concern for her son. Mike placed his arm around his wife's shoulders, looked down at the table and spoke softly, "Yes, I do think that we'd better get Justin working with this guy John as soon as we can."

***

John DiBiaggio had been a school counselor at Mahoney Elementary for 10 years. He really enjoyed his work, but he often admitted that he rarely saw a gifted student in his office, and that frustrated him. He shared with the teachers that one of his greatest joys was counseling gifted children. He was interested in how they viewed the world differently, marveled at their creative ways of expressing themselves, and admired their sensitive and empathic qualities. John was looking forward to meeting Justin Kerry. He'd done his homework in preparing for his first session, and had talked with Justin's parents and teachers.

When Justin arrived, John noticed that he seemed quite nervous. After chatting casually for a few minutes, he turned to a collection of board games in his office and suggested a game of chess. Justin shrugged his shoulders, smiled softly, and agreed to a game. As Justin eyed the chessboard closely and began to plan his strategy, John slowly began his questions for his young client.

"So tell me, how are things going in fifth grade these days?"

Again, Justin shrugged his shoulders and mumbled, "OK, I guess."

"Tell me, what's your favorite subject this year?"

"Art."

"Art class, huh? Tell me about it."

"Miss Winstead's class is cool. I really like her. She let's us work on awesome stuff."

As John DiBiaggio continued the conversation with Justin, he realized the report the Mahoney teachers had presented to him concerning Justin seemed consistent with what he was seeing in his office. John thought to himself, "This gifted little guy has lots of layers I'll have to unravel before I get to the heart of his issues. I wonder how I'll get through."

"So tell me about math class these days."

With that prompt, Justin appeared even more reluctant and said nothing.

John spoke again, "I would think a really sharp guy like you would really enjoy math."

As Justin carried out his next move on the chessboard, he began to divulge his thoughts, "I have a problem with my teacher."

When John encouraged him to continue, Justin described his feelings about Rick McGowan: "I don't like him as a person. I just don't respect him at all."

John questioned him further, asking, "Can you tell me more about that?"

Justin appeared uncomfortable, but nevertheless continued, "He's one of those teachers that picks on kids. Kids like Montoya Marshall. Just because he's different, I guess. Montoya is a little crazy. He's cool. All the kids in fifth grade know that, but Mr. McGowan treats him like an outcast."

John noted the emotion that came across Justin's face as he spoke. He probed further by asking, "An outcast? Tell me about that."

"I think he had to go to the principal's office three times this week. He's always in trouble. Mr. McGowan kicks him out of class every day. He doesn't do anything to try to help Montoya. He just yells at him and says things like, 'If you're gonna' just sit there and be stupid, then sit there and be stupid!' He says those things in front of the whole class."

John commented, "It seems like Mr. McGowan's behavior really bothers you."

Justin responded, "Yeah, it does. He just doesn't treat kids with respect."

As he continued to discuss the insensitivity of the math teacher, Justin explained that if he didn't respect the teacher, there was no way he could motivate himself to work for the man. He finished his comments with an emphatic, "I think he's a real jerk."

John DiBiaggio realized he had made an early breakthrough. He continued, "So, tell me. What's homework like in math these days?"

Justin made a strategic move on the chessboard, placing John's king in check once again. As he enjoyed the exasperated look on Mr. DiBiaggio's face, he smiled and proceeded to explain, "No, it's not tough at all. Math is my best subject."

John continued, "How about math homework?"

Justin smiled slightly and explained, "I have a personal philosophy on homework. If you know how to do it, why bother to do the homework? It's when you don't know how to do the work that you should have to sit down and figure it out, right?"

John smiled in return and didn't reply. He looked at Justin to continue.

"If I've proven in class that I know the stuff, why do I have to continue to prove that I know it by doing 20 more problems at home? I just don't see the logic in that."

John DiBiaggio stifled a laugh as Justin continued to grumble about the unfairness of fifth grade. He knew he was going to really enjoy getting to know Justin even better. He decided that Justin Kerry was a sharp customer, and he would expect some more very interesting conversations with him if the two of them could continue toward resolving Justin's situation. John knew he was in for an interesting ride with Justin, but he was looking forward to the journey.

Questions to Consider in Reflecting on Justin Kerry's Case

Educators, counselors, and parents might propose a number of possible explanations to understand what was happening with Justin. In considering individual or psychological factors, one might wonder what role his relationship with Coach Fitzgerald played in how he felt about himself. One might also ask how Justin's sensitivity and empathy for others influenced his school experience. Many might raise questions concerning his attraction to surrealism and attempt to understand what that fascination says about him. Concerned adults might want to know more about his parents' expectations for him. Another important question is how the accomplishments of Justin's older sibling influenced his situation. When thinking about peer group influences, concerned adults might ask why Justin seemed to be looking for a new group of friends. Educators and counselors would likely want to know if Justin's educational needs were being addressed appropriately.

I have called attention to a number of issues in Justin's case; however, there remain many more questions that educators and counselors like John DiBiaggio would want to know before attempting to design an intervention. Multiple factors may interact within the lives of gifted students that would contribute to underachievement. As it might have been in Justin's case, sibling rivalry combined with an inappropriate curriculum could be enough to begin the problem. Several insensitive teachers could exacerbate the problem. Negative peer group influences could worsen the situation. In addition to understanding the interaction of multiple factors occurring within an underachievement case, there is a need to consider designing a multifaceted plan or intervention to reverse underachievement.

Young people underachieve for many reasons. Therefore, no one intervention strategy can possibly reverse underachieving behaviors in all bright students. Educators need to individualize programs for underachieving gifted students just as they do for any other population of students in school.

In my work at the University of Georgia, I teach a graduate seminar entitled Underachievement in High-Ability Students. As my students and I spend a semester delving into theory and research on this complex phenomenon, we inevitably reach the same conclusion. Each case of underachievement involves various issues that are colliding and potentially creating a multitude of difficult situations. To highlight this point, I bring to class a deck of circular cards labeled with factors that contribute to underachievement. I begin my discussion by tossing out several randomly selected cards on the seminar table. These three or four cards become Venn diagrams used to reflect what might be occurring in a student's life. For example, the cards may represent lack of challenge in curriculum, an impending divorce of parents, peer group perceptions about school, and sibling rivalry with a high-achieving older brother. This class activity may seem rather simplistic; however, as my students examine the possible interactions that may be occurring with each of the situations the cards represent, they realize that designing an intervention plan to address the problematic issues will require that each factor within the Venn diagram be considered. For example, it becomes obvious that a study skills course is not a cure for a situation as complex as that represented by the factors described above. From there, my students and I begin to consider strategies and methods that may be combined to create an intervention plan for reversing underachievement. Several of these strategies and approaches to addressing underachievement are discussed below.

Strategies and Methods for Addressing Underachievement

In order to address the needs of students like Justin, teachers, school counselors, and parents need to be well versed in a variety of interventions. Interventions need to be individually designed to address the unique situation of the underachieving student. A review of the literature indicates that there are two major approaches to intervention: counseling and education. Each approach has strengths as well as drawbacks. My objective is to present several field-tested counseling methods and research-based educational strategies and highlight how both may be incorporated into individualized interventions for underachieving students.

Include Type III Investigations

Details about the adolescent years of Colin Powell and Christine Todd Whitman in the introduction of this chapter remind us that young people often develop passionate interests. Powell made a connection with the Pershing Rifles, and, as a result, his fascination with the military became his passion and eventually shaped his career. Whitman was miserable in boarding schools, where she was unable to pursue her fascination with politics. She desperately craved being connected to her mother and her mother's political work. This early interest in the political system influenced Whitman's career path. These adolescent snapshots of Colin Powell and Christine Todd Whitman speak to the importance of making connections with the interests of students. Many intelligent young people have interests that are not addressed in school. Tapping into such interests of students is one approach that educators may want to consider in addressing underachievement.

I joined my colleagues and mentors Joseph Renzulli and Susan Baum in a research study that examined the effect of exploring students' interests using Type III enrichment as a systematic intervention in reversing underachievement (Baum et al., 1994; Baum, Renzulli, & Hébert, 1995). This type of enrichment is a major component of the Enrichment Triad Model (Renzulli, 1977). This model provides students with (a) general exploratory experiences that might stimulate a new area of interest (Type I enrichment); (b) authentic research skills and learning-how-to-learn skills necessary for pursuing an interest in greater depth (Type II enrichment); and (c) guidance in the pursuit of individual and small-group investigations that are designed to have an impact on an authentic audience (Type III enrichment).

Twelve teachers in school districts throughout the country assisted us in identifying 17 gifted underachievers. Following the identification of the participants, the teachers spent an academic year facilitating the Type III investigation with 5 girls and 12 boys, ranging in age from 8 to 12. The teachers identified the students' strengths and interests and assisted them in developing their creative projects. In working with the teachers in this study, we had three objectives in mind: (a) to examine the dynamics of underachievement through a systematic intervention program using Type III investigations; (b) to analyze the effect of the intervention on the participating students, and (c) to examine successful teacher strategies for working with gifted underachievers. We found there were five factors contributing to the underachievement of the students involved in the study: emotional issues, social and behavioral issues, lack of an appropriate curriculum, undetected learning disabilities, and poor self-regulation. These findings were consistent with the body of literature on underachievement.

The most compelling finding of our study was that involvement in Type III enrichment reversed the cycle of underachievement. Of the 17 students involved, 14 improved academically during that year and in the year following the intervention. In the course of pursuing the Type III investigation, the students developed a mentoring relationship with a significant teacher who focused on their strengths. For many of the students, the investigation provided an opportunity to select a topic of interest and create new knowledge in a preferred learning style. The Type III work provided several of the participants an opportunity to interact with an achievement-oriented peer group. For students with poor learning or organizational skills, completing an investigation helped them become aware of self-regulation strategies that facilitated learning. Several of the participants also had an opportunity to investigate issues related to their own underachievement .

In addition to our findings on the benefits of a Type III intervention, my colleagues and I found that the teacher was crucial to the success of this approach. (For an in-depth description of how this occurred, see Hébert, 1997). We discovered that teachers who were most effective in reversing the underachievement pattern:

- Took time to get to know the student before initiating an investigation.
- Used their time with students to facilitate the process rather than counsel them regarding their underachievement.
- Saw their role as a facilitator of the process. In doing so, they arranged conferences with the students, provided resources, allocated time for the students to complete the project, and offered suggestions when students seemed to be at a standstill.
- Understood that students needed to feel like practicing professionals and share their products with authentic audiences.
- Recognized the dynamic nature of the underachievement problem by observing students, reflecting on their behaviors as they worked on their projects, and identifying strategies to help them overcome problems.
- Consistently demonstrated patience and believed in the student.

The teachers involved in this study should inspire us. The evidence suggests that facilitating a Type III investigation enables a supportive adult to guide a student in such a way that the child's life may be changed significantly. I encourage all teachers of gifted underachieving students to consider this strategy as a possible intervention.

Seek Counseling

The scholarly literature includes substantial work focusing on counseling as a strategy for reversing underachievement. Counseling interventions involve changing the personal or family dynamics that contribute to a student's underachievement. Counseling interventions may involve individual, group, or family counseling (Mandel & Marcus, 1995; Moon, 2002a; Rathvon, 1996). Rather than trying to challenge the underachiever to become a more successful student, the counselor's role is to assist the young person in deciding whether success is a desirable goal. If the student decides it is, then the counselor helps to reverse habits or cognitions that are counterproductive (Reis & McCoach, 2000).

Counseling psychologist Barbara Kerr (1991) noted that while gifted underachievers may be socially and emotionally immature, antisocial in their behavior, and suffering from low self-concepts, "it is also likely that they have a deep need for understanding the world and themselves, a thirst for knowledge, and the capacity to change negative behaviors when intellectually challenged" (p. 67). Kerr maintained that some underachieving students in need of counseling were students who had been frustrated for so long by the lack of challenge in their education that they had become "embittered and pessimistic about the possibility of ever loving learning again" (p. 66). She believed that such students may be suffering from existential depression, characterized by alienation and a sense of meaninglessness. Kerr argued that an attentive short-term counseling program designed to assist students in defining a sense of meaning and purpose could be effective. She also cautioned that some underachieving students with serious personality or behavior disorders, and others suffering from depression, substance abuse, or family dysfunction were likely to require more time in counseling.

Colangelo (2003) reported that in the family counseling program at The Connie Belin and Jacqueline N. Blank International Center for Gifted Education and Talent Development underachievement was the problem counselors addressed most often. Colangelo (2003) maintained that for school counselors the issue of underachievement was more than simply a discrepancy between scores measuring ability and achievement. He called attention to the need to look beyond how we define underachievement and consider the dynamics involved in the problem. He indicated, "Rather than looking at underachievement as a psychometric event, it can be seen as a relationship between the gifted student and teachers, parent(s), and sometimes peers" (Colangelo, 2003, p. 383). Colangelo (2003) proposed that for some gifted students underachievement could be viewed as "a way to express either a need for attention or a need for control over a situation" (p. 383).

Colangelo and Peterson (1993) provided a strong rationale for the use of group counseling with gifted young students. In their extensive experience with counseling gifted children and adolescents, they found that these students often camouflage who they are, including their intellect, and often hide distress and fears behind a façade of self-confidence. For this reason, they maintained that in counseling groups, gifted students are encouraged to share their vulnerabilities and anxieties as well as their strengths and successes. Within these groups, they can also share their unique passions with others who understand and accept them.

> Counseling groups can take gifted students momentarily out of the competitive academic realm, where personal issues are not dealt with, and give them an experience in the less judgmental affective realm, where no one dominates and where no grades are given. (Colangelo & Peterson, 1993, p. 113)

Colangelo and Peterson also explained the value of counseling groups for underachieving students:

> gifted students who have not embraced the inherently competitive academic environment can find, in nurturant groups, affirmation for intelligence that may not be affirmed elsewhere. Nonschool achievement can be communicated and celebrated, and various kinds of intelligence can be recognized. Personal worth can be defined in terms other than academic results. . . . Achievers and underachievers can break down stereotypes of each other in counseling groups. When underachievers share fears and disillusionment, they are seen as more than just stereotypical bravado, insolence, laziness, or rebellion, if, in fact, one of these is their "label." Achievers become more than a gradepoint. (p. 113)

Colangelo and Peterson (1993) reported that their best experience with facilitating discussion/counseling groups with gifted students was with groups including both achievers and underachievers. Their rationale for such an approach was that high achievers who are perfectionistic and competitive may appear articulate and confident, but are not necessarily comfortable with expressing their own social and emotional concerns. These counselors noted that underachievers were especially sensitive and expressive about emotions and often enhanced group interaction. They also concluded that both achievers and underachievers benefit from mixed groups because it allows all participants to compare stress levels, values, and coping styles. Moreover, underachieving students have a chance to be known by achievers and achievers, are provided an opportunity to learn to know those with priorities different from theirs.

Colangelo and Peterson (1993) found that although gifted students may have intellectual interests that are similar across age levels it is wise to strive for homogeneity of age when facilitating conversations about social and emotional concerns. The developmental issues faced by a bright high school sophomore are likely quite different than those of a senior leaving for college soon. In addition, these authors maintained that mixing genders in groups is suitable for most purposes. Colangelo and Peterson indicated that when counselors work with all-male groups they face the challenge of getting boys to remove their protective facades. Mixed-gender groups also offer females an opportunity to practice appropriate assertiveness in a group situation involving males. Mixed-gender groups become opportunities to practice social skills. It is important to realize, however, that some situations and particular issues make single-sex discussion groups more appropriate. For example, Colangelo and Peterson found that optimal group size varies according to the age level and the composition of the group. They recommended high school groups of 8–12 members, and elementary or middle school groups of 6–8 students. They also have found that 40–60 minutes is an appropriate length of time for any group.

In designing discussion groups for gifted students, Colangelo and Peterson (1993) found that it is best for groups to be somewhat focused in content yet flexible. An effective facilitator can guide conversations to accommodate a variety of issues, helping group members remain focused and leading them to closure. Colangelo and Peterson facilitated discussions on a wide variety of topics and issues and provided a rich menu of appropriate topics for groups of gifted students, both achievers and underachievers. A sampling from their menu included "understanding giftedness," "dealing with our own and others' expectations," "managing stress," "understanding one's learning style," and "learning to deal effectively with the 'system'" (Colangelo & Peterson, 1993, pp. 119–120).

Colangelo and Peterson (1993) suggested that group discussion leaders receive counselor training or some academic work in counseling. However, these experienced counselors acknowledged that teachers who are sensitive to the needs of gifted students, who are not intimidated by them or in awe of their intelligence, who hold no personal agendas, and are willing to learn by doing can become effective group discussion facilitators. Because gifted education teachers often understand the special needs of highly intelligent individuals, gifted students are likely to participate openly. For educators interested in learning more about the process of facilitating discussion groups with young people, Peterson's (2008) book, *The Essential Guide to Talking With Gifted Teens*, is an excellent resource. Incorporated in this guidebook are many sessions that focus on issues related to underachievement. Peterson, Betts, and Bradley (2009) offered additional topics and pertinent guidelines.

Find Mentors for Students

Consider Tom Brokaw's story, introduced earlier. Given how he described his adolescence in his autobiography, he may have benefited from the guidance of a male mentor during his senior year in high school and his early days at The University of Iowa. Guidance from an adult figure in his life other than a parent may have enabled him to remain achievement-oriented. With students like Tom, educators and counselors may want to consider mentoring as an appropriate intervention. Mentoring has long been recognized as a helpful process for educating and guiding gifted youth. Torrance's (1980, 1984) seminal study of mentor relationships presents conclusive evidence that mentorships have a significant impact on later creative achievements of gifted individuals. This 22-year longitudinal study strongly suggested that a critical component in facilitating achievement among students experiencing difficulties is having a mentor (Torrance et al., 1998).

What transpires in a mentorship is a supportive relationship between a child or young adult and someone more senior in age and experience who offers support, guidance, and assistance. The protégé may be experiencing difficulties, entering a new area of experience, taking on an important task, or addressing an earlier problem. In general, during mentoring, protégés identify with or form a strong interpersonal attachment to their mentors; as a result, they become able to do for themselves what their mentors have done for them (Clasen & Clasen, 2003; Hébert & Olenchak, 2000; Siegle & McCoach, 2005a).

Rick Olenchak and I (2000) collaborated on a series of three case studies of gifted underachieving males working under the guidance of mentors. In each case the students pursued an area of their interest, with the mentor providing support, and reversed their pattern of underachievement. The overarching finding in this research was the powerful influence of a significant adult. Another compelling finding was the open-minded and nonjudgmental characteristics of the mentors required to sustain an ongoing relationship. As a caring adult friend, each mentor provided consistent and personalized social and emotional support and advocacy beyond that associated with simple instructor-student relationships. In addition, a plan involving strength- and interest-based strategies for reversing the underachievement was successful in each case.

Stephen, a participant in our case study research, was mentored by a university professor who also served as Stephen's college advisor. After leaving the university, Stephen sent a letter to his mentor expressing appreciation. The following excerpt highlights the powerful impact of a significant relationship between the student and a caring adult:

> There was always something more that made me feel we had a friendship rather than just a student-advisor relationship. We had a comfortable relationship. You believed in me from the beginning. You weren't just trying to cheer me up and make me feel better. You believed in me from the beginning, from day one. I picked up on that right away. I appreciated what you were doing for me. You were always checking in with me to see that things were okay. Not just in my classes, but other things outside of school, like my social life and whether I was meeting new people and making new friends. You were concerned about my development as a person. Just knowing that there was a person out there who cared about me was important to me. I'll be honest, every time I hear that someone has a doctorate, that's pretty intimidating to me. To have someone at that level listening to me and telling me that he believed in me, and telling me he knew that I could do it really made me feel good. (Hébert & Olenchak, 2000, p. 205)

I was involved in a second study examining mentoring in an elementary classroom (Hébert & Speirs Neumeister, 2000). I spent 4 months observing Judy Wood's classroom at Maple Grove Elementary School. This study examined Judy's implementation of a mentoring program involving fourth graders and 18 university students. The teacher's objective was to have the university students facilitate a biographical research project in which the children investigated significant historical figures in order to produce a pageant on famous people from their state's history. During the program, I found that the relationships between the children and their mentors enabled the mentors to provide intellectual, motivational, and emotional support to their young protégés (Hébert & Speirs Neumeister, 2000).

The mentors worked with the children for a semester. The project included researching biographical materials in the school's media center, scavenging the local public libraries with the children for authentic historical information, teaching the youngsters the research process, writing several drafts of their biographical reports, composing their individual vignettes for the pageant, memorizing their lines, and preparing a historically accurate costume to wear as they appeared on stage. In observing this mentorship program in action, I was especially curious about the role the mentors played for underachieving gifted students. For example, Vanessa, a mentor working with two young girls, faced the challenge of keeping her students on task and admitted that they challenged her repertoire of pedagogical strategies weekly. She described how, as a mentor, she played an important role in keeping the girls focused and motivated to work on their research:

> I learned that I really had to come well prepared and organized each week. Otherwise, it was too easy for them to lose interest if they weren't stimulated or I wasn't prepared. The two students I worked with were a real handful at times. One little girl was ADD and had such a hard time concentrating on what she was supposed to be doing. My challenge was keeping her on task and keeping her motivated. I really learned that I had to separate them in order to keep them focused and actively involved in what they were supposed to be doing while I was working with the other. (Hébert & Speirs Neumeister, 2000, p. 137)

With these two young girls Vanessa discovered that breaking the task into small parts helped them to feel good about their progress. Vanessa also learned that locating primary sources of historical information helped to excite both students. The children appreciated learning about historical figures from diaries and historical photographs acquired from local and state historical societies. In addition, Vanessa and several other mentors pointed out the importance of field trips to sites throughout the state to study the biographical backgrounds of the historical figures. They maintained that field trips made a difference in keeping the children enthusiastic about their efforts.

Within the population of gifted students in Judy Wood's classroom were children with complex emotional needs. I observed how the mentors' emotional support played an important role in the children's success. One mentor, John, was a vivacious, easygoing young man who worked with three bright, energetic boys. A business administration major, John did not have a teacher education background, yet he appeared to be a natural in working with children. In one work session I watched as Matt composed a finished draft of his biography of Charles Goodyear at the computer. John stood behind him and encouraged with comments such as, "That sentence really has improved, but what have you forgotten at the end?" When the student discovered he had overlooked a question mark and corrected himself, John ruffled Matt's hair and cheered, "All right, Matt!" He watched over the shoulder of his other student at the computer and commented, "You've really worked hard since your last draft. That sentence wasn't there before. I like it, Darius!" Following my observations of this mentor who apparently felt comfortable in his work with the three boys, John shared his thoughts about how he may have been helping to fill an emotional void in the boys' lives:

> Whether or not I served as a father figure, I'm not sure. I noticed that Darius tried to demand more of my time. He was clingy at times. He was constantly checking to see if I'd be coming the following week. Judy mentioned that on the days I couldn't make it in, he would have a bad day. I listened, and I was always respectful. By respecting them and treating them like young men, they respected me. Once I had established that, their behavior was amazing. (Hébert & Speirs Neumeister, 2000, p. 139)

The relationship this energetic college student had created with the three boys was apparently special. I often observed the boys standing at the windows of their classroom overlooking the front lawn of the school's campus. They were watching for John's SUV to pull into the school parking lot. The three boys knew the make, year, model of the Jeep, how much John had paid for it, how much gas it consumed, and what John had recently paid to repair it. They also reported to me the upsetting events of one weekend when the Jeep was stolen from a parking lot at a nearby sports coliseum. However, although they admired the vehicle, they admired John even more. Describing him as "awesome," they looked forward to every session with him; and, if he appeared as much as 2 minutes late for their scheduled time, John heard about it from the three upset boys.

When the pageant day arrived, it was evident that the relationships between students and mentors had become important, and Judy Wood was comfortable with these relationships. I questioned her about "letting go" of her relationships with students and sharing them with other adults, and she explained as follows:

> You often get the feeling as a teacher that you need to be with them, you need to guide them through every paper, you need to be in control of what they are doing. . . . Some of them have a lot of emotional needs, really letting go, and letting them hook onto someone who is going to spend a lot of time, just one on one, or one on two, and really develop a special relationship with that adult from outside the classroom [was healthy]. . . . It gave them a break away from me, the person who is demanding and has requirements for them every day. It gave them a treat, being able to work with someone else in a quiet atmosphere and really be guided at their own level. (Hébert & Speirs Neumeister, 2000, p. 140)

Judy Wood's experience with implementing a mentorship program in a heterogeneous elementary classroom may inspire educators to consider how they might implement a similar approach in their work with a variety of student populations. Mentoring has long been established as an effective strategy for working with students. Those concerned with gifted underachieving students should consider this strategy as a possible intervention.

Implement Rimm's Tri-Focal Model

Another well-recognized approach to reversing underachievement is Sylvia Rimm's (1995) Tri-Focal Model. According to this model, gifted students are at greater risk than others for becoming underachievers because they are often given too much attention and power in the early years of schooling. Rimm (1995) maintains that gifted children are also more likely to experience boredom in school as they soon discover that assignments are not challenging and they realize that they only have to put forth minimal effort to succeed academically. In her approach to addressing underachievement, Rimm's model consists of six steps for reversing it: assessment, communication, changing expectations, role-model identification, correction of skill deficiencies, and modifications at home and school.

To implement the Tri-Focal Model, the clinician begins by facilitating a comprehensive assessment including an individual intelligence test, individual achievement tests to identify strengths and deficits, creativity tests, inventories to identify characteristics of achievement or underachievement, and interviews with parents. Following the assessment, communication between parents and teachers begins with serious discussion of the results of the assessment through which clinician, parents, and teachers come to better understand the student's strengths and share evidence of giftedness. Important others—parents, teachers, and siblings—then have an opportunity to express that they believe in the child's ability to achieve. These messages regarding expectations can help young people change their self-expectations. The clinician, family, and teachers work together to match children with achievers who may serve as role models: tutors, mentors, companions, scout leaders, ministers, other teachers, or relatives. Tutoring designed to address skill deficiencies is incorporated into each student's program. Parents and teachers collaborate on long-term goals and short-term objectives that ensure immediate small successes for the student at home as well as at school.

The Tri-Focal Model has been successful in approximately 80% of clinic cases (Rimm, 2003). Based on her extensive experience facilitating this approach, Rimm (2003) indicated that although reversal of gifted underachievement is difficult, the satisfaction felt by the child and family members is worth the long-term commitment and effort by all those involved in the process.

Implement the Achievement Orientation Model

Another approach that educators and counselors may want to consider is the Achievement Orientation Model conceptualized by Del Siegle and Betsy McCoach (2005b). Siegle and McCoach designed their model based on extensive research in educational psychology. They maintained that achievement is shaped by a relationship among four factors: task value, self-efficacy, environmental perceptions, and self-regulation. Siegle and McCoach argued that although there may be many factors that contribute to achievement, motivated youngsters appear to exhibit three perceptions and a resulting behavior. To begin, these students see value in academics, for school is meaningful to them and they believe that what they are doing will result in beneficial outcomes. In addition, these students believe they have the skills that lead to success. Finally, they trust their environment and believe that they can succeed within it. Siegle and McCoach explained,

"When students value the task or outcome and have positive perceptions of themselves and their opportunities for success, they are more likely to implement self-regulatory behavior by setting realistic expectations and applying appropriate strategies for academic success" (p. 5).

These two researchers maintained that, with concerted effort, educators and parents can help gifted students to see that what they are doing serves a purpose, to believe that they have the skills to perform successfully in school, to trust that their environment will encourage productivity, and to set realistic expectations for themselves. In addition to conceptualizing the model, Siegle and McCoach (2005b) provided educators and parents with a selection of motivation tips designed to keep young people focused on their academic goals and succeeding in school. To provide a flavor of this innovative model here, I highlight several of their suggested strategies below. Teachers and counselors interested in learning more about the model should refer to *Motivating Gifted Students* by Siegle and McCoach (2005b).

Task Value

- Parents and educators can help students see beyond the present activity to the long-term benefits it produces. A school assignment may seem unimportant, but acceptance into a prestigious university, earning a lucrative college scholarship, or obtaining a rewarding occupation may be outcomes that students value and are willing to strive toward. (Siegle & McCoach, 2005b, p. 12)

Self-Efficacy

- Educators and parents should save samples of previous academic work and periodically review the students' earlier work with them to show growth and improvement. Students are amazed at how easy their earlier work now appears and how much better they are now able to perform. Student portfolios are a popular educational practice that promotes this activity. (Siegle & McCoach, 2005b, p. 18)

Environmental Perceptions

- Educators and parents can discuss with students the obstacles they believe are keeping them from doing well and what options exist for them. This includes a discussion of what is within the student's control, as well as what is beyond their control. Teaching students to appreciate multiple viewpoints should be part of the discussion. (Siegle & McCoach, 2005b, p. 33)

Self-Regulation

🐦 Teachers and parents can teach students to set attainable short-term goals and reward themselves once they are completed. For example, a student might reward herself with a half-hour of conversation on the phone with a friend after reading a chapter for social studies homework. (Siegle & McCoach, 2005b, pp. 38–39)

In conceptualizing their model, Siegle and McCoach (2005b) saw their objective as promoting motivation and an achievement orientation that will enable students to pursue their interests and passions. They believed that teachers and parents can support students through this process and that the "encouragement of these behaviors is a major step toward helping young people lead productive and fulfilling lives" (Siegle & McCoach, 2005b, p. 40).

For Further Thought and Discussion

🐦 What insights regarding underachievement do we gain from the adolescent experiences of Colin Powell, Christine Todd Whitman, and Tom Brokaw? How might sharing their stories help gifted adolescents today?

🐦 The findings regarding selective achievement described in this chapter came from two research studies involving university students. Do you think this phenomenon could also occur during childhood or early adolescence? If so, what might it look like? How might educators and counselors address the selective achievement of gifted K–12 students?

🐦 The selective achievement involved gifted young males. What might this phenomenon look like in gifted females? How might it be different? Why?

🐦 In Justin Kerry's case:
- What would you identify as Justin's most pressing concern?
- What would you propose as possible solutions to Justin's situation?
- What wisdom does Justin bring to the situation? How would you personally respond to the situation described?
- What does your response to the situation reveal about your views on underachievement in gifted students?
- What does your response to the situation reveal about your philosophy of education?

❧ Consider each of the following strategies for addressing under-achievement suggested in this chapter: facilitating Type III enrichment, counseling, implementing the Tri-Focal Model, mentoring, and implementing the Achievement Orientation Model. Discuss the strengths of each approach. Discuss the challenges or limitations of each approach.

Resources to Expand Your Thinking and Extend Your Support to Gifted Students

Brophy, J. (2010). *Motivating students to learn* (3rd ed.). New York, NY: Routledge.

Neihart, M. (2008). *Peak performance for smart kids: Strategies and tips for ensuring school success.* Waco, TX: Prufrock Press.

Rimm, S. B. (2008). *Why bright kids get poor grades: And what you can do about it* (3rd ed.). Scottsdale, AZ: Great Potential Press.

Siegle, D., & McCoach, D. B. (2005). *Motivating gifted students.* Waco, TX: Prufrock Press.

Spevak, P. A., & Karinch, M. (2006). *Empowering underachievers: New strategies to guide kids (8–18) to personal excellence.* Far Hills, NJ: New Horizon Press.

CHAPTER 8

Supporting the Social and Emotional Development of Gifted Students With Learning and Attention Difficulties

My goals for this chapter are to:
- Introduce you to the various types of gifted students with learning disabilities.
- Acquaint you with gifted students with attention difficulties.
- Present the issues related to social and emotional development facing this special population of gifted students.
- Present the survival techniques that gifted students with learning disabilities implement.
- Present strategies and methods for supporting gifted students with learning and attention difficulties.

We are all just pilgrims on the same journey . . . but some pilgrims have better road maps.

—Nelson DeMille

Terry Bradshaw is a former NFL quarterback, who led the Pittsburgh Steelers to six division titles and four Super Bowls in six seasons. This Hall of Fame athlete became a successful sports commentator for the NFL and a national consultant to the sports industry. Of several autobiographical works, his most recent, *It's Only a Game* (Bradshaw & Fisher, 2001), included information about his schooling experiences that gifted students might appreciate knowing, including the following:

> My very first day in school I got my hand spanked with a ruler because I couldn't sit still. That never changed. If I enjoyed a subject, like history, I did well in the course; but for the most part learning wasn't fun for me. If I didn't understand a subject, I just ignored it. I went for an entire semester without ever opening my geometry textbook, so I flunked every geometry test. The only good thing about that was that I showed consistency. For a long time I believed that I wasn't as smart as the other kids. It was a horrible feeling. Awful. But my real problem was that I could not sit calmly in my seat and focus on the subject for any period of time. I was always moving, always pulling at my hair or biting my fingernails. My mother used to say I was a squirmer. "My little boy is a very energetic young man. He really likes to hang from the ceiling." (pp. 8–9)

Much later in life, the energetic boy learned that there was a name for his problem. He explained, "It's called attention deficit disorder, ADD, and I could have been the poster boy for it. Of course my picture on the poster would have been blurred" (Bradshaw & Fisher, 2001, p. 9). Bradshaw allowed his reader to see the human side of this stellar athlete including challenges he faced in school. He empathized with young people who may be faced with an attention disorder, a condition that prevents children from reaching their intellectual potential and may affect their entire lives. He explained, "It doesn't mean they're not every bit as smart as the other kids, it means they have difficulty processing certain information. They have difficulty focusing on one task for any length of time. For a child, it makes learning hard" (Bradshaw & Fisher, 2001, p. 9).

Terry Bradshaw grew up in the 1950s in rural Louisiana. During that period, his mother took her little squirmer to several doctors, but they had no idea what was wrong. Although the medical community recognized that a problem existed, there was little they could do. Medicines like Ritalin or Dexedrine did not exist. Long after Bradshaw finished his career in professional football, he decided he wanted to understand what was wrong with him. He underwent a battery of tests and learned that he had had ADD his entire life. He reflected, "I truly wish I had been tested when I was a child so I might have been able to reach my potential academically. I wouldn't have had to struggle quite so much. But I wasn't tested, I struggled, and in football I found my answers" (Bradshaw & Fisher, 2001, p. 10). Bradshaw realized that his attention difficulties may have been the reason he had difficulty with standardized testing. When taking an exam for a scholarship to Louisiana State University, Bradshaw missed qualifying by one point.

Bradshaw is only one of many prominent men and women of high achievement who struggled with a learning difference that influenced their school experience and how they viewed their intellectual abilities. The Internet offers a wealth of documented cases of gifted individuals who struggled with learning difficulties. These successful adults are prominent politicians, writers, artists, musicians, composers, athletes, business leaders, entertainers, and community advocates and activists. Table 6 provides a list of prominent individuals with learning disabilities who made significant contributions to society for generations. Students in our classrooms should be made aware of them.

Children identified as learning disabled comprise 4.49% of the total school population (Smith, Polloway, Patton, & Dowdy, 2004). Kampwirth (2006) reported that advocates for individuals with learning disabilities (LD) celebrate this statistic, for they interpret it as recognition of the reality of the condition and an acknowledgement of the needs of these students. Advocates for gifted students with LD celebrate for the same reasons. Although there is no doubt that students with LD exist in our schools, the notion of gifted students with learning disabilities has been discussed in the literature since the early 1980s (Baum, 1984; Fox, Brody, & Tobin, 1983). Since then, research studies and scholars have revealed an extensive body of knowledge about the identification of these students, their learning characteristics, and what is required in school to help them fulfill their academic potential (Baum, Cooper, & Neu, 2001; Baum & Owen, 2004; McCoach, Kehle, Bray, & Siegle, 2004; Neu, 2003; Olenchak & Reis, 2002; Reis & Ruban, 2004; Sternberg & Grigorenko, 2004). Although the experiences of gifted students with LD have improved in schools with

TABLE 6

Successful Individuals With Learning Disabilities or ADHD

Harry Belafonte	African American singer, actor, and political activist promoting human rights worldwide.
Terry Bradshaw	Former NFL quarterback. Television host of NFL pre-game show on FOX.
Erin Brockovich	Consumer advocate. Inspiration for the movie by the same name.
Fannie Flagg	Author and actress most famous for her novel *Fried Green Tomatoes*.
Danny Glover	Film and theatre actor and activist promoting AIDS awareness in South Africa and the advancement of minority youth.
Whoopi Goldberg	Hollywood actress, comedienne, and community activist working to eliminate homelessness.
Woody Harrelson	Hollywood movie and television actor.
Tommy Hilfiger	Internationally known fashion designer.
John Irving	Novelist and screenplay writer of *The World According to Garp*, *Hotel New Hampshire*, and *The Cider House Rules*.
Bruce Jenner	1976 gold medalist in the Olympic decathlon.
Dexter Scott King	Son of civil rights leader Dr. Martin Luther King, Jr. President and CEO of The King Center.
Ingvar Kamprad	Founder of IKEA furniture chain. One of the world's wealthiest men.
Jay Leno	Popular comedian and host of a late night talk show.
Greg Louganis	Olympic gold medalist in diving in 1984 and 1988. AIDS awareness activist.
David Neeleman	Founder and former CEO of JetBlue Airways.
Edward James Olmos	Hollywood actor, political activist, and entrepreneur promoting Latino culture in the United States.
Patricia Pollacco	Award-winning children's author and illustrator.
Charles Schwab	Founder and CEO of the Charles Schwab Corporation, the largest brokerage firm in the United States.
Robert Toth	Artist whose paintings and sculptures are featured in museums internationally including the Smithsonian's National Portrait Gallery.
Henry Winkler	Hollywood movie and television producer, actor, and children's book author.

Note. Adapted from GreatSchools Staff (n.d.).

increased knowledge and awareness, more needs to be done for this population. As educators and researchers work to improve educational programming for gifted students with learning and attention difficulties, we must not overlook the need to provide support systems to address their social and emotional development. Mendaglio (1993) reviewed the literature on gifted students with LD and reported that insufficient attention has been paid to the affective needs of this population. Therefore, the focus of this chapter is to examine how the interaction of giftedness and learning disabilities has an impact on the social and emotional development of these students and what educators and counselors can do to provide support.

The term *twice-exceptional*, often abbreviated as 2e, is commonly applied to gifted students with learning and attention difficulties. This term refers to the fact that these children are exceptional because of both their intellectual gifts as well as their special needs. In this chapter, I will use the term twice-exceptional and gifted students with LD interchangeably. I will briefly summarize definitions and types of gifted students with learning disabilities and review their characteristics. I will also discuss students with attention deficit disorders. I will then explore pertinent social and emotional issues, in and out of school, and look at ways that gifted students with LD learn to survive academically. I will introduce the voices of students who have faced challenges related to being both gifted and learning disabled. Some of these students have contributed to research studies involving this population and others have shared their experiences through published memoirs, personal narratives, and autobiographies. This chapter concludes with a discussion of strategies that educators and counselors might consider when addressing the social and emotional development of twice-exceptional students.

Definition of Gifted and Learning Disabled

The research community has come to terms with defining gifted students with learning disabilities. Definitions in the literature are fairly consistent, and the following two definitions are representative. Baum and Owen (2004) defined the gifted student with learning disabilities as "a child who exhibits remarkable talents or strengths in some areas and problematic weaknesses in others" (p. 29). McCoach and her colleagues (2004) specified that "gifted/LD students are students of superior intellectual ability who exhibit a significant discrepancy in their level of performance in a particular academic area such as reading, mathematics, spelling, or written expression" (p. 36).

Three Types of Gifted Students With Learning Disabilities

The literature regarding gifted students with learning disabilities highlights three different types (Baum & Owen, 2004; Brody & Mills, 1997): identified gifted students with subtle learning disabilities, students identified with learning disabilities who are also gifted, and students not identified as learning disabled or gifted.

Identified gifted students with subtle learning disabilities are placed in gifted programs based on their high grades, high achievement, and impressive IQ scores. As work becomes more demanding and the academic tasks depend more on the skills hindered by their disability, these students begin to struggle. They may put forth more effort, but their situations do not improve because they have not learned how to study. They become confused and discouraged, struggle to keep up with class assignments, and begin to doubt their abilities. Baum and Owen (2004) maintained that if the learning disability is not detected early enough and addressed, social and emotional problems will emerge.

Identified students with learning disabilities who are also gifted, the second type, are initially noticed by teachers for what they cannot do and are officially identified as learning disabled. These students have severe learning disabilities along with outstanding aptitudes in specific academic or intellectual areas, although they are seldom formally identified as gifted (Baum & Owen, 2004; Brody & Mills, 1997). Baum and Owen (2004) indicated that these students are at serious academic risk because the implicit message behind the LD label says to them, "You are broken." This negative message is often reinforced by the school. The typical approach in these situations is to work on the disability until the student is "fixed" before any focus on the special gift or talent occurs. Acquisition of basic skills becomes the sole objective of school. Baum and Owen noted, "Reading, spelling, writing, and math take precedence over a student's talent in building bridges, gift of using art to explain conflict, or commitment to save the whales by starting a city-wide campaign" (p. 32). If the emphasis is on the disability and surpasses any positive feelings connected to the special gift or talent, these students may view themselves as inadequate.

The third profile is of students not identified as either gifted or learning disabled. Their learning disabilities have been hidden by their high intellectual ability. Their talents have enabled them to compensate effectively, and they are performing at grade level. Baum and Owen (2004) noted, "In an on-going tug-of-war, their intellectual ability hides the disability and the disability hides the gift" (p. 31). As a result, these students are difficult to identify because they do not display exceptional behaviors noticed by teachers. The discrepancy between their IQs and their performance goes undetected, and they appear average to their teachers. Baum and Owen have found that the hidden gifts of these students emerge in specific content areas in classrooms where the teacher uses creative approaches to teaching and learning. For example, a teacher may spot talent in a learning environment in which written work is minimized in favor of debates, discussions, role-playing, art, and individual projects. For those who have learned to compensate, their hidden disability may not be uncovered until college or adulthood. By that time these students may have little confidence in their abilities and may be discouraged about school and learning.

Given the complexity of the issue of appropriately identifying these three specific types of gifted students with learning difficulties, it is important that educators and counselors become aware of their educational and affective needs. Silverman's (2003) poignant call for help for these children serves as a cogent reminder of their need for support:

> there is a group of disabled children who remain virtually defenseless. These children are physically healthy and highly intelligent, but poorly coordinated, dyslexic, dysgraphic, anxious, or hyperactive. They are often teased by their classmates, misunderstood by their teachers, disqualified for gifted programs due to their deficiencies, and unserved by special education because of their strengths. Twice exceptional learners can become casualties of a system that refuses to acknowledge their existence, fails to identify them, and does not support their strengths or assist them with their weaknesses. Too often, they are left on their own to cope with their differences. (p. 534)

Students With Attention Difficulties

Terry Bradshaw's childhood experience highlighted in the introduction of this chapter is not uncommon. Many bright children in schools today may not be all that different from the little squirmer growing up in

Louisiana in the 1950s. Bradshaw described the lack of knowledge concerning attention deficits at that time, and unfortunately, the medical and psychological communities continue to struggle to understand this complex phenomenon.

Attention deficit/hyperactivity disorder (ADHD) is currently viewed as an executive function disorder, a "dysfunction of that part of the brain that attends to, organizes, processes, and outputs information" (Lovecky, 2004, p. 44). The symptoms associated with ADHD—inattention, impulsivity, and hyperactivity—shape a disorder that has impact on an individual's life in multiple settings. Because symptoms displayed may differ from one setting to another (e.g., classroom vs. home), subtle symptoms may be overlooked in certain environments (Lovecky, 2004; Moon, 2002b).

The American Psychiatric Association's (2000) text revision of the fourth edition of the *Diagnostic and Statistical Manual* (*DSM-IV-TR*) specifies criteria required for the diagnosis of ADHD. This manual describes three types of attention deficit/hyperactivity disorder:

- **ADHD Inattentive Type**—An individual displays symptoms of inattention.
- **ADHD Combined Type**—An individual displays symptoms of inattention, impulsivity, and hyperactivity.
- **ADHD Hyperactive/Impulsive Type**—An individual displays few symptoms of inattention; however, impulsivity and hyperactivity override the inattention.

There are no definitive explanations for ADHD. Most researchers who have examined the phenomenon suggest that it results from both genetic predisposition and environmental factors (Kaufmann, Kalbfleisch, & Castellanos, 2000). Moon (2002b) indicated that it appears to be a neurobiological disorder that impairs executive functioning and influences behavior at school and at home. Some researchers have concluded that the major cognitive impairments of ADHD are in impulse-control processes (Barkley, 1997), while others place more emphasis on attention processes (Brown, 2000). The condition is commonly associated with other psychiatric conditions (Lovecky, 2004). Moreover, learning disabilities, reading difficulties, and language deficits often appear to coexist with ADHD. Tannock and Brown (2000) have estimated that 20% to 25% of all children with ADHD have some type of learning disability.

Because some symptoms of ADHD resemble characteristics of giftedness, scholars in the field of gifted education have theorized that gifted children may be misidentified and treated for attention difficulties when they do not actually have ADHD (Baum et al., 1998; Cramond, 1995). Such a situation potentially has negative consequences for the social and emotional development of these children. Another problematic misidentification is the failure to correctly identify ADHD, giftedness, or both in young people who actually have both exceptionalities (Moon, 2002b).

Characteristics commonly associated with giftedness and ADHD may mask one or both of the exceptionalities, which can result in underidentification for gifted education programming, and misunderstanding of their behaviors. When they do not understand their own behaviors, and when teachers, parents, and friends cannot explain or appreciate their behaviors, these children may experience distress. In the limited gifted education research on this area, a number of emotional problems within the gifted/ADHD population have been recognized. Listed below are emotional problems identified by researchers through case study investigations (Moon, Zentall, Grskovic, Hall, & Stormont-Spurgin, 2001; Zentall, Moon, Hall, & Grskovic, 2001):

- difficulty with emotional regulation;
- emotional immaturity;
- social immaturity;
- internal asynchrony between cognitive and affective abilities;
- problems with labeling, controlling, and appropriately expressing their emotions;
- displaying annoying and aggressive behaviors that are disliked by their peers;
- family stress; and
- school stress.

Researchers working with gifted students with ADHD indicate that a comprehensive approach must be taken to address the needs of this special population (Lovecky, 2004). Gifted students with attention difficulties require a plan that adjusts the academic curriculum of the schools and trains them in areas of deficits, such as skills related to executive functions, interpersonal skills, and emotional control. Life in and out of schools for these individuals may be complex, and they need emotionally supportive adults who understand the special challenges they face.

Social and Emotional Issues Facing Gifted Students With Learning and Attention Difficulties

The research literature on identification and academic programming is extensive, yet no researcher or university theorist can help teachers and counselors understand the feeling responses or experiences of young people who struggle with being twice-exceptional. Concerned educators should be pleased that the educational community has recently been provided several outstanding resources describing the experience of being gifted and learning disabled. Several books written by gifted young adults describe their experiences growing up with a learning disability. Samantha Abeel's (2003) autobiography, *My Thirteenth Winter: A Memoir*, was published several years following her college graduation. It is a compelling account of a resilient young woman with fierce determination, sensitivity, creativity, and personal vision who overcame childhood adversity and was successful. She graduated with honors from Mt. Holyoke with a degree in creative writing. This young woman captured the attention of the national media following her publication at the age of 15 of a children's picture book of poetry, *Reach for the Moon* (Abeel & Murphy, 1994). Her book earned her the 1994 Orton Dyslexia Society Margot Marek Award for the best book written on the subject of learning disabilities. Following the publication of her book, Samantha was invited to speak to audiences throughout the country about her experiences as a gifted child with learning disabilities.

In addition to Abeel's work, educators can benefit from the work of Jonathan Mooney and David Cole (2000), *Learning Outside the Lines*. Jonathan, a young man with dyslexia, struggled to read until he was 12 years old. Later, following one year of study at Loyola Marymount University in Los Angeles, he transferred to Brown University, where he graduated with an honors degree in English. He was awarded the distinguished Truman Fellowship for graduate study in learning disabilities and special education. While at Brown University he met David Cole, a student with ADHD. At age 15 David had dropped out of high school and later returned to the Putney School in Vermont. He then attended Landmark College, a 2-year college in Putney, and eventually transferred to Brown University, where he graduated with an honors degree in visual arts. Although the two young men shared similar difficulties in learning, their approaches to dealing with the issue differed. Jonathan directed his energies toward playing soccer, while David enjoyed nonconformity, rebellion, and, in his words, "empowerment-through-self-destruction-trainwreck of getting high" (Mooney & Cole, 2000, p. 56).

The two Ivy League college students wrote of their school experiences as unusual learners in an educational system that was not understanding or willing to provide them an unconventional approach that respected their learning differences. At Brown University, they thrived in a learner-centered and self-directed environment that highly valued personal empowerment. In addition to sharing their experiences in a book, Mooney and Cole (2000) have provided other unconventional learners with a guidebook for navigating university life. Both *My Thirteenth Winter: A Memoir* and *Learning Outside the Lines* provide twice-exceptional students with an important message that schools do not have to be one-size-fits-all in their approach to learning. By reading the stories shared by these young authors, readers can better understand and appreciate the social and emotional issues twice-exceptional students experience during adolescence.

The gifted education community is also fortunate to have researchers in special education who have examined twice-exceptional populations in their work. Rodis, Garrod, and Boscardin (2001), in *Learning Disabilities and Life Stories,* offered a rich anthology of riveting autobiographical essays that inform the professional discourse on learning disabilities. Their work offers practitioners and scholars in education and psychology a phenomenological perspective—that is, a perspective that conveys authentically the way learning disabilities are experienced by those who have them. These scholars worked for 2 years with young adults attending four different universities in the northeastern United States. Within the context of a two-semester independent study course in writing, 30 college students met weekly with the researchers/instructors in one-on-one sessions, discussing their experiences with a wide range of specific learning disabilities and crafting their autobiographical narratives. Selected from this anthology are the voices of Christie Jackson and Kevin Marshall, which will be shared later in this chapter. Their stories are told frankly and with the intention of revealing what they experienced as well as what they felt.

In addition, Susan Baum and Mary Rizza, two researchers in gifted education, collaborated with Sara Renzulli, a twice-exceptional college student, to shed light on the unique challenges of adolescents with coexisting talents and deficits. Baum, Rizza, and Renzulli (2005) offered Sara's personal narrative, in which she described her experiences as a gifted adolescent with a learning disability who eventually learned to focus on her strengths, and compensate for her weaknesses, and who had success academically in college.

In addition to the autobiographical materials described above, findings in a study conducted by the National Research Center on the Gifted and Talented (NRC/GT) entitled *Talents in Two Places: Case Studies of High Ability Students With Learning Disabilities Who Have Achieved* (Reis, Neu, & McGuire, 1995) can help educators and counselors better understand the experiences of gifted students with learning disabilities. In this study, researchers examined the life experiences of 12 young adults with disabilities who were successful at the college level. Reis and her colleagues (1995) conducted extensive interviews with the university students and a thorough review of their school records in order to provide portraits of the challenges and problems faced by these twice-exceptional students. The interview data from this study also shed light on several of the social and emotional issues challenging these students. The following discussion describes issues related to social and emotional development.

Stress and Frustration That Impact Self-Esteem

Imagine a young child who arrives in school after having been told by parents and family members throughout his preschool years that his artwork was beautiful enough to hang on the family refrigerator. His wonderful sense of humor has entertained relatives and family friends for years, his use of kitchen gadgets in building inventions is clever and appreciated, and his ability to solve problems creatively is celebrated by his neighborhood friends. Suddenly in school he discovers that he is not so wonderful after all. He struggles with mathematical concepts the teacher presents, and time spent in reading is a time of anxiety and discomfort. The former superstar feels frustrated and begins to question his abilities, a rather frightening experience for one who just a short time ago was both confident and enthusiastic about learning. For example, Jonathan Mooney (Mooney & Cole, 2000) highlighted how he began to question his abilities early in elementary school when he detected differences in the experiences of students in various reading groups. He realized his status in his "blue jay reading circle" was lower than the robins, hawks, and sparrows as his group read "See Spot Run" from one day to the next and the books that other children carried to their reading circles appeared to be getting thicker. He noted that the teacher talked differently to the children in the other groups and her body language indicated that they were smart. He explained that looking at the pages of his book made his head hurt and he felt dizzy. When he attempted to unscramble the words and was unsuccessful he felt trapped. Wanting desperately to be like everyone else, he learned to escape to the boys' bathroom to prevent having to read out loud. In the bathroom, he hoped no one would walk in and see him crying.

Christie Jackson (2001) described her experiences in *Learning Disabilities and Life Stories* and reflected on similar frustration and its effect. Although her eagerness to learn was recognized by her teachers and family, there were times when she saw herself as inferior to her classmates and felt ashamed. She reflected, "I remember Sister Maria's first grade class and being the last to get my spelling words corrected. You had to write each word you spelled wrong five times; when you were done, you could play" (Jackson, 2001, p. 40). Christie noted that she seldom got to play.

Sara Renzulli (Baum et al., 2005) also described her frustration and stress as she coped with her inconsistent performance in school:

> Even with the constant reassurance of my parents that I was smart, I still felt dumb. The few teachers who bothered to really get to know me in the regular level classes noticed right away that I was smart and not challenged in these classes. They saw me as a "fish out of water." Yet, even with these statements, which were reassuring in some small way, my grades continued to be poor because I could not take traditional tests. I couldn't help wondering why, if I were as smart as everyone was telling me, I could not get good grades in these non-challenging classes. (p. 148)

Diane, a participant in the Reis et al. (1995) study, reflected on her situation in elementary school and provided insights regarding what might have been done to improve it:

> I remember being so angry at the kids who would get the As . . . because I actually knew more than they did, but nobody would let me say anything. If they had given me oral tests, I could tell them anything they wanted to know about, but they always gave me the written stuff. I would be on question 3 or 4, and the time would be gone, because it took me so long to figure out what the questions were. (p. 53)

Peggy, another participant from the study, sought counseling as a young adult to understand her situation and cope with her disability. Her reflections also highlight the stressful situations with teachers:

I am still very angry. I've discussed this with my psychologist. I carried a lot of anger towards my second grade teacher, towards my fourth grade teacher. I was upset. I used to sit in the front of the classroom and cry, because I couldn't get my work done, and she would send me from my desk to another desk in front of the class and I would sit there and my friends would come over and say, "What is wrong?" And she would say, "Leave her alone. She just feels like crying." I never got my work done. I would never get to do the things that people got to do . . . . I think the only day I ever got to play was the last day of school and everyone did. (Reis et al., 1995, pp. 53–54)

Consider the frustration and stress that Samantha Abeel experienced every day as she struggled with life skills and competencies that most teenagers her age had acquired. She had to continue to present an image to those around her that she was in control of her situation:

No one understands the sinking feeling of lost helplessness when I lose track of time and the only clock I can find, I can't read. Or the anxious confusion I feel when a cashier looks into my face and wonders why I, a perfectly normal-looking person, have handed him fifty cents when he asked for seventy-five. They don't understand the embarrassment I feel at not being able to keep score in my gym class, never knowing how much of a tip to leave in a restaurant, forgetting how to fill out a deposit slip at the bank. Or the terrifying idea of riding a bus alone because I may not be able to figure out the schedule. Or always knowing that no matter how good my paper's content, I will get marked down for my grammar and spelling mistakes. . . . Many people have never heard of the learning disability I have—dyscalculia. When they look at me or talk to me they don't think it's possible. Everyone assumes I am normal, that I can do things that every grown-up can do. I don't want to be different. I just want to fit in! I don't want to feel helpless and embarrassed or look stupid. No one really understands." (Abeel, 2003, p. 175)

When a student continues to experience such intense frustration with everyday tasks that seem overwhelming, imagine the frustration experienced with difficult tasks in school. Baum and Owen (2004) noted that these young people "must often function and survive in an unfriendly world where they are judged and judge themselves according to what they cannot do" (p. 250). As a result, they routinely experience frustration and stress. The tendency toward intense frustration may eventually produce a lack of motivation, disruptive or withdrawn behavior, feelings of low self-esteem, and a sense of learned helplessness (Olenchak & Reis, 2002). According to Olenchak (1994), living through successive years of school-related frustration may eventually require in-depth individual counseling to explore challenging issues. Mendaglio (1993) offered examples of students whose emotions go unexpressed for long periods of time who later "explode" at trivial comments from parents, teachers, or friends, giving the student a "Jekyll and Hyde" quality (p. 134).

Reis and Ruban (2004) reported on a study of university students identified as gifted and learning disabled. These researchers highlighted how participants in the study were affected by what happened to them during their K–12 school experiences as a result of discrepancy between their high ability and their learning disability. Complex emotions continued to affect them as young adults. Several of them sought counseling to reconcile some of the problems they experienced. One young woman described how she contemplated suicide:

> What I did as a senior was, I watched all these kids apply at schools. They were my best friends applying to schools . . . they were 1st, 2nd, 3rd, and 4th in class, and I said, "what the hell am I going to do?" My father has this nice job. My uncle is a professor at Cornell, and I am this real shameful thing in the family, I mean, it was really awful and I knew there wasn't anything that I could do. I couldn't take notes. There were so many things that I couldn't do, so I decided that suicide was the answer, and I planned to do it before graduation. I carried it right out. . . I gave all my stuff away. I did all the things that kids do when they are planning to kill themselves. I decided I'd make peace with everyone. I had a teacher pull me in, and she said, "Are you thinking about suicide?" It was so abrupt and straightforward. I didn't know what to do except say "yes." (Reis & Ruban, 2004, p. 169)

Reis and Ruban noted that appropriate interventions were pursued for this young woman, who eventually developed compensation strategies to cope with her disability and to succeed in college and graduate school.

Challenges With Identity Development

Another critical issue that gifted students with LD experience is a struggle with identity development (Dole, 2001). Given their experiences with feeling smart in some areas of their lives and feeling incapable in others, they may constantly question their abilities and struggle to understand just who they are. Mendaglio (1993) explained that gifted students with learning disabilities experience "an added dimension of uncertainty with respect to their self perception" (p. 133). Throughout their early experiences in school, these students have had their identity defined by whether or not they were successful. Samantha Abeel (2003) described her experiences with learning to read and the impact they had on her view of self. She started out the academic year in one of the more advanced reading groups but eventually was moved to one of the slower groups when she struggled to master skills. Embarrassed by this, she started to question her abilities. She explained,

> I also felt anxious about maintaining my identity. I felt very strongly that I did not want anyone to know that I didn't get it, and that I should pretend I did. Everyone thought I was smart and I didn't want them thinking otherwise; *I* didn't want to think otherwise. (Abeel, 2003, p. 11)

For these young people, the effect on identity development continues through later adolescence. This struggle is evident in Christie Jackson's (2001) description of her college application process, a time during which she questioned who she was as a student:

> I was an overachiever, I admit, and the college admissions process was just another one of my extensive projects. I applied to 12 colleges, thinking I would not get in anywhere and wondering why any school would want me. I remember I cried a lot during this year. At times I cried because I felt I was faking my intelligence, somehow slipping through the cracks. I cried because I felt I would fail. I kept repeating, "Let me get in somewhere, anywhere, please God." Somehow I was admitted to a prestigious East Coast college, and I became known as the "Ivy Girl." I tried to keep the news low-key, but soon everyone assumed I was God's gift to academia.

Yeah, right! Everyone saw me as valedictorian. I saw myself as a fraud. (p. 43)

Mooney and Cole (2000) reflected on their early school experiences and described the role that school environments played in shaping their view of self. Teachers influenced the shaping of their identity as young boys. They explained, "We were taught that sitting still and getting gold stars on our math homework were more important than art and ideas, and much more important than what kind of people we were and how we treated other kids" (Mooney & Cole, 2000, p. 68). They highlighted how their success in school, their performance and behavior, defined who they were. "From our first days in school, we are given an idea of what it means to succeed. It does not mean having compassion for the kid who falls down on the playground or questioning why we have to spell correctly. Instead, success means reaching for those gold stars at any cost" (Mooney & Cole, 2000, pp. 70–71).

Sara Renzulli highlighted how she resolved her struggle with identity development and how this resolution influenced her relationships with her peers in her private high school. She explained:

The friends that I made at my private high school are a second family to me: They are the people I look forward to seeing the most when on vacation, and often the people I want to tell big news to first. I believe I was able to make these friends because I became comfortable with who I was. A large part of that was figuring out on my own how to deal with my learning disability and be as successful as I possibly could become. My friends know that I have a learning disability, but it is not how they define me. They define me by all my weird, quirky traits that make up my character. (Baum et al., 2005, p. 153)

Perception of Self May Be Influenced by Extracurricular Talents and Strengths

How they see themselves in school versus how they view themselves out of school can be significant in shaping the identity of twice-exceptional students. Some will find salvation in extracurricular activities. Rather than see themselves as intelligent young people who may be struggling learners in mathematics or language arts, they prefer to view themselves as superstars on the athletic field or the theatrical stage. Their engagement in a sport or extracurricular activity provides them the feeling of what it must be like to be a smart student. Their identity is shaped by their experiences with such successes.

To help students maintain a positive self-esteem, it is critical that parents, educators, and counselors not allow gifted students with learning disabilities to think of themselves in a one-dimensional way. Realistically, success in extracurricular activities will not last forever and adults do students a disservice when promoting the view that their abilities in other domains will totally counteract the struggles with learning. Jonathan Mooney (Mooney & Cole, 2000) highlighted this issue when he described his experience withdrawing from school in sixth grade, frustrated with his academic life and subsequently dedicating himself to soccer. Jonathan considered this sport as his only hope for the future. During this period, he saw family being affected by his need to achieve in this domain, and his extreme involvement in the sport actually led him to question his abilities further. He feared that his athletic ability might quickly fade. He described being haunted by images of his mother on the sidelines screaming at him as he played. His father coached his teams and he adopted his father's obsession with athletic training. The obsession eventually undermined Jonathan's belief in his talents and the regimentation took away his love of soccer, a sport that had initially brought him joy and experiences with success.

Difficulties With Peer Relationships

Along with struggling with identity development, relationships with peers become difficult for twice-exceptional students as they progress through school. Many of them feel isolated as they struggle to establish satisfying relationships with friends. Daniels (1991) called attention to this issue with three possible scenarios these students might experience in the course of a school day. Daniels asked that we consider the dilemma of the child who is in three classroom settings as a result of being identified as gifted and learning disabled. Because a child may be receiving services in the LD resource room, he misses important social activities in the regular classroom. While he is in the LD resource room, he cannot find a peer to identify with intellectually. During his gifted and talented classroom activities, he may not be able to make the quick responses that other students do because he must compensate for his disability. Daniels (1991) noted that gifted students with learning disabilities may respond in a number of ways. The child may act out or become the comedian in the regular classroom to divert attention away from his disability. In the gifted and talented class-room, he protects himself by denigrating the interests and ideas of others, and in the LD resource room, he seeks out friendships by identifying with the negative behaviors of others struggling academically.

The stress and frustration experienced in school by many twice-exceptional students may have social ramifications. As their battle with academics continues and as they begin to have negative views of themselves, their peer relationships may change. The friends they had during the earlier period in their lives when they saw themselves as competent and smart are no longer in their reading groups and classes or sitting with them in the school cafeteria. Those friends may become participants in the school's gifted program, and the gifted child with learning disabilities is left feeling deserted, especially if he or she is not in the program. These students may then take a defensive approach in coping with this upsetting situation.

Samantha Abeel (2003) described how she did not qualify for the gifted program because of her low math scores. When her friends qualified for the program, she coped with her jealousy by making fun of them with names like "Nerd Herd." Although she realized that those students were her social group, she chose to retreat from her old friends. She withdrew into herself. This withdrawal continued to plague her during middle and high school and remained a concern even as an undergraduate. This issue affected her at a time in her life when other young women were ready to explore new relationships and discover new places in their college commu-nity to have fun. She excused herself from parties and dances with excuses that she had a paper to write or she escaped to the library at the last minute so her friends would not find her in time for a party.

Many of these students withdraw from their peer group. Christie Jackson (2001) described how she felt like an outsider among her peers:

> During grade school, I was a very quiet, shy student. I had many passions inside of me and about four friends, but I was always afraid of interacting with a large group, turning violently crimson whenever called upon. Everyone saw me as the class brain, who was quiet and always slightly out of the cool group. I was not into the normal early teen fascinations. I would rather watch NOVA than MTV, rather hear Mozart than Madonna, and read classical books than *Sweet Valley High*. (p. 41)

Gifted young people with learning disabilities often describe know-ing an answer in class but not being able to deliver it because they cannot articulate the words, resulting in ridicule. Fred, a participant in the Reis et al. (1995) study, explained, "I could know the word, know it well and say it wrong. I felt dumb in elementary school. I believed and trusted what the other kids told me. The kids would say, 'You're so dumb.' I believed them" (p. 54). Fred explained that he did not have friends because he said things in class that were not correct and his peers perceived him as strange. He responded by turning inward and withdrawing from others: "I would spend a lot of time alone because I was comfortable alone, and when you go out at recess walking alone being comfortable by yourself people start to think you are strange" (Reis et al., 1995, p. 55). Fred saw this situation as an unfortunate cycle that only worsened: "I had to be comfortable alone because I wasn't accepted into a group, because they saw me comfortable alone" (Reis et al., 1995, p. 55).

Numerous participants in the Reis et al. (1995) study recalled painful incidents related to peer pressure. Kate recalled one particularly traumatic event:

> I remember an instance when I wanted to die. My girlfriend sat next to me in history class. I don't think she even knew what she did. My history teacher was tough on us. . . . He asked me to read out loud, so I had to read. I only read like one paragraph and I stopped, and he picked someone else in class and my girlfriend turned to me and said, "What's wrong with you, you can't even read?" And I thought, "You're my friend. Why did you have to embarrass me like this?" It was so hard. (Reis et al., 1995, p. 55)

A Need to Understand the Diagnosis

With gifted students with learning disabilities, their life experiences have such a dichotomous quality and the sooner they realize that will persist, the healthier they will be. There is a need to understand the experience of both being gifted and having a disability in order to help these students accept their situation, move forward, and live life deliberately. The official diagnosis of the learning disability provides a concrete explanation for why school has been such a struggle, and they feel relief when they understand their diagnosis. Kevin Marshall (2001) described the need to understand this dichotomy:

I was first diagnosed with dyslexia in college. Dyslexia comes in many different forms, and mine is auditory. The disability makes it difficult to hear and recite, read problems, and digest speech quickly. For me, Spanish recitation sessions were problematic because they involve call-and-response. . . . When I was first diagnosed with the disability, I felt that a weight had been lifted from my back. I had been having a terrible time in Spanish class, and I was becoming almost depressed with the thought of not being able to do well in a language class. While trying to learn Spanish, I feared that perhaps I was not academically "up to par" with the rest of my classmates. But learning that many of the problems that I encountered were actually not caused by my lack of intelligence or lack of effort, but by a learning problem that I could not control, helped to alleviate some of my fears. (p. 119)

These students are finally able to say to the world, "See! This problem is real! There really has been something wrong with me all these years. I want everyone to know and understand that about me." With this new understanding it becomes easier to accept that they will need support from the learning disabilities program in their schools. Moreover, they are better able to cope with their peers' questions at school. For example, Samantha Abeel (2003) described how she felt empowered with her new understanding of her abilities and when friends asked what math class she was taking, she enjoyed being able to tell them the truth, "Special education math." She realized that her friends realized that she was intelligent and fun and they would understand that her math placement was where she needed to be.

Learning to Live With the Disability

When students are officially diagnosed as having a learning disability and understand that they are not to blame for the problem, they are likely to feel a sense of relief. Once they understand their brain works differently, they are able to acknowledge the learning disability and work with it. However, they must come to understand that the disability will have an impact on many aspects of their lives. Samantha Abeel (2003) highlighted this as she explained:

I need to acknowledge that my learning disability is an innate part of who I am. I can't ignore it. I can't do things like everyone else at this pace. I need to slow down, get the help and support I need. It's OK to ask for help—and I'm OK just the way I am . . . (p. 179)

After this acknowledgment, gifted students with LD must begin to work with supportive adults to understand how the disability will impact various aspects of their lives. Particular skills may be challenging for them, skills that will be required in summer jobs, college courses, or daily activities. Balancing a checkbook, maintaining a schedule, acquiring a driver's license, and dealing with combination locks on a high school locker are just a few that some face. As they move into adulthood, the challenges may change; however, the issue of the disability does not. As Samantha explained, "I have had to learn to make peace with the concept that I will always be working within myself to accept how my learning disability affects me as the circumstances in my life change" (Abeel, 2003, p. 202).

Survival Techniques That Gifted Learning-Disabled Students Implement

The following discussion highlights insights gained from examining the experiences of Samantha Abeel, Jonathan Mooney, David Cole, Sara Renzulli, Christie Jackson, and others included in research studies highlighted in this chapter. The descriptions of their experiences provide examples of techniques they implemented to be successful in school.

Understand That Being a Different Type of Learner Does Not Mean It Is a Deficit

Gifted students with learning disabilities typically come to terms with their disability after being officially diagnosed. They come to understand that the disability is with them for life and it will help shape their lives. What they must also understand is that their learning differences are not deficits. Their differences can be appreciated as an important part of their identity. This notion of "different does not equal deficit" is highlighted in David Cole's story of his admissions interview at Brown University. The creative young artist provided the university administrators with a delightful surprise:

I lifted a heavy cardboard box out of the trunk of my car, and walked into the admissions building at Brown University. In the spacious waiting room, once the living room of a Victorian house, I carefully cleared off the coffee table. I started removing the items from the box, and before I had them even half set up, I realized that I was being watched. A passing admissions officer, weary from the final rounds of freshman applicants, was engrossed, watching me, a young man in a proper blue blazer, kneeling down on the carpet and setting out an assortment of welded steel sculptures on his coffee table. It was my "writing process." I stood up, introduced myself, and began to explain what I had brought with me. . . . By the end of the day I had cleared off two more coffee tables—in the office of the dean of disability support services, and in the office of the chair of the Art Department. Not your average college application story, but then again, I've never been much at being average. (Mooney & Cole, 2000, p. 60)

Focus on Gifts and Celebrate Strengths

For gifted students with learning disabilities, tapping into their strengths becomes a salvation from the struggles they experience in school. For Samantha Abeel writing became a creative outlet for self-expression, affording her an ego boost during adolescence and an emotional outlet that enabled her to express the melancholy she experienced as she struggled to cope with her learning disability. By middle school, "the discovery of writing was my lifeline. My writing gave me some sanity amidst the increasingly difficult challenges I was facing to keep up in my other school classes" (Abeel, 2003, p. 39). She described her seventh-grade writing class as her "life preserver." She explained, "It was the one thing that got me through the anxiety and fear that plagued me. No matter what I couldn't do, I could write. I found an identity in that skill and I clung to it. I told myself again and again that I was special, that I was different and my ability to write was proof" (Abeel, 2003, pp. 77–78). In the introduction of her book *Reach for the Moon*, Abeel and Murphy (1994) spoke to readers who may also be struggling to understand their learning disability, and encouraged them to focus on their strengths:

If you struggle with a disability, the first thing you need to do is find something that you are good at, whether it's singing or skate boarding, an interest in science or acting, even just being good with people. Then do something with that. If you are good with people, then volunteer at a nursing home or at a day care center; if you love skate boarding, work toward a competition. If it's singing, join a school choir. Even if you can't read music (like me) or read a script, you can always find ways of coping and compensating.

Find Supportive Teachers

Teachers can make a great difference in the life of a child, and many gifted students with learning disabilities have found that connecting with a supportive teacher was critical to their success (Baum & Owen, 2004; Reis et al., 1995). Professionals working with these students and their families can advocate for them by selecting teachers who are sensitive to the needs of this population. Teachers who focus on the strengths of students and do not concentrate solely on closing the gaps in their skills can help ensure success. With their intuition, gifted students with LD may be able to identify teachers who are empathetic and reach out to them for social and emotional support. Jonathan Mooney spoke warmly of an elementary teacher who made a difference for him. "Mr. R" created a classroom environment where he could be successful with science and social studies projects. In this classroom there were no reading groups and children read at their own individualized pace. There were no spelling tests and students used computers for writing. Jonathan explained, "Most of all Mr. R. respected me. When I struggled during reading lessons, he sat next to me and put his arm around me. *That arm saved my life*" (Mooney & Coles, 2000, p. 34).

For Samantha Abeel, her seventh-grade writing teacher, Roberta Williams, was instrumental to her development. The attention she paid to the aspiring writer and her willingness to overlook the spelling and grammar mistakes for the content and ideas made a difference. In her book of poetry, *Reach for the Moon* (Abeel & Murphy, 1994), Samantha included a brief essay from her teacher. Mrs. Williams pointed out that Samantha Abeel's story should serve as a reminder to educators that when they look for and nurture "possibilities and potential" in every student, their students are likely to become successful learners. She calls attention to teacher responsibility to discover students like Samantha:

> I suspect that many more Samanthas sit in our classrooms: the quiet ones who hide out in the back, the ones who always "forget" their homework or constantly apologize, the ones who cover up by distracting us with their behavior, their language, or their attitude. How many have we missed because we didn't have the right key,

didn't know a key existed, didn't even know the door was locked? ... The willingness to help them should define the word "teacher."

Recognize Intuition as a Strength

Gifted students with learning disabilities have been recognized for their intuition. Guyer (2000) maintained that many learning-disabled individuals have a unique understanding of the problems faced by others, an attunement to the needs of other people, and a high level of empathy. They have developed these characteristics as a result of their dichotomous situations. These individuals spend their childhood years honing their observation skills, learning to read the small facial gestures of people, and studying the changing moods, reactions, and patterns of behavior. These skills enable them to survive in a world that may not always understand learning disabilities. Samantha Abeel (2003) described her experiences in middle school when a popular girl, who was often in trouble, would often invite her to sit at a separate table in the school cafeteria after they were finished eating lunch. Referring to their conversations as her "counseling sessions," she would share her latest problem or friendship crisis with Samantha, and she expressed awe at Samantha's wisdom.

Take Pride in Resilience

Resilience theory attempts to explain the academic success of students who encounter negative psychological situations. Resilience has been described as a protective mechanism that modifies an individual's response to a risk (Rutter, 1981, 1987) or as adjustment despite negative life events. Rutter (1987) defined resilience as a "positive role of individual differences in people's response to stress and adversity" (p. 316). McMillan and Reed (1994) maintained that resilient students are those who "have a set of personality characteristics, dispositions, and beliefs that promote their academic success regardless of their backgrounds or current circumstances" (p. 139).

To define *adversity* is to describe the experience of gifted students with learning and attention difficulties. These young people often experience a negative psychological situation filled with stress and frustration; therefore, developing the ability to bounce back from adversity and overcome challenges is critical to success. These students need to be educated about resilience and asked to look for it within themselves. As noted in Figure 4, many successful individuals in American society have overcome a learning disability or attention disorder. Their life stories are stories of resilience.

This trait is not a fixed attribute in individuals, and the successful negotiation of psychological risks at one point in a person's life does not guarantee that the individual will not respond adversely to other stresses when situations change (Reis, Colbert & Hébert, 2005); however, resilience can be developed within young people and assist them in life. Mooney and Cole (2000) highlighted how resilience shaped them, "Our struggles make us stronger, and our wounds heal and knit together to constitute the strength of the fabric of our character" (p. 264).

It is important to note that students featured in the research literature highlighted in this chapter often described their resilience. Representative of this were reflections from Kevin Marshall (2001), in which he spoke with pride of the resilience he recognized in himself:

> I am open to offering people my disability history when someone speaks about obstacles they face. It feels good to let people know that there are sometimes invisible obstacles that can hold you back . . . I like to let people, especially children or family, know that they can overcome any obstacle . . . In defining myself, I have never let the diagnosis of my learning disability play a role. Having a learning disability is only a small part of who I am. And even though the disability explains some of the frustrations that I have experienced academically, I refuse to let it stand in the way of my achievements and my goals. I take pride in my athletic abilities and how far they have taken me, helping me get into college and be successful. I am also equally proud of my academic achievements, which have allowed me to attend a prestigious school and reap the benefits and rewards of determination and hard work. (p. 120)

How Can Educators and Counselors Support Gifted Students With Learning and Attention Difficulties?

Understanding what we have learned from the gifted individuals with learning disabilities highlighted in this chapter, it remains clear that twice-exceptional students need support to help them cope socially and emotionally with the combination of high ability and disability. After several years of struggling with failure, many with disabilities lose confidence in their ability, and their academic self-efficacy diminishes over time (Baum & Owen, 2004). This situation seems even more troublesome for gifted students with LD, for they often have a heightened awareness and sensitivity to failure and are distressed by the discrepancy between what they are capable of doing and their struggles related to learning. More serious problems may develop.

Twice-exceptional students may feel overwhelmed and be unable to cope effectively. They then may begin to manifest negative behaviors such as acting out in class, procrastinating, failing to turn in work, skipping school, and seeking an inappropriate peer group. Should the stress continue, the students may experience physical manifestations such as digestive problems, body aches, headaches, or eye strain. Such ailments are not imagined and serve as indicators of emotional difficulties. If these symptoms are not addressed, the situation may deteriorate further, resulting in serious anxiety, severe depression, obsessive-compulsive behavior, or extreme inattentiveness and hyperactivity (Kauffman, 2001). In order to prevent such burnout from occurring, teachers and counselors need to facilitate a number of strategies designed to support twice-exceptional students. Below are several that educators may want to consider.

Offer Group Counseling

Gifted students with learning disabilities "need opportunities to talk about their feelings, to learn to advocate for themselves, and to set goals that align to their gifts and talents" (Baum et al., 2005, p. 159). Group counseling in schools offers numerous benefits. In small-group sessions, students can safely discuss their concerns with others in similar situations. They learn that they are not alone, that others share their frustrations and problems. Their perceptions of self improve as they have an opportunity to be listened to and accepted by others. Group members can form a positive prosocial group for students who have long felt isolated. Moreover, within the group, they may actually be more willing to consider others' observations and accept suggestions than listen to the recommendations of adults elsewhere. Christie Jackson (2001) described how she felt when she shared the same learning disability with a friend:

> Like long-lost family reunited, we understood each other. We spoke of the feeling of failure, about the pain of isolation. Nothing is more comforting than to hear someone else speak the words you are unable to express. She let me talk mostly, yet her eyes told me that she wanted to soak in all I said, as if my words were what she longed to hear another human utter. Then she thanked me, and I

will remember this as the only time I have ever been happy to have a learning disability. (p. 49)

In group counseling sessions facilitated by an empathic school counselor, gifted students like Christie have opportunities to experience similar conversations, receive support, and make connections with other students who can identify with their feelings.

Counseling can help students like Christie deal with depression and anger associated with the struggle to understand their inconsistent performance in school. Through regularly scheduled group sessions, counselors are able to help students understand unique challenges and develop strategies for coping with these challenges. Involving gifted students with LD in counseling approaches involving the arts is effective, because many have nonverbal communication strengths. Music, photography, and art therapies offer students outlets to explore difficulties and develop coping techniques (Henley, 2000; Patterson, 2003).

Groups foster self-efficacy, as supportive counselors can help to establish an expectation within students that they can master particular tasks. During group sessions members have opportunities to rehearse skills and role-play conversations that enable them to become their own advocates. Through such activities they build important communication skills. Educators and counselors in higher education have long advocated for support groups for college students with LD and have noted that groups make a difference in recruitment and retention of twice-exceptional students (Cobb, 2003; Knab, Cashman, & Sullivan, 2000). Cobb (2003) noted that a support group may be simply an informal gathering where students with learning disabilities get together and just listen to each other, a place to hear "horror stories" of "fellow sufferers" (p. 89). Such an exchange can be helpful in identifying instructors who are "disability friendly" and an important time for students to vent to those who understand what they are experiencing.

Share Biographies and Biographical Movies of Successful Gifted Individuals With Learning Disabilities

Middle and high school gifted students with LD will benefit from sessions in which teachers and counselors share biographies and autobiographies of successful and famous individuals who grew up with disabilities, as well as ADHD. Inspirational stories of these men and women who overcame their challenges can provide students with emotional support.

Novelist Fannie Flagg, Olympic diver Greg Louganis, NFL star Terry Bradshaw, and fashion designer Tommy Hilfiger, to name a few, are all inspirational models. Teachers may want to consider focusing on the childhood and teenage years of these successful individuals so that they are likely to identify with them. A helpful resource for teachers and counselors pursuing this approach is Lauren and Verdick's (2004) *Succeeding With LD: 20 True Stories About Real People With LD*. Educators with limited time will welcome this edited collection of short biographical sketches that can be shared with students. Teachers and counselors would be remiss if they did not share Samantha Abeel's (2003) *My Thirteenth Winter: A Memoir*, and Jonathan Mooney and David Cole's (2000) *Learning Outside the Lines*. These two books provide twice-exceptional learners with three life stories that may foster self-understanding.

Teachers and counselors may also want to consider sharing biographical films of successful gifted individuals with LD. Biographical videos appeal to visual learners more than books do, as film appeals to multiple senses (Hébert & Sergent, 2005). Moreover, gifted students with dyslexia think mainly in pictures rather than in words (Silverman, 2003). Such an approach is an appropriate strategy for a resource room teacher, school counselor, or gifted education teacher. When watching videos of success stories and discussing issues highlighted in the video in a safe, relaxed environment, students are likely to be receptive to discussing the issues in their own lives. Commercial bookstores and home entertainment stores feature collections of biographical videos appropriate for classroom use on the lives of people such as Patricia Polacco and Whoopi Goldberg.

Facilitate Discussions That Guide Students to Self-Understanding Using Literature

Classroom teachers have long used children's literature to address affective concerns of their students. Teachers working with twice-exceptional students are no exception. Discussing characters who face similar challenges is a strategy the special education community has advocated for many years (Anderson, 2000; Halsted, 2009; Lindsey & Frith, 1981). Appendix A contains an annotated bibliography of children's literature appropriate for facilitating therapeutic discussions with gifted young people with disabilities, including picture books that focus on the experiences of being twice exceptional. For example, Ross and Barron (1994) offered young readers a delightful picture book entitled *Eggbert: The Slightly Cracked Egg*. Another resource is a picture book by Polacco (1998), an author and illustrator of children's literature. In *Thank you, Mr. Falker*, Polacco's childhood autobiography, we learn of her experiences as a gifted artist who struggled with a disability. Samantha Abeel's (Abeel & Murphy, 1994) *Reach for the Moon*, is a collection of beautiful poetry and breathtaking art reflecting Samantha's remarkable journey of growth and self-discovery.

Esham's (2008a, 2008b, 2008c, 2008d) series entitled the Adventures of Everyday Geniuses, is a delightful collection of picture books that address learning difficulties of elementary school children. Esham's work helps young children understand and appreciate their issues with math facts and memorization, handwriting, attention, and dyslexia, for example, while appreciating their gifts, special talents, and creativity. The following books are highly recommended for classroom picture book collections to provide support for twice-exceptional students:

- *If You're So Smart, How Come You Can't Spell Mississippi?*
- *Last to Finish: A Story About the Smartest Boy in Math Class*
- *Mrs. Gorski, I Think I Have the Wiggle Fidgets*
- *Stacey Coolidge's Fancy-Smancy Cursive Handwriting*

In addition to these picture books are several trade books for elementary students. *My Name is ~~Brain~~ Brian* by Jeanne Betancourt (1993) is the story of Brian Toomey, a sixth-grade student with dyslexia who discovers his creative ability to write poetry. Henry Winkler, the well-known actor, producer, and director, coauthored with Lin Oliver a series of compassionate books describing the experiences of the fictitious Hank Zipper. The books are advertised as "the mostly true confessions of the world's greatest underachiever." Readers appreciate the authors' sensitivity in depicting the delightful and highly creative adventures of the protagonist, a young man with a zest for life who comes to understand the role of his learning differences in and out of school. Teachers and counselors may want to begin their discussion groups with Winkler and Oliver's (2003a, 2003b) *I got a "D" in Salami* and *Niagara Falls, or Does It?*

Teach Stress Management

Because gifted students with LD experience high stress, one of the most helpful strategies educators, parents, and counselors can employ is to teach stress management techniques. Stress management may be incorporated into group counseling sessions or the classroom and reinforced by the learning disabilities specialist, teacher of the gifted, classroom teacher, or school counselor. Peterson's (2008) *The Essential Guide to Talking With*

Gifted Teens provides educators and counselors with a helpful resource for facilitating guided discussions and counseling groups. In sessions focusing on stress, the objectives are to help students learn that it can feel good to talk about their stressors and the feelings associated with them. When students hear about the stressors of other group members, it enables them to put their own stressors into perspective. The sharing also helps participants feel less alone in dealing with their stress. Students learn to focus on the present rather than looking anxiously toward the future. They also consider making adjustments in their lives to relieve stress. Moreover, they realize that responses to stress and coping strategies are often learned from adult role models. Peterson's (2008) guide for counseling groups can be applied effectively to working with gifted students with LD.

Educators and counselors offering instruction in stress management to children and teenagers will find that commercial bookstores provide extensive collections of books that teach stress reduction. These self-help books provide a common-sense approach that adults have long appreciated (see Olivier, 2003, Powell, 2002). Many of them are written in a style that appeals to a teenage audience and are packed with insights and techniques that empower young people to gain control of their lives. Teachers and counselors can use this material to address the stressors of children and teenagers. The menu of stress-reducing strategies below is compiled from such materials and represents important concepts that twice-exceptional students need to understand in order to better cope with the stressors in their lives. Teachers and counselors can support young people with stress management easily by passing on the following helpful tips:

- Enjoy a healthy diet that helps your body manage stress.
- Eliminate caffeinated beverages.
- Spend time in a quiet private place for reflection at the end of a school day.
- Enjoy any form of physical exercise or sports.
- Unwind from the challenges of the day by tuning into your favorite music.
- Enjoy time with your pets.
- Spend time talking with a good friend.
- Keep a journal and spend time working through your feelings.
- Write poetry.
- Enjoy a warm and relaxing bubble bath.
- Learn yoga and take time after school to unwind from your day.
- Enjoy a good book.
- Spend time reading something that makes you laugh.

   ❧ Spend quiet time sketching, drawing, or cartooning.

   ❧ Enjoy a hobby.

Provide a Safe Haven

David Cole, the successful visual artist in *Learning Outside the Lines* (Mooney & Cole, 2000), described a middle school art teacher who provided him a safe environment to escape to when he needed an outlet for dealing with the stress and frustration of struggling with attention difficulties in school: "Jan the art teacher let me hang around, and it would be okay. I would walk out of math class sometimes and go into the art room." He explained, "I didn't make any art (except for two little paintings and a batik mask), but I knew that she liked me" (Mooney & Cole, 2000, p. 54).

As in David's case, there may be times when twice-exceptional students may become overwhelmed with stress and frustration. When stress overpowers them and they are feeling emotionally fragile, having an empathic adult to turn to may make a huge difference in a child's school day. Baum and Owen (2004) referred to this approach as providing a safe haven. Knowing that there is someone in the building who cares about them may enable some to survive another day in school. A school counselor, teacher of the gifted, resource room teacher, or administrator can offer support by providing space, time, and strategies for reducing stress. For some students, simply sharing positive and negative news of the day, whether it is success on multiplication facts or an embarrassing moment in the cafeteria, may make a difference.

Help Students Appreciate Their Intuitive Qualities, Celebrate Their Creativity, and See the Value of Developing Resilience

Intuition, creativity, and resilience, three qualities of many gifted young people with learning and attention difficulties, should be celebrated as often as possible. The twice-exceptional students in our classrooms who are living out the dichotomous experience of being highly intelligent and having a disability need to be reminded often that they have special traits that will enable them to succeed.

These young people have usually developed observation skills, learned to read facial gestures, and understand body language. They notice changing moods, reactions, and behavior patterns. These finely tuned intuitive skills allow them to be able to read people accurately, and this special ability will likely serve them well professionally and interpersonally as adults.

For example, reading the demeanor and body language of a university professor and knowing whether or not she appreciates students stopping by her office unexpectedly may serve a college student well. Being able to read the mood of an employer and realize when it is the right time to ask for an increase in salary may come in handy. Teachers and counselors can call attention to these skills. Straightforward discussions with students about how their intuition serves them well are important, for twice-exceptional students need to take note of how this special human quality supports them and feel pride in it.

In addition to celebrating their intuitive qualities, teachers can celebrate the creativity of their gifted students with LD. Having them apply their creative strengths to academic tasks and celebrating their success as creative problem solvers can boost self-esteem. A twice-exceptional student benefits greatly when parents and teachers highlight his or her creativity. A young artist benefits more from praise for the original cartoon script he publishes in a national children's magazine than from an adult's concern about his poor spelling. A young kinesthetic learner profits when teachers and friends appreciate his original inventive contraptions. A student who determines accurate directions for her directionally challenged teacher and chaperones, who are guiding her classmates to the theatre district in New York, enjoys recognition for her ability to solve a spatial problem creatively.

Finally, it is important that teachers and counselors openly celebrate the resilience of twice-exceptional students. This special trait they are developing when young is another quality that will serve them well as adults. Highlighting resilience in the biographies of successful individuals with LD and drawing parallels to their lives allows them to see how valuable this trait is. They may be inspired by the powerful message that Mooney and Cole (2000) delivered in the conclusion of their book:

> When our report cards fade from our memory, and we have healed the wounds from our past, and when college rankings and our GPA bleed into oblivion, what stays is a beautiful and profound struggle to be true to ourselves that no one, not even time, can ever take away from us. (pp. 264–265)

For Further Thought and Discussion

- Imagine you were able to invite Samantha Abeel to your classroom as a guest speaker. What message would you want her to deliver to your students? Why?
- What can educators, school counselors, and parents do to help gifted students with learning disabilities find supportive friendships?
- Explain your philosophical view of the role of extracurricular activities in the lives of gifted students with LD.
- The description of David Cole's experience with the admissions interview at Brown University may serve as a significant discussion starter with gifted students with learning disabilities. How might you facilitate this discussion?
- How do you think teachers in your school would respond to the notion of providing gifted students with learning disabilities the "safe haven" advocated by Baum and Owen (2004)? How would you respond?
- Imagine you could plan a dinner party for gifted students with learning disabilities. Your invitation list may include several individuals listed in Figure 4. Who would you invite to dine with the students? What topics would you hope would emerge during the dinner conversation? Why?

Resources to Expand Your Thinking and Extend Your Support to Gifted Students

Baum, S. M., & Owen, S. V. (2004). *To be gifted and learning disabled: Strategies for helping bright students with LD, ADHD, and more.* Mansfield Center, CT: Creative Learning Press.

Lavoie, R. (2005). *It's so much work to be your friend: Helping the child with learning disabilities find social success.* New York, NY: Simon & Schuster.

CHAPTER 9

Supporting the Social and Emotional Development of Gifted Culturally Diverse Students

My goals for this chapter are to:
- ❧ Introduce you to within-group heterogeneity in understanding culturally diverse populations.
- ❧ Discuss the role played by contextual influences on the experiences of culturally diverse students.
- ❧ Examine ethnic identity development in culturally diverse students.
- ❧ Examine the challenges related to social and emotional development facing gifted culturally diverse students.
- ❧ Present strategies and methods for supporting gifted culturally diverse students.

Guided by my heritage of a love of beauty and a respect for strength—in search of my mother's garden, I found my own.

—Alice Walker

Walter Wallace, a young African American child, attended classes in Manhattan and enjoyed his educational experiences in a special program for gifted students. His journey to school every morning involved dodging crowds of adults as he maneuvered his way through the New York City subways; however, the young child knew that his school experiences would be worthwhile, so he didn't mind the hectic daily journey. Walter knew his school day would be filled with exciting classroom activities, an intellectually stimulating curriculum that was accelerated and challenging, and plenty of time to interact with intellectual peers who were also enthusiastic about learning. Moreover, he enjoyed the times his teacher held discussions centered on emotional issues in their lives. For Walter, the only African American male in the class, these discussions were important because they related to his life as a highly gifted culturally diverse child in a metropolitan community.

Today Dr. Walter Wallace is a retired professor of sociology living in Pennsylvania. His recollections of the Speyer School in New York City include many wonderful stories of his dedicated teacher, Leta Sutter Hollingworth, and he considers himself fortunate to have been her student. As a participant in a special program for highly gifted children, he attended classes with other children who also journeyed from New York's ethnically diverse neighborhoods in the 1920s; together these students pursued an education that included opportunities for independent investigations, biographical studies, and individualized learning. Dr. Wallace cherished these memories of his early years at the Speyer School and realized that his teacher and her teaching methods were far ahead of their time (W. Wallace, personal communication, February 2005; W. White, personal communication, July 2010).

Walter Wallace was a very fortunate child. A review of the gifted education movement in this country reveals that Leta Hollingworth (1926, 1942) was the first educator to advocate educational programming that addressed the counseling needs of gifted children with sensitivity to the needs of the culturally diverse. Although Leta Hollingworth accurately anticipated some of the social and emotional issues that educators in gifted education are concerned about today, not until the 1950s were concentrated efforts in counseling directed at gifted students. With the leadership of scholars such as John Rothney, Charles Pulvino, Nicholas Colangelo, and

Phillip Berrone, researchers began to address issues related to counseling gifted individuals (Colangelo, 2003), and labs and guidance degree programs were established. From the 1950s through the 1970s, John Curtis Gowan played a significant role in advocating for counseling programs for gifted young people and initiated a conversation about gifted underachievers (see Gowan, 1955). With the advent of the Civil Rights Movement in the 1960s, increased sensitivity to the issues and counseling needs of gifted minority students emerged.

In 1979, Nicolas Colangelo and R. T. Zaffran edited a definitive collection entitled *New Voices in Counseling the Gifted* that addressed the counseling needs of gifted students. Colangelo and Zaffran invited leading researchers and theorists of gifted education to offer their expertise on the most compelling issues related to counseling high-ability youth. In response to that invitation, Mary Frasier contributed a chapter entitled "Counseling the Culturally Diverse Gifted." Frasier (1979) identified four major areas of focus in the counseling of gifted culturally diverse children: identity as gifted individuals, difficulty making academic and vocational decisions, problems of social adjustments within their own culture and the dominant culture, and problems in facing and resolving interpersonal conflicts.

Colangelo and Lafrenz (1981) added to the conversation by highlighting several additional concerns. They called for helping culturally diverse students to address ethnic identity issues, noting that in order to realize their potential, these students would need support to maintain their cultural identity while also remaining a part of the majority culture. They observed that these young people might face peer pressure that discouraged them from succeeding in the dominant culture. Continuing with this line of inquiry, Colangelo (1985) called for counselors to work with parents of gifted culturally diverse students to help them become effective advocates for their children as well to preserve family and community values that support the children. Ford and Harris (1999) reinvigorated the dialogue by calling attention to several new issues. They saw a critical need for educators and counselors to focus on questions related to underachievement within minority populations, ethnic identity development, and social injustice and discrimination faced by gifted culturally diverse youth.

The underrepresentation of culturally diverse students in gifted education programs has been well documented (Castellano, 2003; Dixon, 2003; Foley & Skenandore, 2003; Moore, Ford, & Milner, 2005a; Whiting, 2009). The gifted education community continues to struggle with solutions to this problem and to seek innovative ways of identifying gifts and talents in diverse students. As educators continue the work of discovering these gifts, however, they must simultaneously look for ways to address the affective needs of talented young people from diverse backgrounds whose gifts have already been identified. To retain culturally diverse young people in gifted programs, it is essential to provide services that support their social and emotional development.

Understanding Within-Group Heterogeneity

It is critical to understand the complexity of within-group heterogeneity, particularly because the diversity of American society is richer than ever before. The phrase *culturally diverse students* does not capture the essence of just how diverse our schools have become. The question today is, "Just how diverse is culturally diverse?" The answer to this question is astounding. Consider the following: Asian Americans come from 32 different cultural groups (Dana, 1998). Hispanic students in our schools represent all 22 Spanish-speaking countries and territories in the world (Castellano, 2003). The Native American population in the U.S. encompasses 562 distinct federally recognized tribes (Hayden, 2004). Native Hawaiians are also heterogeneous, encompassing Korean, Chinese, Japanese, and African ancestry, with only 1% considered "pure-blooded" (Banks, 1997). Children of Arab ancestry are now a visible ethnic group in our schools and include those whose cultural and ethnic origins can be traced to more than 20 countries in the Middle East and northern Africa (Nassar-McMillan, 2003). A prerequisite for working with children of African descent is an understanding of the term *African American*. Historically, the term was used to describe people of African descent born in the United States, who either experienced or inherited a history of slavery. The contemporary understanding of the term includes those persons who have immigrated to the United States and who chose the term African American because it best fits their group identity. This includes individuals from African countries, the West Indies, the Caribbean, and South America who do not classify themselves as Caucasian, Asian, Hispanic, or Native American (Brooks, Haskins, & Kehe, 2004).

With such a broad spectrum, we must understand and appreciate the rich variety and heterogeneity within each of these groups whose members may differ in history, immigration experience, language, religion, customs, socioeconomic status, degree of acculturation, and ethnic identity. We cannot examine issues facing culturally diverse gifted young people appropriately if our view of their cultural backgrounds is clouded by erroneous assumptions of intergroup homogeneity. Frasier and Passow (1994) maintained that within-group cultural differences are often as great as or greater than the differences among the four major "minorities"—African Americans, Hispanics, Asian Americans, and Native Americans—or the differences between those four groups and the equally diverse dominant majority. They indicated that these differences may include socioeconomic status; English proficiency; residency in an urban, suburban, rural or inner-city environment; and recency of immigration or migration. For example, within groups that might be considered living in communities that place them "at risk," Frasier (1989) noted, "there are many well-adjusted, well-cared for children even in inner city environments who are reinforced in their intellectual pursuits" (p. 222).

Educators and counselors must become more aware of and sensitive to the existence of individual differences within diverse populations if they are to educate children in settings that are becoming increasingly multicultural. In light of this need to recognize intergroup heterogeneity, this chapter examines the issues in counseling gifted culturally diverse students identified by Mary Frasier, Nicholas Colangelo, and Donna Ford as they relate to the diverse populations in our schools. In exploring these issues, we consider the role of environmental context in order to understand the challenges faced by gifted culturally diverse youths. We then hear the voices of gifted young people who have faced such challenges in their adolescence, some who have contributed to research studies involving culturally diverse students and others who have shared their experiences through published autobiographies. This chapter concludes with a discussion of teacher-friendly strategies to address the social and emotional development of gifted culturally diverse students.

Contextual Influences on the Experiences of Culturally Diverse Students

As discussed in an earlier chapter of this book, Bronfenbrenner's (1979) ecological model of the environment helps us understand the powerful role of context in shaping the experiences of young people. Bronfenbrenner views the environment as a series of nested and interrelated structures. The connections or interrelationships among structures such as homes, schools, and peer groups help explain why some culturally diverse gifted students have positive experiences in schools while others do not. For example, adolescents who have secure and harmonious relationships with their parents are more inclined to be accepted by their peers and to develop supportive friendships. Parents who have chosen to live in a suburban neighborhood made up of many different ethnic groups may encourage their children at a young age to play with other children of many different races and ethnic backgrounds. Early experiences with a racially integrated peer group enable children to feel more comfortable among a diverse group of students.

Findings from my research study of gifted African American males in a predominantly White university setting revealed that all of the young men in the study benefited from supportive mothers who insisted that their sons associate with friends who were academically oriented, regardless of racial or ethnic background. They received messages from their mothers such as, "You can never have too many friends. Never discriminate. Be a good person, and be accepting of all people" (Hébert, 2002, p. 40).

Although exposure to diverse populations allowed these young men to feel comfortable establishing friendships with others from a variety of ethnic backgrounds, some parents may discourage interaction with other young people beyond the immediate family circles. Hébert and Reis (1999) found that Hispanic parents in an urban community in Connecticut were often very protective of their daughters, not wanting them to venture out to major universities beyond their urban setting. They feared that living in university dormitories would expose their daughters to lifestyles that were not aligned with the family's value system. Instead, they wanted their daughters to attend community colleges within the city in order to remain at home with their families. With such expectations imposed by protective parents, these young women may be placed at a disadvantage when competing with others later in life.

Bronfenbrenner's (1979) theory also helps illuminate how a school's environment may influence the attitudes and experiences of gifted culturally diverse young people. At schools where members of the dominant culture are in the minority, attitudes regarding academic achievement are influenced in positive ways (Hébert & Reis, 1999). An environment that allows for a network of high-achieving peers to thrive is a contextual phenomenon that may positively influence the experiences of gifted culturally diverse students (Fries-Britt, 1997; Hébert & Reis, 1999). An ecological theoretical model such as Bronfenbrenner's (1979) underscores how individual contexts shape not only the experiences of gifted students, but also their self-concepts, their gifts, and their talents.

Ethnic Identity Development

Given the significance of contextual influences, a number of issues emerge as critical in understanding the social and emotional development of gifted culturally diverse students. Along with identity issues that all young people confront, culturally diverse adolescents must also establish an ethnic identity—a personal identification with an ethnic group and the value system and traditions maintained by the group (Phinney, 1996). For some this task may be difficult. Researchers who examine ethnic identity issues indicate that a commitment to an ethnic identity is an important component of the self-concept of culturally diverse teenagers and helps to prepare them for success in a multicultural society (Phinney, 1996).

Researchers have proposed general models of racial/ethnic identity development (see Atkinson et al., 1993; Phinney et. al, 1990) as well as culture-specific models of racial/ethnic identity (see Arce, 1981; Cross, 1995; Kim, 1981). Discussed in Chapter 5 on identity development was the work of Ponterotto and Pederson (1993) who examined these five models, identified commonalities across the various theories, and proposed a four-stage integrative model: Identification With the White Majority; Awareness, Encounter, and Search; Identification and Immersion; and Integration and Internalization.

The emergence of an ethnic identity is evidenced in many of the life stories of gifted culturally diverse individuals; therefore, examining their biographies and autobiographies enables us to more fully appreciate the significance of this developmental process. It is important to bear in mind the contextual and historical influences that shape the emergence of an ethnic identity. In his autobiography entitled *My American Journey*, former Secretary of State Colin Powell (1995) reflected on his adolescent experience growing up in Banana Kelly, a neighborhood in the South Bronx in the late 1940s:

> I have been asked when I felt a sense of racial identity, when I first understood that I belonged to a minority. In those early years, I had no such sense, because on Banana Kelly there was no majority. Everybody was either a Jew, an Italian, a Pole, a Greek, a Puerto Rican, or, as we said in those days, a Negro. Among my boyhood friends were Victor Ramirez, Walter Schwartz, Manny Garcia, Melvin Klein. The Kleins were the first family in our building to have a television set. Every Tuesday night, we crowded into Mel's

living room to watch Milton Berle. On Thursdays we watched *Amos 'n' Andy*. We thought the show was marvelous, the best thing on television. It was another age, and we did not know that we were not supposed to like *Amos 'n' Andy*. (p. 19)

This passage illuminates the role of historical context in understanding various attitudes toward race and ethnicity. With increased understanding of the significance of one's ethnic identity, contemporary teenagers would respond strongly to Colin Powell's experience and appreciate the journey he traveled to during more difficult times for African Americans.

Another example of ethnic identity taking shape within a gifted young person can be seen in the life story of Esmeralda Santiago. A gifted young woman who graduated from New York City's High School of Performing Arts, Santiago went on to earn a degree from Harvard University. She shared her adolescent experiences in her autobiography entitled *When I Was Puerto Rican* (1993). In her memoir, Santiago reflects on her transition from Puerto Rico to the public schools of Brooklyn and the difficulty she faced in understanding the behavior of other Puerto Rican young women:

There were two kinds of Puerto Ricans in school: the newly arrived, like myself, and the ones born in Brooklyn of Puerto Rican parents. The two types didn't mix. The Brooklyn Puerto Ricans spoke English, and often no Spanish at all. To them, Puerto Rico was a place where their grandparents lived, a place they visited on school and summer vacations, a place which they complained was backward and mosquito-ridden. Those of us for whom Puerto Rico was still a recent memory were also split into two groups: the ones who longed for the island and the ones who wanted to forget it as soon as possible.

I felt disloyal for wanting to learn English, for liking pizza, for studying the girls with big hair and trying out their styles at home, locked in the bathroom where no one could watch. I practiced walking with the peculiar little hop of the *morenas*, but felt as if I were limping.

I didn't feel comfortable with the newly arrived Puerto Ricans who stuck together in suspicious little groups, criticizing everyone, afraid of everything. And I was not accepted by the Brooklyn Puerto Ricans, who held the secret of coolness. They walked the halls between the Italians and the *morenos*, neither one nor the other, but looking and acting like a combination of both, depending on the texture of their hair, the shade of their skin, their makeup, and the way they walked down the hall. (Santiago, 1993, p. 230)

Santiago's reflections highlight the struggle many adolescents face in understanding the rules established by the peer groups that determine social acceptance. In addition to those rules, culturally diverse students may find an additional layer of rules that are specific to their cultural group.

Wilma Mankiller (Mankiller & Wallis, 1993), the first female chief of the Cherokee nation, describes experiences consistent with the model posited by Ponterroto and Pederson in her autobiography entitled *Mankiller: A Chief and Her People*. In reflecting on her adolescent experience during which she struggled with the transition from the Oklahoma outland to the urban neighborhoods of San Francisco, she shared one coping mechanism that was closely connected to her identity as a young Cherokee female. Mankiller explained:

When the going got especially difficult, I allowed my mind to slip away to the past. Going back in time and space can sometimes help remedy a person's troubles. . . . This is a technique that I developed when I was older and had learned more about my tribe's history. Today, I often consider the old days of the Cherokees. I allow myself to think about "the trail where they cried," and the federal government's forced removal of our people and the other southeastern tribes. I compare the upheaval in the late 1830s to my own family's relocation in the 1950s. Remembering those Cherokees and others who were forced to move to Indian Territory and how they persisted brings me to some relief whenever I feel distressed or afraid. Through the years, I have learned to use my memory and the historical memory of my people to help me endure the most difficult and trying periods of my life. (Mankiller & Wallis, 1993, p. 77)

In sharing her life story, Mankiller relates a traditional Cherokee tale that influenced her view of her culture. She tells the story of an Indian prophet called Charley who had received a message from the Great Spirit, the Creator of Life and Breath. The prophet emerged from the mountains accompanied by two wolves and reported that the Great Spirit was displeased with Cherokees, who had given up their traditions in favor of the White man's factories, clothing, and culture. Mankiller described the significance of this Indian tale in her life:

Among the artworks I keep in my home are a painting and a wood sculpture. They are depictions of Charley and the wolves appearing before the council of the Cherokee. Having Charley in my home reminds me every single day of the need for contemporary Cherokees to be on guard. Having Charley nearby reminds us to be sure to do everything we can to hold onto our language, our ceremonies, our culture. For we are a people of today—people of the so-called modern world. But first and foremost, and forever, we are also Cherokees. (Mankiller & Wallis, 1993, p. 257)

Navigating the Dominant Culture While Remaining True to One's Own Culture

Regardless of where culturally diverse students attend school—whether on an Indian reservation, at a historically Black university, in a multicultural high school environment, or at an elite preparatory high school—there will be times when they will find themselves in settings dominated by the majority White culture. During these times, the ability to navigate comfortably within the dominant culture and remain true to their minority culture will become important. Success in these efforts requires an ability to be flexible and to practice a bicultural method of operation. A key characteristic of an intelligent individual is the ability to adapt to one's environment and to different contexts (Sternberg, 1985). For culturally diverse students, this involves learning to be culturally flexible. In other words, young people have to understand which behaviors are appropriate for one situation and inappropriate for another. This adaptive skill of being able to interact effectively in a variety of social realms and contexts is referred to as *biculturality* (Banks, 1979). Developing this ability to juggle two cultures and succeed within both may be a difficult journey for some and may involve painful experiences along the way. Bicultural identities allow gifted culturally diverse students to maintain their cultural identities while engaging in achievement-oriented behaviors (Banks, 1979; Rowley & Moore, 2002).

Although biculturality may seem like an emotionally healthy compromise for culturally diverse young people, the literature on the psychosocial health of students with strong bicultural competence is rather ambiguous. Many theorists view biculturalism as the healthiest resolution of identity in a pluralistic society while others view it as abandoning one's cultural heritage (Gopaul-McNicol & Thomas-Presswood, 1998). Some researchers see the individual's ability to appreciate multiple cultures, overcome stereotypes, and maintain role-flexibility as adaptive, resilient, and capable of strengthening self-esteem. The student is able to call upon the experiences of two cultural groups to function most effectively in a given situation. Friendships are not limited by race, culture, or gender and a broader perspective is established (Gopaul-McNicol & Thomas-Presswood, 1998). Others have argued that biculturality may lead to identity confusion and emotional conflict (Arroyo & Zigler, 1995). Such mixed reports of this phenomenon suggest that the influence of a bicultural identity on a young person's life may vary from one individual to the next (Rowley & Moore, 2002).

This issue is illustrated by the experiences of Marcus Mabry, a political commentator for CNN. Prior to his work with CNN, Mabry served as an international correspondent for *Newsweek* magazine. Mabry was born and raised in "White City," an all-Black enclave in Trenton, NJ, and a community of families struggling with poverty. The son of a single mother on welfare, Mabry was awarded a full academic scholarship to attend a prestigious preparatory high school, the Lawrenceville School in Lawrenceville, NJ. As he excelled within Lawrenceville's ivy-clad walls, he grew painfully aware of the racial ignorance that surrounded him.

From Lawrenceville, Mabry moved on to Stanford University, where he double majored in international relations and French and English literatures. He entered Stanford with Advanced Placement credits, which enabled him to use his fourth year at Stanford to earn a master's degree in English. After graduating from Stanford, he spent the early part of his career as a foreign correspondent in Paris. His autobiography (Mabry, 1995), entitled *White Bucks and Black-Eyed Peas: Growing Up Black in White America*, provides poignant examples of his struggles to learn to navigate the dominant White culture of both his prep school and his university campus. The challenges he faced are evidenced in the following description of his graduation day from Lawrenceville:

> Clasping my diploma, I said, "Thank you" to the headmaster for his gentle stewardship. (He had been the man who had worked courageously to integrate Lawrenceville in the sixties.) Looking out across the sea of faculty faces sitting just before the podium, I found Ms. McKay, who was beaming, and Mr. Graham, who gave me a thumbs up. But when I crossed Mr. Megna's face, he was staring straight ahead, coldly peering through me, an ice pick. Troubled, I walked back to my seat and tried to recapture the feeling of triumph that had slipped away. Only later did I understand that I

had again broken an unwritten tenet of the WASP code. Seniors did not graduate in cap and gown, but in coat and tie, and I took this to mean that as long as we were neat and stylish there would be no need for further formalities. I wore my white linen pants and a snappy blue Lawrenceville blazer. I rolled my shirt sleeves over my jacket cuffs, flipped up my shirt collar, and loosened my thin white tie a la Miami Vice. I thought it symbolic, imitating the California cool of my future university, bridging worlds, past and future. Mr. Megna must have believed I was disrespecting Lawrenceville, broadcasting one final "up yours!" Friends told me that parents and teachers were shocked by my outrageous political act. I thought (incorrectly) I was being stylish; they thought I was making a Black Power statement. After the ceremony, a friend's father asked him, "What was Mabry trying to prove? Is that the latest in ghetto fashion?" (Mabry, 1995, pp. 148–149)

Remaining True to the Family

Marcus Mabry's (1995) autobiography sheds light on the challenges of navigating two distinct cultures. In addition, culturally diverse students may also face challenges within the context of their families. As gifted culturally diverse students excel in school and pursue their goals, some may benefit from supportive parents and family members, while others may not be so fortunate. In a study in which I examined resilience within gifted Latino males (Hébert, 1996), I related the experiences of young men who excelled in an urban high school in Connecticut. One of these young men, Carlos, was the oldest of seven children in a Puerto Rican family. Carlos lived with his three brothers and three sisters in a small two-family duplex of cement brick in the city's projects. In conversations with Carlos, he referred to feelings of "such desolation and despair" when he looked out at his neighborhood and realized how many teenagers in that community had turned off to school and given in to the culture of the streets (Hébert, 1996, p. 86). "They feel the system has failed them. They act so indifferent," he said in discouragement. "I feel isolated here. I'm really alone" (Hébert, 1996, p. 86).

Carlos was born in Ponce, Puerto Rico, and immigrated to the United States when he was 8 years old. Carlos's parents spoke only Spanish, so he was placed in a self-contained bilingual program upon starting school. By sixth grade, Carlos was mainstreamed into a regular classroom. Teachers in elementary school were impressed with Carlos's commitment to his studies.

He worked diligently and, by his freshman year in high school, he ranked seventh in his class of 472, carrying a full load of college preparatory and Advanced Placement courses.

This high-achieving student who saw desolation in his urban community tried to make a difference. Influenced by a male Hispanic teacher who had served as a role model to him in the fifth grade, he returned to his elementary school and offered his services as a volunteer tutor. He worked with bilingual students because he could relate to the challenges they were facing. After working with young children, Carlos decided he wanted to major in early childhood education in college. Upon graduation from high school, he was awarded a 4-year scholarship of $100,000 to the highly selective Connecticut College in New London, CT. Carlos is currently teaching elementary school children in the Connecticut public schools.

As Carlos reflected on his success in high school, he explained how the love of family provided him with the motivation he needed to meet the challenges faced by an urban teenager:

> I realized the burdens my parents had taken. I realized that they had made so many sacrifices for me. It had been so many years. Just to give up now would be such a disappointment, not just to me, but to my parents . . . I found encouragement from their situation, where they came from, where they were born. They were born in the countryside and were very poor. I got the motivation from knowing how they struggled and the sacrifices they made. (Hébert, 1996, p. 87)

Lucio joined Carlos in my research study. Lucio also excelled academically and athletically in his high school. He ranked 10th in a class of 490, completed accelerated mathematics coursework at a nearby college, was a leader on the men's swim team, and served as an executive board member of the National Honor Society. A visit to Lucio's home revealed that he came from a warm and loving Latino household. As Spanish music from a radio competed with the cartoons on television, Lucio's extended family members traveled through the family's modest apartment and stopped to pinch his cheeks or kiss him as he sat at the family kitchen table during an interview.

Lucio was Cuban-American and the younger of two sons from his mother's first marriage. Lucio's mother had remarried, and he enjoyed the companionship of a 3-year-old half brother. Lucio's father had not been heard from in years, and Lucio's older brother was living on his own. When Lucio was 13, he was legally adopted by his stepfather, and he indicated that this was a turning point in his adolescence. Lucio had a tremendous amount of love and respect for his stepfather, who had made his mother and his family very happy. Lucio's mother had come to the U.S. from Cuba when she was 18 and had lived in Texas with her first husband for a number of years. She then came to Connecticut and was employed in clerical work. Lucio's stepfather was from El Salvador and worked as a postal assistant. Lucio's family lived in an immaculate two-story apartment building, with his grandparents living downstairs from them. Like Rafael, Lucio also worked hard to achieve. His motivation appeared to be influenced by his family's experiences. He was clearly aware of the hardships his parents faced and he appreciated all they had done for him:

> They came over with so little and then gave us all the time and so many opportunities. It's because of them that I try and get good grades. I see my father working 60–70 hours a week and I see him killing himself. My mother comes home exhausted. I look at them. They try so hard for me and my younger brother. I do owe them a lot. . . . They accomplished so much knowing so little. Just imagine what I can do knowing so much. (Hébert, 1996, p. 87)

Rafael and Lucio understood the struggles their parents had faced, and their parents emotionally supported them in their efforts to achieve academically. These two young men were fortunate; however, not all gifted culturally diverse teenagers have parents who are as understanding. Rockey Robbins, coordinator of a summer residential enrichment program for gifted American Indian high school students called, Explorations in Creativity (EIC), shared a poignant story of one student's experience related to this difficult issue. In his role as coordinator of the summer program, Robbins was available to the students in their residential setting. He reported how he overheard a conversation late one evening that highlighted the difficulties American Indian students may face with their families:

> One night I discovered a student on the phone long after he was supposed to have been in bed. The anguish in his voice kept me from telling him to discontinue his conversation and get into bed. He kept repeating, "I'm not going white. I'm not going white." Hesitantly, I approached him when he had finished his conversation. He did not want to talk a lot, but said that his mother and his uncle were having fears that the EIC program would result in his forgetting of their teachings and maybe even his eventual leaving of

the reservation. He also argued with his mom about the computer class he was in, assuring her that it was not a skill that he would use in some city someday. He told them that he had danced at the EIC pow-wow that night and that he missed singing his tribe's songs and that he would always be Indian. (Robbins, 1991, p. 17)

Expressing One's Talents in Ways That Challenge Family Expectations

The young man described in Robbins's (1991) research study calls attention to another important issue. Culturally diverse students may also have to negotiate the culturally specific expectations of their parents and families. Parents often have very definite plans for their children's futures. Within culturally diverse groups who have immigrated to the United States for a better quality of life, parents may have high expectations for their children and high hopes for their children's success in achieving a higher standard of living for their own families. This is especially the case when the children are the first generation in the family to pursue college degrees. Moreover, certain professions may be more highly valued or respected within a particular cultural group. For example, within Asian cultures, technical fields and the hard sciences are often highly valued. Asian youngsters who question the need to pursue academic excellence or the career choices deemed "appropriate" by their parents may therefore cause conflict among family members (Sue & Sue, 2003).

This problem was noted by a participant in Olenchak and Hébert's (2002) research study on gifted underachieving males in university settings. Jimmy was an undergraduate student at a major urban university in the Southeast whose family had immigrated to the United States from Vietnam. As the eldest son in his family, Jimmy was expected "to make something of himself." Jimmy's parents insisted that his educational preparation should lead him to a career that would guarantee, at minimum, a middle-class lifestyle. Jimmy's parents had decided early on that he would become a physician and this message was delivered early in his adolescence. He explained:

From my earliest awareness, I knew that I had to become a doctor to make my parents happy and proud. They made me feel like it was, you know, like my destiny to be a successful doctor and that I really had to use my brain to get there. All along, it was science fair after science fair, working on science kits at home, and even joining science clubs as early as I could . . . I wasn't all that upset about it—it was fun for me, but the bad news was that I could never even think about anything else. It was going to be science so that someday I would be ready for college to become a doctor. Period! (Olenchak & Hébert, 2002, p. 200)

Once he entered college, Jimmy was disturbed by the rigidity of a premedical program that allowed little room for exploration of topics and disciplines outside the university's core curriculum or the requirements of his biology major. He was much more passionate about his interests in another, less academic domain. As he struggled with the prescribed curriculum, he faced another dilemma. Jimmy explained:

The basic program is as narrow as a tightrope. If you step too far in any direction but straight, you fall. I have thought about getting involved in some things that don't have anything to do with studying. I am really interested in my parents' restaurant business, but they think that is not good enough for me. I'd like to try my hand at cooking more; I remember times as a kid when I'd help them out, and I loved it! But if I ever did anything like that, I'd have two huge obstacles: getting up the nerve to tell them and then getting them not to think I let them down. Besides, where on this campus is anybody going to work with me on cooking? It sure isn't in my program, and I don't think too many universities have cooking schools. (Olenchak & Hébert, 2002, p. 202)

Jimmy's disappointment and frustration with his circumstances at the university reinforced a pattern of underachievement that persisted through his junior year. Although fluctuations in his grade performance altered the downward trend, Jimmy's grade point average was a 2.3 after completing 3 years of university work. For a student who had graduated with high honors from a rigorous high school program, his collegiate performance became an emotional issue for Jimmy and his family.

Jimmy explained that he was originally dedicated to fulfilling his parents' wish for him; however, his academic commitment eroded soon after he arrived at the university. He grappled with a mediocre academic record in college and his need to develop his own identity apart from that based on parental expectations. He explained, "I feel bad about what I have done here these past three years. My grades are so bad that I have lost my scholarships and have to rely on working at [a local restaurant]" (Olenchak & Hébert, 2002, p. 203). He pointed out that his restaurant work didn't get in his way academically, but he was feeling guilty about how much he enjoyed working there. He commented, "I know that I could be a great chef if I had that opportunity, but I guess I need to hang in there and finish my bachelor's" (Olenchak & Hébert, 2002, p. 203). He thought of his future and struggled with his plans for medical school. "I just hope I can do so great on the medical boards that my grades won't be such a big deal. I just wonder when I can get to tackle my own goals" (Olenchak & Hébert, 2002, p. 203).

Challenges of Peer Group Expectations and Academic Achievement

Jimmy's experience highlights just how crippling a set of rigid parental expectations can become for a talented young person with goals and aspirations that differ from those of his parents. In addition, culturally diverse students may also receive crippling messages from peers regarding academic achievement. These students often experience conflicts between the values of their culture and those of the dominant culture, and members of their cultural peer group may discourage identity explorations that are at odds with the traditions of their cultural group. Members of the cultural peer group who feel insecure about their own abilities may be threatened by the successes of the gifted students and lash out at them. Additionally, through associating success in school with assimilation into the dominant culture, peers may direct abusive and derogatory remarks toward academically oriented students. Shaffer (2000) highlighted this abusive treatment succinctly:

> Virtually all North American minorities have a term for community members who are "too white" in orientation, be it the "apple" (red on the outside, white on the inside) for Native Americans, the Hispanic "coconut," the Asian "banana," or the African American "Oreo." Clearly, minority adolescents must resolve these value conflicts and decide for themselves what they are inside. (p. 187)

Researchers have examined the issue of culturally diverse students being accused by their peers of "acting White." Ethnographic research has indicated that urban Black youth defined academic success as more appropriate for Whites. Fordham (1988) and Fordham and Ogbu (1986) examined the concept of racelessness as a factor in the academic achievement of African American students in a high school in Washington, DC, fictitiously named Capitol High School. They found that high-achieving students were more willing to identify with the cultural beliefs and value systems of the dominant culture than less successful students. Fordham and Ogbu found that to "act White" wasn't merely to achieve academically; instead, the concept incorporated a variety of attitudes and behaviors, including speaking standard English; listening to White rock and roll radio stations; spending a lot of time in the library studying; working hard to get good grades in school; going to the Smithsonian Institution; doing volunteer work; going camping, hiking, or mountain climbing; being on time; and reading and writing poetry. Fordham described the problem further as she spoke of her research experience at Capital High School:

> given the Black community's penchant for collectivity, what kind of support from peers can be expected by Black adolescents whose behaviors and values in the school context appear to be at odds with the indigenous social organization of Black people? At Capital High School, there is not much support for students who adopt the individualistic ethos, because succeeding in school is invariably associated with movement away from the community and is seen as a sign of having been co-opted by the dominant society. Hence, even those high achievers who camouflage their efforts at academic excellence are viewed with suspicion. (p. 81)

Marcus Mabry's experiences growing up in Trenton, NJ, and his transition to the Lawrenceville School underscore the findings of Fordham and Ogbu (1986). Mabry described his return to his Trenton neighborhood following a semester away at the private school. Before he left for Lawrenceville, elderly members of his community wished him success and encouraged him to "do us all proud." Some of his peers expressed admiration and predicted that he would be in the White House one day. He struggled to understand the response he received when he arrived back in Trenton:

> But when I returned home, I felt all black America had turned on me; like they had made common cause with white society to convince me that I couldn't, or I shouldn't, succeed. Success meant somehow losing my blackness. Speaking standard English, lik-

ing school, getting good grades—all indicated whiteness. As if because I spoke differently meant I thought I was better than poor black folks.

I had left the community because my mother thought it would be best, not because I wanted to escape being black. No one seemed to remember that. It was like leaving the earth to live on the moon and coming home only to be crushed under the weight of the gravity I was no longer accustomed to. (Mabry, 1995, pp. 103–104)

The research conducted by Fordham and Ogbu (1986) has been supported by follow-up studies conducted by other researchers, yet their work remains controversial because it does not explain the success of many students from involuntary minority backgrounds. Researchers have pointed out that many culturally diverse young people succeed in school without losing their cultural identity. Sally Reis and I (1999) examined high-ability students in an urban high school and found that the high-achieving students in that setting had a strong multicultural awareness and appreciation. Moreover, we found that because of the diversity within that setting, academic achievement was not viewed strictly as the domain of White students. The high achievers maintained that gifted students in their school were aware of significant scholarship money available to minority youth; therefore, a focus on academic achievement was positively valued by the gifted students from all ethnic and racial backgrounds. Being smart and maintaining a strong achievement orientation was considered "cool" in this setting (Hébert & Reis, 1999).

These findings contrasted with those of Fordham (1988) and Fordham and Ogbu (1986); however, the contextual influences should be noted. Whereas the Hébert and Reis (1999) study took place in a diverse setting that included students from many cultural backgrounds, Fordham and Ogbu's research was conducted in a high school environment comprised primarily of two cultures, Black and White. Less diversity appeared to have a powerful effect on how young people viewed academic achievement.

Darrell Dawsey (1996) has also examined the controversial issue of culturally diverse students "acting White." In his book entitled *Living to Tell About It: Young Black Men in America Speak Their Piece*, Dawsey highlighted how the popular press has reported how African American children discourage their high-achieving peers from earning A's. He maintained that precocious African American children are often recruited by talk shows and journalists to tell how they have had textbooks knocked from their hands, gotten bullied, and suffered merciless teasing from classmates accusing them of "acting White." Dawsey commented:

> Such reports have always struck me as racist nonsense. To be sure, I've met young people who don't grasp fully the importance of education. I've met kids who, out of jealousy or embarrassment, may lob barbs at a classmate who reads regularly or who fares better on his report card. And I've met kids who cringe at the thought of being singled out at a pinning ceremony or an honor-roll call. But this is nowhere near the same as accusing our children of loathing intellectual pursuits because they think only white people should engage in them. I've never met any such Black kids, kids who hate good grades and harbor no dreams of life in a better world. I've yet to meet a Black child who wouldn't like to get an A on his math test. I've yet to encounter the young sister or brother who thinks the honor roll is shameful. I've yet to run across the student who thinks only white folks should have white-collar jobs, high salaries or an Ivy League degree. (Dawsey, 1996, pp. 212–213)

In his work, Dawsey offered a snapshot of a high-achieving African American male named John Copeland who shared his thoughts on his personal experiences. Copeland, a Harvard graduate, grew up in a working-class Black community in Miami. A stellar honor roll student, Copeland scored 1500 on his SAT's. He was high school valedictorian and later went on to a career as a corporate executive. Copeland maintained that he was never accused of trying to mimic a White boy:

> "I was never criticized about that," he recalls. "People respected my accomplishments. At the free-throw line, they would crack jokes, always calculating the trajectory to the front of the rim and all this type of stuff. It didn't really discourage me. I actually kind of liked it. My boys recognized that I was hooking it up in the classroom." (Dawsey, 1996, pp. 213–214)

In his interviews with Dawsey, John Copeland shared his belief that criticism for "acting White" related less to perceptions of academic achievement and more to community standards governing the social behavior of students. Copeland explained, "Precocious kids can be introverts, and few people of any color take to hermits. Hell, even white folks have names for scholars who don't place themselves within the active social context of their immediate communities: nerds" (Dawsey, 1996, p. 214). He maintained that this is what African American teenagers mean when they accuse one another of "acting White."

Reflecting on his high school experiences, Copeland described how his striving for academic excellence, his involvement in the high school band, and his role as a football quarterback were respected by his community. Copeland credited his social skills with enabling him to navigate any environment in which he found himself. He explained that students who are accused of "acting White" are those who are not respectful of their communities:

> We are part of a community. You only get ostracized when you decide that you are not going to be part of the community. It is probably not the people's fault, but if you see another Black person and you look down at the floor and just don't want to face whatever, then that is when people start reacting that way. When you, by the way you act or speak in a roundabout way, try to demean them. A lot of people who speak "correctly" do it with attitude. "I am speaking proper English, what the hell is wrong with you?" (Dawsey, 1996, p. 214)

Confronting Stereotypes, Social Injustices, and Discrimination

Defining, being aware of, and understanding prejudice and racism are critical if educators are to understand the experiences of many culturally diverse students in schools. In his book *Increasing Multicultural Understanding*, Locke (1998) defined prejudice as "judging before fully examining the object of evaluation." (p. 9) and racial prejudice as "judgment based on racial/ethnic/cultural group membership before getting to know the person" (p. 9). According to Locke, racism "combines prejudice with power—power to do something based on prejudiced beliefs" (p. 9).

With these definitions in mind, educators must realize that the impact of prejudice in the lives of culturally diverse students cannot be denied or ignored. Many students from diverse racial and ethnic backgrounds experience racism on a daily basis, a problem that could adversely affect their school performance (Ford, 1995). This racism may occur as negative messages concerning their ability to achieve academically. Communication of low expectations may come from teachers, peers, or society in general (Fordham & Ogbu, 1986). These messages are bound to have a negative impact on the self-concepts of young people. Students who are unable to deal effectively with prejudice may become totally disenchanted with school.

Gifted culturally diverse students are not immune to this problem. Moreover, because of the heightened sensitivities (Piechowski, 1997) that are part of the emotional makeup of these young people, they may be more aware of and sensitive to social injustices and prejudice, and this problem may affect them emotionally even more deeply. Consider the reflections of Wilma Mankiller as she described her experiences as a young Native American student in a California public school:

> I was placed in the fifth grade, and I immediately noticed that everyone in my class considered me different. When the teacher came to my name during roll call each morning, every single person laughed. Mankiller had not been a strange name back in Adair County, Oklahoma, but it was a very odd name in San Francisco. The other kids also teased me about the way I talked and dressed. It was not that I was so much poorer than the others, but I was definitely from another culture. . . . My sister Linda and I sat up late every night reading aloud to each other to get rid of our accents. We tried to talk like the other kids at school. . . . Like most young people everywhere, we wanted to belong. (Mankiller & Wallis, 1993, pp. 73, 103)

A vignette from Ruben Navaratte's (1993) autobiography *A Darker Shade of Crimson: Odyssey of a Harvard Chicano* further illuminates this critical issue. Navarette, a young man of Mexican heritage, graduated from Harvard University in 1990 and went on to become a successful journalist and lecturer. In his autobiography, he poignantly described a scenario that occurred during his senior year of high school as he was pursuing admission to Ivy League universities. His high school principal had heard faculty rumors about the high caliber of colleges to which he was applying and decided to counsel Ruben concerning his plan. He arrived in Advanced Placement English as Ruben was immersed in reading and began a conversation concerning a sensitive subject. The principal questioned Ruben about his applications to Harvard University, Yale University, and Stanford University and suggested that he should also consider applying to Fresno State.

I stopped smiling. *State college?* Here I was, class valedictorian with straight As and scattered A+s on my transcript, high SATs, strong recommendations, the works . . . and the man wanted me to apply to a state school, anyone-with-high-school-diploma-and-four-hundred-bucks-accepted state school! There were classmates of mine, white classmates, who were also rumored to be applying to highly competitive colleges. Stanford. Cornell. The Naval Academy. And Harvard. As I struggled with my composure, I wondered why he had chosen me as the lucky recipient of his little speech sprung of low expectation. The sort of low expectation that his predecessors had for decades heaped upon people like me. A speech, I suspected, that he would not have dared repeat to one of my white friends with credentials like mine. . . .

Biting off my words, I politely, if disingenuously, thanked him for his advice and unusual concern. I told him that I was confident I could hold my own in the admissions process, and so I would disregard his advice. Rebuffed, the principal cast his spear. "You may be right," he said with a faint grin. "After all . . . your race should help you a lot."

In five short seconds, my high school's top administrator had casually dismissed four long years of hard work and sacrifice and the perfect grades they had produced in the toughest courses that the place had to offer. He opted instead for a more simplistic, race-conscious explanation of why he presumed I might be accepted to an elite college. My classmates had their qualifications, Navarette had his race on his side. And, on yeah, a near-perfect high school record.

To his last remark, I said nothing. Maybe a polite, insincere smile to end the awkward episode. I looked away, afraid of his scornful glare. I resumed reading Conrad. *Blindfolded bearers of light destroy what they profess to enlighten . . .*

His work done, the principal lifted himself from the tiny wooden desk and walked from the classroom. He was most likely completely unaware of the sting of his words and the damage that they had done to the self-image of a young man whose talent and arrogance was supposed to make him immune to such pain. Supposed to. (pp. 12–13)

How Can Educators and Counselors Support Gifted Culturally Diverse Students?

Having heard from young people who have confronted the challenges highlighted by Mary Frasier, Nicholas Colangelo, and Donna Ford at the beginning of this chapter, we must now consider how we can best help other students who may face these same challenges. Educators and counselors working with gifted culturally diverse students will need a rich repertoire of pedagogical strategies to effectively teach and guide these students. The following classroom methods and strategies are designed to support diverse students.

Design Culturally Meaningful Classrooms

To work with culturally diverse students in gifted education classrooms, educators must become skilled in culturally responsive teaching. Gay (2000) defined such teaching as, "Using the cultural knowledge, prior experiences, frames of reference, and performance styles of ethnically diverse students to make learning encounters more relevant to and effective for them" (p. 29). She maintained that such an approach is based on the assumption that "positive self-concepts, knowledge of and pride in one's own ethnic identity, and improved academic achievement are interactional" (Gay, 2000, p. 29). Moreover, Gay argued that two desirable goals to be addressed in schools are incorporated within this approach: (a) cultural understanding and (b) the knowledge and skills necessary to challenge the existing social order and power structures. She maintained that when academic knowledge and skills are situated within the lived experiences and frames of reference of students, they carry more personal meaning for students, increase the interest appeal, and are learned naturally and more efficiently. Ford and Harris (1999) have also found that for culturally diverse students, school is more engaging, motivating, and relevant when they examine their own culture and the culture of others. Ladson-Billings (2006) incorporated the notion of teaching cultural competence as a component of culturally relevant pedagogy. She defined this as helping young people to "recognize and honor their own cultural beliefs and practices while acquiring access to the wider culture, where they are likely to have a chance of improving their socioeconomic status and making informed decisions about the lives they wish to lead" (p. 36). Moreover, Ladson-Billings (2006) noted that educators have an "obligation to expose their students to the very culture that oppresses them" (p. 36). Although this seems paradoxical, she argued that "without the skills and knowledge of the dominant culture, students are unlikely to engage that culture to effect meaningful change" (Ladson-Billings, 2006, p. 36). Nieto and Bode (2008) pointed out that such an approach is simply good pedagogy. They posited "all good education takes students seriously, uses their experiences as a basis for further learning, and helps them develop into informed, critically aware, and empowered citizens" (Nieto & Bode, 2008, p. 59).

To deliver culturally relevant pedagogy takes culturally responsive teachers. According to Larke, Elbert, Webb-Johnson, Larke, and Brisco (2006), responsive teaching involves designing effective, culturally meaningful classrooms. These researchers maintained that effective, culturally responsive teachers exhibit the following characteristics:

- They are sensitive to the needs of all students and recognize that cultural congruence between the teacher and student is critical to student success.
- They consider students' differences equitably.
- They have a desire to know the historical and cultural backgrounds of their students because that information increases their sensitivity, awareness, and knowledge base to supplement their instructional materials.
- They modify their teaching styles to address the learning styles of their students.
- They maintain high expectations for all students and work to provide the necessary experiences that enable their students to meet them.
- They strive to develop positive working relationships with parents.
- They appreciate the economic status of their students and make connections to the student's environment, regardless of economic conditions, in designing instruction.
- They recognize the isms—racism, classism, and sexism in the curriculum and work to eliminate them in their classrooms and schools.
- They incorporate a wide variety of instructional strategies.
- They affirm cultural differences by incorporating classroom experiences that enable students to become successful without having to give up their cultural identity and conform to the dominant culture (p. 162).

Larke and her colleagues (2006) highlighted five culturally responsive best practices to ensure success in designing culturally meaningful classrooms: commitment, coresponsibility, communication, cultural under-standing, and courage. Next, I ask that teachers in gifted education consider each of these five components of a culturally meaningful classroom, and I pose questions that require educators to reflect on their teaching of diverse students.

Commitment. Educators demonstrate high levels of commitment to empower students.

- As a teacher of gifted students, do I integrate issues of race, diversity, and social justice as integral components of my classroom?
- In designing curriculum, do I organize concepts and content around the contributions, perspectives, and life experiences of the multitude of groups that make up American society?
- Do I view my students through differences and not deficits?

Coresponsibility. Educators demonstrate shared responsibility among administrators, families, and communities to guarantee the best outcomes for students.

- As a teacher of gifted students, do I work with administrators, colleagues, parents and families, and community members in providing the best educational program possible?
- Do I work cooperatively with parents and families to enhance out-of-school learning that supports student achievement?

Communication. Educators maintain open channels of communication between students, families, and administrators in developing and maintaining their classrooms.

- As a teacher of gifted students, do I understand the significance of my nonverbal means of communicating with students?
- Do I understand the nuance of communication across cultures? Am I aware of the messages being delivered to my students through my body language?
- Are my actions consistent with my words? If I say I care for my students, is my behavior genuine?
- Do I use language that is affirming?

Cultural understanding. The behaviors of educators clearly honor the values of culture, language, and therefore, their students.

- As a teacher of gifted students, are my students invited to bring their culture and language into the classroom?

   ➤ Do I value cultural pluralism? Do I recognize that all cultures have made valuable contributions?

   ➤ Am I working to develop my own understanding of all of the cultures represented in my classroom?

   ➤ Do I design culturally relevant curricula?

Courage. Educators remain comfortable in passionately pursuing their nontraditional ways of reaching students and advocating on their behalf.

   ➤ As a teacher of gifted students, do I view my work as a calling?

   ➤ Do I serve as a change agent in my school?

   ➤ Do I work enthusiastically to teach those bright young people who are labeled as not caring about school?

   ➤ Do I help my coworkers in reexamining the worthiness of all students?

   ➤ Do I confront my colleagues in the school's place of gossip, the teacher's lounge?

Examine Biographies of Gifted Culturally Diverse Individuals

My beloved colleague, the late Mary Frasier, shared with me that she believed a carefully selected biography could serve as an important mentor to a gifted child (M. Frasier, personal communication, September 1998). She pointed out that the person whose life story is being shared through biography may serve as a role model for intelligent young people and assist them in reflecting upon issues that require analyzing a problem in a safe environment. The use of biographies and autobiographies of culturally diverse men and women of achievement represents culturally responsive teaching. As the poignant vignettes from the autobiographies of Marcus Mabry, Ruben Navarette, Esmeralda Santiago, and Wilma Mankiller have illustrated, biographies and autobiographies offer teachers and counselors enlightening stories to share with their students. The gifted education community has maintained that encounters with biographies or autobiographies can have positive effects on gifted students (Flack, 1993; Hébert, 1995b, 2009; Hébert et al., 2001; Piirto, 1992; Robinson & Butler Schatz, 2002). Flack (1993) highlighted the critical importance of identification young people can find in both biography and autobiography: "Identification occurs when readers discover that they are not singularly alone in either their dreams and aspirations or their loneliness, frustrations, and disappointments (p. 2).

Along with the identification Flack (1993) described, gifted culturally diverse students enjoy additional benefits from biographies. Through them, diverse students are exposed to role models who may not exist in their immediate lives. They appreciate the realistic portrayal of the lives of high-achieving culturally diverse men and women, providing them with significant lessons and influential messages for succeeding in life. In addition, biographies expose young people to new ways of thinking and diverse perspectives of the world around them. They benefit from exposure to a variety of philosophical views of life; various liberal and conservative worldviews; and a diversity of socioeconomic backgrounds, cultures, and religions. Moreover, many biographies of individuals whose lives were filled with adversity often provide young people with realistic strategies for developing resilience (Hébert, 2009).

The biography section of any high quality bookstore or library offers many fine examples of biographical materials that are appreciated by gifted culturally diverse adolescents. Appendix B offers a collection of biographies of significant men and women of achievement and includes numerous culturally diverse individuals. These materials are recommended for facilitating class discussions on the difficult challenges highlighted in this chapter. Appendix C offers a collection of picture book biographies appropriate for use with young gifted children.

The discussion below presents an example of how teachers or counselors might facilitate a class discussion using a biography with gifted secondary students. The biography featured is Felix's (2002) work entitled *Condi: The Condoleezza Rice Story*. This well-respected biographer presents a compelling portrait of an influential political leader who overcame all barriers to excel as an African American woman in a field dominated by White males. This biography offers the fascinating life story of one of the most powerful women in international politics. Gifted students will enjoy learning of her childhood in segregated Birmingham, AL, where her parents nurtured her many talents, her love of learning, and her striving for excellence in everything she did.

In facilitating a discussion to accompany the reading of *Condi*, teachers have a wealth of significant issues in the story that students will appreciate and draw parallels to their lives. Key issues that emerge in this biography include: experiencing racism, developing resilience, finding emotional support from family, understanding the important role played by mentors, applying one's intelligence to solve life's challenges, having a strong belief in self, and maintaining a balanced lifestyle.

In my work facilitating discussions of biographies, I have found that having a list of prepared discussion questions to pose during the conversation with students is critical to success. I suggest that introductory questions should appear nonthreatening to students. As the conversation unfolds and students are engaged in discussion of the life story under investigation, I then pose more sensitive questions that focus on the problematic situations faced by both the central figure of the biography and the students involved in the discussion. I always make a point to conclude the discussion with a question that enables the students to capture the essence of one important message delivered through the biography. This final question may be helpful for students to need to decompress from any emotionally laden discussion that occurred. A sensitively crafted menu of questions is needed for cathartic conversation. Below is a list of discussion questions I suggest for use with *Condi: The Condoleezza Rice Story:*

- What did you know about Condoleezza Rice before reading this biography? What surprises have you discovered in reading her life story?

- How would you describe the challenges she faced during her childhood and adolescence? What do you think helped her overcome these challenges?

- Condoleezza Rice is a multitalented woman. What do you think helped to develop and support her many talents? How are your gifts and talents nurtured and supported? How are support systems important to multitalented young people?

- From what you know of Condoleezza Rice's adult life, how do you think her early strengths as an adolescent contributed to her future? What lessons can we learn from this?

- How did Condoleezza's multipotentiality influence her search for a college major? How might you learn from her story in determining a college major that matches your talents?

- What important lessons do the parents of Condoleezza Rice have for parents of gifted children? For parents of gifted culturally diverse children? Consider yourself as a parent in the years to come. How might these lessons influence your approach to parenting?

- What do we learn about the role of mentors in developing talent from reading this biography? How might this apply to your life?

- How was Condoleezza Rice resilient? How do you think this resilience supports her in her professional domain? Have their been times in your life when you needed to develop resilience to overcome adversity? How did that evolve?

- What important message does Antonia Felix's biography of Condoleezza Rice deliver to gifted culturally diverse young women?

❧ As you leave school today, what will you remember most about Condoleezza's story that will shape the remainder of your day? (Hébert, 2009, pp. 274–275)

In addition to preparing a menu of questions, I also select several thought-provoking or inspirational quotes from the biography as prompts for discussion. I mark these significant passages in my copy of the biography and have them readily available. An example of such a powerful passage from *Condi* is one in which Felix (2002) described a critical incident in Condoleezza's university classroom as a 15-year-old undergraduate:

> What went through Condi's mind as the professor described and appeared to support Shockley's view of blacks as "genetically disadvantaged"? Rather than crouch down in her seat and avoid the onslaught, she sprang out of her chair and defended herself. "I'm the one who speaks French!" she said to the professor. "I'm the one who plays Beethoven. I'm better at your culture than you are. This can be taught!" (p. 69)

Given the sensitivity of the challenges faced by diverse individuals and the parallel experiences of students, it is critical that teachers and counselors provide students time to digest the conversation that evolves. Following a thoughtful discussion of a biography, I suggest that teachers or counselors conclude a lesson with follow-up activities that enable the students to acknowledge and evaluate their feelings about the emotionally charged topics addressed. These activities are designed to be enjoyable and provide opportunities for students to continue conversations in which they provide support for each other. I have found that providing students with a variety of options is also effective. The following is a suggested menu of follow-up activities to consider with Felix's (2002) book:

❧ Reflect on the following prompt in your journal: What was most inspirational in this life story? How might this biography influence you?

❧ You are inspired by Condoleezza Rice. Write a poem about overcoming difficult obstacles in life and dedicate it to her. Submit it to your school's literary magazine.

❧ Imagine that Condoleezza Rice was visiting your community. As a reporter for your school newspaper, you have been assigned to interview her for the leading story. Generate a list of interview questions and role-play the interview.

- Design an artistic representation of Condoleezza's life story and the significant lessons learned from her.
- Write an essay in which you compare and contrast the challenges faced by Condoleezza Rice with an inspirational woman in your life. How are these two women similar? How are they different?
- Craft an e-mail message to Condoleezza Rice seeking her advice about growing up gifted. How will your message read? Write her response.
- Condoleezza Rice has agreed to present the commencement speech at your high school graduation! Write the speech she will deliver. (Hébert, 2009, pp. 276–277)

In using biographies such as Felix's (2002) *Condi* to conduct affective discussions, I have found that combining the book with biographical videos adds richness to the students' experience with the life story. Collections of contemporary biographies are now available in DVD format and can be acquired inexpensively in commercial bookstores as well as through the Internet. I have found that such material is thoroughly researched and is consistent with the published biographical materials.

Combining a biography with a guest speaker is another approach teachers or counselors may want to consider. Some students may read the biographies of men and women of achievement whom they perceive as "larger than life" and struggle to identify with them. I suggest that teachers invite younger individuals as guest speakers, from backgrounds similar to the person featured in the biography yet at an earlier stage of their self-actualization. For example, when enjoying Felix's (2002) *Condi* with students, an appropriate guest speaker for the class might be a local African American female graduate student in international studies or a law school student who could share her experiences as a member of the community. A visit from a young professional would surely inspire gifted culturally diverse students.

Another strategy I discovered using biographical materials enabled me to deliver an important lesson efficiently. As a secondary teacher, when I could not dedicate the allotted time it might take for my students to read a complete biography, I chose to share a single chapter that focused on the individual's childhood and adolescent years. This "slice" of the biography is where my high school students identified with the gifted individual featured, and I was able to facilitate discussions focusing on affective concerns effectively and efficiently. When my students became intrigued with the life story of the individual, I encouraged them to read the entire biography. As a result, I maintained an extensive collection of biographies in my classroom.

In addition to using a portion of a biography, teachers and counselors may want to consider using children's picture books to facilitate the same type of class discussions efficiently. This approach of guiding young people to self-understanding through literature was described in Chapter 2. Gifted culturally diverse students enjoy talking about books that feature gifted minority students as the main characters. Public libraries offer comprehensive directories of children's literature that can help identify picture books and young adult literature featuring gifted culturally diverse youngsters as main characters (see Jweid & Rizzo, 2004; Lee, 2003; Norton, 2004; Rand, Trent-Parker, & Foster, 2001). Appendix A offers a comprehensive annotated bibliography of literature appropriate for use with gifted students in grades K–12. Literature featuring culturally diverse young people is incorporated throughout the collection.

Implement Guided Viewing of Film

There may be no more powerful way to address the challenges faced by gifted culturally diverse young people than to facilitate discussions of these issues through movies. I described guided viewing of film in Chapter 3. I believe that films are an important component of the contemporary culture of diverse students and gifted young people respond positively to this counseling approach. Because movies are such an important part of their lives, culturally diverse students may be more receptive to the notion of discussing sensitive topics through popular films. Appendix D offers an annotated bibliography of excellent movies that provide a starting point for educators who want to use guided viewing of film to support their students. Included in the bibliography are the following movies that specifically feature gifted culturally diverse children and teenagers:

- *Akeelah and The Bee* (2006)
- *The Ernest Green Story* (2005)
- *Finding Forrester* (2000)
- *Freedom Writers* (2007)
- *The Great Debaters* (2007)
- *Mad Hot Ballroom* (2005)
- *Pride* (2007)
- *The Red Sneakers* (2002)
- *Ruby Bridges* (2004)
- *Selma, Lord, Selma* (1999)

>❧ *Stand and Deliver* (1988)
>❧ *Smoke Signals* (1998)

Provide Support Groups for Diverse Students

In an article entitled "The Breakfast Club: Poetry and Pancakes," former high school English teacher Jean Peterson (1996) shared her experiences starting a poetry breakfast club in which aspiring poets and creative writers arrived at their high school early to share their poems with one another. Peterson (1996) highlighted the benefits of bringing together a group of like-minded teenagers to engage in a common task. She found that many of the participants in the breakfast club were dealing with complex adolescent emotions and welcomed the opportunity to express themselves, to be heard by other young poets, and to receive feedback and support from new friends. Teachers and counselors may want to consider Peterson's approach and begin a support group for gifted culturally diverse students by selecting a similar activity that appeals to these students. Counselors have found that much healthy social and emotional development can be nurtured through art or music therapy. A support group centered on artistic expression or music appreciation may easily bring culturally diverse young people together in a supportive fashion.

Another possibility would be the study of poetry written by ethnically diverse poets. Such poetry may enable a teacher or counselor to enjoy an investigation of ethnic identity development with a group of intelligent adolescents.

Take Advantage of Community Resources

Teachers can reach out to their communities and take advantage of the wealth of resources available to support them in addressing the needs of all students. Students in gifted programs benefit when their teachers invite representatives of various cultures to share their expertise. Manning and Baruth (2009) indicated that teachers enhance the curriculum of a gifted program by inviting guest actors, musicians, and even dance groups representative of various cultural backgrounds. Teachers can search the community and recruit high-achieving culturally diverse gifted adults to the classroom to share their experiences of growing up gifted. Teachers and counselors in school districts within close proximity to colleges or universities may discover cultural organizations of diverse undergraduate or graduate students who would be delighted to share their experiences with students. Many of these groups are expected to conduct outreach activities such as working with local schools. On many college campuses teachers will discover culturally specific sororities and fraternities of high academic achievers. These collegians would enjoy visiting schools, sharing their expertise with younger students, and serving as mentors for gifted diverse students in elementary and secondary classrooms.

Encourage Mentoring Programs and E-Mail Pals

Teachers and counselors who recruit gifted culturally diverse university students into their classrooms soon discover that they serve as expert mentors on research or independent study projects. As mentioned earlier, a Big Brother–Big Sister approach has the capacity to change lives in very positive ways. Young people may receive "work hard and you will achieve" messages from their parents and teachers daily; however, they will listen much more attentively to a 20-year-old college student they respect. There appears to be something almost magical about a relationship between an intelligent child or teenager and a high-achieving young adult. These supportive relationships often continue long after the research project is completed, as young people will continue the connection through e-mail. Today's e-mail pals can make a significant difference for children and adolescents in need of emotional support. College students who serve as powerful role models for success can support gifted culturally diverse students as they learn to cope with the difficult issues described in this chapter.

For Further Thought and Discussion

- ❧ Imagine you were having a conversation with Marcus Mabry following his graduation from the Lawrenceville School. In light of the unfavorable response Marcus received from adults to the way he presented himself during the commencement ceremony, what advice would you want to offer Marcus?
- ❧ Reflect on the experience described by Ruben Navarette in which his high school principal approached him with questions regarding his college applications. Do you think this scenario could occur today? What advice would you give to students like Ruben who might encounter such attitudes?
- ❧ Consider the early acculturation experience of Esmeralda Santiago. Would a young Latina arriving in our schools today experience

something similar? How might educators and counselors support her?

≋ The description of Wilma Mankiller's ethnic identity development may serve as a good discussion starter with culturally diverse students. How might they respond to her thinking?

≋ Describe the contextual influences that may shape the experiences of culturally diverse students in your school. How might teachers, counselors, and administrators respond to your description? What advice would you provide them?

Resources to Expand Your Thinking and Extend Your Support to Gifted Students

Ford, D. Y., & Harris, J. J., III (1999). *Multicultural gifted education.* New York, NY: Teachers College Press.

Gay, G. (2000). *Culturally responsive teaching: Theory, research and practice.* New York, NY: Teachers College Press.

Graham, S. (2000). *Teens can make it happen: Nine steps for success.* New York, NY: Fireside.

Graham, S. (2001). *Teens can make it happen workbook.* New York, NY: Fireside.

Ladson-Billings, G. J. (2009). *The dreamkeepers: Successful teachers of African-American children* (2nd ed.). San Francisco, CA: Jossey-Bass.

Ladson-Billings, G. J. (2001). *Crossing over to Canaan: The journey of new teachers in diverse classrooms.* San Francisco, CA: Jossey-Bass.

Nieto, S., & Bode, P. (2008). *Affirming diversity: The sociopolitical context of multicultural education* (5th ed.). Boston, MA: Pearson.

CHAPTER **10**

Designing Gifted and Creative-Friendly Classroom Environments for Social and Emotional Development

My goals for this chapter are to:
- ➴ Acquaint you with theory guiding the design of gifted and creative-friendly classroom environments.
- ➴ Provide you with information regarding how I learned to design my classroom environment in teaching gifted students.
- ➴ Present additional strategies offered by teachers for designing supportive classroom environments.

[R]elationships are to youth development what location is to real estate: We need relationship, relationship, relationship. The best instructional methods, curricula, and equipment are not going to produce good outcomes in bad relationship environments.

—James Comer

I was fortunate to encounter the work of Albert Cullum early in my teaching career. As a first-year teacher, I attended a workshop on using creative drama in the classroom. The facilitator of the session began the training by reading Cullum's (1971) book of poetry entitled, *The Geranium on the Windowsill Just Died, But Teacher You Went Right on.* The book features children's experiences with schools and their teachers through the eyes of young boys and girls. Each poem offers a snapshot of school and reminds us how children might view their lives in school and how they feel about their teachers. A few poems provide a taste of the important message Cullum (1971) was delivering:

Of course your classroom is not a circus!
Of course you have rules we have to follow!
Of course there's lots of stuff we must learn!
But, Teacher, can't you smile when you tell us all this?

I want you to come to our house, Teach, and yet I don't.
You're so important, but our back door has a hole in it.
And my mother has no fancy cake to serve.
I want you to come to our house, Teacher, and yet I don't.
My brother chews with his mouth open, and sometimes my dad burps.
I wish I could trust you enough, Teacher, to invite you to my house.

Teacher, let me swim in a puddle!
Let me race a cloud across the sky!
Let me build a house without a single wall!
Let me leap, let me whirl, let me fly! . . .
"Turn to page sixty-seven," you say,
"paragraph two."

I was good at everything until I started being here with you.
I was good at laughing, playing dead, being king!
Honest, I was good at everything!
And now?

Now I'm only good at everything
on Saturdays and Sundays . . .

As I listened to the facilitator read the poems, I was struck by Cullum's ability to capture the reality of the school life experiences of many young children. As a child I had enjoyed school; however, I recognized many of my childhood friends in Cullum's poems. They felt the same way about school and their teachers. Determined to become an excellent teacher, I vowed that day that I would make my classroom a place where I would not hesitate to smile, a place where my students would feel comfortable sharing their families with me, and a place where they could laugh, play dead, or be king. I was determined to create a psychologically safe environment for all young people who passed through my classroom door. Years later when I became involved in gifted education, I realized that this notion of design-ing classroom environments where young people feel comfortable being themselves remained important. I worked hard to make my gifted educa-tion classroom a place where students would feel at home. My work with gifted children and teenagers throughout the years reinforced my philo-sophical view of classroom environments and why I continue to believe in Albert Culllum's message. In this chapter, I discuss the theoretical litera-ture that has influenced my thinking on designing supportive classroom environments for gifted students and offer a smorgasbord of pedagogical strategies I have used with gifted elementary, middle, and high school stu-dents in creating gifted and creative-friendly classrooms.

Related Theoretical Literature

Palmer (1993) describes teaching as creating a space. This may strike people as a poetic metaphor until we understand that it describes everyday life. As Palmer noted, we know what it means to run through an open field and we can compare that experience to a ride on a crowded rush-hour sub-way. On the crowded subway, we struggle to find the space to breathe and think; yet, in an open field, we can also be open as our ideas and feelings emerge within us. According to Palmer, these experiences with space are parallel to our relationships with people in our lives. We know how it feels to feel crowded by the urgency of deadlines and stressed by the competitive-ness of colleagues. We have also experienced other times when colleagues collaborate effectively and people feel comfortable creating, inventing, and solving problems with enthusiasm and energy. The same feelings apply to our experiences with family and friends. We may have been overwhelmed by the expectations of those who are closest to us and at other times when we feel accepted, supported, and loved for who we are as well as who we want to become. Palmer drew a parallel to schools:

> Similar experiences of crowding and space are found in education. To sit in a class where the teacher stuffs our minds with information, organizes it with finality, insists on having the answers while getting utterly uninterested in our views, and forces us into a grim competition for grades—to sit in such a class is to experience a lack of space for learning. But to study with a teacher who not only speaks but listens, who not only gives answers but asks questions and welcomes our insights, who provides information and theories that do not close doors but open new ones, who encourages students to help each other learn—to study with such a teacher is to know the power of a learning space. (pp. 70–71)

Palmer's (1993) notion of learning space includes three important characteristics: openness, boundaries, and an air of hospitality. Openness refers to removing any barriers to learning. The teacher who wants to design an open learning space also must define and protect its boundaries. A learning space must also have some structure. Without it, we are openly inviting confusion and chaos. Such a space must also include hospitality. Palmer describes this as being open to receiving each other and our new ideas. This space needs to be hospitable to make learning enjoyable but also to provide room for students to experience the difficult challenges of learning such as testing hypotheses, questioning false information, and handling mutual criticism.

Palmer's (1993) learning space is consistent with what Kennedy (1995) described as a gifted-friendly classroom environment in which "a bright child feels valued and comfortable, free to develop socially and emotionally, as well as intellectually" (p. 232). She defined it as "an environment in which a child is encouraged both to ask and to answer complex questions . . . an environment in which individual differences are honored, and no one is ostracized . . . an environment in which the child can expect to learn new things every day—and to enjoy learning" (Kennedy, 1995, p. 232). More recently, Fogarty (1998) has proposed that educators consider designing what she refers to as intelligence-friendly classrooms. She defined such a classroom as one "in which the teaching/learning process is governed by what is known about developing the intellectual potential of human beings" (Fogarty, 1998, p. 655). Such classrooms are friendly to the learner in fostering all that is associated with problem solving, decision making, and creative thinking, and serve as a supportive friend in fostering the development of the student's intellectual potential. Moreover, intelligence-friendly classrooms are environments that "celebrate the joy of the learner's emotional and intellectual world . . . through richness and relationships" (Fogarty, 1998, p. 655).

Noddings (1995) maintained that teachers should strive for the development of caring people and encouraged educators to focus on "developing relations of trust, talking with students about problems that are essential to their lives, and guiding them toward greater sensitivity and competence across all domains of care" (p. 679). She argued that caring "is the glue that binds teachers and students together and makes life in classrooms meaningful" (Noddings, 1995, p. 681). With the construct of caring as a foundation, Smith and Emigh (2005) described the construction of a caring classroom community. In a caring classroom, children experience an orderly environment; a climate of mutual trust, honesty, and respect; and psychological protection and care in their work with others. These are family like environments in which students know one another and share a sense of purpose. From their teachers students receive positive messages of concern, affection, and security. Students are involved in decision making and create rituals that highlight the significance of the important work they accomplish in their everyday activities. In addition, individual differences and diversity are respected and valued in caring classrooms.

Tomlinson (1999) offered several principles of teaching that guide educators in creating healthy learning environments. Several of these significant principles are parallel to the philosophical approaches presented above and become significant as educators work to build community (Tomlinson, Brimijoin, & Narvaez, 2008). Tomlinson (1999) shared these principles as starting points for reflection as teachers begin to plan their instruction:

- *The teacher appreciates each child as an individual.* Educators work hard to understand who their students really are as unique human beings and they allow the children to know them as people.
- *The teacher remembers to teach whole children.* Educators are sensitive in their understanding of young people with individual intellects, emotions, and ever-changing physical needs. They realize that they teach children about science, not that they are science teachers.
- *The teacher continues to develop expertise.* Educators are passionate about the big ideas of their discipline and strive to learn all they can in the discipline to share with their young protégés.

- ❧ *The teacher strives for joyful learning.* Educators realize that children are still full of energy and naturally respond to joy; therefore, they strive to ensure that their students are actively engaged in what they are learning.

- ❧ *The teacher helps students make their own sense of ideas.* Educators find ways to help young people take responsibility for creating their own understanding of the world.

- ❧ *The teacher shares the teaching with students.* Educators who create healthy classroom environments are comfortable with having their students become a part of the teaching. They do this by having young people teach one another. They provide them opportunities to collaboratively design the boundaries to maintain order and respect in the classroom. They ask for feedback from their students in order to assess the effectiveness of the learning experiences.

- ❧ *The teacher clearly strives for student independence.* Educators work to become the guide on the side—facilitators of learning rather than instructors who orchestrate every move made by students. They offer directions, advice, and guidelines for quality, but they allow for flexibility, choice, and some ambiguity in order that students become responsible for their own learning.

- ❧ *The teacher uses positive energy and humor.* Educators in healthy classrooms laugh with their students. Humor happens with spontaneity, in celebrating creativity, and when mistakes lead to surprising and insightful new discoveries.

Throughout my career, I have often reflected on the childlike poetry of Albert Cullum and the important message he instilled within me as a beginning teacher. I have found support from educational researchers and theorists such as Palmer, Kennedy, Fogarty, Noddings, and Tomlinson for this philosophical view and have felt validated in my beliefs. Moreover, I have also been heavily influenced by the work of William Purkey, a counselor educator whose research and philosophical approach have helped to influence the design of many gifted education classrooms. Purkey (1978) has defined good teaching as "the process of inviting students to see themselves as able, valuable, and self-directing and of encouraging them to act in accordance with these self-perceptions" (p. vi). He believed the teacher's most important role is to view students in positive ways and invite them to act accordingly. The Invitational Learning concept, developed by Purkey and his colleagues is a paradigm that provides educators, counselors, and administrators with a plan for enriching the physical and psychological environments of schools and encouraging the development of the people who work there. Invitational learning is centered on four assumptions regarding the nature of people and their potential and the nature of professional helping (Novak & Purkey, 2001; Purkey, 1978; Purkey & Novak, 2008; Purkey & Strahan, 2002):

- *Respect.* People are able, valuable, and responsible and should be treated accordingly.
- *Trust.* Education should be a collaborative, cooperative activity where process is as important as product.
- *Optimism.* People possess untapped potential in all areas of human endeavor.
- *Intentionality.* Human potential can best be realized by places, policies, programs, and processes that are specifically designed to invite development, and by people who are intentionally inviting with themselves and others, personally and professionally.

Respect for the uniqueness, value, and integrity of each and every one of us is the cornerstone of invitational learning. Only when teachers accept their students as they are, recognize their unlimited potential, and invite them to take responsibility for their lives and make appropriate decisions regarding their learning, do they contribute to their development. Trust, the second important quality in invitational learning, acknowledges the interdependence of human beings and emphasizes that teaching should become a collaborative and cooperative activity in which process is celebrated as much as product.

Optimism is the belief that human potential is endless and always there, waiting to be discovered and realized. Optimistic teachers have a vision of what is possible for students to become. They see the child who struggles in math overcoming his phobia and succeeding in algebra. The fourth principle, intentionality, is the ability we have to link our perceptions with our overt behaviors. Intentionality is an important element in any helping relationship. It encourages educators to become aware of the helpful or harmful potential of every intentional or unintentional action. It also supports teachers and counselors in maintaining inviting attitudes in all of their interactions, consistently inviting well-being in themselves as well as the young people they teach (Novak & Purkey, 2001; Purkey & Novak, 2008; Purkey & Schmidt, 1992).

Invitational learning maintains that the easiest way to positively influence people to is improve the many messages they receive. These messages may be formal or informal, intentional and unintentional. Positive messages must be delivered that invite people to feel able, valuable, and responsible rather than negative messages that inform people they are not capable, worthless, and irresponsible. These positive and negative messages are categorized as four levels of personal and professional functioning.

Intentionally disinviting messages or behaviors are those that are purposefully designed to discourage, defeat, or demean people, the kinds of behaviors that invitational learning seeks to eliminate. Individuals who send such messages are frustrated by their circumstances and make negative remarks based on their feelings. They may justify their bully behavior with rationales sprinkled with phrases such as "being good for them," "fight fire with fire," and "the only language they understand" (Novak & Purkey, 2001; Purkey & Novak, 2008; Purkey & Schmidt, 1992).

Unintentionally disinviting behaviors are seen in people who simply do not reflect on what they are doing. Educators functioning at this level simply are clueless about the damage they are doing through their insensitivity, abrupt behavior, or lack of forethought. Their classrooms are places where irrelevant busywork and boredom thrive (Novak & Purkey, 2001; Purkey & Novak, 2008).

Unintentionally inviting educators are often outgoing, good-natured people who do whatever comes naturally; however, their approach is inconsistent and lacks thoughtful commitment. They have forgotten the importance of the intentionality. These teachers may be entertaining and enthusiastic when things are working well in their lives but when things are not running smoothly, they become frustrated and cynical. They have not been reflective about their practice and subsequently have not modified their approach (Novak & Purkey, 2001; Purkey & Novak, 2008; Purkey & Schmidt, 1992).

Intentionally inviting educators consistently demonstrate integrity in everything they do. They reflect on their practice and they grow continuously. They constantly remind themselves of why they entered teaching: their authentic appreciation of others and their development. They maintain a high level of personal dignity and self-respect in order to respect and trust others. They have a deep commitment to caring for people. Educators who operate at this level display respect, trust, optimism, and intentionality in everything they do. They conduct themselves graciously without drawing attention to themselves. Successful intentionally inviting educators are individuals who continue to grow and develop throughout their lives and enjoy the process (Novak & Purkey, 2001; Purkey & Novak, 2008).

Educational researchers and theorists have offered insightful suggestions regarding how educators should create classroom environments that are supportive of the social and emotional development of young people. It is the task of teachers to implement the approaches suggested in ways that will benefit students in gifted education classrooms. The following is a discussion of how educators can translate theory into practice by designing both the physical and psychological classroom environment needed for supporting able learners.

Translating Theory Into Practice: Creating the Physical Classroom Environment

Although people are most influential in shaping how students think about themselves, the physical environment of the school or classroom is also important. Aesthetically pleasant environments actually influence behavior and performance (Stewart, Evans, and Kaczynski, 1997). The landscape, aesthetics, and even the sounds and smells of the school can deliver a message that says to children, "We care about you and we're glad you're here" (Purkey, 2000). Gladwell (2000) maintained that environmental conditions strongly influence how young people behave and he argued that "children are powerfully shaped by their external environment [and] that the features of our immediate social and physical world . . . play a huge role in shaping who we are and how we act" (p. 168). Johns (1997) highlighted this issue as she suggested,

> Schools need to be attractive places. We can unintentionally send a very negative message to students when we do not keep our schools well maintained—"We don't care enough about you to clean or paint." Just the opposite message is sent when schools are decorated with items such as plants, when walls and bulletin boards are decorated with student art and photographs, and when student and staff awards and recognition for accomplishments are on display. (p. 35)

Bothmer (2003) spoke to educators when she said, "Creating a nurturing and supportive classroom environment comes from the heart: love for yourself, love for your students, and love for teaching and learning" (p. 1). She noted that looking at the classroom environment is the first step to creating a psychologically safe classroom. She recommended that teachers begin preparing their classrooms by asking themselves what they can do to create an environment that will make both the teacher and the children feel good and assist them in doing their best work. To design such an environment, Bothmer suggested feng shui, an ancient Chinese practice stemming from an awareness that the elements of the natural world affect our being. She explained,

> We are affected by the caress of the breeze, the sun shining on our faces, and the plants in our yards. Because most of us spend the majority of our time indoors, we are not as closely connected to the earth or as stimulated by the rhythms of the outdoor elements as we once were. Feng shui symbolically brings the outdoors inside, allowing you and your students to experience the elements daily. A nurturing and supportive environment is the result. (p. 3)

The three tenets of feng shui—connectedness, balance, and vitality—provide guidelines for designing a classroom that promotes a nurturing environment for both the teacher and students. *Connectedness* relates to the feeling of being connected to the natural world, one's ancestors and family, and even the role models who have inspired us. It is important that students and teachers feel connected to the classroom space and to one another. *Balance* is created by providing space where both quiet and active experiences and activities may take place. A classroom space needs to be stimulating but not too stimulating, relaxing but not too relaxing. *Vitality* is understood as aliveness. A vital classroom space feels uplifting and comfortable (Bothmer, 2003). The following list serves as a menu of suggestions for designing a vital and balanced classroom where students and their teachers can feel connected to one another and work as a community of learners.

- Display student products.
- Hang framed class photographs in a prominent place in the classroom.
- Hang several favorite pictures of family and friends near the teacher's desk.
- Bring a sofa or upholstered chairs as a reading corner, a place for students to snuggle up and read, or a space for quiet conversation.
- Provide a round table covered with a tablecloth and decorated with flowers. This special space becomes a favorite "kitchen table" place for quiet study or private student-teacher conferences.
- Place a colorful rug in a classroom meeting area. The rug defines the space where teacher and students gather and promotes a feeling of safety.
- Create a classroom display piece by hanging a tree branch from the ceiling and use it to hang student artwork or poetry.

- Decorate the room with some colorful posters and prints related to the popular interests of the students.
- Have an author's chair for student sharing with the class.
- Add vitality to the classroom with lush green plants.
- Hang student-designed posters containing positive messages or affirmations at eye level for students.
- Incorporate lamps for soft lighting in strategic places.
- Arrange the student furniture flexibly for collaborative work.
- Provide quiet work spaces.
- Incorporate space for a student museum where students have opportunities to share something about themselves and their extra-curricular lives.

With the design of the physical environment in place, the teacher's next challenge is the critical task of creating an emotional climate in the classroom that enables students to feel they are valued for their intelligence and creativity, and respected as individuals by both their teacher and class-mates. The design of this emotional climate is presented below.

Translating Theory Into Practice: Creating the Emotional Classroom Environment

The Opening Day of School

Classroom teachers who invest serious energy in designing psycho-logically safe classroom environments begin their work before the first day of school. I recently met Daniel Henderson, a dedicated teacher from Hagerstown, MD, at an education conference. Daniel shared with me how much he enjoyed preparing his fifth-grade classroom for the first day of school. During the summer Daniel sends out personal letters introducing himself to his incoming group of students and their families. His letter includes an invitation to parents to join their children for a family break-fast in his classroom on the morning of the first day of school. Daniel asks the students to reply to his letter with a letter in which they introduce themselves and share important information about their strengths, hobbies, talents, and interests. Recently, as the families arrived in the classroom to meet Mr. Henderson, they were greeted with a red carpet and a bright spotlight. Daniel had turned his classroom into an Oscars-night event and the spotlight was on the individual fifth graders who were treated like celebrities as they walked the red carpet into fifth grade. Following the family breakfast prepared and served by Mr. Henderson, each student was introduced and awarded a replica of the Oscars statue celebrating his or her individual talents and interests. Mr. Henderson was certainly letting his students know that in his classroom each and every student was a star! In my conversation with this dedicated teacher, it was obvious to me that Daniel was passionate about his profession and derived much pleasure from his work. As we chatted, he went on to describe his new creative plan for the opening day of the upcoming school year.

Several years ago, I enjoyed working with another dedicated educator, Linda McNair, a student in my graduate course in gifted education. Linda was a first-grade teacher in Fort Worth, TX. That semester she shared with her colleagues in the class how she welcomed her first graders on the opening day of school. Linda spent a little time at a local dollar store. She purchased simple items that were included in small brown paper sacks that she decorated with ribbons and delivered to the children. One year Linda included a rubber band, a band-aid, a cookie, an eraser, and a pencil. To accompany the items, Linda included the following note to the children:

You're Someone Special

In this sack, you will find special things for special you.
First, a rubber band to wear and remind you that you may have a hug at any time.
A band-aid to help you with any hurts. Remember, you can talk about your feelings at any time, when you feel happy or when you are hurt.
A cookie, because you are a smart cookie!
An eraser to erase any mistakes and begin the new school year with renewed vitality.
Last, you will find a pencil to sharpen your thinking skills and write down all of your wonderful thoughts.
You're special!

Linda's delightful strategy is one that I have enjoyed passing on to educators in my graduate classes. In doing so, I have asked them to generate a list of items they might want to include in their opening day of school sacks. The following are several that middle and high school teachers have suggested:

- A blank CD—In this classroom, you will burn your own path to success.
- Laffy Taffy—Remember to always keep your sense of humor.
- A jigsaw puzzle piece—Everyone in this classroom is unique, but together we can make something great.
- A jumbo paper clip—In this classroom, we will all help each other keep it together.
- Miniature Post-it® Notes—You'll need these to capture your important "Aha!s."
- A free homework pass—For that one day when you will really need to cash it in.

With a small amount of preparation and creative brainstorming, teachers enjoy designing "welcome to my classroom" sacks that help students realize that they are about to embark upon a wonderful academic year in their new teacher's classroom.

In addition to sharing these first day of school activities from Daniel and Linda, I will pass on several of my favorite field-tested methods. The following strategies are from my years of teaching in gifted education classrooms and include methods and activities I found successful with elementary, middle, and high school students. The strategies I offer are described in the order in which they occurred in my classroom, and I begin with those typically used as "getting to know each other" activities that helped to create a sense of community.

Business Cards

One of the first activities I facilitated in my classroom during the first week of school was "Business Cards." I explained to the students how professionals have business cards that present an image to the world of what they are all about. I then shared with them my collection of business cards and highlighted how many of them send a very clear message. I have collected cards from all over the country and have enjoyed showing students how Ann Marie McGranaghan's card from "The Courtesy Cleaning Company" in Bowling Green, OH, speaks to me with its clear, clean, crisp lines that say Ms. McGranaghan offers a housecleaning service that is meticulous and that she would be the kind of woman I would want taking care of my new home. My card from "Cakes Extraordinaire" in Portland, ME, is a simple and elegant looking card. I chose to order my parents' 50th wedding anniversary cake from this bakery because I wanted the perfect cake—something simple and elegant looking, not a huge monstrosity with blue roses. I made the right choice. The cake was beautiful and made a big hit on my parents' special day.

After my short introduction, I had students reflect on a question: "What does a business card say about you?" I then handed out large sheets of construction paper and provided them the time to design their personal business cards. My objective behind this activity is to have gifted students find a friend. I wanted science fiction buffs to find each other. I wanted the baseball card collectors to locate other sports junkies. I wanted the girls who designed step dance routines to find other dancers. I wanted the computer experts to discover each other. I wanted the gymnasts and horse-back-riding students to find others who enjoyed those sports. Through their common interests or passions, new friendships may evolve. The business cards were proudly displayed on the walls of the classroom and children were able to make new friendship connections. Older students who were savvy in their knowledge of technology enjoyed creating professional-looking cards, having them printed, and exchanging them amongst the group. This simple, nonthreatening activity was exactly what I needed to begin building community. In today's high-tech classrooms, teachers can enjoy having students post their cards on the class website and begin to help them build important relationships.

Little-Known Facts

A second activity that I discovered guaranteed me rich information about each of my students was one known as "Little-Known Facts." Students are asked to jot down on an index card five interesting facts or items of information about themselves. Within those five, one of the items must be a lie. Students then exchange the index cards and they must determine which one of the items is the lie. I always included myself in this activity. Here is my list of interesting bits of information about me:

- I enjoy country music.
- I drive a red Volkswagen Beetle.
- I was once bowled over by a bully on the skating rink as I was skating around the ice rink holding hands with my new seventh-grade sweetheart and she remained standing!
- I was President of the Golden Gavel Civics Club in fifth grade.
- I once lived in Bad Kreuznach, Germany.

The students always enjoyed sharing their interesting lives with each other and with their teacher. They also enjoyed seeing that their teacher

was capable of telling a lie. I had ea
mate to the class following a conversati
laughter evolved throughout the sharing th
deal about each other, and this time spent
through "Little-Known Facts" provided us all
starters in the beginning of the year. I continue to
university graduate students today and it has never bee
I recently discovered that I had the honor of having the C
the Vidalia, GA, Onion Festival in one of my graduate sem
case you're wondering, the second item on my list is the lie. I w
to drive a red VW Beetle one day, but right now I drive something
more conservative in appearance.

Wanted Posters

I also had fun experimenting with another strategy I referred to as "Wanted Posters." I had students think about how they would want to advertise for a new friend by highlighting their personal interests, hobbies, and passions. With a disposable camera and a classroom set of individual snapshots, we had what we needed to advertise each new member of the classroom community. Several text examples of Wanted Posters are provided below:

Wanted
A friend for trading baseball cards,
playing computer games, and organizing campaigns
to save endangered species.

Call John Jenkins
555-9649

Wanted
Friends who love reading good books,
writing stories, and creating puppet shows and plays.

Call Shanika Johnson
555-8853
Or look for me on the school playground.
I'm in Mrs. Thurston's room.

ch student introduce their new class-
on in dyads. Lots of good-natured
me. We quickly learned a great
etting to know each other
with many conversation
use this strategy with
a disappointment.
Onion Queen of
nars. Just in
ould like
a little

s!

y mother.
lls.

several additional
students and their
ative writing and
scovered a helpful
resource, *If You're Going to Teach Kids How to Write, You Gotta' Have This Book* by Marjorie Frank. Frank's (1979) classic work provided me with a smorgasbord of simple, nonthreatening poetry activities that I could implement without a lot of training.

The students enjoyed writing "I used to be . . . but now I . . ." poems. I had them think back to the "good old days" when they were much younger and had them generate phrases that described their physical appearance, favorite ways of having fun, music, food, people they admired, and beliefs. They were then to do the same in describing themselves today. With that information collected, we then infused the information into a simple poetic structure. Danny Albanese and Veronica Ducci were elementary students I worked with in Connecticut and their responses to this activity are provided below:

I used to be a very fat baby,
But now I'm tall and thin.

I used to wear diapers,
But now I wear He-Man underwear.

I used to believe in the Easter bunny,
But now I have my own rabbit.

I used to like nursery rhyme songs,
But now I listen to Van Halen.

I used to be afraid of ghosts,
But now I'm afraid of when report cards come out.

—Danny Albanese (Grade 3)

I used to be skinny,
But now I am medium sized.

I used to like good food,
But now I like junk food.

I used to be smart,
And I am still smart.

I used to be a fussy eater,
But now I eat a lot.

I used to take lots of naps,
But now I have a lot of homework.

—Veronica Ducci (Grade 4)

When poems were completed, my students enjoyed incorporating their artwork that reflected scenes of themselves from "the good old days" to accompany their poem. Other times, I was successful in having them bring in baby pictures and their most recent school photographs to use in displaying their poems in the classroom. Wonderful conversations evolved from these poems as the new classroom community came together in the beginning of the school year.

I am . . . but I wish . . . Frank (1979) offered another poetry strategy that I found was always successful with students of any age. I had students brainstorm five or six different ways of describing themselves. For example, "I am a fifth grader, a Boy Scout, the oldest boy in my family, a student in Mr. Connell's room, and a science whiz." Students were then asked to brainstorm and generate five or six wishes, dreams, or aspirations. This information was infused into a simple poetic structure and "I am . . . but

I wish I were . . ." poems resulted. Examples from Jessica Nickerson and Kyung-Hee Linn are provided below:

> I am a second grader,
> But I wish I were in college so I wouldn't have to go to school every day.

> I am 7 years old,
> But I wish I were 20 and I had a job so I wouldn't have to worry about an allowance.

> I am in Mrs. Capitanio's room,
> But I wish I were back in Kindergarten so I wouldn't have so much work.

> I am in East School,
> But I wish I were in Bermuda swimming in Horseshoe Bay.

> I am living in Torrington, Connecticut,
> But I wish I lived in New York City so I could see the Statue of Liberty every day.
>
> —Jessica Nickerson (Grade 2)

> I am a 4th grader,
> But I wish I were a computer genius so I could rule the world.

> I am a 9-year-old girl,
> But I wish I were 13 years old so I could go to middle school and get even smarter.

> I am a ballet student,
> But I wish I were a prima ballerina performing on stages all over the world.

> I am a fan of Britney Spears,
> But I wish I could sing in my own concert.

I am a girl living in Georgia,
But I wish I were living in North Carolina because I am sick of the humidity.

—Kyung-Hee Linn (Grade 4)

Two-word poems. Two-word poems offered by Frank (1979) were also effective strategies with students of all levels of writing ability. These poems had to describe the students in the classroom. I paired the students and provided them the time to get to know each other in quiet conversation. Once they had spent time gathering information about each other's lives beyond the classroom, they were asked to write a two-word poem describing their classroom colleague. Each line of the poem was limited to two words. After time sharing these poems and introducing new friends to the class, student artwork or personal snapshots could accompany the poems. These poems were proudly displayed on a classroom bulletin board. The following poems are examples of what evolved from this activity:

Becky Swanson
Sensitive girl
Vivacious personality
Pretty eyes
Brown hair
Loves dancing
Spelling champion
Chocolate lover
Awesome friend

—Julie Rogalla

Jimmy Kirkwood
Skateboard dude
Rugged muscles
Curly hair
Army brat
Soccer player
Yankees fan
Neat guy

—Roderick Johnson

Interest Inventories

Along with strategies designed to have students come to know each other and their teacher, I also discovered that important information could be learned by conducting interest inventories with my students. In order to plan appropriate instructional activities that would engage students, the facilitation of interest surveys enabled me to make connections with the interests of my students and the curriculum. Joseph Renzulli (1997) and his colleagues have developed a series of commercially available interest inventories known as Interest-a-Lyzers, questionnaires designed for students to become more familiar with their interests and potential interests. The series includes the original Interest-a-Lyzer (Renzulli, 1997), appropriate for elementary students; the Secondary Interest-a-Lyzer (Hébert, Sorenson, & Renzulli, 1997), designed for middle and high school students; and the *Primary Interest-a-Lyzer* (Renzulli & Rizza, 1997), created for children in grades K–3. These three questionnaires assist educators in providing young people with meaningful educational experiences that further develop their interests, nurture their talents, and challenge their learning potential. The following are examples of the types of questions posed in the surveys designed to uncover the authentic interests of young people.

From the Primary Interest-a-Lyzer (Renzulli & Rizza, 1997):

- Do you like to collect things? What do you collect?
- You are a famous author about to write your next book. What will it be about?

From the Interest-a-Lyzer (Renzulli, 1997):

- Imagine that a time machine has been invented that will allow famous people from the past to travel through time. If you could invite some of these people to visit your class, whom would you invite?
- Imagine that you have been assigned to a space station for your next school year. You are allowed to take a few personal possessions (books, games, hobbies, projects) with you to help you spend your free time. List the things you would take.

From the Secondary Interest-a-Lyzer (Hébert et al., 1997):

- Teenagers in your community have been asked to prepare individual time capsules for future generations. You are allowed to include

10 personal possessions that are representative of you. What will you include in your capsule?

∾ If you could be an exchange student in another country for half a school year, what country would you like to visit as a student? Why?

By learning the students' interests, I was able to modify the curriculum to meet their individual needs. I was also sending an important message to students that said, "I care about you and what you are interested in." In addition to the commercially available materials, Nugent (2005) recommended that teachers consider developing their own interest inventories by asking questions of students regarding what they enjoy doing after school, sports they enjoy, who are the important people in their lives, and how they feel about particular school subjects. Applying a bit of personal creativity to a series of questions for young people in the beginning of an academic year can go a long way in uncovering information that will be helpful to teachers in planning for successful school experiences and creating a supportive classroom community. Recently, I have enjoyed working with educators in my graduate classes in designing personalized inventories they will use with their students. I have discovered that high school teachers enjoy designing these in such a way that they learn much-needed information about their students' interests, personalities, learning styles, and lives beyond the classroom. The following are examples of questions that secondary educators have incorporated in their inventories:

∾ Two prominent politicians running for office, one conservative and one liberal, are holding a debate in our high school's gym and it's open to the public. They have asked the students to contribute topics to be the subjects for debate. You are provided the opportunity to select three debate topics over current issues facing our society. What three topics would you choose? Why do you think they are important? (Jamie Atkins, high school science teacher)

∾ Oprah Winfrey has asked you to select a person for her to interview on her show. Who would you choose? Write two questions you would have her ask this person.

∾ What picture is on your screen-saver on your computer? Or the background picture on your cell phone? Why? (Katie Gilbert, high school math teacher)

- How would you describe your ideal friend? What characteristics do you look for in a best friend?
- Describe your biggest fear in life.
- Describe a typical week in your life. What are you doing each day, besides coming to school and loving every minute of AP biology?
- If you could ask me any three questions, what would you ask me? (Matt Dahlke, high school AP biology teacher)

- What qualities in a teacher help you learn the most? What qualities in a teacher harm your learning the most?
- When, where, and with who do you feel the happiest? (Joseph Palmour, high school computer technology teacher)

- You are stuck in Walmart as your mom's "this will only take a minute" promise has turned into 45 minutes. So, to ease frustration, you browse through the magazines. Which magazines are you most likely to pick up and flip through to see what's new this month?
- As part of your senior project, you are asked to create a "Soundtrack of Your Life." The songs you compile represent the music you love, and the lyrics might reflect the events in your life for the past 17 or 18 years. Which songs and artists would be included on your soundtrack?
- America is famous for being a melting pot of cultures. What is your ancestral background? Were your parents immigrants? Your great-grandparents? What are some family customs and celebrations that stem from your family's background? (Holly Sewell, high school British literature and composition teacher)

- This Saturday, you have no homework or chores to worry about. You can spend the day however you want. What will you do?
- If you could change one thing about your high school, what would it be? (Steve Kuninsky, high school science teacher)

Heavy Bags

An activity I incorporated in my classroom later in the school year was one I called "Heavy Bags." I offered this activity when I saw students becoming overwhelmed by their responsibilities or stressed out over school or their busy lifestyles after school.

After I distributed a handout with an artistic sketch of a student book bag, I discussed how we all entered the classroom every day with something heavy in our bags. We were all worried or anxious about something in our lives, whether it was happening at school or at home. Perhaps we were worried about an upcoming exam in a difficult subject, or someone in our family who was dealing with a difficult illness, or a relationship with a friend that was currently troubled. I asked the students to jot down on the sheet of paper one stressor that they were carrying into the classroom that day. I insisted that they submit anonymous responses. After I collected the responses, I read them aloud, making a point to use a soft tone of voice. As I read them, I also made sure to provide empathic comments that accentuated how we all could understand why the stressor would be difficult.

Each time I conducted this activity my students realized that they all had stressors in common. They realized that everyone in the class had something that they were worried about. As a classroom community, they realized that we are all facing the challenges of life together and we need to support each other. I highlighted how we all needed to be kinder and gentler with each other and respectful of that fact that someone in the classroom may be having a bad day because of the heavy baggage being carried. I noticed that following such an activity the classroom temperature changed. Students spoke in softer voices, were more often respectful and polite, and were gentler in their dealings with each other. At the end of the school day, class period, or block of time that we were together, I handed out a second copy of the same book bag, and asked the students to jot down one new insight they learned that day that they would carry away as a result of being together as a community. The responses varied from insightful responses related to the curricular activities to more personal responses related to having learned something about themselves. The second round of responding to the "Heavy Bags" prompt enabled me to conclude our time together on a positive note following the earlier sharing of something rather "heavy." I discovered that students appreciated the activity and recognized that sometimes they needed to be reminded that everyone faces challenges in their lives that are difficult and may influence how they behave. I found that "Heavy Bags" worked with very young children as well as high school seniors and university students.

Celebrating Friendships

Throughout the academic year, I found it helpful to incorporate activities in my classroom that highlighted the importance of the friendships that were forming amongst my students. I found it was especially easy to do this by incorporating children's literature that featured stories revolving around friendships. Taking a bit of time to share a children's picture book with my students and facilitating an artistic activity following the reading of the book about friendship was often valuable in maintaining a culture of respect and appreciation for each other.

The graduate students in my university classroom today enjoy my sharing Pam Muñoz Ryan's (2003) *A Box of Friends*. She has written a heart-warming story about a young girl adjusting to a new home in a new community. When Annie's family moves to the beach, she misses her friends and worries that she will not be able to make new ones. Fortunately, her grandmother knows exactly what to do. She shows Annie a box filled with mementos—a feather, a small bouquet of dried flowers, and a smooth white stone—and she explains how each of these wonderful items reminds her of a special day with one of her friends. Together Annie and her grandmother decorate a box and fill it with things that will remind Annie of the friends she misses so much.

After reading the literary selection to my students, I present an example of a box of friends that I have created to remind me of the important people in my life. Students of all ages enjoy creating a classroom box of friends. Each student in the class becomes responsible for creating one item for the box that represents how he or she contributes to the friendships within the class. Items might be of an artistic nature or students may enjoy contributing a poem about the important friendships in the class. Items might include mementos from a class field trip, photographs taken during special class activities, or souvenir programs from special events they experienced as a group. Students also enjoy spending time decorating the class friendship box in a creative manner. The symbolic box of friendship is displayed in a prominent place in the classroom as a daily reminder of how important it is to maintain supportive relationships with each other. The friendship box activity often leads to students creating their friendship boxes.

With a quick visit to the children's section in the library, a teacher at any grade level can easily locate many fine children's picture books that teach important lessons regarding friendship. With a little creativity applied to a follow-up activity, the students in a classroom can enjoy the lesson reminding them why relationships are so highly valued within the classroom.

Mr. Hébert's Mailbox

Early in my teaching career in gifted education, I incorporated a classroom mailbox that enabled students to communicate with me privately. I covered a Quaker Oats oatmeal box with colorful contact paper, and explained to my students that if they were to leave a letter in my mailbox, I would guarantee that they would find a letter from me the next day in a sealed envelope. In the beginning I was deluged with letters; however, I managed to respond to all of them. Typically, I received notes that read, "Mr. Hébert, I really liked the detective activity we did in class yesterday. Can we do more mini-mysteries this week?" or " Dear Mr. Hébert, You really looked like a dork in that silly red bowtie you wore last week. Don't ever do that again!" The letters were always enjoyable and helpful to me in understanding how students were feeling about their experiences in my classroom. More important to me were the letters I received that were calls for help. I shall always remember the letter I received from a student that read, "Dear Mr. Hébert, My mom and dad are getting a divorce. They want me to choose who I want to live with. Can you help me decide? Your student, Dustin." I responded to Dustin's letter the next day with a private conversation and an explanation of the special training Mrs. Jones, our school counselor, had undergone in order to help children who were faced with situations like his. Together Dustin and I then walked to the counselor's office, where I introduced them to each other and saw that he spent time with her during this difficult period in his fifth-grade year. My classroom mailbox became an important outlet for children to share their personal lives with me when they needed support, encouragement, or a significant adult to listen to what was on their minds. Many classroom teachers have incorporated similar approaches to student-teacher communication and have shared how having students maintain private journals have allowed them to conduct private student-teacher conversations through an approach that may be comfortable for young people.

Going to Boston

One of my favorite strategies from Canfield and Wells (1994) in *100 Ways to Enhance Self-Concept in the Classroom* is an activity referred to as "Going to Boston" that I implemented often in my classroom. In conducting this activity, the first student says, "I'm going to Boston with my suitcase and in it I have my high energy." The student offers some characteristic or talent that he or she values. The next student then says, "I'm going to Boston and in my suitcase I'm carrying Bethany's high energy and my skill at calligraphy." The third youngster says, "I'm going to Boston and in my suitcase I'm carrying Bethany's high energy, Joel's skill at calligraphy and my talent for talking with elderly people." This continues until all of the students in the class have had their opportunity to add their special gift to the suitcase. Canfield and Wells highlighted a variation of this activity for older students in which they pack the suitcase with personal successes. Teachers may want to ask teenagers to identify their most outstanding success to date. For example, "I'm going to Boston with my suitcase and in it I have my trophy from last year's state science fair."

I discovered that this activity took little time and students appreciated hearing others repeat their strength or celebrate their success. I also found that often when a student was humble and struggled to come up with a particular positive characteristic or strength, another student in the class would be ready to offer what he or she saw as a strength in their classmate. When this occurred, smiles quickly emerged.

Appreciative Feedback

I learned another important lesson from Canfield and Wells (1994) concerning the difference between evaluative and appreciative feedback. They noted that evaluative feedback is characterized by judgment. The teacher judges the student: "This is a B+ lab report." "You are a good line leader." " You are a class comedian." Appreciative feedback is characterized by letting the student know how you have been personally affected by something he or she has done. Examples of appreciative feedback are: "I was moved by your poem, *Worried on a Summer Evening*. As I read it, I could identify with the many fears you expressed. I now understand that we are similar in many ways." "I really enjoy your quick wit and I'm happy to have you in class each time you relax the tension in the room with one of your funny jokes." The important issue to remember is that most evaluative feedback begins with the word *you* while most appreciative feedback begins with the word *I*.

I learned that it was useful to incorporate appreciative feedback in written formal evaluations of my students' products as well as in informal personal conversations and group discussions. As the year progressed, I noticed that my students picked up on my cues and began to use appreciative feedback rather than evaluative comments with each other. When that occurred, I could not have been happier.

Summary

The theoretical literature that grounds the design of a psychologically safe classroom environment is extensive. Much has been written to convince educators of the value of addressing the affective needs of gifted students by designing classroom environments that support social and emotional development. With the theory as a foundation, I have offered practical strategies that I found were useful to me in carrying out the design of such an environment. I encourage teachers to consider the approaches presented in this chapter and experiment with them in their classrooms. Moreover, teachers may want to apply their personal creativity and design their own.

In conducting the activities with my students, I learned much from them about the importance of addressing affective development. Moreover, from my students I learned to celebrate the joy of learning together and the authentic childlike qualities in each and every one of us. As I highlighted at the beginning of the chapter, I wanted to make my classroom a place where I would not hesitate to smile, a place where my students would feel comfortable sharing their families with me, and a place where they could laugh, play dead, or be king. I am reminded of the joy I experienced in creating that place and the process of learning from my students each time I read my favorite Albert Cullum (1971) poem:

> Teacher, push back the desk and come outside!
> I'll race you to the swings!
> Don't be afraid, Teacher.
> Just grab my hand and follow me.
> You can learn all over again!

Resources to Expand Your Thinking and Extend Your Support to Gifted Students

Betts, G. T., & Kercher, J. J. (1999). *The Autonomous Learner Model: Optimizing ability.* Greeley, CO: ALPS.

Bothmer, S. (2003). *Creating the peaceable classroom: Techniques to calm, uplift, and focus teachers and students.* Tucson, AZ: Zephyr Press.

Galbraith, J. (2009). *The gifted kid's survival guide* (3rd ed.). Minneapolis, MN: Free Spirit.

Packer, A. J. (2006). *Wise highs: How to thrill, chill, and get away from it all without alcohol and other drugs.* Minneapolis, MN: Free Spirit.

Epilogue

You met me as the young teacher from Auburn, ME, ready to begin my journey. I was excited about the adventure I was embarking on as I left home for southeast Georgia. That journey has taken me to the University of Georgia, where I enjoy my work preparing young scholars and teachers in gifted education. It is the end of another academic year, and I am enjoying the warm sunshine on an April afternoon. Final exams are about to begin and a pile of student papers await my evaluation. The dogwoods and azaleas have come and gone as summer approaches but I still enjoy the quiet of my backyard where I sit with a tall glass of iced tea and my trusty laptop to write this final reflection.

Just as the end of an academic year is a good time to look back on where we have been in our work with students, the epilogue of a book provides a good place to share final reflections, lessons learned, and hopes for the future. In writing this text, I have become more convinced of the need to understand and appreciate the life experiences of gifted young people. In doing so, we honor their social and emotional lives. I have learned that the work we do in gifted education is important and influence lives in significant ways.

My hope is that in my writing this text many aspiring scholars in graduate classes will be inspired to raise new questions and pursue answers to those questions through research. In describing my experiences with participants in my research, I hope that others will want to design studies that extend my work. In addition, my hope is that practitioners enrolled in those same classes have enjoyed the stories I have shared about my students and have taken time to reflect on their own practice. I hope they will consider the strategies and methods I have recommended and enjoy experimenting with them in their classrooms. Moreover, I hope that young scholars will continue their conversation with practitioners in gifted education. With researchers and teachers and counselors maintaining a dialogue about the social and emotional experiences of gifted students, many more lives will be influenced in positive ways.

Before writing this book, I realized that the field of gifted education is still in the early developmental stages of research related to the social and emotional experiences of gifted students. Because we have much more work ahead of us, it is important that theorists and researchers continue to examine literature from other fields that help to inform our research and practice. There is a critical need for more scholars to examine the issues I have highlighted in this book, and I invite them to join me. The work is both important and rewarding.

I was reminded of the importance of our work recently as I listened to an interview with a motivational speaker. She reminded us to consider the recommendation made by airline attendants in describing safety procedures right before take off: "Secure your oxygen mask before assisting others." That simple message is an important one for the work we do with gifted students. In order for us to be effective in supporting the social and emotional development of children, we must also take good care of ourselves. As teachers and scholars in gifted education, self-nurturing is important. With that understood, I need to adjust my oxygen mask. I will shut down this laptop, sip my iced tea, and enjoy the Georgia sunshine.

Please take good care,
Tom
April 30, 2010

References

Abdelnoor, A., & Hollins, S. (2004). The effect of childhood bereavement on secondary school performance. *Educational Psychology in Practice, 20,* 43–54.

Abeel, S. (2003). *My thirteenth winter: A memoir.* New York, NY: Orchard Books.

Abeel, S., & Murphy, C. R. (1994). *Reach for the moon.* Scranton, PA: Scholastic.

Ackerman, C. M. (1997). Identifying gifted adolescents using personality characteristics: Dabrowski's overexcitabilities. *Roeper Review, 19,* 229–236.

Adderholdt, M. R., & Goldberg, J. (1999). *Perfectionism: What's bad about being too good?* Minneapolis, MN: Free Spirit.

Akhtar, S., & Kramer, S. (1997). *The seasons of life: Separation-individuation perspectives.* Northvale, NJ: Aronson.

Alabama Department of Archives and History. (1998).

Milledge County. Retrieved from http://www.asc.edu/archives/populate/[milledge].html

Allès-Jardel, M., Fourdrinier, C., Roux, A., & Schneider, B. H. (2002). Parents' structuring of children's daily lives and the stability of children's friendships. *International Journal of Psychology, 37,* 65–73.

Altermatt, E. R., & Pomerantz, E. M. (2005). The implications of having high-achieving versus low-achieving friends: A longitudinal analysis. *Social Development, 14,* 61–81.

American Psychiatric Association. (2000). *Diagnostic and statistical manual of mental disorders, fourth edition, text revision* (DSM-IV-TR). Washington, DC: Author

Anderson, K. (1993). A queen and her court. *Sports Illustrated, 79*(22), 68–71.

Anderson, P. L. (2000). Using literature to teach social skills to adolescents with LD. *Intervention in School and Clinic, 35,* 271–279.

Anthony, E. J., & Cohler, B. J. (Eds.). (1987). *The invulnerable child.* New York, NY: Guilford Press.

Arce, C. A. (1981). A reconsideration of Chicano culture and identity. *Daedalus, 110,* 177–192.

Armstrong, D. C. (1994). A gifted child's education requires real dialogue: The use of interactive writing for collaborative education. *Gifted Child Quarterly, 38,* 136–144.

Arroyo, C. G., & Zigler, E. (1995). Racial identity, academic achievement, and the psychological well-being of economically disadvantaged adolescents. *Journal of Personality and Social Psychology, 69,* 903–915.

Atkinson, D. R., Morten, G., & Sue, D. W. (Eds.). (1993). *Counseling American minorities: A cross-cultural perspective* (3rd ed.). Dubuque, IA: William C. Brown.

Aukett, R., Ritchie, J., & Mill, K. (1988). Gender differences in friendship patterns. *Sex Roles, 19,* 57–66.

Bagwell, C. L., Newcomb, A. F., & Bukowski, W. M. (1998). Preadolescent friendship and peer rejection as predictors of adult adjustment. *Child Development, 69,* 140–153.

Baker, J. A., Bridger, R., & Evans, K. (1998). Models of underachievement among gifted preadolescents: The role of personal, family, and school factors. *Gifted Child Quarterly, 42,* 5–15.

Bank, B. J., & Hansford, S. L. (2000). Gender and friendship: Why are men's best same-sex friendships less intimate and supportive? *Personal Relationships, 7,* 63–78.

Banks, J. A. (1979). *Teaching strategies for ethnic studies* (2nd ed.). Boston, MA: Allyn & Bacon.

Banks, J. A. (1997). *Teaching strategies for ethnic studies* (6th ed.). Boston, MA: Allyn & Bacon.

Bar-On, R. (2007). How important is it to educate people to be emotionally intelligent, and can it be done? In R. Bar-On, J. G. Maree, & M. J. Elias (Eds.), *Educating people to be emotionally intelligent* (pp. 1–14). Westport, CT: Praeger.

Bar-On, R., & Parker, J. D. (Eds.). (2000). *The handbook of emotional intelligence: Theory, development, assessment, and application at home, school, and in the workplace.* San Francisco, CA: Jossey-Bass.

Barkley, R. A. (1997). *ADHD and the nature of self-control.* New York, NY: Guilford.

Barry, C. M., & Wentzel, K. R. (2006). Friend influence on prosocial behavior: The role of motivational factors and friendship characteristics. *Developmental Psychology, 42,* 153–163.

Basco, M. R. (1999). *Never good enough: Freeing yourself from the chains of perfectionism.* New York, NY: The Free Press.

Batson, C. D., Ahmad, N., Lishner, D. A., & Tsang, J. (2002). Empathy and altruism. In C. R. Snyder & S. J. Lopez (Eds.), *Handbook of positive psychology* (pp. 485–498). New York, NY: Oxford University Press.

Baum, S. M. (1984). Meeting the needs of learning disabled gifted students. *Roeper Review, 7,* 16–19.

Baum, S. M., Cooper, C. R., & Neu, T. W. (2001). Dual differentiation: An approach for meeting the curricular needs of gifted students with learning disabilities. *Psychology in the Schools, 38,* 477–490.

Baum, S. M., Olenchak, F. R., & Owen, S. V. (1998). Gifted students with attention deficits: Fact or fiction? Or, can we see the forest from the trees? *Gifted Child Quarterly, 42,* 96–104.

Baum, S. M., & Owen, S. V. (2004). *To be gifted and learning disabled: Strategies for helping bright students with learning and attention difficulties.* Mansfield Center, CT: Creative Learning Press.

Baum, S. M., Renzulli, J. S., & Hébert, T. P. (1994). Reversing underachievement: Stories of success. *Educational Leadership, 52*(3), 48–53.

Baum, S. M., Renzulli, J. S., & Hébert, T. P. (1995). Reversing underachievement: Creative productivity as a systematic intervention. *Gifted Child Quarterly, 39,* 224–235.

Baum, S. M., Rizza, M. G., & Renzulli, S. (2005). Twice-exceptional adolescents: Who are they? What do they need? In F. A. Dixon & S. M.

Moon (Eds.), *The handbook of secondary gifted education* (pp. 137–164). Waco, TX: Prufrock Press.

Baum, S., Viens, J., Slatin, B., & Gardner, H. (2005). *Multiple intelligences in the elementary classroom.* New York, NY: Teachers College Press.

Bayless, K. (2006). Dare to dream big. *Creative Kids, 24*(3), 5.

Beard, P. (1996). *Growing up Republican: Christie Whitman: The politics of character.* New York, NY: HarperCollins.

Bego, M. (2002). *Bette Midler: Still divine.* New York, NY: Cooper Square Press.

Beiles, N. (2006, April). She's feeding her community. *Teen People Magazine, 9,* 106–125.

Berg-Cross, L., Jennings, P., & Baruch, R. (1990). Cinematherapy: Theory and application. *Psychotherapy in Private Practice, 8,* 135–156.

Betancourt, J. (1993). *My name is ~~Brain~~ Brian.* New York, NY: Scholastic.

Bleedorn, B. B. (1982). Humor as an indicator of giftedness. *Roeper Review, 4,* 33–34.

Bloom, B. S. (Ed.). (1985). *Developing talent in young people.* New York, NY: Ballantine Books.

Blum, R., & Rinehart, P. (2000). *Reducing the risk: Connections that make a difference in the lives of youth.* Minneapolis, MN: University of Minnesota. Division of General Pediatrics and Adolescent Health.

Boehm, L. (1962). The development of conscience: A comparison of American children of different mental and socioeconomic levels. *Child Development, 33,* 575–590.

Bond, R. M. (1994, November 5). School holds anti-gang rally: Eastland Elementary School students petition mayor. *Fort Worth Star Telegram,* pp. 23–24.

Bothmer, S. (2003). *Creating the peaceable classroom: Techniques to calm, uplift, and focus teachers and students.* Tucson, AZ: Zephyr Press.

Bouchard, L. L. (2004). An instrument for the measure of Dabrowskian overexcitabilities to identify gifted elementary students. *Gifted Child Quarterly, 45,* 260–267.

Brackett, M. A., & Geher, G. (2006). Measuring emotional intelligence: Paradigmatic diversity and common ground. In J. Ciarrochi, J. P. Forgas, & J. D. Mayer (Eds.), *Emotional intelligence in everyday life* (2nd ed., pp. 27–50). New York, NY: Psychology Press.

Bradshaw, T., & Fisher, D. (2001). *It's only a game.* New York, NY: Simon & Schuster.

Breard, N. S. (1994). *Exploring a different way to identify gifted African-*

American students (Unpublished doctoral dissertation). University of Georgia, Athens.

Brendgen, M., Markiewicz, D., Doyle, A. B., & Bukowski, W. M. (2001). The relations between friendship quality, ranked-friendship preference, and adolescents' behavior with their friends. *Merrill-Palmer Quarterly, 47,* 395–415.

Brody, G., Stoneman, Z., & McCoy, J. (1994). Forecasting sibling relationships in early adolescence from child temperaments and family processes in middle childhood. *Child Development, 65,* 771–784.

Brody, L. E., & Mills, C. J. (1997). Gifted children with learning disabilities: A review of the issues. *Journal of Learning Disabilities, 30,* 282–296.

Brokaw, T. (2002). *A long way from home: Growing up in the American heartland in the forties and fifties.* New York, NY: Random House.

Bronfenbrenner, U. (1979). *The ecology of human development: Experiments by nature and design.* Cambridge, MA: Harvard University Press.

Bronfenbrenner, U. (1989). Ecological systems theory. In R. Vasta (Ed.), *Annals of child development* (Vol. 6, pp. 187–249). Greenwich, CT: Jai Press.

Bronfenbrenner, U. (1993). The ecology of cognitive development: Research models and fugitive findings. In R. H. Wozniak & K. Fischer (Eds.), *Development in context: Acting and thinking in specific environments* (pp. 3–46). Hillsdale, NJ: Lawrence Erlbaum.

Bronfenbrenner, U., & Ceci, S. J. (1994). Nature-nurture reconceptualized in developmental perspective: A bioecological model. *Psychological Review, 101,* 568–586.

Brooks, L. J., Haskins, D. G., & Kehe, J. V. (2004). Counseling and psychotherapy with African American clients. In T. B. Smith (Ed.), *Practicing multiculturalism: Affirming diversity in counseling and psychology* (pp. 145–166). Boston, MA: Allyn & Bacon.

Brown, B. (1990). Peer groups. In S. Feldman & G. Elliott (Eds.), *At the threshold: The developing adolescent* (pp. 171–196). Cambridge, MA: Harvard University Press.

Brown, B. (2004). Adolescent relationships with peers. In R. Lerner & L. Steinberg (Eds.), *Handbook of adolescent psychology* (pp. 363–394). New York, NY: Wiley.

Brown, B. B., & Steinberg, L. (1990). Skirting the "brain-nerd" connection: Academic achievement and social acceptance. *Education Digest, 55,* 57–60.

Brown, K., & Greer, S. (2007, Winter). Laughing together for 15 years. *The Challenge: Magazine of the Center for Gifted Studies, 18,* 2–3.

Brown, L. M., & Gilligan, C. (1992). *Meeting at the crossroads: Women's psychology and girls' development.* Cambridge, MA: Harvard University Press.

Brown, T. E. (2000). Emerging understandings of attention-deficit disorders and comorbidities. In T. E. Brown (Ed.). *Attention-deficit disorders and comorbidities in children, adolescents, and adults* (pp. 3–55). Washington, DC: American Psychiatric Press.

Bucknavage, L. B., & Worrell, F. C. (2005). A study of academically talented students' participation in extracurricular activities. *Journal of Secondary Gifted Education, 16,* 74–86.

Buhrmester, D. (1996). Need fulfillment, interpersonal competence, and the developmental contexts of early adolescent friendship. In W. M. Bukowski, A. F. Newcomb, & W. W. Hartup (Eds.), *The company they keep: Friendship in childhood and adolescence* (pp. 158–185). New York, NY: Cambridge University Press.

Calvert, E., & Cleveland, E. (2006). Extracurricular activities. In F. A. Dixon & S. M. Moon (Eds.), *The handbook of secondary gifted education* (pp. 527–546). Waco, TX: Prufrock Press.

Camarena, P. M., Sarigiani, P. A., & Peterson, A. C. (1990). Gender-specific pathways to intimacy in early adolescence. *Journal of Youth and Adolescence, 19,* 19–32.

Canfield, J., & Wells, H. C. (1994). *100 ways to enhance self-concept in the classroom* (2nd ed.). Boston, MA: Allyn & Bacon.

Castellano, J. A. (2002). Renavigating the waters: The identification and assessment of culturally and linguistically diverse students for gifted and talented education. In J. A. Castellano & E. I. Diaz (Eds.), *Reaching new horizons: Gifted and talented education for culturally and linguistically diverse students* (pp. 94–116). Boston, MA: Allyn & Bacon.

Castellano, J. A. (2003). The "browning" of American schools: Identifying and educating gifted Hispanic students. In J. A. Castellano & A. D. Frazier (Eds.), *Special populations in gifted education: Working with diverse gifted learners* (pp. 29–43). Boston, MA: Allyn & Bacon.

Clark, B. (2002). *Growing up gifted* (6th ed.). Upper Saddle River, NJ: Merrill/Prentice Hall.

Clasen, D. R., & Clasen, R. E. (2003). Mentoring the gifted and talented. In N. Colangelo & G. A. Davis (Eds.), *Handbook of gifted education* (3rd ed., pp. 254–267). Boston, MA: Allyn & Bacon.

Clinkenbeard, P. R. (1991). Unfair expectations: A pilot study of middle school students' comparisons of gifted and regular classes. *Journal for the Education of the Gifted, 15,* 56–63.

Cobb, J. (2003). *Learning how to learn: Getting into and surviving college when you have a learning disability.* Washington, DC: Child & Family Press.

Colangelo, N. (1982). Characteristics of moral problems as formulated by gifted adolescents. *Journal of Moral Education, 11,* 219–232.

Colangelo, N. (1985). Counseling needs of culturally diverse gifted students. *Roeper Review, 8,* 33–35.

Colangelo, N. (2003). Counseling gifted students. In N. Colangelo & G. A. Davis (Eds.), *Handbook of gifted education* (pp. 373–387). Boston, MA: Allyn & Bacon.

Colangelo, N., & Assouline, S. G. (2000). Counseling gifted students. In K. A. Heller, F. J. Mönks, R. J. Sternberg, & R. F. Subotnik (Eds.), *International handbook of giftedness and talent* (2nd ed., pp. 595–607). New York, NY: Elsevier Science.

Colangelo, N., Assouline, S. G., & Gross, M. U. M. (2004). *A nation deceived: How schools hold back America's brightest students* (Vol. 1). Iowa City: The University of Iowa, The Connie Belin & Jacqueline N. Blank International Center for Gifted Education and Talent Development.

Colangelo, N., & Lafrenz, N. (1981). Counseling the culturally diverse gifted. *Gifted Child Quarterly, 25,* 27–30.

Colangelo, N., & Peterson, J. S. (1993). Group counseling with gifted students. In L. K. Silverman (Ed.), *Counseling the gifted and talented* (pp. 111–129). Denver, CO: Love.

Colangelo, N., & Zaffran, R. T. (Eds.). (1979). *New voices in counseling the gifted.* Dubuque, IA: Kendall/Hunt.

Coleman, J. M., & Fults, B. A. (1982). Self-concept and the gifted classroom: The role of social comparisons. *Gifted Child Quarterly, 26,* 116–120.

Coleman, L. J., & Cross, T. (1988). Is being gifted a social handicap? *Journal for the Education of the Gifted, 11,* 41–56.

Coleman, L. J., & Cross, T. L. (2001). *Being gifted in school: An introduction to development, guidance, and teaching.* Waco, TX: Prufrock Press.

Coleman, L. J., & Sanders, M. D. (1993). Understanding the needs of gifted students: Social needs, social choices and masking one's giftedness. *Journal of Secondary Gifted Education, 5,* 22–25.

Coles, R. (1997). *The moral intelligence of children.* New York, NY: Random House.

Conklin, A. M. (1940). *Failure of highly intelligent pupils: A study of their behavior.* New York, NY: Teachers College, Columbia University.

Connery, S., Mark, L., Tollefson, R. (Producers), & Van Sant, G. (Director).

Finding Forrester [Motion Picture] (Available from Columbia Pictures, 10202 W. Washington Boulevard, Culver City, CA 90232)

Cornell, D. G. (1984). *Families of gifted children.* Ann Arbor, MI: UMI Research Press.

Cornell, D. G., & Grossberg, I. W. (1987). Family environment and personality adjustment in gifted program children. *Gifted Child Quarterly, 31,* 59–64.

Costello, A. (2005, March). The ten greatest actors of our generation. *Gentleman's Quarterly,* 238–255, 315.

Covey, S. (1998). *The 7 habits of highly effective teens.* New York, NY: Simon & Schuster.

Cramond, B. L. (1995). *The coincidence of Attention Deficit Hyperactivity Disorder and creativity.* Storrs: University of Connecticut, The National Research Center on the Gifted and Talented.

Crosnoe, R., Cavanaugh, S., & Elder, G. H. (2003). Adolescent friendships as academic resources: The intersection of friendship, race, and school disadvantage. *Sociological Perspectives, 46,* 331–352.

Cross, W. E., Jr. (1995). The psychology of Nigrescence: Revising the Cross model. In J. G. Ponterotto, J. M. Casas, L. A. Suzuki, & C. M. Alexander (Eds.), *Handbook of multicultural counseling* (pp. 93–122). Thousand Oaks, CA: Sage.

Cross, T. L. (2004). *On the social and emotional lives of gifted children: Issues and factors in their psychological development* (2nd ed.). Waco, TX: Prufrock Press.

Cullum, A. (1971). *The geranium on the windowsill just died, but teacher you went right on.* Paris, France: Harlin Quist Books.

Dabrowski, K. (1964). *Positive disintegration.* Boston, MA: Little, Brown.

Dabrowski, K. (1972). *Psychoneurosis is not an illness.* London, England: Gryf.

Dai, D. Y., & Feldhusen, J. F. (1996). Goal orientations of gifted students. *Gifted and Talented International, 11,* 84–88.

Dana, R. H. (1998). *Understanding cultural identity in intervention and assessment.* Thousand Oaks, CA: Sage.

Daniels, P. R. (1991). Educating the learning-disabled gifted child. In R. M. Milgram (Ed.), *Counseling gifted and talented children* (pp. 207–222). Norwood, NJ: Ablex.

Davalos, R. A., & Haensly, P. A. (1997). After the dust has settled: Youth reflect on their high school mentored research experience. *Roeper Review, 19,* 204–207.

Davis, G. A. (1998). *Creativity is forever* (4th ed.). Dubuque, IA: Kendall/ Hunt.

Davis, G. A., Rimm, S. B., & Siegle, D. (2011). *Education of the gifted and talented* (6th ed.). New York, NY: Pearson.

Dawsey, D. (1996). *Living to tell about it: Young Black men in America speak their piece.* New York, NY: Doubleday.

DeHaan, R. F., & Havinghurst, R. J. (1961). *Educating gifted children* (2nd ed.). Chicago, IL: University of Chicago Press.

DeSalvo, L. (1999). *Writing as a way of healing.* San Francisco, CA: Harper.

Devito, D., Shamberg, M., Sher, S. (Producers), & Lagravense, R. (Director). (2007). *Freedom writers.* [Motion Picture]. (Available from Paramount Pictures, 5555 Melrose Avenue, Hollywood, CA 90038)

Diaz, E. I. (1998). Perceived factors influencing the academic under-achievement of talented students of Puerto Rican descent. *Gifted Child Quarterly, 42,* 105–122.

Diaz, E. I. (2002). Framing a contemporary context for the education of culturally and linguistically diverse students with gifted potential: 1990s to the present. In J. A. Castellano & E. I. Diaz (Eds.), *Reaching new horizons: Gifted and talented education for culturally and linguistically diverse students* (pp. 29–46). Boston, MA: Allyn & Bacon.

Dimeler, K. (1995). Learning to be me. *Creative Kids, 13*(5), 5.

Dixon, K. (2003). Gifted education and African American learners: An equity perspective. In J. A. Castellano (Ed.), *Special populations in gifted education: Working with diverse gifted learners* (pp. 45–63). Boston, MA: Allyn & Bacon.

Dole, S. (2001). Reconciling contradictions: Identity formation in individuals with giftedness and learning disabilities. *Journal for the Education of the Gifted, 25,* 103–137.

Dornbusch, S., Erickson, K., Laird, J., & Wong, C. (2001). The relation of family and school attachment to adolescent deviance in diverse groups and communities. *Journal of Adolescent Research, 16,* 392–422.

Doyle, A. B., & Markiewicz, D. (1996). Parents' interpersonal relationships and children's friendships. In W. M. Bukowski, A. F. Newcomb, & W. W. Hartup (Eds.), *The company they keep: Friendship in childhood and adolescence* (pp. 115–136). New York, NY: Cambridge University Press.

Eakin, E. (2002, March 30). Listening for the voices of women. *New York Times,* p. 9.

Edwards, J. (2004). *Four trials.* New York, NY: Simon & Schuster.

Edwards, O. (2009). A new frame of mind: Howard Gardner reflects on his once-radical theory. *Edutopia, 5,* 32–33.

Emerick, L. J. (1992). Academic underachievement among the gifted: Students' perceptions of factors that reverse the pattern. *Gifted Child Quarterly, 36,* 140–146.

Erikson, E. H. (1968). *Identity: Youth and crisis.* New York, NY: W.W. Norton.

Erman, J. (Producer & Director). (2002). *Ellen Foster* [Motion picture]. (Available from Hallmark Home Entertainment, 6100 Wilshire Boulevard, Ste. 1400, Los Angeles, CA 90048)

Esham, B. (2008a). *If you're so smart, how come you can't spell Mississippi?* Ocean City, MD: Mainstream Connections.

Esham, B. (2008b). *Last to finish: A story about the smartest boy in math class.* Ocean City, MD: Mainstream Connections.

Esham, B. (2008c). *Mrs. Gorski, I think I have the wiggle fidgets.* Ocean City, MD: Mainstream Connections.

Esham, B. (2008d). *Stacey Coolidge's fancy-smancy cursive handwriting.* Ocean City, MD: Mainstream Connections.

Estes, L., Rosenfelt, S. (Producers), & Eyre, C. (Director). (1998). *Smoke signals* [Motion Picture] (Available from Miramax Films, 375 Greenwich Street, New York, NY 10013)

Falk, R. F., Lind, S., Miller, N. B., Piechowski, M. M., & Silverman, L. K. (1999). *The overexcitability questionnaire—II: Manual, scoring system and questionnaire.* Unpublished manuscript.

Fehrenbach, C. R. (1993). Underachieving gifted students: Intervention programs that work. *Roeper Review, 16,* 88–90.

Feldhusen, J. F., Sayler, M. F., Nielsen, M. E., & Kolloff, P. B. (1990). Self-concepts of gifted children in enrichment programs. *Journal for the Education of the Gifted, 13,* 380–387.

Felix, A. (2002). *Condi: The Condoleezza Rice story.* New York, NY: Newmarket Press.

Ferguson, S. K. (2009). Affective education: Addressing the social and emotional needs of gifted students in the classroom. In F. A. Karnes & S. M. Bean (Eds.), *Methods and materials for teaching the gifted* (3rd ed., pp. 447–482). Waco, TX: Prufrock Press.

Fern, T. L. (1991). Identifying the gifted child humorist. *Roeper Review, 14,* 30–34.

Field, T., Harding. J., Yando, R., Gonzalez, K., Lasko, D., Bendell, D., & Marks, C. (1998). Feelings and attitudes of gifted students. *Adolescence, 33,* 331–342.

Flack, J. (1993). Autobiography as a pathway to creativity. *Connections, 2*(3), 1–2, 9.

Flack, J. (2003). Twenty-five teaching strategies that promote learning success for underserved gifted populations. In J. F. Smutny (Ed.), *Underserved gifted populations: Responding to their needs and abilities* (pp. 7–26). Cresskill, NJ: Hampton Press.

Fogarty, R. (1998, May). The intelligence-friendly classroom: It just makes sense. *Phi Delta Kappan,* 655–657.

Foley, K., & Skenandore, O. (2003). Gifted education for the Native American student. In J. A. Castellano & A. D. Frazier (Eds.), *Special populations in gifted education: Working with diverse gifted learners* (pp. 113–122). Boston, MA: Allyn & Bacon.

Fonzi, A., Schneider, B. H., Tani, F., & Tomada, G. (1997). Predicting children's friendship status from their dyadic interaction in structured situations of potential conflict. *Child Development, 68,* 496–506.

Forbes, B., Rizzotti, P., Oboven, M., Rosenfelt, A., Hall, P. (Producers), & Gonera, S. (Director). (2007). *Pride* [Motion Picture]. (Available from Lionsgate Entertainment, 2700 Colorado Avenue, Santa Monica, CA 90404)

Ford, D. Y. (1995). *Counseling gifted African American students: Promoting achievement, identity, and social and emotional well-being* (RBDM 9506). Storrs: University of Connecticut, The National Research Center on the Gifted and Talented.

Ford, D. Y. (1996). *Reversing underachievement among gifted Black students: Promising practices and programs.* New York, NY: Teachers College Press.

Ford, D. Y., & Harris, J. J., III (1999). *Multicultural gifted education.* New York, NY: Teachers College Press.

Fordham, S. (1988). Racelessness as a strategy in Black students' school success: Pragmatic strategy or pyrrhic victory? *Harvard Educational Review, 58,* 54–84.

Fordham, S., & Ogbu, J. U. (1986). Black students' school success: Coping with the "burden of 'acting White.'" *The Urban Review, 18,* 176–206.

Fox, L. H., Brody, L., & Tobin, D. (Eds.). (1983). *Learning-disabled gifted children: Identification and programming.* Baltimore, MD: University Park Press.

Fox, M. (1985). *Wilfrid Gordon McDonald Partridge.* Brooklyn, NY: Kane Miller.

Frank, M. (1979). *If you're trying to teach kids how to write, you've gotta have this book.* Nashville, TN: Incentive Publications.

Frasier, M. M. (1979). Counseling the culturally diverse gifted. In N. Colangelo & R. T. Zaffran (Eds.), *New voices in counseling the gifted* (pp. 304–311). Dubuque, IA: Kendall/Hunt.

Frasier, M. M. (1989). Identification of gifted Black students: Developing new perspectives. In C. J. Maker & S. S. Schiever (Eds.), *Critical issues in gifted education: Defensible programs for cultural and ethnic minorities* (pp. 213–225). Austin, TX: Pro-Ed.

Frasier, M. M., & Passow, A. H. (1994). *Toward a new paradigm for identifying talent potential* (Research Monograph No. 94112). Storrs: University of Connecticut, The National Research Center on the Gifted and Talented.

Friedman, D. (2006, November). The unbearable awkwardness of being. *Gentleman's Quarterly,* 315–319, 334–336.

Fries-Britt, S. (1997). Identifying and supporting gifted African American men. In M. J. Cuyjet (Ed.), *Helping African American men succeed in college* (pp. 65–78). San Francisco, CA: Jossey-Bass.

Frost, R. P., Marten, P., Lahart, C., & Rosenblate, R. (1990). The dimensions of perfectionism. *Cognitive Therapy and Research, 14,* 449–468.

Gains, N. H., Gains, S., Fishburne, L., Romersa, M., Llewelyn, D. (Producers), & Atchison, D. (Director). (2006). *Akeelah and the bee* [Motion Picture]. (Available from Lionsgate Entertainment, 2700 Colorado Avenue, Santa Monica, CA 90404)

Gallagher, J. J. (1958). Peer acceptance of highly gifted children in elementary school. *Elementary School Journal, 58,* 465–470.

Gallagher, S. (1985). A comparison of the concept of overexcitabilities with measures of creativity and school achievement in sixth-grade students. *Roeper Review, 8,* 115–119.

Gallen, D. (1994). *Bill Clinton as they know him: An oral biography.* New York, NY: Gallen.

Gándara, P. (2005). *Fragile futures: Risk and vulnerability among Latino high achievers.* Princeton, NJ: Policy Information Center, Educational Testing Service.

Gardner, H. (1983). *Frames of mind: The theory of multiple intelligences.* New York, NY: Basic Books.

Gardner, H. (1999). *Intelligence reframed: Multiple intelligences for the 21st century.* New York, NY: Basic Books.

Gardner, H., & Checkley, K. (1997). The first seven . . . and the eighth: A conversation with Howard Gardner. *Educational Leadership, 55*(1), 8–13.

Gardner, H., & Walters, J. (1993). A rounded version. In H. Gardner (Ed.),

Multiple intelligences: The theory in practice (pp. 13–34). New York, NY: Basic Books.

Garmezy, N. (1985). Stress resistant children: The search for protective factors. In J. E. Stevenson (Ed.), *Recent research in developmental psychopathology* (pp. 213–233). Oxford, England: Pergamon.

Garnefski, N. (2000). Age differences in depressive symptoms, antisocial behavior, and negative perceptions of family, school, and peers among adolescents. *Journal of the American Academy of Child and Adolescent Psychiatry, 39*, 1175–1181.

Gavin, L. N., & Furman, W. (1996). Adolescent girls' relationships with mothers and best friends. *Child Development, 67*, 375–386.

Gay, G. (2000). *Culturally responsive teaching: Theory, research, and practice.* New York, NY: Teachers College Press.

Gilligan, C. (1982). *In a different voice.* Cambridge, MA: Harvard University Press.

Gilligan, C. (1993). *In a different voice* (2nd ed.). Cambridge, MA: Harvard University Press.

Gisselbrecht, L. (1985). Recipe for the perfect friendship. In Talented and Gifted Program (Ed.)., *Treasures unlimited* (p. 22). Torrington, CT: Talented and Gifted Program.

Gladwell, M. (2000). *The tipping point: How little things can make a big difference.* New York, NY: Little Brown.

Goff, K., & Torrance, E. P. (1999). Discovering and developing giftedness through mentoring. *Gifted Child Today, 22*(3), 14–15, 52–53.

Gohm, C. L., Humphreys, L. G., & Yao, G. (1998). Underachievement among spatially gifted students. *American Educational Research Journal, 35*, 515–531.

Goldberg, M. D., & Cornell, D. G. (1998). The influence of intrinsic motivation and self-concept on academic achievement in second- and third-grade students. *Journal for the Education of the Gifted, 21*, 179–205.

Goleman, D. (1995). *Emotional intelligence.* New York, NY: Bantam Books.

Golombok, S., & Fivush, R. (1994). *Gender development.* New York, NY: Cambridge University Press.

Gonzalez, J., & Hayes, A. (1988). Psychosocial aspects of the development of gifted underachievers: Review and implications. *Exceptional Child, 35*(1), 39–51.

Gopaul-McNicol, S., & Thomas-Presswood, T. (1998). *Working with linguistically and culturally different children.* Boston, MA: Allyn & Bacon.

Gowan, J. C. (1955). The underachieving gifted child—A problem for everyone. *Exceptional Children, 21*, 247–249, 270–271.

Granada, A. J. (2002). Addressing the curriculum, instruction, and assessment needs of the gifted bilingual/bicultural student. In J. A. Castellano & E. I. Diaz (Eds.), *Reaching new horizons: Gifted and talented education for culturally and linguistically diverse students* (pp. 133–153). Boston, MA: Allyn & Bacon.

GreatSchools Staff. (n.d.). *Famous people with LD and AD/HD.* Retrieved from http://www.greatschools.org/special-education/health/famous-people-dyslexia-ld-or-ad-hd.gs?content=696

Greeno, C. G., & Macoby, E. E. (1986). How different is the "different voice"? *Signs: Journal of Women in Culture and Society, 11,* 310–316.

Greenspon, T. S. (2002). *Freeing our families from perfectionism.* Minneapolis, MN: Free Spirit.

Gross, M. U. M. (1992). The use of radical acceleration in cases of extreme intellectual precocity. *Gifted Child Quarterly, 36,* 91–99.

Gross, M. U. M. (1993). *Exceptionally gifted children.* London, England: Routledge.

Gross, M. U. M. (2000). Issues in the cognitive development of exceptionally and profoundly gifted individuals. In K. A. Heller, F. J. Mönks, & A. H. Passow (Eds.), *International handbook of research and development of giftedness and talent* (pp. 473–490). New York, NY: Pergamon.

Gross, M. U. M. (2002a). Musings: Gifted children and the gift of friendship. *Understanding Our Gifted, 14*(3), 27–29.

Gross, M. U. M. (2002b). Social and emotional issues for exceptionally intellectually gifted students. In M. Neihart, S. M. Reis, N. M. Robinson, & S. M. Moon (Eds.), *The social and emotional development of gifted children: What do we know?* (pp. 19–29). Waco, TX: Prufrock Press.

Gross, M. U. M. (2004). *Exceptionally gifted children* (2nd ed.). New York, NY: RoutledgeFalmer.

Gross, M. U. M., & van Vliet, H. E. (2005). Radical acceleration and early entrance to college: A review of the research. *Gifted Child Quarterly, 49,* 154–171.

Gurian, M. (1996). *The wonder of boys.* New York, NY: Putnam Books.

Guyer, B. P. (2000). Is there a place in college for the student with learning disabilities? In K. Kay (Ed.), *Uniquely gifted: Identifying and meeting the needs of the twice-exceptional student* (pp. 104–112). Gilsum, NH: Avocus.

Halpern, R. (1992). The role of after-school programs in the lives of inner-city children: A study of the "urban youth network." *Child Welfare, 71,* 215–230.

Halsted, J. W. (2009). *Some of my best friends are books: Guiding gifted readers from preschool to high school* (3rd ed.). Scottsdale, AZ: Great Potential Press.

Hamachek, D. E. (1978). Psychodynamics of normal and neurotic perfectionism. *Psychology, 15,* 27–33.

Hart, D., Atkins, R., & Donnelly, T. M. (2006). Community service and moral development. In M. Killen & J. G. Smetana (Eds.), *Handbook of moral development* (pp. 633–656). Mahwah, NJ: Lawrence Erlbaum.

Hart, D., Matsuba, M. K., & Atkins, R. (2008). The moral and civic effects of learning to serve. In L. P. Nucci & D. Narvaez (Eds.), *Handbook of moral and character education* (pp. 484–499). New York, NY: Routledge.

Hawk, T., & Mortimer, S. (2002). *Tony Hawk: Professional skateboarder.* New York, NY: Regan Books.

Hayden, T. (2004). The modern life of American Indians. *U.S. News & World Report, 137*(11), 42–50.

Heath, S. B., & McLaughlin, M. W. (1993). *Identity and inner-city youth: Beyond ethnicity and gender.* New York, NY: Teachers College Press.

Hébert, T. P. (1993). *An ethnographic description of the high school experiences of high ability males in an urban environment* (Unpublished doctoral dissertation). The University of Connecticut, Storrs.

Hébert, T. P. (1995a). Coach Brogan: South Central High School's answer to academic achievement. *Journal of Secondary Gifted Education, 7,* 310–323.

Hébert, T. P. (1995b). Using biography to counsel gifted young men. *Journal of Secondary Gifted Education, 6,* 209–219.

Hébert, T. P. (1996). Portraits of resilience: The urban life experience of gifted Latino young men. *Roeper Review, 19,* 82–90.

Hébert, T. P. (1997). Jamison's story: Talent nurtured in troubled times. *Roeper Review, 19,* 142–147.

Hébert, T. P. (1998). Gifted Black males in an urban high school: Factors that influence achievement and underachievement. *Journal for the Education of the Gifted, 21,* 385–414.

Hébert, T. P. (2000a). Defining belief in self: Intelligent young men in an urban high school. *Gifted Child Quarterly, 44,* 91–114.

Hébert, T. P. (2000b). Gifted males pursuing careers in elementary education. *Journal for the Education of the Gifted, 24,* 7–45.

Hébert, T. P. (2001). "If I had a new notebook, I know things would change": Bright underachieving young men in urban classrooms. *Gifted Child Quarterly, 45,* 174–194.

Hébert, T. P. (2002). Gifted Black males in a predominantly White university: Portraits of high achievement. *Journal for the Education of the Gifted, 26,* 25–64.

Hébert, T. P. (2006). Gifted university males in a Greek fraternity: Creating a culture of achievement. *Gifted Child Quarterly, 50,* 26–41.

Hébert, T. P. (2009). Guiding gifted teenagers to self-understanding through biography. In J. L. VanTassel-Baska, T. L. Cross, & F. R. Olenchak (Eds.), *Social-emotional curriculum with gifted and talented students* (pp. 259–287). Waco, TX: Prufrock Press.

Hébert, T. P., & Beardsley, T. M. (2001). Jermaine: A critical case study of a gifted Black child living in rural poverty. *Gifted Child Quarterly, 45,* 85–103.

Hébert, T. P., & Furner, J. M. (1997). Helping high ability students overcome math anxiety through bibliotherapy. *Journal of Secondary Gifted Education, 8,* 164–178.

Hébert, T. P., & Hammond, D. R. (2006). Guided viewing of film with gifted students: Resources for educators and counselors. *Gifted Child Today, 29*(3), 14–27.

Hébert, T. P., & Kelly, K. R. (2006). Identity and career development in gifted students. In F. A. Dixon & S. M. Moon (Eds.), *The handbook of secondary gifted education* (pp. 35–63). Waco, TX: Prufrock Press.

Hébert, T. P., & Kent, R. (2000). Nurturing social and emotional development in gifted teenagers through young adult literature. *Roeper Review, 22,* 167–171.

Hébert, T. P., Long, L. A., & Speirs Neumeister, K. L. (2001). Using biography to counsel gifted young women. *Journal of Secondary Gifted Education, 12,* 62–79.

Hébert, T. P., & McBee, M. T. (2007). The impact of an undergraduate honors program on gifted university students. *Gifted Child Quarterly, 51,* 136–151.

Hébert, T. P., & Olenchak, F. R. (2000). Mentors for gifted underachieving males: Developing potential and realizing promise. *Gifted Child Quarterly, 44,* 196–207.

Hébert, T. P., & Reis, S. M. (1999). Culturally diverse high-achieving students in an urban high school. *Urban Education, 34,* 428–457.

Hébert, T. P., & Schreiber, C. M. (2010). An examination of selective achievement in gifted males. *Journal for the Education of the Gifted, 33,* 570–605.

Hébert, T. P., & Sergent, D. (2005). Using movies to guide: Teachers and counselors collaborating to support gifted students. *Gifted Child Today, 28*(4), 14–25.

Hébert, T. P., Sorenson, M. F., & Renzulli, J. S. (1997). *The secondary inter-est-a-lyzer.* Mansfield Center, CT: Creative Learning Press.

Hébert, T. P., & Speirs Neumeister, K. L. (2000). University mentors in the elementary classroom: Supporting the intellectual, motivational, and emotional needs of high-ability students. *Journal for the Education of the Gifted, 24,* 122–148.

Hébert, T. P., & Speirs Neumeister, K. L. (2001). Guided viewing of film: A strategy for counseling gifted teenagers. *Journal of Secondary Gifted Education, 14,* 224–235.

Hébert, T. P., & Speirs Neumeister, K. L. (2002). Fostering social and emotional development of gifted children through guided viewing of film. *Roeper Review, 25,* 17–21.

Henley, D. R. (2000). Blessings in disguise: Idiomatic expression as a stim-ulus in group therapy with children. *Art Therapy, 17,* 270–275.

Herrera, J. F. (1998). *Laughing out loud, I fly: Poems in English and Spanish.* New York, NY: Joanna Cotler Books.

Hetherington, E. M., Bridges, M., & Insabella, G. M. (1998). What mat-ters? What does not? Five perspectives on the association between marital transitions and children's adjustment. *American Psychologist, 53,* 167–184.

Hewitt, P. L., & Flett, G. L. (1991). Perfectionism in the self and social contexts: Conceptualization, assessment, and association with psycho-pathology. *Journal of Personality and Social Psychology, 60,* 456–470.

Heydt, S. (2004). Dear diary: Don't be alarmed . . . I'm a boy. *Gifted Child Today, 27*(3), 16–27.

Higgins, J. (Producer), & Laneuville, E. (Director). (2005). *The Ernest Green story* [Motion Picture]. (Available from Disney Educational Productions, 1200 Thorndike Avenue, Elk Grove Village, IL 60007)

Hilderbrandt, C., & Zan, B. (2008). Constructivist approaches to moral education in early childhood. In L. P. Nucci & D. Narvaez (Eds.), *Handbook of moral and character education* (pp. 352–369). New York, NY: Routledge.

Hodges, E. V. E., Boivin, M., Vitaro, F., & Bukowski, W. M. (1999). The power of friendship: Protection against an escalating cycle of peer vic-timization. *Developmental Psychology, 35,* 94–104.

Hollingworth, L. S. (1926). *Gifted children: Their nature and nurture.* New York, NY: Macmillan.

Hollingworth, L. S. (1939). What we know about the early selection and training of leaders. *Teachers College Record, 40,* 575–592.

Hollingworth, L. S. (1942). *Children above 180 IQ Stanford Binet: Origin and development.* Yonkers-on-Hudson, NY: World Book.

Howard-Hamilton, M., & Franks, B. A. (1995). Gifted adolescents: Psychological behaviors, values, and developmental implications. *Roeper Review, 17,* 186–191.

Howard-Hamilton, M. F. (1994). An assessment of moral development in gifted adolescents. *Roeper Review, 17,* 57–59.

Hynes, A. M., & Hynes-Berry, M. (1986). *Bibliotherapy: The interactive process.* Boulder, CO: Westview.

Jackson, C. (2001). Look in the mirror and see what I see. In P. Rodis, A. Garrod, & M. L. Boscardin (Eds.), *Learning disabilities and life stories* (pp. 39–50). Boston, MA: Allyn & Bacon.

Janos, P. M. (1983). *The psychological vulnerabilities of children of very superior intellectual ability* (Unpublished doctoral dissertation). The Ohio State University, Columbus.

Janos, P. M., Marwood, K. A., & Robinson, N. M. (1985). Friendship patterns in highly intelligent children. *Roeper Review, 8,* 46–49.

Janos, P. M., Robinson, N. M., & Lunnenborg, C. E. (1989). Markedly early entrance to college: A multi-year comparative study of academic performance and psychological adjustment. *Journal of Higher Education, 60,* 496–518.

Janus, S. S. (1975). The great comedians: Personality and other factors. *The American Journal of Psychoanalysis, 35,* 169–174.

Jenkins-Friedman, R. (1992). Families of gifted children and youth. In M. J. Fine & C. Carlson (Eds.), *The handbook of family school interventions: A systems perspective* (pp. 175–187). Boston, MA: Allyn & Bacon.

Johns, B. (1997, Fall). Making school a place to call home. *Reaching Today's Youth,* 34–36.

Johnson, H. D. (2004). Gender, grade, and relationship differences in emotional closeness within adolescent friendships. *Adolescence, 39,* 243–255.

Jones, D. J., Bibbins, V. E., & Henderson, R. D. (1993). Reaffirming young African American males: Mentoring and community involvement by fraternities and other groups. *The Urban League Review, 16*(2), 9–19.

Jones, S. R. (1997). Voices of identity and difference: A qualitative exploration of the multiple dimensions of identity development in women college students. *Journal of College Student Development, 38,* 376–385.

Jones, S. R., & McEwen, M. K. (2000). A conceptual model of multiple dimensions of identity. *Journal of College Student Development, 41,* 405–413.

Josselson, R. (1987). *Finding herself: Pathways to identity development in women.* San Francisco, CA: Jossey-Bass.

Josselson, R. (1996). *Revising herself.* New York, NY: Oxford University Press.

Jweid, R., & Rizzo, M. (2004). *Building character through multicultural literature: A guide for middle school readers.* Lanham, MD: Scarecrow Press.

Kampwirth, T. J. (2006). *Collaborative consultation in the schools: Effective practices for students with learning and behavior problems* (3rd ed.). Upper Saddle River, NJ: Pearson Education.

Kanevsky, L., & Keighley, T. (2003). To produce or not to produce? Understanding boredom and the honor in underachievement. *Roeper Review, 26,* 20–28.

Karnes, F. A., & McGinnis, J. C. (1996). Self-actualization and locus of control with academically talented adolescents. *Journal of Secondary Gifted Education, 7,* 369–372.

Karnes, F. A., & D'Illio, V. R. (1990). Self-actualization of gifted youth as measured on the Reflections of Self by Youth. *Psychological Reports, 67,* 465–466.

Kauffman, J. (2001). *Characteristics of emotional and behavioral disorders of childhood and youth* (7th ed.). Upper Saddle River, NJ: Merrill/Prentice Hall.

Kaufman, F., Kalbfleisch, M. L., & Castellanos, F. X. (2000). *Attention deficit disorders and gifted students: What do we really know?* Storrs: University of Connecticut, The National Research Center on the Gifted and Talented.

Kennedy, D. M. (1995). Plain talk about creating a gifted-friendly classroom. *Roeper Review, 17,* 232–234.

Kerns, K. A., Klepec, L., & Cole, A. (1996). Peer relationships and pre-adolescents' perceptions of security in the child-mother relationship. *Developmental Psychology, 32,* 457–466.

Kerr, B. A. (1991). *A handbook for counseling the gifted and talented.* Alexandria, VA: American Counseling Association.

Kessler, G. R., Ibrahim, F. A., & Kahn, H. (1986). Character development in adolescents. *Adolescence, 21,* 1–9.

Keyes, R. (1976). *Is there life after high school?* New York, NY: Warner Books.

Kim, J. (1981). *Process of Asian-American identity development: A study of Japanese American women's perceptions of their struggle to achieve positive identities* (Unpublished doctoral dissertation). University of Massachusetts, Amherst.

Kindlon, D., & Thompson, M. (1999). *Raising Cain: Protecting the emotional life of boys.* New York, NY: Ballantine.

Kinney, D. (1993). From nerds to normals: The recovery of identity among adolescents from middle school to high school. *Sociology of Education, 66,* 21–40.

Kitano, M. K. (1990). Intellectual abilities and psychological intensities in young children: Implications for the gifted. *Roeper Review, 13,* 5–10.

Kitano, M. K., & Espinosa, R. (1995). Language diversity and giftedness: Working with gifted English language learners. *Journal for the Education of the Gifted, 18,* 234–254.

Kluger, J. (2006). The new science of siblings. *TIME, 168*(2), 47–55.

Knab, J., Cashman, J., & Sullivan, M. (2000). Choosing options for success: A student's guide to admissions, support, and counseling. In J. M. Taymans, L. L. West, & M. Sullivan (Eds.), *Unlocking potential: College and other choices for people with LD and AD/HD* (pp. 153–197). Bethesda, MD: Woodbine House.

Knelman, M. (2000). *Jim Carrey: The joker is wild.* Buffalo, NY: Firefly Books.

Kolloff, P. B., & Moore, A. D. (1989). Effects of summer programs on self-concepts of gifted children. *Journal for the Education of the Gifted, 12,* 268–276.

Kuttler, A. F., La Greca, A. M., & Prinstein, M. J. (1999). Friendship qualities and social-emotional functioning of adolescents with close, cross-sex friendships. *Journal of Research on Adolescence, 9,* 339–366.

Labonte, R. (1999). Social capital and community development: Practitioner emptor. *Australian New Zealand Journal of Public Health, 23,* 430–433.

Ladson-Billings, G. (2002). But that's just good teaching! The case for culturally relevant pedagogy. In S. J. Denbo & L. Moore Beaulieu (Eds.), *Improving schools for African American students: A reader for educational leaders* (pp. 95–102). Springfield, IL: Charles C. Thomas.

Ladson-Billings, G. (2006). "Yes, but how do we do it?": Practicing culturally relevant pedagogy. In J. Landsman & C. W. Lewis (Eds.), *White teachers/diverse classrooms* (pp. 29–42). Sterling, VA: Stylus.

Lael, S. (1995). To have a friend. *Creative Kids, 14*(2), 26.

Laffoon, K. S., Jenkins-Friedman, R., & Tollefson, N. (1989). Causal attributions of underachieving gifted, achieving gifted, and nongifted students. *Journal for the Education of the Gifted, 13,* 4–21.

Langerman, D. (1990, March). Books and boys: Gender preferences and book selection. *School Library Journal,* 132–136.

Larke, J., Elbert, C., Webb-Johnson, G., Larke, A. W., & Brisco, M.

(2006). Culturally meaningful classrooms: The five Cs of best practice. In V. O. Pang (Ed.), *Race, ethnicity and education: Principles and practices of multicultural education* (Vol. 1, pp. 161–179). Westport, CT: Praeger.

Lauren, J., & Verdick, E. (Eds.). (2004). *Succeeding with LD: 20 true stories about real people with LD*. Bloomington, IN: AuthorHouse.

Lee, A. R. (2003). *Multicultural American literature: Comparative Black, Native, Latino/a and Asian fictions.* Jackson: University Press of Mississippi.

Lenkowsky, R. S. (1987). Bibliotherapy: A review and analysis of the literature. *The Journal of Special Education, 21,* 123–132.

Leno, J., & Zehme, B. (1996). *Leading with my chin.* New York, NY: HarperCollins.

Leppien, J. H., & Bobbitt, C. (2006). Using biography and autobiography to understand challenge, choice and chance: A unit for high school students incorporating all four parallels. In C. A. Tomlinson, S. N. Kaplan, J. H. Purcell, J. H. Leppien, D. E. Burns, & C. A. Strickland (Eds.), *The parallel curriculum in the classroom: Units for application across the content areas, K–12* (pp. 293–362). Thousand Oaks, CA: Corwin Press.

Levin-Epstein, A. (2006). Two scoops of quinoa: Why a man with ice cream in his blood swapped the 31 flavors for grains and fruits. *Best Life, 111*(8), 66.

Lewis, B. A. (1992). *Kids with courage: True stories about young people making a difference.* Minneapolis, MN: Free Spirit.

Lewis, B. A. (1998). *The kid's guide to social action* (2nd ed.). Minneapolis, MN: Free Spirit.

Lewis, B. A. (1998). *What do you stand for?* Minneapolis, MN: Free Spirit.

Lewis, B. A. (2009). *The kid's guide to service projects: Over 500 service ideas for young people who want to make a difference* (2nd ed.). Minneapolis, MN: Free Spirit.

Lewis, J. D., Karnes, F. A., & Knight, H. V. (1995). A study of self-actualization and self-concept in intellectually gifted students. *Psychology in the Schools, 32,* 52–61.

Lindsey, J. D., & Frith, G. H. (1981). Bibliotherapy and the learning disabled. *Clearing House, 54,* 322–325.

Locke, D. C. (1998). *Increasing multicultural understanding: A comprehensive model.* Thousand Oaks, CA: Sage.

Lopez, S. J., & Gallagher, M. W. (2009). A case for positive psychology. In S. J. Lopez & C. R. Snyder (Eds.), *Oxford handbook of positive psychology* (2nd ed., pp. 3–6). New York, NY: Oxford University Press.

Lovecky, D. V. (1992). Exploring social and emotional aspects of gifted-ness in children. *Roeper Review, 15,* 18–25.

Lovecky, D. V. (1993). The quest for meaning: Counseling issues with gifted children and adolescents. In L. K. Silverman (Ed.), *Counseling the gifted and talented* (pp. 29–50). Denver, CO: Love.

Lovecky, D. V. (2004). *Different minds: Gifted children with AD/HD, Asperger Syndrome, and other learning deficits.* New York, NY: Jessica Kingsley.

Lundsteen, S. (1972, April). A thinking improvement program through literature. *Elementary English, 49,* 505.

Luria, Z. (1986). A methodological critique. *Signs: Journal of Women in Culture and Society, 11,* 321–324.

Luster, T., & McAdoo, H. (1996). Family and child influences on educational attainment: A secondary analysis of the High/Scope Perry preschool data. *Developmental Psychology, 32,* 26–39.

Lysy, K. Z., & Piechowski, M. M. (1983). Personal growth: An empirical study using Jungian and Dabrowskian measures. *Genetic Psychology Monographs, 108,* 267–320.

Mabry, M. (1995). *White bucks and black-eyed peas: Coming of age Black in White America.* New York, NY: Scribner.

Maccoby, E. E. (1990). Gender and relationships: A developmental account. *American Psychologist, 45,* 513–520.

Malikow, M. (Ed.). (2007). *Profiles in character: Twenty-six stories that will instruct and inspire teenagers.* New York, NY: University Press of America.

Mandel, H. P., & Marcus, S. I. (1995). *Could do better: Why children underachieve and what you can do about it.* New York, NY: John Wiley & Sons.

Mankiller, W., & Wallis, M. (1993). *Mankiller: A chief and her people.* New York, NY: St. Martin's Press.

Manning, M. L., & Baruth, L. G. (2009). *Multicultural education of children and adolescents* (5th ed.). Boston, MA: Pearson.

Marcia, J. E. (1980). Identity in adolescence. In J. Adelson (Ed.), *Handbook of adolescent psychology* (pp. 159–187). New York, NY: Wiley.

Marcia, J. E. (1993). The ego identity status approach to ego identity. In J. E. Marcia, A. S. Waterman, D. R. Matteson, S. L. Archer, & J. L. Orlofsky (Eds.), *Ego identity: A handbook for psychosocial research* (pp. 3–21). New York, NY: Springer-Verlag.

Marcia, J. E. (1994). The empirical study of ego identity. In H. A. Bosma,

T. L. G. Graafsma, H. D. Grotevant, & D. J. de Levita (Eds.), *Identity and development* (pp. 67–80). Thousand Oaks, CA: Sage.

Marshall, K. (2001). I will not succumb to obstacles. In P. Rodis, A. Garrod, & M. L. Boscardin (Eds.), *Learning disabilities and life stories* (pp. 110–121). Boston, MA: Allyn & Bacon.

Mascia, K. (2006, April). He's saving lives with music. In *Teen People Magazine, 9*(3), 106–125.

Maslow, A. H. (1954). *Motivation and personality*. New York, NY: Harper.

Masten, A. S., & Garmezy, N. (1990). Resilience and development: Contributions from the study of children who overcome adversity. *Development and Psychopathology, 2*, 425–444.

Mayer, J. D., & Salovey, P. (1997). What is emotional intelligence? In P. Salovey & D. J. Sluyter (Eds.), *Emotional development and emotional intelligence: Educational implications* (pp. 3–31). New York, NY: Basic Books.

Mayer, J. D., Salovey, P., & Caruso, D. R. (2000). Emotional intelligence as Zeitgeist, as personality, and as a mental ability. In R. Bar-On & J. D. Parker (Eds.), *The handbook of emotional intelligence: Theory, development, assessment, and application at home, school, and in the workplace* (pp. 92–117). San Francisco, CA: Jossey-Bass.

McCoach, D. B., & Siegle, D. (2003). Factors that differentiate underachieving gifted students from high-achieving gifted students. *Gifted Child Quarterly, 47*, 144–154.

McCoach, D. B., Kehle, T. J., Bray, M. A., & Siegle, D. (2004). The identification of gifted students with learning disabilities: Challenges, controversies, and promising practices. In T. M. Newmann & R. J. Sternberg (Eds.), *Students with both gifts and learning disabilities: Identification, assessment, and outcomes* (pp. 31–48). New York, NY: Kluwer Academic/Plenum Publishers.

McKay, H., & Dudley, B. (1996). *About storytelling*. Sydney, NSW, Australia: Hale & Iremonger.

McLaughlin, S. C., & Saccuzzo, D. P. (1997). Ethnic and gender differences in locus of control in children referred for gifted programs: The effect of vulnerability factors. *Journal for the Education of the Gifted, 20*, 268–283.

McMillan, J. H., & Reed, D. F. (1994). At risk students and resiliency: Factors contributing to academic success. *Clearing House, 67*, 137–140.

McNelles, L. R., & Connolly, J. A. (1999). Intimacy between adolescent friends: Age and gender differences in intimate affect and intimate behaviors. *Journal of Research on Adolescence, 9*, 143–159.

Mendaglio, S. (1993). Counseling gifted learning disabled: Individual and group counseling techniques. In L. K. Silverman (Ed.), *Counseling the gifted and talented* (pp. 131–149). Denver, CO: Love.

Mendaglio, S. (2008). Dabrowski's theory of positive disintegration: A personality theory for the 21st century. In S. Mendaglio (Ed.), *Dabrowski's theory of positive disintegration* (pp. 13–40). Scottsdale, AZ: Great Potential Press.

Mendaglio, S., & Tillier, W. (2006). Dabrowski's theory of positive disintegration and giftedness: Overexcitability research findings. *Journal for the Education of the Gifted, 30,* 68–87.

Merriam-Webster's collegiate dictionary (10th ed.). (1998). Springfield, MA: Merriam-Webster.

Montgomery, D. (2000). Inclusive education for able underachievers: Changing teaching for learning. In D. Montgomery (Ed.), *Able underachievers* (pp. 127–149). London, England: Whurr.

Moon, S. M. (2002a). Counseling needs and strategies. In M. Neihart, S. M. Reis, N. M. Robinson, & S. M. Moon (Eds.), *The social and emotional development of gifted children: What do we know?* (pp. 213–222). Waco, TX: Prufrock Press.

Moon, S. M. (2002b). Gifted children with Attention-Deficit/Hyperactivity Disorder. In M. Neihart, S. M. Reis, N. M. Robinson & S. M. Moon (Eds.), *The social and emotional development of gifted children: What do we know?* (pp. 193–201). Waco, TX: Prufrock Press.

Moon, S. M. (2009). Theories to guide affective curriculum development. In J. L. VanTassel-Baska, T. L. Cross, & F. R. Olenchak (Eds.), *Social-emotional curriculum with gifted and talented students* (pp. 11–39). Waco, TX: Prufrock Press.

Moon, S. M., & Hall, A. S. (1998). Family therapy with intellectually and creatively gifted children. *Journal of Marital and Family Therapy, 24,* 59–80.

Moon, S. M., Zentall, S., Grskovic, J., Hall, A., & Stormont-Spurgin, M. (2001). Emotional, social, and family characteristics of boys with AD/HD and giftedness: A comparative case study. *Journal for the Education of the Gifted, 24,* 207–247.

Mooney, J., & Cole, D. (2000). *Learning outside the lines.* New York, NY: Simon & Schuster.

Moore, J. L., III, Ford, D. Y., & Milner, H. R. (2005a). Recruitment is not enough: Retaining African American students in gifted education. *Gifted Child Quarterly, 49,* 51–67.

Moore, J. L., III, Ford, D. Y., & Milner, H. R. (2005b). Underachievement among gifted students of color: Implications for educators. *Theory Into Practice, 44,* 167–177.

Moran, S., Kornhaber, M., & Gardner, H. (2008). Orchestrating multiple intelligences. In L. Abbeduto & F. Symons (Eds.), *Taking sides: Clashing views in educational psychology* (5th ed., pp. 220–226). Boston, MA: McGraw-Hill.

Musca, T. (Producer), & Menéndez, R. (Director). (1988). *Stand and deliver* [Motion Picture]. (Available from Warner Brothers, 4000 Warner Boulevard, Burbank, CA 91522)

Narváez, D. (1993). High achieving students and moral judgment. *Journal for the Education of the Gifted, 16,* 268–279.

Nash, D. (2001, December). Enter the mentor. *Parenting for High Potential,* 18–21.

Nassar-McMillan, S. C. (2003). Counseling Arab Americans. In N. A. Vacc, S. B. DeVaney, & J. M. Brendel (Eds.), *Counseling multicultural and diverse populations: Strategies for practitioners* (4th ed., pp. 117–140). New York, NY: Brunner-Routledge.

Navarette, R., Jr. (1993). *A darker shade of crimson: Odyssey of a Harvard Chicano.* New York, NY: Bantam Books.

Neihart, M. (2002). Risk and resilience in gifted children: A conceptual framework. In M. Neihart, S. M. Reis, N. M. Robinson, S. M. Moon (Eds.), *The social and emotional development of gifted children: What do we know?* (pp. 113–122). Waco, TX: Prufrock Press.

Neihart, M., & Cramond, B. L. (Eds.). (2000). Perfectionism: Conceptual definitions, research, and dialogue [Special issue]. *Journal of Secondary Gifted Education, 11,* 172.

Neihart, M., Reis, S. M., Robinson, N. M., & Moon, S. M. (Eds.). (2002). *The social and emotional development of gifted children: What do we know?* Waco, TX: Prufrock Press.

Nelson, K. (1989). Dabrowski's theory of positive disintegration. *Advanced Development, 1,* 5–9.

Neu, T. (2003). When the gifts are camouflaged by disability: Identifying and developing the talent in gifted students with disabilities. In J. A. Castellano & A. D. Frazier (Eds.), *Special populations in gifted education: Working with diverse gifted learners* (pp. 151–162). Boston, MA: Allyn & Bacon.

Nevitt, H. (1997, November). *Scholar outreach groups: Everyone benefits.* Paper presented at the annual meeting of the National Association for Gifted Children, Little Rock, Arkansas.

Nieto, S., & Bode, P. (2008). *Affirming diversity: The sociopolitical context of multicultural education* (5th ed.). Boston, MA: Pearson.

Noddings, N. (1995). Teaching themes of care. *Phi Delta Kappan, 76,* 675–679.

Norton, D. E. (2004). *Multicultural children's literature: Through the eyes of many children.* Upper Saddle River, NJ: Merrill-Prentice Hall.

Novak, J. M., & Purkey, W. W. (2001). *Invitational education.* Bloomington, IN: Phi Delta Kappa Educational Foundation.

Nugent, S. A. (2000). Perfectionism: Its manifestations and classroom-based interventions. *Journal of Secondary Gifted Education, 11,* 214–221.

Nugent, S. A. (2005). *Social and emotional teaching strategies.* Waco, TX: Prufrock Press.

Oboven, M., Rosenfelt, A. (Producers), & Gonera, S. (Director). (2007). *Pride* [Motion Picture]. (Available from Lions Gate Entertainment, 2700 Colorado Avenue, Santa Monica, CA 90404)

Olenchak, F. R. (1994). Talent development: Accommodating the social and emotional needs of secondary gifted/learning disabled students. *Journal of Secondary Gifted Education, 5,* 40–52.

Olenchak, F. R. (1995). Effects of enrichment on gifted/learning disabled students. *Journal for the Education of the Gifted, 18,* 385–399.

Olenchak, F. R., & Hébert, T. P. (2002). Endangered academic talent: Lessons learned from gifted first-generation college males. *Journal of College Student Development, 43,* 195–212.

Olenchak, F. R., & Reis, S. M. (2002). Gifted students with learning disabilities. In M. Neihart, S. M. Reis, N. M. Robinson, & S. M. Moon (Eds.), *The social and emotional development of gifted children: What do we know?* (pp. 177–191). Waco, TX: Prufrock Press.

Olivier, S. (2003). *101 ways to stress-free living: How to declutter your mind, body, and soul.* New York, NY: Barnes and Noble Books.

Olszewski-Kubilius, P., & Lee, S. (2004). The role of participation in in-school and outside-of-school activities in the talent development of gifted students. *Journal of Secondary Gifted Education, 15,* 107–123.

Olszewski-Kubilius, P. M. (1989). Development of academic talent: The role of summer programs. In J. VanTassel-Baska & P. M. Olszewski-Kubilius (Eds.), *Patterns of influence on gifted learners: The home, the self, and the school* (pp. 214–230). New York, NY: Teachers College Press.

Olszewski-Kubilius, P. M. (2002a). Parenting practices that promote talent development, creativity, and optimal adjustment. In M. Neihart, S. M. Reis, N. M. Robinson, S. M. Moon (Eds.), *The social and emotional development of gifted children: What do we know?* (pp. 205–212). Waco, TX: Prufrock Press.

Olszewski-Kubilius, P. M. (2002b). A summary of research regarding early entrance to college. *Roeper Review, 24,* 152–157.

Olszewski-Kubilius, P. M. (2003). Special summer and Saturday programs for gifted students. In N. Colangelo & G. A. Davis (Eds.), *The handbook of gifted education* (3rd ed., pp. 219–228). Boston, MA: Allyn & Bacon.

Olszewski-Kubilius, P. M., & Limburg-Weber, L. (1999). Options for middle school and secondary level gifted students. *Journal of Secondary Gifted Education, 11,* 4–10.

Oswald, D. L., & Clark, E. M. (2003). Best friends forever? High school best friendships and the transition to college. *Personal Relationships, 10,* 187–196.

Paley, B., Conger, R., & Harold, G. (2000). Parents' affect, adolescent cognitive representations, and adolescent social development. *Journal of Marriage and the Family, 62,* 761–776.

Palmer, P. J. (1993). *To know as we are known: Education as a spiritual journey.* San Francisco, CA: HarperCollins.

Parker, W. D. (2000). Healthy perfectionism in the gifted. *Journal of Secondary Gifted Education, 11,* 173–182.

Parker, W. D., & Adkins, K. K. (1995). Perfectionism and the gifted. *Roeper Review, 17,* 173–175.

Parker, W. D., & Mills, C. J. (1996). The incidence of perfectionism in gifted students. *Gifted Child Quarterly, 40,* 194–199.

Parton, D. (1994). *Dolly: My life and other unfinished business.* New York, NY: HarperCollins.

Passow, A. H. (1988). Educating gifted persons who are caring and concerned. *Roeper Review, 11,* 13–15.

Passow, A. H. (1990). Leta Stetter Hollingworth: A real original. *Roeper Review, 12,* 134–136.

Patterson, A. (2003). Music teachers and music therapists: Helping children together. *Music Educators Journal, 89*(4), 35–38.

Pellegrini, A. D. (1995). A longitudinal study of boys' rough-and-tumble play and dominance during early adolescence. *Journal of Applied Developmental Psychology, 16,* 77–93.

Perdomo, W. (2002). *Visiting Langston.* New York, NY: Henry Holt and Company.

Perosa, L. M., Perosa, S. L., & Tam, H. P. (1996). The contribution of family structure and differentiation to identity development in females. *Journal of Youth & Adolescence, 25,* 817–837.

Peterson, J. S. (1996). The breakfast club: Poetry and pancakes. *Gifted Child Today, 19*(4), 16–19, 49.

Peterson, J. S. (2001). Successful adults who were once adolescent under-achievers. *Gifted Child Quarterly, 45,* 236–250.

Peterson, J. S. (2008). *The essential guide to talking with gifted teens: Ready-to-use discussions about identity, stress, relationships, and more.* Minneapolis, MN: Free Spirit.

Peterson, J. S., Betts, G., & Bradley, T. (2009). Discussion groups as a component of affective curriculum for gifted students. In J. L. VanTassel-Baska, T. L. Cross & F. R. Olenchak (Eds.), *Social-emotional curriculum with gifted and talented students* (pp. 289–320). Waco, TX: Prufrock Press.

Peterson, J. S., & Colangelo, N. (1996). Gifted achievers and underachievers: A comparison of patterns found in school files. *Journal of Counseling and Development, 74,* 399–407.

Phinney, J. S. (1996). When we talk about American ethnic groups, what do we mean? *American Psychologist, 51,* 918–927.

Phinney, J. S., Lochner, B. T., & Murphy, R. (1990). Ethnic identity development and psychological adjustment in adolescence. In A. R. Stiffman & L. E. Davis (Eds.), *Ethnic issues in adolescent mental health* (pp. 53–72). Newbury Park, CA: Sage.

Phipps, J. J. (2005). E-journaling: Achieving interactive education online. *Educause Quarterly, 28*(1), 62–65.

Piechowski, M. M. (1991). Emotional development and emotional giftedness. In N. Colangelo & G. A. Davis (Eds.), *Handbook of gifted education* (pp. 285–306). Boston, MA: Allyn & Bacon.

Piechowski, M. M. (1997). Emotional giftedness: The measure of intrapersonal intelligence. In N. Colangelo & G. A. Davis (Eds.), *Handbook of gifted education* (2nd ed., pp. 366–381). Boston, MA: Allyn & Bacon.

Piechowski, M. M. (1999). Overexcitabilities. In M. A. Runco & S. R. Pritzker (Eds.), *Encyclopedia of creativity* (Vol. 2, pp. 325–334). San Diego, CA: Academic Press.

Piechowski, M. M. (2002). Experiencing in a higher key: Dabrowski's theory of and for the gifted. *Gifted Education Communicator, 33*(1), 28–31, 35.

Piechowski, M. M. (2003). Emotional and spiritual giftedness. In N. Colangelo & G. A. Davis (Eds.), *Handbook of gifted education* (3rd ed., pp. 403–416). Boston, MA: Allyn & Bacon.

Piechowski, M. M. (2006). *"Mellow out," they say. If only I could: Intensities and sensitivities of the young and bright.* Madison, WI: Yunasa Books.

Piechowski, M. M. (2008). Discovering Dabrowski's theory. In S. Mendaglio (Ed.), *Dabrowski's theory of positive disintegration* (pp. 41–77). Scottsdale, AZ: Great Potential Press.

Piechowski, M. M., & Colangelo, N. (1984). Developmental potential of the gifted. *Gifted Child Quarterly, 28,* 80–88.

Piirto, J. (1992). *Understanding those who create.* Dayton, OH: Ohio Psychology Press.

Polacco, P. (1998). *Thank you, Mr. Falker.* New York, NY: Philomel Books.

Pollack, W. S. (1998). *Real boys: Rescuing our sons from the myths of boyhood.* New York, NY: Random House.

Pollack, W. S., & Shuster, T. (2000). *Real boys' voices.* New York, NY: Penguin Books.

Ponterotto, J. G., & Pedersen, P. B. (1993). *Preventing prejudice: A guide for counselors and educators.* Newbury Park, CA: Sage.

Porter, L. (2005). *Gifted young children: A guide for teachers and parents* (2nd ed.). New York, NY: Open University Press.

Powell, C. (1995). *My American journey.* New York, NY: Random House.

Powell, M. (2002). *Stress relief: The ultimate teen guide.* Lanham, MD: The Scarecrow Press.

Pufal-Struzik, I. (1999). Self-actualization and other personality dimensions as predictors of mental health of intellectually gifted students. *Roeper Review, 22,* 44–47.

Purcell, J. H., Renzulli, J. S., McCoach, D. B., & Spottiswoode, H. (2001, December). The magic of mentorships. *Parenting for High Potential,* 22–26.

Purkey, W. W. (1978). *Inviting school success: A self-concept approach to teaching and learning.* Belmont, CA: Wadsworth.

Purkey, W. W. (2000). *What students say to themselves: Internal dialogue and school success.* Thousand Oaks, CA: Corwin Press.

Purkey, W. W., & Novak, J. M. (2008). *Fundamentals of invitational education.* Kennesaw, GA: International Alliance for Invitational Education.

Purkey, W. W., & Schmidt, J. J. (1992). Invitational learning for counseling and development. In G. R. Walz & T. I. Ellis (Eds.), *Counseling and guidance in the schools* (pp. 45–60). Washington, DC: National Educational Association.

Purkey, W. W., & Strahan, D. B. (2002). *Inviting positive classroom discipline.* Westerville, OH: National Middle School Association.

Rand, D., Trent-Parker, T., & Foster, S. (2001). *Black books galore! Guide to more great African American children's books.* New York, NY: John Wiley & Sons.

Rasmussen, J. E. (1964). Relationship of ego identity to psychosocial effectiveness. *Psychological Reports, 15,* 815–825.

Rathvon, N. (1996). *The unmotivated child: Helping your underachiever become a successful student.* New York, NY: Simon & Schuster.

Reed, T., & Brown, M. (2000). The expression of care in the rough and tumble play of boys. *Journal of Research in Childhood Education, 15,* 104–116.

Rees, M., Hopkins, A. (Producers), & Palcy, E. (Director). (2004). *Ruby Bridges* [Motion Picture]. (Available from Walt Disney Pictures, 500 S. Buena Vista, Burbank, CA 90232)

Reese-Weber, M. (2000). Middle and late adolescents' conflict resolution skills with siblings: Associations with interparental and parent adolescent conflict resolutions. *Journal of Youth and Adolescence, 29,* 697–711.

Reis, S. M., Colbert, R. D., & Hébert, T. P. (2005). Understanding resilience in diverse, talented students in an urban high school. *Roeper Review, 27,* 110–120.

Reis, S. M., Hébert, T. P., Diaz, E. I., Maxfield, L. R., & Ratley, M. E. (1995). *Case studies of talented students who achieve and underachieve in an urban high school* [Research Monograph No. 95120]. Storrs: University of Connecticut, The National Research Center on the Gifted and Talented.

Reis, S. M., & McCoach, D. B. (2000). The underachievement of gifted students: What do we know and where do we go? *Gifted Child Quarterly, 44,* 152–170.

Reis, S. M., & McCoach, D. B. (2002). Underachievement in gifted students. In M. Neihart, S. M. Reis, N. M. Robinson, & S. M. Moon (Eds.), *The social and emotional development of gifted children: What do we know?* (pp. 81–91). Waco, TX: Prufrock Press.

Reis, S. M., Neu, T. W., & McGuire, J. M. (1995). *Talents in two places: Case studies of high ability students with learning disabilities who have achieved* (Research Monograph No. 95114). Storrs: University of Connecticut, The National Research Center on the Gifted and Talented.

Reis, S. M., & Ruban, L. M. (2004). Compensation strategies used by high-ability students with learning disabilities. In T. M. Newmann & R. J. Sternberg (Eds.), *Students with both gifts and learning disabilities: Identification, assessment, and outcomes* (pp. 155–198). New York, NY: Kluwer Academic/Plenum Publishers.

Reis, S. M., & Sullivan, E. E. (2009). Characteristics of gifted learners:

Consistently varied; Refreshingly diverse. In F. A. Karnes & S. M. Bean (Eds.), *Methods and materials for teaching the gifted* (3rd ed., pp. 3–35). Waco, TX: Prufrock Press.

Reisman, J. M. (1990). Intimacy in same-sex friendships. *Sex Roles, 23,* 65–82.

Renzulli, J. S., Smith, L., White, A., Callahan, C., Hartman, R., & Westberg, K. (2001). *Scales for rating the behavioral characteristics of superior students.* Mansfield Center, CT: Creative Learning Press.

Renzulli, J. S. (1977). *The Enrichment Triad Model: A guide for developing defensible programs for the gifted.* Mansfield Center, CT: Creative Learning Press.

Renzulli, J. S. (1997). *The interest-a-lyzer.* Mansfield Center, CT: Creative Learning Press.

Renzulli, J. S. (2003). Conception of giftedness and its relationship to the development of social capital. In N. Colangelo & G. A. Davis (Eds.), *Handbook of gifted education* (3rd ed., pp. 75–87). Boston, MA: Allyn & Bacon.

Renzulli, J. S. (2009). Operation Houndstooth: A positive perspective on developing social intelligence. In J. L. VanTassel-Baska, T. L. Cross, & F. R. Olenchak (Eds.), *Social-emotional curriculum with gifted and talented students* (pp. 79–112). Waco, TX: Prufrock Press.

Renzulli, J. S., Koehler, J. L., & Fogarty, E. A. (2006). Operation Houndstooth intervention theory: Social capital in today's schools. *Gifted Child Today, 29*(1), 15–24.

Renzulli, J. S., & Rizza, M. G. (1997). *The primary interest-a-lyzer.* Mansfield Center, CT: Creative Learning Press.

Renzulli, J. S., Sytsma, R. E., & Schader, R. M. (2003, December). Developing giftedness for a better world. *Parenting for High Potential,* 18–22.

Rest, J. (1986). *Moral development: Advances in research and theory.* New York, NY: Praeger.

Rhodes, J. E. (1994). Older and wiser: Mentoring relationships in childhood and adolescence. *The Journal of Primary Prevention, 14,* 187–196.

Rimm, S. B. (1995). *Why bright kids get poor grades and what you can do about it.* New York, NY: Three Rivers Press.

Rimm, S. B. (2003). Underachievement: A national epidemic. In N. Colangelo & G. A. Davis (Eds.), *The handbook of gifted education* (3rd ed., pp. 424–443). Boston, MA: Allyn & Bacon.

Rinn, A. N. (2008). College programming. In J. A. Plucker & C. M.

Callahan (Eds.), *Critical issues and practices in gifted education: What the research says* (pp. 97–106). Waco, TX: Prufrock Press.

Robbins, R. (1991). American Indian gifted and talented students: Their problems and proposed solutions. *Journal of American Indian Education, 31,* 15–24.

Roberts, J., & Inman, T. (2001, December). Mentoring and your child: Developing a successful relationship. *Parenting for High Potential,* 8–10.

Robinson, A., & Butler Schatz, A. (2002). Biography for talented learners: Enriching the curriculum across the disciplines. *Gifted Education Communicator, 33*(3), 12–15, 38–39.

Robinson, N. M., & Noble, K. D. (1991). Social-emotional development and adjustment of gifted children. In M. C. Wang, M. C. Reynolds, & H. J. Walberg (Eds.), *Handbook of special education: Research and practice: Emerging programs* (Vol. 4, pp. 57–76). New York, NY: Pergamon Press.

Rodis, P., Garrod, A., & Boscardin, M. L. (Eds.). (2001). *Learning disabilities and life stories.* Boston, MA: Allyn & Bacon.

Rogers, K. B. (2002). *Re-forming gifted education: Matching the program to the child.* Scottsdale, AZ: Great Potential Press.

Romey, E. A. (2000). *A study of common themes in reading selections of gifted girls: Implications for bibliotherapy* (Unpublished thesis). The University of Georgia, Athens.

Ross, T., & Barron, R. (1994). *Eggbert: The slightly cracked egg.* New York, NY: Paper Star Books.

Rotter, J. (1966). Generalized expectancies for internal versus external control of reinforcements. *Psychological Monographs, 80,* Whole No. 609.

Rowe, J. W., & Kahn, R. L. (1998). *Successful aging.* New York, NY: Pantheon.

Rowley, S. J., & Moore, J. A. (2002). Racial identity in context for the gifted African American student. *Roeper Review, 24,* 63–67.

Rusch, E. (2002). *Generation fix: Young ideas for a better world.* Hillsboro, OR: Beyond Words.

Rutter, M. (1981). Stress, coping and development: Some issues and some questions. *Journal of Child Psychology and Psychiatry and Allied Disciplines, 22,* 323–356.

Rutter, M. (1987). Psychosocial resilience and protective mechanisms. *American Journal of Orthopsychiatry, 57,* 316–331.

Ryan, P. M. (2003). *A box of friends.* Columbus, OH: McGraw-Hill Children's.

Salovey, P., & Mayer, J. D. (1990). Emotional intelligence. *Imagination, Cognition, and Personality, 9*, 185–211.

Santiago, E. (1993). *When I was Puerto Rican.* New York, NY: Random House.

Santrock, J. W. (2003). *Adolescence* (9th ed.). Boston, MA: McGraw-Hill.

Scheid, J. (2006). My type. *Creative Kids, 25*(1), 32.

Schuler, P. A. (2000). Perfectionism and the gifted adolescent. *Journal of Secondary Gifted Education, 11*, 183–196.

Schultze, R., & Roberts, R. D. (Eds.). (2006). *Emotional intelligence: An international handbook.* Cambridge, MA: Hogrefe.

Seeley, K. (1993). Gifted students at risk. In L. K. Silverman (Ed.), *Counseling the gifted and talented* (pp. 263–276). Denver, CO: Love.

Seider, S. (2009). An MI odyssey. *Edutopia, 5*(2), 26–30.

Seitz, C. (Producer), & Burnett, C. (Director). (1999). *Selma, Lord, Selma* [Motion Picture]. (Available from Buena Vista Television, 500 S. Buena Vista, Burbank, CA 91521)

Seligman, M. E. P. (1991). *Learned optimism.* New York, NY: Knopf.

Seligman, M. E. P., & Csikszentmihalyi, M. (2000). Positive psychology. *American Psychologist, 55*, 5–14.

Sewell, A., Agrelo, M. (Producers), & Agrelo, M. (Director). (2005). *Mad hot ballroom* [Motion Picture]. (Available from Paramount Classics, 5555 Melrose Avenue, Hollywood, CA 90038)

Shade, R. (1991). Verbal humor in gifted students and students in the general population: A comparison of spontaneous mirth and comprehension. *Journal for the Education of the Gifted, 14*, 134–150.

Shaffer, D. R. (2000). *Social and personality development* (4th ed.). Belmont, CA: Wadsworth/Thomson Learning.

Sheely, A. R. (1998, Fall). A circle of friends: The nature and nurturing of social relationships among gifted children. *Understanding Our Gifted,* 3–8.

Sherman, A. M., DeVries, B., & Lansford, J. E. (2000). Friendship in childhood and adulthood: Lessons across the life span. *International Journal of Aging and Human Development, 51*, 31–51.

Siegle, D., & McCoach, D. B. (2005a). Extending learning through mentorships. In F. A. Karnes & S. M. Bean (Eds.), *Methods and materials for teaching the gifted* (2nd ed., pp. 473–518). Waco, TX: Prufrock Press.

Siegle, D., & McCoach, D. B. (2005b). *Motivating gifted students.* Waco, TX: Prufrock Press.

Siegle, D., & Schuler, P. A. (2000). Perfectionism differences in gifted middle school students. *Roeper Review, 23*, 39–44.

Siegle, D., McCoach, D. B., & Wilson, H. E. (2009). Extending learning through mentorships. In F. A. Karnes & S. M. Bean (Eds.), *Methods and materials for teaching the gifted* (3rd ed., pp. 519–563). Waco, TX: Prufrock Press.

Silverman, L. K. (1989, January). Perfectionism. *Understanding Our Gifted,* 11.

Silverman, L. K. (1990). Social and emotional development of the gifted: The discoveries of Leta Hollingworth. *Roeper Review, 12,* 171–177.

Silverman, L. K. (1992, September/October). Social development or socialization? *Understanding Our Gifted,* 15.

Silverman, L. K. (1993a). A developmental model for counseling the gifted. In L. K. Silverman (Ed.), *Counseling the gifted and talented* (pp. 51–78). Denver, CO: Love.

Silverman, L. K. (1993b). The gifted individual. In L. K. Silverman (Ed.), *Counseling the gifted and talented* (pp. 3–28). Denver, CO: Love.

Silverman, L. K. (2003). Gifted children with learning disabilities. In N. Colangelo & G. A. Davis (Eds.), *Handbook of gifted education* (3rd ed., pp. 533–543). Boston, MA: Allyn & Bacon.

Silverman, L. K., & Kearney, K. (1989). Parents of the extraordinarily gifted. *Advanced Development, 1,* 41–56.

Smith, C. (1986). Nurturing kindness through storytelling. *Young Children, 41,* 46–51.

Smith, R. L., & Emigh, L. (2005). A model for defining the construct of caring in teacher education. In R. L. Smith, D. Skarbek, & J. Hurst (Eds.), *The passion of teaching: Dispositions in the schools* (pp. 27–39). Lanham, MD: Scarecrow Education.

Smith, T., Polloway, E., Patton, J., & Dowdy, C. (2004). *Teaching students with special needs in inclusive settings.* Boston, MA: Allyn & Bacon.

Spada, J. (1984). *The divine Bette Midler.* New York, NY: Collier Books.

Speirs Neumeister, K. L. (2002). Shaping an identity: Factors influencing the achievement of newly married, gifted young women. *Gifted Child Quarterly, 46,* 291–305.

Speirs Neumeister, K. L. (2004a). Interpreting successes and failures: The influence of perfectionism on perspective. *Journal for the Education of the Gifted, 27,* 311–335.

Speirs Neumeister, K. L. (2004b). Understanding the relationship between perfectionism and achievement motivation in gifted college students. *Gifted Child Quarterly, 48,* 219–231.

Speirs Neumeister, K. L. (2004c). Factors influencing the development of perfectionism in gifted college students. *Gifted Child Quarterly, 48,* 259–274.

Speirs Neumeister, K. L., & Hébert, T. P. (2003). Underachievement versus selective achievement: Delving deeper and discovering the difference. *Journal for the Education of the Gifted, 26,* 221–238.

Staton, J. (1988). An introduction to dialogue journal communication. In J. Staton, R. W. Shuy, J. K. Peyton, & L. Reed (Eds.), *Dialogue journal communication: Classroom, linguistic, social, and cognitive views* (pp. 1–32). Norwood, NJ: Ablex.

Steinberg, L. (2005). *Adolescence* (7th ed.). Boston, MA: McGraw Hill.

Steinberg, L., Dornbusch, S. M., & Brown, B. B. (1992). Ethnic differences in adolescent achievement: An ecological perspective. *American Psychologist, 47,* 723–729.

Stephenson, G. L. (Producer), & Hines, G. (Director). (2002). *The red sneakers* [Motion Picture]. (Available from Showtime Networks, 1633 Broadway, New York, NY 10019)

Sternberg, R. J. (1985). *Beyond IQ: A triarchic theory of human intelligence.* Cambridge, England: Cambridge University Press.

Sternberg, R. J. (1990). Preface. In R. J. Sternberg (Ed.), *Wisdom: Its nature, origins, and development* (pp. ix–x). New York, NY: Cambridge University Press.

Sternberg, R. J. (1998). A balance theory of wisdom. *Review of General Psychology, 2,* 347–365.

Sternberg, R. J. (2000). Wisdom as a form of giftedness. *Gifted Child Quarterly, 44,* 252–260.

Sternberg, R. J. (2003). *Wisdom, intelligence, and creativity synthesized.* New York, NY: Cambridge University Press.

Sternberg, R. J., & Grigorenko, E. L. (2004). Learning disabilities, giftedness, and gifted/LD. In T. M. Newmann & R. J. Sternberg (Eds.), *Students with both gifts and learning disabilities: Identification, assessment, and outcomes* (pp. 31–48). New York, NY: Kluwer Academic/Plenum Publishers.

Sternberg, R. J., Jarvin, L., & Grigorenko, E. L. (2009). *Teaching for wisdom, intelligence, creativity, and success.* Thousand Oaks, CA: Sage.

Sternberg, R. J., Wagner, R. K., Williams, W. M., & Horvath, J. A. (1995). Testing and common sense. *American Psychologist, 50,* 912–927.

Stewart, S., Evans, W., & Kaczynski, D. (1997). Setting the stage for success: Assessing the instructional environment. *Preventing School Failure, 41*(2), 53–56.

Stieg, B. (2006, June). Take it from me: An interview with Al Gore. *Men's Health,* 96–97.

Strickland, C. A. (2006). With liberty and justice for all: A U.S. government unit based on the core and identity parallels for middle or high school students. In C. A. Tomlinson, S. N. Kaplan, J. H. Purcell, J. H. Leppien, D. E. Burns, & C. A. Strickland (Eds.), *The parallel curriculum in the classroom, book 2: Units for application across the content areas, K–12* (pp. 249–292). Thousand Oaks, CA: Corwin Press.

Subotnik, R. (2003). Through another's eyes: The Pinnacle Project. *Gifted Child Today, 26*(2), 14–17.

Subotnik, R. F., & Olszewski-Kubilius, P. (1997). Restructuring special programs to reflect the distinctions between children's and adults' experiences with giftedness. *Peabody Journal of Education, 72,* 101–116.

Sue, D. W., & Sue, D. (2003). *Counseling the culturally diverse: Theory and practice* (4th ed.). New York, NY: John Wiley & Sons.

Sundem, G. (2010). *Real kids, real stories, real change: Courageous actions around the world.* Minneapolis, MN: Free Spirit.

Tannen, D. (1990). Gender differences in topical coherence: Creating involvement in best friends' talk. *Discourse Processes, 13,* 73–90.

Tannock, R., & Brown, T. E. (2000). Attention-deficit disorders with learning disorders in children and adolescents. In T. E. Brown (Ed.), *Attention-deficit disorders and comorbidities in children, adolescents, and adults* (pp. 231–295). Washington, DC: American Psychiatric Press.

Taradash, A., Connolly, J., Pepler, D., Craig, W., & Costa, M. (2001). The interpersonal context of romantic autonomy in adolescence. *Journal of Adolescence, 24,* 365–377.

Tavris, C. (1992). *The mismeasure of women.* New York, NY: Simon & Schuster.

Terman, L. M. (1925). *Mental and physical traits of a thousand gifted children: Vol. 1: Genetic studies of genius.* Stanford, CA: Stanford University Press.

Thomas, J. C. (1993). *Brown honey in broomwheat tea.* New York, NY: HarperCollins.

Thomas, J. J., & Daubman, K. A. (2001). The relationship between friendship quality and self-esteem in adolescent girls and boys. *Sex Roles, 45,* 53–65.

Tieso, C. L. (2007). Patterns of overexcitabilities in identified gifted students and their parents. *Gifted Child Quarterly, 51,* 11–22.

Tomlinson, C. A. (1999). *The differentiated classroom: Responding to the needs of all students.* Alexandria, VA: Association for Supervision and Curriculum Development.

Tomlinson, C. A. (2001, December). President's column. *Parenting for High Potential,* 27.

Tomlinson, C. A., Brimijoin, K., & Narvaez, L. (2008). *The differentiated school: Making revolutionary changes in teaching and learning.* Alexandria, VA: Association for Supervision and Curriculum Development.

Tomlinson, C. A., Callahan, C. M., & Lelli, K. M. (1997). Challenging expectations: Case studies of culturally diverse young children. *Gifted Child Quarterly, 41,* 5–17.

Tomlinson, C. A., Kaplan, S. N., Purcell, J. H., Leppien, J. H., Burns, D. E., & Strickland, C. A. (Eds.). (2006). *The parallel curriculum in the classroom: Units for application across the content areas, K–12.* Thousand Oaks, CA: Corwin Press.

Tomlinson, C. A., Kaplan, S. N., Renzulli, J. S., Purcell, J. H., Leppien, J. H., Burns, D. E., . . . Imbeau, M. B. (2008). *The parallel curriculum: A design to develop learner potential and challenge advanced learners* (2nd ed.). Thousand Oaks, CA: Corwin Press.

Torrance, E. P. (1969). Creative positives of disadvantaged children and youth. *Gifted Child Quarterly, 13,* 71–81.

Torrance, E. P. (1980). Growing up creatively gifted: A 22-year longitudinal study. *Creative Child and Adult Quarterly, 5,* 148–158, 170.

Torrance, E. P. (1984). *Mentor relationships: How they aid creative achievement, endure, change, and die.* Buffalo, NY: Bearly Limited.

Torrance, E. P., Goff, K., & Satterfield, N. B. (1998). *Multicultural mentoring of the gifted and talented.* Waco, TX: Prufrock Press.

Troxclair, D. (1999, December). Recognizing perfectionism in gifted children. *Parenting for High Potential,* 18–21.

Tucker, B., & Hafenstein, N. L. (1997). Psychological intensities in young gifted children. *Gifted Child Quarterly, 41,* 66–75.

Updergraff, K., McHale, S., & Crouter, A. (2000). Adolescents' sex-typed friendship experiences: Does having a sister versus brother matter? *Child Development, 71,* 1597–1610.

van Aken, M. A. G., & Asendorpf, J. B. (1997). Support by parents, classmates, friends, and siblings in preadolescence: Covariation and compensation across relationships. *Journal of Social and Personal Relationships, 14,* 79–93.

VanTassel-Baska, J. (1991). Teachers as counselors for gifted students. In R. M. Milgram (Ed.), *Counseling gifted and talented children: A guide for teachers, counselors and parents* (pp. 37–52). Norwood, NJ: Ablex.

VanTassel-Baska, J. (1998). Characteristics and needs of talented learners.

In J. VanTassel-Baska (Ed.), *Excellence in educating gifted and talented learners* (3rd ed., pp. 173–191). Denver: Love.

VanTassel-Baska, J. (2006). Secondary affective curriculum and instruction for gifted learners. In F. A. Dixon & S. M. Moon (Eds.), *The handbook of secondary gifted education* (pp. 481–503). Waco, TX: Prufrock Press.

Vare, J. V. (1979). Moral education for the gifted: A confluent model. *Gifted Child Quarterly, 23,* 487–499.

Waldrup, L. (2006). Black. *Creative Kids, 24*(3), 19.

Way, N., & Chen, L. (2000). Close and general friendships among African American, Latino, and Asian American adolescents from low income families. *Journal of Adolescent Research, 15,* 274–301.

Webb, J. T., Amend, E. R., Webb, N. E., Goerss, J., Beljan, P., & Olenchak, F. R. (2005). *Misdiagnosis and dual diagnoses of gifted children and adults: ADHD, bipolar, OCD, Asperger's, depression, and other disorders.* Scottsdale, AZ: Great Potential Press.

Webb, J. T., Meckstroth, E. A., & Tolan, S. S. (1982). *Guiding the gifted child.* Columbus, OH: Ohio Psychology.

Werner, E. E., & Smith, R. S. (1982). *Vulnerable but invincible: A study of resilient children.* New York, NY: McGraw–Hill.

Whiting, G. (2009). Gifted Black males: Understanding and decreasing barriers to achievement and identity. *Roeper Review, 31,* 224–233.

Whitmore, J. R. (1980). *Giftedness, conflict, and underachievement.* Boston, MA: Allyn & Bacon.

Whitmore, J. R. (1986). Understanding a lack of motivation to excel. *Gifted Child* Quarterly, *30,* 66–69.

Winkler, H., & Oliver, L. (2003a). *I got a "D" in salami.* New York, NY: Grosset & Dunlap.

Winkler, H., & Oliver, L. (2003b). *Niagara Falls, or does it?* New York, NY: Grosset & Dunlap.

Wolfle, J. A. (1991). Underachieving gifted males: Are we missing the boat? *Roeper Review, 13,* 181–184.

Yong, F. L. (1994). Self-concepts, locus of control, and Machiavellianism of ethically diverse middle school students who are gifted. *Roeper Review, 16,* 192–194.

Zentall, S. S., Moon, S. M., Hall, A. M., & Grskovic, J. A. (2001). Learning and motivational characteristics of boys with AD/HD and giftedness. *Exceptional Children, 67,* 499–519.

Ziv, A., & Gadish, O. (1990). Humor and giftedness. *Journal for the Education of the Gifted, 13,* 332–345.

Zuo, L., & Cramond, B. L. (2001). An examination of Terman's gifted children from the theory of identity. *Gifted Child Quarterly, 45,* 251–259.

Zuo, L., & Tao, L. (2001). Importance of personality in gifted children's identity formation. *Journal of Secondary Gifted Education, 12,* 212–223.

APPENDIX A

Literature to Guide Gifted Students

Picture Books

Jane and the Dragon by Martin Baynton (2001)
Key Issue(s): gender role expectations; leadership
Description: Jane wants to be a knight, but everyone in the kingdom laughs at her, saying that girls can't be knights. The court jester takes her seriously and lends her a suit of armor that turns out to be just what she needs.

Anna Banana and Me by Lenore Blegvad (1985)
Key Issue(s): individuality; gender role expectations; creativity; peer relationships
Description: Anna is a fearless young girl who swings high on the playground, invents stories, and believes in magic. She inspires a playmate to face his own fears.

Michael by Tony Bradman (2009)
Key Issue(s): behavior problems; precocity; underachievement; individuality
Description: Always late, always scruffy, and always misbehaving, Michael was the worst boy in school, but he surprises his teachers one day.

The Summer My Father Was Ten by Pat Brisson (1998)
Key Issue(s): relationships with others; coming of age; image management
Description: A girl's father recounts the tale of how his childish carelessness deeply bruised an elderly neighbor's well-being, and what he did to make things better.

Odd Velvet by Mary E. Whitcomb (1998)
Key Issue(s): image management; creativity; being alone; peer relationships
Description: Velvet doesn't exactly fit in, but soon she is able to show her classmates just how empowering it can be to simply be yourself.

Prince Cinders by Babette Cole (1997)
Key Issue(s): family relationships; creativity; image management; gender role expectations
Description: Prince Cinders is always forced to do the dirty work for his tough, strong, hairy older brothers until one day a well-intentioned fairy falls down his chimney and tries her best to grant his wishes.

Princess Smartypants by Babette Cole (2005)
Key Issue(s): gender role expectations; leadership
Description: Princess Smartypants outfoxes Prince Swashbuckle and convinces the people of the kingdom that she doesn't have to get married to live happily ever after.

Norma Jean, Jumping Bean by Joanna Cole (1987)
Key Issue(s): gender role expectations; image management; overexcitabilities
Description: Norma Jean, a nice kangaroo, tries to control her rambunctious behavior to please people but eventually realizes that she must be herself, a kangaroo who never stops jumping!

Miss Rumphius by Barbara Cooney (1985)
Key Issue(s): individuality; gender role expectations; being alone; family relationships
Description: Alice Rumphius learns of faraway places from her grandfather at a very early age. As an older woman, she lives a complete life, traveling to

many different parts of the world. She leaves the world a little more beautiful by leaving behind her garden of lupines.

Paul and Sebastian by Rene Escudie (1994)
Key Issue(s): being labeled "different"; relationships with others
Description: Paul's and Sebastian's mothers forbid them from playing together. Each parent insists that "they are not our kind of people." When the two boys become lost on a school field trip, they support each other until they are rescued. As a result, the boys' mothers realize the significance of their friendship and change their attitudes.

Weslandia by Paul Fleischman (2002)
Key Issue(s): being labeled "different"; creativity; image management; heightened sensitivity; individuality
Description: Entrepreneurial, creative Wesley stays true to himself when others want him to fit in. Eventually his teasers and tormenters realize that conformity may not be the best way to go.

Wilfrid Gordon McDonald Partridge by Mem Fox (1995)
Key Issue(s): heightened sensitivity; relationships with others
Description: A young boy and an elderly woman share a warm relationship that allows them to appreciate the beauty of life together.

Elena's Serenade by Campbell Geeslin (2004)
Key Issue(s): creativity in young gifted girls; gender role expectations; individuality
Description: Elena is a young girl in Mexico who learns to be a glassblower and develops self-confidence.

Ronald Morgan Goes to Bat by Patricia Reilly Giff (1990)
Key Issue(s): gender role expectations; peer relationships
Description: Ronald Morgan, a nonathletic young boy, comes to realize that he is an important part of his team.

Watch Out, Ronald Morgan by Patricia Reilly Giff (1986)
Key Issue(s): being labeled "different"; relationships with others; self-inflicted pressure
Description: Ronald Morgan bumbles his way through second grade, until Miss Tyler recommends glasses. Ronald is thrilled. With glasses, he'll be

the superkid of the school. Glasses can't do everything, but with Miss Tyler's help, Ronald sees how super he can be.

Teammates by Peter Golenbock (1992)
Key Issue(s): coping skills; peer relationships; athletic giftedness
Description: The story of the friendship between Jackie Robinson and Pee Wee Reese of the 1947 Brooklyn Dodgers has several important messages for young men.

Jamaica Tag-Along by Juanita Havill (1990)
Key Issue(s): image management; being alone; peer relationships
Description: When her older brother refuses to let her tag along with him, Jamaica goes off and finds her own friends and fun.

Woolbur by Leslie Helakoski (2008)
Key Issue(s): free-spirited children enjoying their unique approach to life
Description: Woolbur is not like other sheep. He hangs out with wild dogs, cards and spins his own wool, and even dyes it blue. When his parents try to get Woolbur to follow the flock, the other sheep decide to follow Woolbur!

Chrysanthemum by Kevin Henkes (1996)
Key Issues: image management; family relationships; peer relationships
Description: As she enters kindergarten, Chrysanthemum's once-perfect name seems to her less than ideal when her classmates begin to tease her relentlessly.

Amazing Grace by Mary Hoffman (1995)
Key Issue(s): individuality; theatrical giftedness; leadership
Description: Grace loves stories. She acts out the most exciting parts of all sorts of tales. So when there is a chance to play a part in *Peter Pan*, Grace knows exactly what she must do. Grace's classmates are doubtful, but with the support of her wise grandmother who bolsters her independence, she gives an amazing performance.

Sweet Clara and the Freedom Quilt by Deborah Hopkinson (1995)
Key Issue(s): creativity; leadership; culturally diverse learners
Description: Clara, a young slave in the South, stitches a quilt with a map pattern that guides her to freedom in the North during the Civil War.

My Great-Aunt Arizona by Gloria Houston (1997)
Key Issue(s): gender role stereotypes; being alone; relationships with others; creativity
Description: Raised as an only child in Appalachia, Arizona spends her time outdoors, exploring and reading, and eventually becomes the most influential teacher the town has ever encountered.

Ben's Trumpet by Rachel Isadora (1991)
Key Issue(s): positive role models; image management; musical giftedness; creativity
Description: Ben loves to hear the Zig Zag Club musicians play, filling the air with sounds and the rhythms of jazz. When he hears it, he plays along on a trumpet that nobody else can see—except one man who opens the door to his dreams.

Max by Rachel Isadora (1984)
Key Issue(s): gender role expectations; athletic giftedness
Description: Max, a baseball player, discovers that his sister's ballet class is a great way to warm up for a home run.

Like Jake and Me by Mavis Jukes (2005)
Key Issue(s): heightened sensitivity; positive role models; family relationships
Description: A young boy comes to terms with a stepfather whose cowboy style is much different from his own.

The Story of Ferdinand by Munro Leaf (2007)
Key Issue(s): heightened sensitivity; gender role expectations
Description: Ferdinand the bull does not butt heads with the other bulls in the pasture yet he is chosen to appear in the bull ring against the mighty matador. He decides he cannot be fierce and fight the matador. Instead, he would rather remain in the pasture smelling flowers.

Josefina Javelina: A Hairy Tale by Susan Lowell (2005)
Key Issue(s): pursuing your dreams; creativity and problem solving in gifted girls
Description: Josefina, a javelina with a dream of becoming a famous ballerina, journeys to California in hopes of being discovered. Eventually she finds a special place where her talent is appreciated.

Annie's Gifts by Angela Medearis (1997)
Key Issue(s): artistic giftedness; creativity; perseverance
Description: A young girl whose determination to bring happiness and beauty to her world helps her to discover the happiness and beauty in herself.

Secret of the Peaceful Warrior by Dan Millman (1991)
Key Issue(s): coping skills; positive role models; peer relationships
Description: Under the guidance of a wise and caring adult, Danny learns to overcome his fears as he confronts a bully.

Tomas and the Library Lady by Pat Mora (2000)
Key Issue(s): culturally diverse learners; positive role models; creativity
Description: Tomas, the young child in a family of migrant workers, develops a meaningful relationship with the librarian as he falls in love with books.

The Boy Who Was Raised by Librarians by Carla Morris (2007)
Key Issue(s): having a passion for learning; finding supportive mentors
Description: Melvin discovers that the public library is the place where he can discover the answers to so many of the questions he asks. In doing so, he becomes friends with three dedicated librarians who support him in his quest for knowledge.

The Paper Bag Princess by Robert Munsch (2005)
Key Issue(s): image management; gender role expectations; individuality
Description: Elizabeth, a strong-willed young princess, fights off a dragon and decides not to marry the arrogant, shallow-minded Prince Ronald.

Stephanie's Ponytail by Robert Munsch (1996)
Key Issue(s): image management; peer relationships; leadership
Description: Stephanie shows up to school each day with a different hairdo, and every subsequent day the whole class has copied her look. She finds a way to maintain her uniqueness while teaching her classmates a lesson on conformity.

The Recess Queen by Alexis O'Neill (2002)
Key Issue(s): Schoolyard bullies
Description: Mean Jean is a bully on the school playground. A new girl

named Katie Sue arrives and becomes the new recess queen by being nice to everyone including Jean.

Coat of Many Colors by Dolly Parton (1996)
Key Issue(s): creativity; family relationships; individuality
Description: A poor girl celebrates her coat of many colors, made by her mother from rags. Despite the ridicule of other children, she cherishes the coat that was made with love.

The Big Orange Splot by Daniel Pinkwater (1999)
Key Issue(s): creativity; identity development
Description: Mr. Plumbean lived on a street where all the houses were identical. When a seagull drops a big splot of orange paint on the top of Mr. Plumbean's home, he decides to paint his house to represent his life dreams. When his neighbors resist his ideas, he succeeds in slowly convincing them to do the same and the neighborhood becomes a far more interesting place where people are comfortable expressing their individuality.

Appelemando's Dreams by Patricia Polacco (1997)
Key Issue(s): creativity; leadership; being labeled "different"; perseverance
Description: Appelemando spends his time enjoying vivid daydreams, and the villagers are convinced that he will never amount to much. Eventually his colorful dreams change the village and all the people living in it.

Mrs. Katz and Tush by Patricia Polacco (2009)
Key Issue(s): positive role models; culturally diverse learners; perseverance
Description: A young African American child and his older Jewish neighbor establish a lifelong friendship.

Pink and Say by Patricia Polacco (1994)
Key Issue(s): culturally diverse learners; peer relationships; individuality; leadership; developing a value system
Description: Pink, an African American Union soldier in the Civil War, discovers a seriously injured Say, a White teenage soldier, and takes him home to make him well.

Thank You, Mr. Falker by Patricia Polacco (2001)
Key Issue(s): gifted/learning disabled; relationships with others; perseverance; artistic giftedness
Description: An autobiographical account of an artistic fifth grader's struggle to learn to read.

Thunder Cake by Patricia Polacco (1997)
Key Issue(s): family relationships; coping skills
Description: Through the use of baking, Grandma finds a way to dispel her grandchild's fear of thunderstorms.

Ish by Peter Reynolds (2004)
Key Issue(s): individuality, creativity
Description: A single reckless comment from an older brother turns a young boy's artistic expressions into painful struggles. A younger sister helps him to recognize and appreciate the unique quality in his creativity.

The Dot by Peter Reynolds (2003)
Key Issue(s): individuality, creativity; self-expression through art
Description: When Vashti becomes frustrated in her elementary art class and announces that she simply cannot draw, her clever teacher succeeds in convincing her to experiment and enjoy self-expression.

Hooray for You! by Marianne Richmond (2008)
Key Issues: image management; individuality
Description: A rhyming celebration of individual differences in young children.

Tar Beach by Faith Ringgold (1996)
Key Issue(s): individuality; culturally diverse learners; perseverance
Description: Cassie Louise Lightfoot, 8 years old in 1939, has a dream to be free to go wherever she wants to for the rest of her life. One night, on the "tar beach," the rooftop of her family's Harlem apartment, her dream comes true. She learns anyone can fly—"All you need is somewhere to go you can't get to any other way."

The Littlest Tall Fellow by Barry Rudner (1989)
Key Issue(s): image management; athletic giftedness; perseverance
Description: A young boy wants to become a basketball star, but his lack

of height will not allow him to play. Through drive and determination he is able to reach his dreams.

An Angel for Solomon Singer by Cynthia Rylant (1996)
Key Issue(s): being alone; image management; relationships with others
Description: Homesick for the Midwest, Solomon Singer spends his days in New York City unhappy and dreaming of a happier life. One night he strolls into a special diner and eventually realizes that, once you find a friend, everything else tends to fall into place.

The Lost Lake by Allen Say (1992)
Key Issue(s): family relationships; perseverance
Description: A father and son embark upon a weeklong hike. At his son's urging, the father continues the journey even after he suffers a hurtful setback.

Brave Irene by William Steig (1988)
Key Issue(s): image management; dealing with stress; coping skills
Description: Irene must deliver a ball gown to the duchess at the palace. She survives a terribly harsh journey through the woods in a snowstorm and accomplishes her task with bravery.

Creativity by John Steptoe (2003)
Key Issue(s): creativity; peer relationships; culturally diverse learners
Description: Charles helps a new student from Puerto Rico get used to life at his new school.

Dear Mrs. LaRue: Letters From Obedience School by Mark Teague (2002)
Key Issue(s): underachievement, individuality; creativity
Description: Doggy Ike's owner sends him to obedience school to change his behavior. Ike attempts to get his way out of the stifling environment and tries to have Mrs. LaRue see that he's OK the way he is.

Alexander and the Terrible, Horrible, No Good, Very Bad Day by Judith Viorst (2009)
Key Issue(s): dealing with stress; coping skills
Description: The trials and tribulations in a young boy's daily life can sometimes be stressful.

Rosie and Michael by Judith Viorst (1988)
Key Issue(s): peer relationships; gender role expectations
Description: Rosie and Michael are the best of friends. They know they can depend on each other. They can even tell what they like about each other—even the bad things!

Ira Sleeps Over by Bernard Waber (2005)
Key Issue(s): image management; heightened sensitivity; gender role expectations
Description: Ira is invited to Reggie's house to sleep over. How will he feel sleeping without his teddy bear for the very first time?

Galimoto by Karen Lynn Williams (1995)
Key Issue(s): perseverance; creativity; culturally diverse learners; family relationships
Description: Kondi, a young African boy, is determined to make a galimoto—a toy vehicle made of wires. His brother laughs at his idea, but all day long Kondi gathers the wire he needs. By nightfall, his wonderful galimoto is ready for the village children.

Tough Eddie by Elizabeth Winthrop (1989)
Key Issue(s): image management; gender role expectations; being labeled "different"
Description: Eddie is afraid he'll be teased for having a dollhouse. When friends admire his bravery, he realizes he can share his favorite plaything and still be tough in their eyes.

The Boy Who Grew Flowers by Jen Wojtowicz (2005)
Key Issue(s): being labeled "different"; empathy in gifted children
Description: A young boy is shunned at school because he sprouts flowers every full moon. He makes a distinctive pair of shoes for a classmate who appreciates his special abilities.

A Quiet Place by Douglas Wood (2005)
Key Issue(s): being alone; identity development; creativity
Description: A vivid description of the special places that a child can go to be quiet, to be alone, and to imagine.

Crow Boy by Taro Yashima (1976)
Key Issue(s): being labeled "different"; culturally diverse learners; creativity
Description: A strange Japanese boy is isolated by his differences from the other children in his village school. Eventually he becomes recognized for his unusual talents.

William's Doll by Charlotte Zolotow (1985)
Key Issue(s): gender role expectations; relationships with others; heightened sensitivity
Description: William wants the forbidden—a doll. William teaches us that he can still be "all boy" and nurture his love for his doll.

I Know a Lady by Charlotte Zolotow (1992)
Key Issue(s): heightened sensitivity; positive role models; individuality
Description: Sally describes a loving and lovable old lady in her neighborhood who grows flowers, waves to children when they pass by, and bakes cookies for them at Christmas.

Literature for Elementary Grades 3–5

Did You Carry the Flag Today, Charley? by Rebecca Caudill (1988)
Key Issue(s): image management; leadership
Description: Charley, a young preschooler from an impoverished Appalachian Mountain family, has a wonderful sense of curiosity that must be channeled in a positive direction.

Dear Mr. Henshaw by Beverly Cleary (1994)
Key Issue(s): positive role models; coming of age
Description: A sixth grader develops a nurturing relationship with an author who helps him deal with several difficult adolescent issues.

The Landry News by Andrew Clements (2007)
Key Issues: creativity; perseverance; using one's talents for positive results; positive role models
Description: A fifth grader writes an editorial about her teacher that inspires many important changes at her school.

Because of Winn-Dixie by Kate DiCamillo (2009)
Key Issue(s): image management; family relationships; coping skills
Description: Because of an ugly, cheerful dog named Winn-Dixie, 10-year-old Opal learns to connect with those around her as she finally begins to cope with the fact that her mother abandoned her several years ago.

Waiting for Normal by Leslie Connor (2008)
Key Issue(s): coping with family challenges; searching for friendship; finding emotional support beyond one's family
Description: Addie must learn to understand her mother's erratic behavior and being separated by her loving stepfather and half-sisters when she and her mother move out to live on their own.

The Great Brain by John D. Fitzgerald (2004)
Key Issue(s): leadership; relationships with others
Description: The Great Brain, age 10, specializes in solving problems that baffle adults in his community. This gifted boy uses his resources to help a less fortunate young man.

Nobody's Family Is Going to Change by Louise Fitzhugh (2008)
Key Issue(s): gender role expectations; family relationships
Description: Emma, who is very intelligent, wants to become a lawyer. Her 7-year-old brother, Willie, wants to become a dancer. Their father is opposed to both of these career choices.

Joey Pigza Loses Control by Jack Gantos (2002)
Key Issue(s): living with attention deficits; father-son relationships
Description: With new medications, Joey believes his attention deficit disorder is under control and he can begin to live as a normal kid. He convinces his skeptical mom to let him spend part of his summer visiting his estranged father. The problem Joey faces is that his dad is just as wired as Joey used to be and believes Joey can deal with his ADD without the help of drugs. Is being friends with his father worth losing his self-control?

Matilda by Roald Dahl (2007)
Key Issue(s): precocity; creativity; gender role expectations
Description: Matilda is a highly gifted child who learns to cope with growing up in an anti-intellectual home.

My Side of the Mountain by Jean Craighead George (2004)
Key Issue(s): coming of age; individuality; being alone
Description: A young man's experiences of life in the wild provide him with an opportunity to learn about the wilderness, and himself, in the process.

Julie of the Wolves by Jean Craighead George (2004)
Key Issue(s): image management; family relationships; being alone; perseverance
Description: Miyax rebels against a home situation that she finds intolerable. She becomes lost in the Alaskan wilderness, without food or a compass. She survives day to day and is forced to redefine the traditional richness of Eskimo life.

Pictures of Hollis Woods by Patricia Reilly Giff (2004)
Key Issue(s): identity development; positive role models; creativity; artistic giftedness
Description: Artistically talented Hollis Woods has a history of running away from foster homes. She discovers a place where she wants to remain. There she bonds with Josie, her new guardian, who is a slightly eccentric, retired art teacher. Through her sketchbook she preserves her memories, develops an understanding of her fears, and experiences catharsis as she searches for a place where she belongs.

Philip Hall Likes Me. I Reckon Maybe by Bette Greene (1999)
Key Issue(s): gender role expectations; peer relationships
Description: Beth Lambert could easily be the best student in her class if she did not let Philip Hall, her first love, have this distinction.

The Gift-Giver by Joyce Hansen (2005)
Key Issue(s): gender role expectations; multicultural learners; image management; perseverance; peer relationships
Description: Gifted loner Amir moves to an inner city neighborhood and teaches Doris, another gifted Black student, and other peers how to feel better about themselves and how to appreciate everyone's talents.

Ida B by Katherine Hannigan (2004)
Key Issue(s): giftedness and creativity in young girls; coping with family challenges; emotional support from teachers
Description: Fourth grader Ida B spends enjoys being homeschooled and

playing in her family's apple orchard, until her mother begins treatment for breast cancer and her parents must sell part of their Wisconsin farm and send her to public school.

Crossing the Wire by Will Hobbs (2007)
Key Issue(s): overcoming adversity and developing resilience; belief in self
Description: When falling corn prices in Mexico threaten his family with starvation, 15-year-old Victor Flores heads north to cross the wire into the United States so he can find employment and send money home. Victor's journey is filled with near-death situations as he must decide whom to trust. Through his desperate struggle Victor learns much about courage and love of family.

Baseball Fever by Johanna Hurwitz (2000)
Key Issue(s): parental expectations; family relationships; coping skills
Description: The only game Ezra's father has any respect for is chess; he cannot understand why his son would rather rot his brains watching baseball than reading a book. How can Ezra ever convince him that cheering for a national pastime isn't completely off base?

Class Clown by Johanna Hurwitz (1995)
Key Issue(s): precocity; perfectionism; behavior problems
Description: A third grader named Lucas is one of the smartest kids in school yet he cannot seem to stay out of trouble. Lucas doesn't mean to be the class clown, and he learns a surprising lesson when he attempts to become a perfect student.

Class President by Johanna Hurwitz (1990)
Key Issue(s): leadership; culturally diverse students; relationships with others
Description: Julio Sanchez, a Puerto Rican young man, is a true friend to his peers and has the natural gift of leadership. He is elected president of his fifth-grade class after his friends realize his special ability to help people.

The Bat-Poet by Randall Jarrell (1996)
Key Issue(s): being labeled "different"; individuality
Description: A little brown bat is thought of as an oddball because he celebrates life in an unusual way. A meaningful allegory provides insight into an artist's life.

The Phantom Tollbooth by Norton Juster (2007)
Key Issue(s): creativity; image management
Description: In this delightful classic, Milo learns that, as long as you have an active imagination, life will never be boring.

From the Mixed–Up Files of Mrs. Basil E. Frankweiler by E. L. Konigsburg (2007)
Key Issue(s): parental expectations; family relationships; image management
Description: Tired of being "Straight A's Claudia Kincaid," Claudia persuades her brother to run away with her. They run away to the Metropolitan Museum of Art for a week where they solve a number of mysteries and learn about themselves in the process.

The View From Saturday by E. L. Konigsburg (2007)
Key Issues: positive role models; peer relationships; creativity; individuality
Description: Four sixth graders, with their own individual gifts and talents, develop a special bond when they are recruited by their teacher to represent their class in an Academic Bowl competition.

... and Now Miguel by Joseph Krumgold (1984)
Key Issue(s): parental expectations; positive role models
Description: Miguel Chavez yearns in his heart to go with the men of his family on a long, hard sheep drive to the mountains.

A Wrinkle in Time by Madeleine L'Engle (2007)
Key Issue(s): creativity; image management; family relationships
Description: A search for a missing parent, involving a fantasy, becomes a search for identity for both a young boy and his sister.

Anastasia Krupnik by Lois Lowry (2009)
Key Issue(s): leadership; creativity
Description: Anastasia Krupnik is left in charge of her very disorganized family. She invents the Krupnik Family Nonsexist Housekeeping Schedule and saves the day.

Be a Perfect Person in Just Three Days! by Stephen Manes (1996)
Key Issue(s): perfectionism; peer relationships; coping skills
Description: Milo Crinkley learns that it's OK to be less than perfect.

Fast Sam, Cool Clyde and Stuff by Walter Dean Myers (1988)
Key Issue(s): culturally diverse learners; peer relationships; image management
Description: "Fast Sam," "Cool Clyde," and "Stuff" grow up in Harlem and learn to know the meaning of friendship as they search for self-identity.

Mrs. Frisby and the Rats of NIMH by Robert C. O'Brien (1986)
Key Issue(s): image management; family relationships; being labeled "different"
Description: A lab experiment produces a community of highly intelligent rats who decide to help Mrs. Frisby, a mouse, save the life of her son.

Skinnybones by Barbara Park (2009)
Key Issue(s): coping skills; image management
Description: Alex "Skinnybones" Frankovitch learns that he's not the best Little League player around and his major-league talent for wisecracking leads him to trouble.

The Great Gilly Hopkins by Katherine Paterson (2007)
Key Issue(s): coming of age; relationships with others
Description: Gilly Hopkins, a foster child, yearns desperately for a real family and a place to call home. In her struggle to escape from her foster home, she learns that life usually isn't the way it is supposed to be.

Bridge to Terabithia by Katherine Paterson (2007)
Key Issue(s): peer relationships; coping skills; dealing with death of a loved one; creativity
Description: A young man can be "different" much more easily if he has a friend with whom he can share his thoughts and feelings.

Come Sing, Jimmy Jo by Katherine Paterson (1995)
Key Issue(s): musical giftedness; peer relationships; individuality
Description: Jimmy Jo is a gifted young musician who must deal with increasing recognition from his audiences as well as problems with his peers.

The Schernoff Discoveries by Gary Paulsen (1998)
Key Issue(s): peer relationships; scientific giftedness
Description: Harold Schernoff is a science whiz and a social nerd. He has a theory for solving every problem, from middle school dating to how to buy

a car when you're under age. When he and his best friend join forces to test his theories, nothing goes according to plan.

A Day No Pigs Would Die by Robert Newton Peck (1994)
Key Issue(s): being labeled "different"; image management; family relationships; developing a value system
Description: Robbie tells of his 13th year growing up in a Shaker family in Vermont. A series of vignettes reveals that Rob is growing up knowing that he is different and learning to value the strengths of his family and himself.

Someday Angeline by Louis Sachar (1994)
Key Issue(s): multipotentiality; prodigies; image management; peer relationships
Description: Angeline is an 8-year-old who has been accelerated to sixth grade, and she must deal with the social issues of "being too smart." The mean kids in school call her a freak, her teacher finds her troublesome, and even her father doesn't know how to handle a gifted girl. Angeline doesn't want to be a freak or genius—she just wants to be herself.

A Taste of Blackberries by Doris Buchanan Smith (2002)
Key Issue(s): coping with death; peer relationships
Description: A touching story about a young boy who deals with the tragic death of his best friend.

Maniac Magee by Jerry Spinelli (1999)
Key Issue(s): being labeled "different"; leadership; relationships with others; positive role models
Description: A boy is so incredibly energetic that "he must be a maniac." He uses his energy and gifts to confront the racial divide in his town that no one else has had the strength to face.

Loser by Jerry Spinelli (2003)
Key Issue(s): self-acceptance; celebrating individual differences; optimism
Description: Donald Zinkoff is a quirky kid who enjoys people, loves school, and giggles constantly. Other fourth graders think he's a loser. Donald's optimism and energy, combined with his family's love, do not allow him to think of himself that way. When he tries to rescue a lost child in a winter blizzard, others see the loser become a hero.

Smiles to Go by Jerry Spinelli (2008)
Key Issue(s): friendships; teenagers searching for self-actualization
Description: Will Tuppence's life has always been driven by rules of science and logic. When he discovers in ninth-grade science class that protons decay, he begins to look at the world differently and develops a new perspective on the important relationships in his life.

Surviving the Applewhites by Stephanie S. Tolan (2002)
Key Issue(s): underachievement; creativity; relationships with others; image management
Description: When Jake Semple is kicked out of his latest school, the Applewhites, an eccentric family of artists, offer to have him move in with them and attend their unstructured Creative Academy. Through his new family life, Jakes explores interests and discovers talents he never knew he had.

Locomotion by Jacqueline Woodson (2003).
Key Issue(s): poetry as catharsis; love of family; overcoming adversity and developing resilience
Description: Through a collection of poems, 11-year-old Lonnie Collins Motion, nicknamed Locomotion, writes about the death of his parents in a fire, being separated from his younger sister, living in a foster home, and finding his voice though poetry.

Peace, Locomotion by Jacqueline Woodson (2009)
Key Issue(s): love of family; overcoming adversity and developing resilience; writing as catharsis
Description: Through writing letters to his younger sister living in a different foster home in Brooklyn, Lonnie maintains a record of their lives while they are apart. In his poignant reflections he expresses his love for his sister, shares his own foster family, and describes his experiences watching his foster brother return home from the Iraq war.

Young Adult Literature—Middle and High School

Some of the following young adult novels have mature themes.

The Absolutely True Diary of a Part-Time Indian by Sherman Alexie (2007)
Key Issue(s): cultural identity development; creativity, twice-exceptionality
Description: Arnold Spirit, also known as "Junior," is a budding cartoonist

growing up on the Spokane Indian reservation. Born with several medical problems, he is often the target of bullies. He leaves the reservation when he transfers to an affluent White school in a neighboring rural community where the only other Indian is the school mascot. When he joins the basketball team and meets his former classmates on the court, he struggles with questions revolving around community, identity, and tribe and discovers an internal strength he never knew he had.

Speak by Laurie Halse Anderson (2006)
Key Issue(s): coping with trauma; image management; underachievement
Description: A creative high school student's world has been shattered so much so that she can no longer speak. A story of perseverance in the face of trauma.

Nothing but the Truth by Avi (2010)
Key Issue(s): gender role expectations; being labeled "different"; relationships with others; underachievement
Description: Philip's teacher wants him to have the same passion for literature as he does for track, but he just doesn't connect to the assigned reading material. When his behavior is viewed as disrespectful and unpatriotic by the teacher, Philip decides to stand up for his rights and ends up in the midst of a national debate.

The Moves Make the Man by Bruce Brooks (1996)
Key Issue(s): image management; culturally diverse learners; athletic giftedness
Description: Jerome Foxworthy, a talented athlete, can handle anything, even being the first Black student to integrate the biggest school in Wilmington, NC. The story deals with a strong character who faces tremendous personal turmoil at home as well as at school and his ability to deal with his problems through a strong, new friendship.

Echoes of the White Giraffe by Sook Nyul Choi (2007)
Key Issue(s): gender role expectations; multicultural learners; image management
Description: Sookan, a Korean young woman coming of age during the Korean War, experiences a forbidden romance with a quiet, thoughtful young man who allows her to think for herself and challenges aspects of a strict society.

Celine by Brock Cole (1991)
Key Issue(s): artistic giftedness; gender role expectations; coping skills
Description: Celine is a 16-year-old girl going through a rather difficult period in her life as she tries to deal with the problems she encounters.

Among Friends by Caroline B. Cooney (1998)
Key Issue(s): multipotentiality; perfectionism; musical giftedness; peer relationships; coping with pressure
Description: Junior Jennie Quint, an amazingly talented composer, writer, and musician, finds herself more isolated with each success. In addition, her parents and school officials display her as a "trophy student," which simply adds to her troubles.

Walk Two Moons by Sharon Creech (2004)
Key Issue(s): peer relationships; family relationships; image management
Description: After her mother leaves the family, Sal embarks upon a week-long trip with her grandparents during which she tells the story of how she became close with someone who at first seemed utterly unlike herself.

Bloomability by Sharon Creech (1999)
Key Issue(s): family relationships; culturally diverse learners
Description: Dinnie spends a year away from her family while attending an international school in Switzerland. With time away from her transient family, she discovers an expanding world and finds her place in it. In her new environment, she learns that life is full of new "bloomabilities."

Chasing Redbird by Sharon Creech (1998)
Key Issue(s): family relationships; coping with death; introversion; image management; heightened sensitivity
Description: Zinny is one of seven kids and often escapes the hustle and bustle of her family by going to the quiet house of her aunt and uncle. When her aunt dies, Zinny thinks it's her fault. She ends up dealing with her feelings during the summer as she clears a long-overgrown trail that parallels her emotions.

Ironman by Chris Crutcher (2004)
Key Issue(s): athletic giftedness; family relationships; image management; coping skills
Description: Triathlete Bo's rocky relationship with his English teacher is frustratingly similar to what remains of his relationship with his father.

With the help of sports, an anger management group, and writing, Bo learns to cope.

The Watsons Go to Birmingham—1963 by Christopher Paul Curtis (2001)
Key Issue(s): family relationships; being alone; image management
Description: Kenny, a gifted boy in 1960s America, spends his time trying to avoid teasing from bullies and his tough older brother, Byron. The family thinks a summer in Birmingham may be what Byron needs to learn to behave, but they learn some lessons about racial barriers and institutionalized bullying instead.

The Cat Ate My Gymsuit by Paula Danzinger (2006)
Key Issue(s): image management; gender role expectations; leadership
Description: Marcy has a poor self-image, largely because of her weight and her unpopularity. She is very bright, however, and begins to use her abilities when her English teacher is removed from class. Marcy takes on the establishment in an attempt to have her reinstated.

Whirligig by Paul Fleischman (2001)
Key Issue(s): relationships with others; image management; coping skills; dealing with tragedy
Description: Popularity-obsessed Brent's quest for a higher social ranking eventually leads to the death of an 18-year-old girl. At the girl's mother's request, Brent begins a journey of atonement that takes him to the corners of the country and into people's lives that will be forever tied with his.

The Curious Incident of the Dog in the Night-Time by Mark Haddon (2004)
Key Issue(s): twice-exceptionality; family relationships; relationships with others; image management; coping skills
Description: A highly gifted student with learning disabilities embarks upon a series of adventures to figure out how his neighbor's dog was killed, learning family secrets and important things about himself along the way.

Cowboys Don't Cry by Marilyn Halvorson (1998)
Key Issue(s): heightened sensitivity; family relationships; image management
Description: Shane Morgan couldn't be happier when he and his father inherit a small ranch. Tired of following the rodeo circuit, Shane looks forward to a calmer lifestyle with his dad. In the new environment, Shane and his father face troubles as they must define manhood.

The Planet of Junior Brown by Virginia Hamilton (2006)
Key Issue(s): image management; artistic giftedness; musical giftedness; relationships with others
Description: Overweight and gifted in the arts, Junior has trouble making real connections with others. Through his relationship with fellow student Buddy, Junior is better able to accept himself and learn to be closer with others.

Hoot by Carl Hiaasen (2005)
Key Issue(s): being labeled "different"; leadership
Description: Roy Eberhardt is the new kid in school once again. He faces the same routine: eating alone at lunch, no real friends, and hassle with bullies pushing him around. He connects with bully-beating Beatrice and together they become involved in another student's attempt to save a colony of burrowing owls from a proposed construction site.

When Zachary Beaver Came to Town by Kimberly Willis Holt (2001)
Key Issue(s): peer relationships; being labeled "different"
Description: When Zachary Beaver, an obese teenager, arrives in a small Texas town as part of a traveling road show, Toby and his friends become fascinated with him and the stories he shares of all the places he's known. In coming to know Zachary, Toby learns to appreciate the boy's difficult life as he develops sensitivity to people who are different from him.

The Mosquito Test by Richard Kent (1994)
Key Issue(s): peer relationships; coping skills; increased sensitivity
Description: Against the background of tennis courts, high school hallways, and hospital wards, two young men discover the meaning of courage and legacy of friendship.

If I Love You, Am I Trapped Forever? by M. E. Kerr (2009)
Key Issue(s): peer and parental expectations; multipotentiality; coping skills
Description: A handsome, multitalented, and popular young man has a great deal of pressure placed on him with expectations from his high school friends, parents, and self. He struggles to maintain his image.

The Outcasts of 19 Schuyler Place by E. L. Konigsburg (2004)
Key Issue(s): artistic giftedness; creativity; image management; being labeled "different"; relationships with others
Description: Margaret's tendency not to bow to authority gets her kicked

out of summer camp. With her parents out of the country, she ends up at her eccentric uncle's house, which is well known in the area for the huge sculptures in the yard. The town starts a movement to get rid of the structures, and soon Margaret's summer gets much more serious and meaningful.

Very Far Away From Anywhere Else by Ursula K. Le Guin (2004)
Key Issue(s): introversion; peer relationships; image management; nonconformity
Description: Owen Griffiths tells his story of being a "bright little jerk" and how he deals with being different. He has discovered that conforming for the sake of conformity will not work for him although he is not yet comfortable being himself. Owen learns from Natalie, and when their friendship shows signs of turning into love, he learns even more about taking charge of his future.

The Giver by Lois Lowry (2006)
Key Issue(s): underachievement; image management; nonconformity
Description: Twelve-year-old Jonas has been taken under the wing of "The Giver," his Utopian society's keeper of all secrets and memories. He must learn to balance his search for identity with his community's wishes for him as he decides if he will fulfill the role society has laid out for him.

Sleeping Freshmen Never Lie by David Lubar (2007)
Key Issue(s): image management; surviving the first year of high school; friendships that change
Description: As Scott Hudson navigates his first year of high school, he awaits the birth of a new baby brother. He decides that high school would be less overwhelming if it came with a survival manual, so he writes his reflections and provides a guide of survival tips for his new sibling.

The Facts and Fictions of Minna Pratt by Patricia MacLachlan (1990)
Key Issue(s): image management; family relationships; musical giftedness; creativity
Description: Minna is surrounded by gifted people: her mother is an author, her father is a psychologist, her younger brother "knows everything," and she plays in a quartet of very talented musicians. She learns to value her family because of their eccentricities and to value herself because of her own.

A Corner of the Universe by Ann M. Martin (2005)
Key Issue(s): family relationships; positive role models; being labeled "different"; image management
Description: Loner Hattie finds a kindred spirit in Uncle Adam, someone whose existence was only revealed to her shortly before he comes home for the summer when his "special home" closes. For as much as she's able to identify with eccentric Adam, Hattie's most difficult challenge is recognizing how they are different.

Jeremy Fink and the Meaning of Life by Wendy Mass (2006)
Key Issue(s): son-father relationships; search for self-actualization
Description: Just before his 13th birthday Jeremy Fink receives a keyless locked box, prepared by his father before his death 5 years earlier. According to the writing on the box, it contains the meaning of life. How will he open the box and what will he discover?

Cut by Patricia McCormick (2002)
Key Issues: perfectionism; image management; being alone
Description: Burdened with the pressure of believing she is responsible for her brother's illness, 15-year-old Callie begins a course of self-destruction that leads to her being admitted a psychiatric hospital. Slowly, she begins emerging from her miserable silence, ultimately understanding the role her dysfunctional family played in her brother's health crisis.

The Member of the Wedding by Carson McCullers (2004)
Key Issue(s): family relationships; image management; being alone
Description: Tomboy Frankie yearns to experience more than her small town will offer her; she thinks she has found the perfect solution when her older brother gets married and asks Frankie to be a "member of the wedding." Frankie misunderstands and thinks she'll be accompanying the couple from now on, and when she realizes her mistake she must reevaluate herself.

Hoops by Walter Dean Myers (1989)
Key Issue(s): culturally diverse learners; image management; athletic giftedness
Description: While growing up on the streets of Harlem, Lonnie Jackson, a talented athlete, finds basketball more than just a sure way out of the city. Through the game, he gains the confidence to deal with everyday realities.

Jacob Have I Loved by Katherine Paterson (2007)
Key Issue(s): image management; family relationships
Description: Louise is convinced that everyone despises her and loves Caroline, her beautiful, musically talented younger sister. Not until she is 17 does Louise realize that she is gifted intellectually and capable of doing anything she chooses.

The Island by Gary Paulsen (2006)
Key Issue(s): image management; being alone
Description: A young man needs his personal space throughout adolescence as he struggles to "find himself."

Dancing Carl by Gary Paulsen (2007)
Key Issue(s): heightened sensitivity; gender role stereotypes; athletic giftedness
Description: A stranger new to a small Minnesota community has a great impact on the lives of two 12-year-old boys when he expresses his inner feelings through ice-skating.

The Car by Gary Paulsen (2006)
Key Issue(s): developing one's independence; problem solving in gifted boys; developing self-understanding; developing resilience to overcome adversity
Description: Terry, a 14-year-old, is abandoned by his parents. He travels west in search of his uncle in a car he built himself. Along the way, he picks up two Vietnam veterans, learns from their experiences, and ultimately learns about himself.

Remembering the Good Times by Richard Peck (1986)
Key Issues(s): coping skills; dealing with death of a friend; peer relationships; image management
Description: Buck Mendenhall, Kate Lucas, and Trav Kirby have been friends since junior high and are about to enjoy their sophomore year together. As school begins, Buck and Kate are told that Trav has killed himself. Despite plentiful foreshadowing, Trav's death is still shocking to his friends.

Zen and the Art of Faking It by Jordan Sonnenblick (2007)
Key Issue(s): searching for friendships; popularity; identity development
Description: San Lee is forced to move again to a new community and a new middle school. He attempts to fit in by becoming known as the

Zen expert of eighth grade. With a little library research and the perfect "meditation" rock outside his school, San fools everyone into believing his Buddhist philosophy.

Taking Sides by Gary Soto (2003)
Key Issue(s): cultural identity; sportsmanship; self-acceptance
Description: When 14-year-old Lincoln Mendoza and his mother move from their California barrio to a more affluent White suburb, he misses his Hispanic friends and his old neighborhood. He feels like a traitor when he plays basketball for his new school and must compete against his former classmates. Ultimately, Lincoln learns to accept challenges in his new environment without compromising his cultural identity.

Stargirl by Jerry Spinelli (2004)
Key Issue(s): nonconformity; image management
Description: When eccentric Stargirl joins the ranks at Mica High School, her utter ignorance of the social order and genuine affection for everyone throws the whole community for a loop.

Wringer by Jerry Spinelli (2004)
Key Issue(s): heightened sensitivity; gender role expectations
Description: Palmer's upcoming birthday signifies the time he'll become a wringer, or pigeon killer, at his town's annual Pigeon Day. Palmer doesn't want to play this role, but will he have the courage to stand up for his beliefs?

Roll of Thunder, Hear My Cry by Mildred D. Taylor (2002)
Key Issue(s): image management; culturally diverse learners; perseverance; family relationships
Description: Cassie is a girl raised by a family determined not to surrender their independence or their humanity simply because they are Black. Through her family struggles, Cassie learns to be true to herself.

Dicey's Song by Cynthia Voigt (2003)
Key Issue(s): being labeled "different"; family relationships; perseverance; leadership
Description: Dicey is the oldest daughter in a family abandoned by their mother. Dicey is courageous and independent when she takes charge of her life to remain supportive to those who depend on her.

Izzy, Willy-Nilly by Cynthia Voigt (2005)
Key Issue(s): image management; peer relationships; perfectionism
Description: A drunk-driving accident leaves pretty, popular Izzy with an amputated leg and a group of friends who no longer know how to connect with her. Through a new friendship with an eccentric classmate, Izzy is able to make the transition back to school and face her new life.

The Runner by Cynthia Voigt (2005)
Key Issue(s): self-inflicted pressure; athletic giftedness; image management
Description: Bullet Tillerman is a gifted athlete. His story is that of a boy who conquers self-doubt and enters adulthood.

A Solitary Blue by Cynthia Voigt (2003)
Key Issue(s): parental pressure; perfectionism; family relationships
Description: Jeff's mother, who deserted the family years before, reenters his life and widens the gap between Jeff and his father. This gap is one only truth, love, and friendship can heal.

Sons From Afar by Cynthia Voigt (1996)
Key Issue(s): family relationships; image management
Description: A search for a father forces two brothers to learn their strengths and weaknesses as well as important knowledge about themselves.

Homeless Bird by Gloria Whelan (2001)
Key Issue(s): artistic giftedness; resilience; search for identity
Description: When Koly's ill-fated arranged marriage leaves her a widow at 13, she forges a life for herself that opposes tradition but highlights her creativity.

Tadpole by Ruth White (2004)
Key Issue(s): musical giftedness; family relationships; leadership; image management
Description: Carolina feels lost in a family of talented sisters. When her guitar-playing cousin Tadpole comes for an unexpected visit, Carolina realizes she has talents to unlock while coming to a deeper understanding of human nature.

Fast Talk on a Slow Track by Rita Williams-Garcia (1998)
Key Issue(s): multicultural learners; self-inflicted pressure; peer relationships
Description: Class valedictorian Denzel Watson has never experienced the

humiliation of failure until he tries to bluff his way through orientation at Princeton. His reaction to failure costs him dearly and forces him to confront himself for the first time in his life.

Like Sisters on the Homefront by Rita Williams-Garcia (1997)
Key Issue(s): support of the extended family; identity development
Description: Troubled 14-year-old Gayle lives for the action of her New York neighborhood. When she gets into trouble, her mother sends her down South to live with her uncle and aunt. Her life changes as she experiences the love of her extended family.

The Mozart Season by Virginia Euwer Wolff (2007)
Key Issue(s): musical giftedness; image management
Description: Allegra Shapiro, a sixth grader, is the youngest violinist in a statewide competition. She spends her summer practicing a Mozart concerto and, through her music, she is able to find many significant conceptions in her world.

Maizon at Blue Hill by Jacqueline Woodson (2002)
Key Issue(s): culturally diverse learners; identity development; peer relationships
Description: Maizon, a gifted African American girl, leaves her grandmother in Brooklyn, NY, to attend a private school in Connecticut on scholarship. She must cope with her fear of leaving her grandmother, losing her best friend, and losing her identity in a school with little diversity.

Millicent Min, Girl Genius by Lisa Yee (2003)
Key Issue(s): accelerated gifted girls coping with social issues; hiding one's intelligence to gain friends
Description: Millie, an 11-year-old, is a highly gifted girl enrolled in a summer college poetry class and waiting for her high school senior year. Because she is socially awkward, her parents sign her up for a volleyball team and enlist her to tutor Stanford Wong, her nemesis. Her volleyball teammate Emily becomes her first true friend but Millie feels compelled to camouflage her intelligence.

Stanford Wong Flunks Big-Time by Lisa Yee (2006)
Key Issue(s): underachievement; family expectations; peer group pressure
Description: From the day his father named him for his alma mater, great things were expected of Stanford Wong. When he flunks sixth-grade

English class and has to attend summer school, he worries that he might lose his star status on the basketball team. His summer is filled with turmoil as he misses out on basketball camp, he observes his beloved grandmother's increasing dementia, and he has to face being tutored by Millicent Min, girl genius.

The Pigman by Paul Zindel (2005)
Key Issue(s): learning love, compassion, and trust; identity development; friendships
Description: Coming from unhappy homes, high school sophomores John and Lorraine spend their days in idle pranks. By accident they meet Angelo Pignati, who is known as "The Pigman." The lonely old man befriends the two teens and through his kindness, they experience more happiness than they've ever had before.

The Amazing and Death-Defying Diary of Eugene Dingman by Paul Zindel (2010)
Key Issue(s): image management; relationships with others
Description: A precocious teenager discovers several truths about himself in the course of a summer that change his future and his view of the world.

Confessions of a Teenage Baboon by Paul Zindel (2010)
Key Issue(s): peer relationships; being alone; image management
Description: A 16-year-old feels depressed. A social outcast, he at last finds answers to questions he has been asking throughout his adolescence.

APPENDIX B

Examining Biographies With Gifted Students

Biographies of Women of Achievement

Madeleine Albright (Secretary of State)
Madam Secretary: A Memoir by Madeleine Albright (2003)
Madeleine Albright: A Twentieth Century Odyssey by Michael
   Dobbs (1999)

Maya Angelou (Author and Poet)
I Know Why the Caged Bird Sings by Maya Angelou (1969)

Melba Patillo Beals (Author and Journalist)
*Warriors Don't Cry: A Searing Memoir of the Battle to Integrate
   Little Rock's Central High* by Melba Patillo Beals (1995)

Erma Bombeck (Author and Humorist)
Erma Bombeck: A Life in Humor by Susan Edwards (1997)

Donna Brazile (Political Strategist)
Cooking With Grease: Stirring the Pots in American Politics by Donna Brazile
(2005)

Rachel Carson (Environmentalist)
Rachel Carson: Witness for Nature by Linda J. Lear (1997)

Sandra Cisneros (Author)
Sandra Cisneros: Latina Writer and Activist by Caryn Mirriam-Goldberg
(1998)

Hillary Rodham Clinton (Secretary of State)
Living History by Hillary Rodham Clinton (2003)

Amelia Earhart (Pilot)
East to Dawn: The Life of Amelia Earhart by Susan Butler (1997)

Anne Frank (Victim of the Holocaust)
*Anne Frank Remembered: The Story of the Woman Who Helped to Hide the
Frank Family* by Miep Gies and Allison Leslie Gold (1987)

Lorraine Hansberry (Playwright)
*To Be Young, Gifted and Black: An Informal Autobiography of Lorraine
Hansberry* by Lorraine Hansberry (1969)

Leta Hollingworth (Educator)
A Forgotten Voice: A Biography of Leta Stetter Hollingworth by Ann G. Klein
(2002)

Charlayne Hunter-Gault (Journalist)
In My Place by Charlayne Hunter-Gault (1992)

Zora Neale Hurston (Author)
Jump at de Sun: The Story of Zora Neale Hurston by A. P. Porter (1992)

Barbara Jordan (Politician)
Barbara Jordan: An American Hero by Mary Beth Rogers (1998)

Helen Keller (Author and Activist)
The Story of My Life by Helen Keller (2003)

Coretta Scott King (Human Rights Activist)
Coretta: The Story of Coretta Scott King by Octavia Vivian (2006)

Rebecca Lobo (Athlete, Sports Analyst)
The Home Team: Of Mothers, Daughters, and American Champions by RuthAnn Lobo and Rebecca Lobo (1996).

Wilma Mankiller (Leader of the Cherokee Nation)
Mankiller: A Chief and Her People by Wilma Mankiller and Michael Wallis (1993)

Margaret Mead (Anthropologist)
With a Daughter's Eye: A. Memoir of Margaret Mead and Gregory Bateson by Mary Catherine Bateson (1985)

Sandra Day O'Connor (Supreme Court Justice)
Lazy B: Growing Up on a Cattle Ranch in the American Southwest by Sandra Day O'Connor and H. Alan Day (2002)
Sandra Day O'Connor: How the First Woman on the Supreme Court Became its Most Influential Justice by Joan Biskupic (2005)

Mary Lou Retton (Athlete)
Mary Lou Retton's Gateways to Happiness: 7 Ways to a More Peaceful, More Prosperous, More Satisfying Life by Mary Lou Retton and David Bender (2000)

Condoleezza Rice (Secretary of State)
Condi: The Condoleezza Rice Story by Antonia Felix (2002)

J. K. Rowling (Author)
J. K. Rowling: A Biography by Connie Ann Kirk (2003)

Esmerelda Santiago (Author and Screenwriter)
Almost a Woman by Esmerelda Santiago (1998)
When I Was Puerto Rican by Esmerelda Santiago (1993)

Pat Schroeder (Politician)
24 Years of House Work . . . and the Place Is Still a Mess: My Life in Politics by
   Pat Schroeder (1998)

Beverly Sills (Opera Singer)
Bubbles: A Self-Portrait by Beverly Sills (1976)
Beverly: An Autobiography by Beverly Sills and Lawrence Linderman (1987)

Barbra Streisand (Actress and Singer)
Her Name Is Barbra by Randall Riese (1993)

Maria Tallchief (Ballerina)
Maria Tallchief: America's Prima Ballerina by Maria Tallchief (1997)

Alice Walker (Author)
Alice Walker: A Life by Evelyn C. White (2004)

Heather Whitestone (Miss America, Motivational Speaker)
Yes, You Can, Heather! The Story of Heather Whitestone, Miss America 1995 by
   Daphne Gray (1995)
Listening With My Heart by Heather Whitestone and Angela Elwell Hunt
   (1998)

Christine Todd Whitman (Politician)
Growing Up Republican: Christie Whitman: The Politics of Character by
   Patricia Beard (1996)

Biographies of Men of Achievement

Lance Armstrong (Athlete)
It's Not About the Bike: My Journey Back to Life by Lance Armstrong and
   Sally Jenkins (2000)

Neil Armstrong (Astronaut)
First Man: The Life of Neil A. Armstrong by James R. Hansen (2005)

Arthur Ashe (Athlete)
Days of Grace: A Memoir by Arthur Ashe and Arnold Rampersad (1993)

Russell Baker (Author)
Growing Up by Russell Baker (1982)

Larry Bird (Athlete)
Drive: The Story of My Life by Larry Bird (1991)

Terry Bradshaw (Athlete and Sports Analyst)
Looking Deep by Terry Bradshaw (1989)
Keep It Simple by Terry Bradshaw and David Fisher (2002)

Tom Brokaw (Television Journalist and Author)
A Long Way From Home: Growing Up in the American Heartland in the Forties and Fifties by Tom Brokaw (2002)

Jim Carrey (Actor)
Jim Carrey: The Joker Is Wild by Martin Knelman (2000)

Ben Carson (Surgeon)
Gifted Hands: The Ben Carson Story by Ben Carson (1990)
Think Big: Unleashing Your Potential for Excellence by Ben Carson (1992)

Jimmy Carter (U.S. President)
An Hour Before Daylight: Memories of a Rural Boyhood by Jimmy Carter (2001)

Bart Conner (Athlete)
Winning the Gold by Bart Conner (1985)

Anderson Cooper (Television Journalist)
Dispatches From the Edge: A Memoir of Wars, Disasters, and Survival by Anderson Cooper (2006)

Bob Dole (Politician)
One Soldier's Story: A Memoir by Bob Dole (2005)

Michael J. Fox (Actor)
Always Looking Up: The Adventures of an Incurable Optimist by Michael J. Fox (2009)

Bill Gates (Entrepreneur)
Gates: How Microsoft's Mogul Reinvented an Industry—and Made Himself the Richest Man in America by Stephen Manes and Paul Andrews (1994)

John Glenn (Astronaut)
John Glenn: A Memoir by John Glenn and Nick Taylor (1999)

Tony Hawk (Athlete)
Hawk: Occupation: Skateboarder by Tony Hawk and Sean Mortimer (2000)

Homer Hickam, Jr. (Aerospace Engineer)
October Sky by Homer Hickam (1998)

Grant Hill (Athlete)
Change the Game: One Athlete's Thoughts on Sports, Dreams, and Growing Up by Grant Hill (1996)

Ron Howard (Film Director)
Ron Howard: From Mayberry to the Moon . . . and Beyond by Beverly Gray (2003)

Derek Jeter (Athlete)
The Life You Imagine: Life Lessons for Achieving Your Dreams by Derek Jeter and Jack Curry (2000)

Michael Jordan (Athlete)
Hang Time: Days and Dreams With Michael Jordan by Bob Greene (1992)

Bob Kerrey (Politician)
When I Was a Young Man by Bob Kerrey (2002)

Martin Luther King, Jr. (Civil Rights Leader)
The Autobiography of Martin Luther King, Jr. by Clayborne Carson (Ed.). (1998)

Carl Lewis (Athlete)
Inside Track: My Professional Life in Amateur Track and Field by Carl Lewis (1990)

Marcus Mabry (Journalist)
White Bucks and Black-Eyed Peas: Coming of Age Black in White America by Marcus Mabry (1995)

John McCain (Politician)
Faith of My Fathers by John McCain and Mark Salter (1999)

Ruben Navarette (Journalist)
A Darker Shade of Crimson: Odyssey of a Harvard Chicano by Ruben Navarette, Jr. (1993)

Barack Obama (U.S. President)
Dreams From My Father: A Story of Race and Inheritance by Barack Obama (2004)

Paul O'Neill (Athlete)
Me and My Dad: A Baseball Memoir by Paul O'Neill and Burton Rocks (2003)

Gordon Parks (Photographer and Film Director)
Voices in the Mirror: An Autobiography by Gordon Parks (1990)

Sidney Poitier (Actor, Film Director, and Author)
Life Beyond Measure: Letters to My Great-Granddaughter by Sidney Poitier (2008)

Colin Powell (Secretary of State)
My American Journey by Colin Powell and Joseph E. Persico (1995)
Colin Powell: A Biography by Richard Steins (2003)
Soldier: The Life of Colin Powell by Karen DeYoung (2006)

Dan Rather (Television Journalist)
I Remember by Dan Rather and Peter Wyden (1991)
Lone Star: The Extraordinary Life and Times of Dan Rather by Alan Weisman (2006)

Richard Rodriguez (Journalist)
Hunger of Memory: The Education of Richard Rodriguez by Richard Rodriguez (1982)

Days of Obligation: An Argument With my Mexican Father by Richard Rodriguez (1992)

Brown: The Last Discovery of America by Richard Rodriguez (2002)

Carl Rowan (Journalist)
Breaking Barriers by Carl Rowan (1991)

Tim Russert (Television Journalist)
Big Russ & Me: Father and Son: Lessons of Life by Tim Russert (2004)

Carlos Santana (Musician)
Carlos Santana: Back on Top by Marc Shapiro (2000)

Jerry Seinfeld (Comedian)
Seinfeld: The Making of an American Icon by Jerry Oppenheimer (2002)

Shel Silverstein (Poet and Cartoonist)
A Boy Named Shel: The Life and Times of Shel Silverstein by Lisa Rogak (2007)

Steven Spielberg (Film Director)
Steven Spielberg: A Biography by Joseph McBride (1997)

Josh Waitzkin (National Chess Champion and Martial Arts Champion)
The Art of Learning: An Inner Journey to Optimal Performance by Josh Waitzkin (2007)

J. C. Watts (Politician)
What Color Is a Conservative? My Life and Politics by J. C. Watts, Jr. (2002).

Carl Yastrzemski (Athlete)
Yaz: Baseball, the Wall, and Me by Carl Yastrzemski (1990)

Picture Book Biographies

Alvin Ailey (Dancer and Choreographer)
Alvin Ailey by Andrea Davis Pinkney (1995)

Buzz Aldrin (Astronaut)
Reaching for the Moon by Buzz Aldrin (2005)

Marian Anderson (Singer)
When Marian Sang: The True Recital of Marian Anderson by
    Pam Muñoz Ryan (2002)

John James Audubon (Naturalist)
The Boy Who Drew Birds: A Story of John James Audubon by
    Jacqueline Davies (2004)

Josephine Baker (Entertainer and Actress)
Ragtime Tumpie by Alan Schroeder (1989)

Ruby Bridges (Participant in the Civil Rights Movement)
The Story of Ruby Bridges by Robert Coles (1995)

Rachel Carson (Environmentalist)
Rachel: The Story of Rachel Carson by Amy Ehrlich (2003)

Marc Chagall (Artist)
I Am Marc Chagall by Bimba Landmann (2006)

César Chávez (Civil Rights Leader)
Harvesting Hope: The Story of Cesar Chavez by Kathleen Krull (2003)

Celia Cruz (Singer)
Celia Cruz: Queen of Salsa by Veronica Chambers (2005)

Leonardo DaVinci (Artist)
Leonardo, Beautiful Dreamer by Robert Byrd (2003)
Leonardo Da Vinci by Diane Stanley (1996)

Emily Dickinson (Writer)
Emily by Michael Bedard (1992)

Isadora Duncan (Dancer)
Isadora Dances by Rachel Isadora (1998)

Amelia Earhart (Aviation Pioneer)
Amelia Earhart: The Legend of the Lost Aviator by Shelley Tanaka (2008)
Amelia and Eleanor Go for a Ride by Pam Muñoz Ryan (1999)

Albert Einstein (Scientist)
Odd Boy Out: Young Albert Einstein by Don Brown (2004)

Duke Ellington (Composer, Pianist, and Big Band Leader)
Duke Ellington: The Piano Prince and His Orchestra by Andrea Davis Pinkney
   (1998)

Ella Fitzgerald (Singer)
Ella Fitzgerald: The Tale of a Vocal Virtuosa by Andrea Davis Pinkney (2002)

Anne Frank (Writer)
Anne Frank by Josephine Poole (2005)

Lou Gehrig (Athlete)
Lou Gehrig: The Luckiest Man by David A. Adler (1997)

Ted Geisel—Dr. Seuss (Writer)
The Boy on Fairfield Street: How Ted Geisel Grew Up to Become Dr. Seuss by
  Kathleen Krull (2004)

Althea Gibson (Athlete)
Nothing but Trouble: The Story of Althea Gibson by Sue Stauffacher (2007)

Dizzy Gillespie (Jazz Trumpet Player)
Dizzy by Jonah Winter (2006)

Woody Guthrie (Singer/Songwriter)
Woody Guthrie: Poet of the People by Bonnie Christensen (2001)

Langston Hughes (Poet, Novelist, and Playwright)
Coming Home: From the Life of Langston Hughes by Floyd Cooper (1994)
Langston Hughes: American Poet by Alice Walker (2002)

Frida Kahlo (Artist)
Frida by Jonah Winter (2002)

Martin Luther King, Jr. (Civil Rights Leader)
I've Seen the Promised Land: The Life of Martin Luther King, Jr. by Walter
  Dean Myers (2004)
Martin's Big Words: The Life of Martin Luther King, Jr. by Doreen Rappaport
  (2001)

Bruce Lee (Martial Artist and Actor)
Be Water, My Friend: The Early Years of Bruce Lee by Ken Mochizuki (2006)

Malcolm X (Civil Rights Leader)
Malcolm X: A Fire Burning Brightly by Walter Dean Myers (2000)

Nelson Mandela (Civil Rights Leader)
Nelson Mandela: Long Walk to Freedom by Chris van Wyk (2009)
Peaceful Protest: The Life of Nelson Mandela by Yona Zeldis McDonough (2002)

Michelangelo (Artist)
Michelangelo by Diane Stanley (2000)

Carlos Montezuma (Physician and Indian Rights Activist)
A Boy Named Beckoning: The True Story of Dr. Carlos Montezuma, Native American Hero by Gina Capaldi (2008)

John Muir (Environmentalist)
John Muir: America's First Environmentalist by Kathryn Lasky (2006)

Barack Obama (U.S. President)
Barack Obama: Son of Promise, Child of Hope by Nikki Grimes (2008)
Barack by Jonah Winter (2008)

Georgia O'Keeffe (Artist)
Georgia's Bones by Jen Bryant (2005)
My Name Is Georgia: A Portrait by Jeannette Winter (1998)

Satchel Paige (Athlete)
Satchel Paige by Lesa Cline-Ransome (2000)

Rosa Parks (Civil Rights Activist)
Rosa by Nikki Giovanni (2005)
If a Bus Could Talk: The Story of Rosa Parks by Faith Ringgold (2003)

Beatrix Potter (Writer and Illustrator)
Beatrix by Jeanette Winter (2003)

Diego Rivera (Artist)
Diego: Bigger Than Life by Carmen T. Bernier-Grand (2009)

Jackie Robinson (Baseball Player)
Testing the Ice: A True Story About Jackie Robinson by Sharon Robinson (2009)

Will Rogers (American Cowboy and Humorist)
Will Rogers: An American Legend by Frank Keating (2002)

Eleanor Roosevelt (First Lady)
Eleanor by Barbara Cooney (1996)

Teddy Roosevelt (U.S. President)
Young Teddy Roosevelt by Cheryl Harness (1998)

Wilma Rudolph (Athlete)
Wilma Unlimited: How Wilma Rudolph Became the World's Fastest Woman by
    Kathleen Krull (2000)

Elizabeth Cady Stanton (Social Activist and Abolitionist)
Elizabeth Leads the Way: Elizabeth Cady Stanton and the Right to Vote by
    Tanya Lee Stone (2008)

Jim Thorpe (Athlete)
Bright Path: Young Jim Thorpe by Don Brown (2006)

Sojourner Truth (Abolitionist)
Only Passing Through: The Story of Sojourner Truth by Anne Rockwell (2000)

Harriet Tubman (Abolitionist)
Minty: A Story of Young Harriet Tubman by Alan Schroeder (1996)
Moses: When Harriet Tubman Led Her People to Freedom by Carole Boston
    Weatherford (2006)

Phillis Wheatley (Poet)
Phillis's Big Test by Catherine Clinton (2008)

Walt Whitman (Poet)
Walt Whitman: Words for America by Barbara Kerley (2004)

Laura Ingalls Wilder (Writer)
Pioneer Girl: The Story of Laura Ingalls Wilder by William Anderson (1998)

Victoria Woodhull (Suffragist)
A Woman for President: The Story of Victoria Woodhull by Kathleen Krull
    (2004)

Orville and Wilbur Wright (Aviation Pioneers)
My Brothers' Flying Machine: Wilbur, Orville, and Me by Jane Yolen (2003)

Richard Wright (Writer)
Richard Wright and the Library Card by William Miller (1997)

Selected Bibliography of Films for Guided Viewing With Gifted Students

The annotated bibliography below contains selected movies that may be used in guided viewing sessions with gifted students. Teachers and counselors will want to consider the community's value system and select movies that are appropriate for use in school settings with children and adolescents. The following films were selected with this consideration in mind. The Motion Picture Association of America (MPAA) rating is provided for each film along with a suggested audience and key issues that might become the focus of a guided viewing lesson.

Akeelah and the Bee (2006)

Akeelah Anderson, a fifth grader in South Los Angeles, is feeling isolated from many students at Crenshaw Middle School because she is perceived as a "brainiac." Her natural aptitude for words spurs her principal to recruit her for competitive spelling bees. She joins forces with a coach,

Dr. Joshua Larabee, who is demanding but supports her as she proves her talent and moves on to compete in the Scripps National Spelling Bee. As Akeelah moves to higher levels of competition she encounters different expectations from family, spelling bee competitors, and her community.

Audience: Elementary/Middle School   MPAA Rating: PG
Key Issues for Discussion: family expectations for culturally diverse students; influence of a significant mentor; influence of peer group; setting high aspirations

Amazing Grace and Chuck (1987)
Chuck, a pitcher for his little league baseball team, learns about nuclear weapons and decides that he will refuse to pitch as a form of protest against them. Chuck's story makes its way to a star basketball player from the Boston Celtics, who agrees to join Chuck's protest and refuses to play as well. One by one, athletes from around the globe follow suit, earning Chuck the chance to sit down and talk with the President of the United States about eliminating nuclear weapons altogether.

Audience: Middle School   MPAA Rating: PG
Key Issues for Discussion: being true to self; influence of a significant mentor; sensitivity and emotionality in gifted students

Because of Winn-Dixie (2005)
Opal is a 10-year-old girl faced with another move with her preacher father. She adopts an orphaned dog, Winn-Dixie, named after the grocery store where she found him. The scruffy pet helps Opal to adjust to her new community, make new friends, and strengthen the troubled relationship with her father.

Audience: Elementary School   MPAA Rating: PG
Key Issues for Discussion: creativity and problem solving in young gifted females; father-daughter relationships

Bend It Like Beckham (2003)
Jess Bhamra is a high school student growing up in West London where her family has maintained their Indian heritage. Her parents have aspirations for their daughter to graduate from law school, learn to cook, and marry a nice Indian boy. Although she has posters of David Beckham covering the walls of her bedroom, her parents do not realize that, in her spare time,

she enjoys playing soccer with the boys in her neighborhood. Her talents in soccer are discovered and she is recruited to play for a local women's team. Jess spins a complex web of lies for her parents as she leads a double life of student and soccer player.

Audience: Middle School   MPAA Rating: PG-13
Key Issues for Discussion: balancing academics and athletics; family expectations for culturally diverse students; gender issues for gifted females; gifted girls supporting each other

The Competition (1980)

Heidi, a protégée of an internationally renowned pianist, earns the opportunity to compete in one of the music world's most challenging competitions. At the competition, Heidi meets and falls in love with Paul, a pianist who hopes to use the competition to help his financially strained family and alleviate stress for his father who has been diagnosed with cancer. Heidi becomes torn between whether or not to remove herself from the competition, knowing how important winning is to Paul. At the same time, Paul struggles with knowing that Heidi is more gifted than he. The two gifted musicians must examine their feelings and decide just where their relationship will take them.

Audience: High School   MPAA Rating: PG
Key Issues for Discussion: gender issues for gifted females; influence of a significant mentor; gifted females balancing careers and relationships

Dead Poets Society (1989)

John Keating is a new teacher whose unusual methods run contrary to the conservative nature of the New England prep academy in which he teaches. His passion for all things literary, however, inspires his students to discover their own love of poetry and to form a secret society with that as the focus. The story primarily follows two students, Neil Perry and Todd Anderson, each of whom goes through a journey of self-discovery with the help of Keating. Todd learns to deal with his substantial shyness and struggles to live up to the legacy of his highly successful older brother, while Neil's true nature emerges despite the best efforts of his extremely controlling father.

Audience: High School   MPAA Rating: PG
Key Issues for Discussion: identity development in gifted males; influence

of a significant mentor; parental expectations for gifted males; setting high aspirations

Dreamer (2006)

Ben Crane was a Kentucky horseman whose talents as a trainer were being wasted. Sonador was a horse with a promising future suddenly cut short by a broken leg. Considered useless by her owner, the injured filly is given to Crane as severance pay when he is fired. Ben's young daughter Cale uses her unwavering love of family and determination to bring her father and Sonador together in her quest to reach what others consider an impossible goal—to win the Breeder's Cup Classic.

Audience: Elementary   MPAA Rating: PG
Key Issues for Discussion: appreciating intelligence in young girls; developing resilience to overcome adversity; father-daughter relationships; leadership talent in young girls

Ellen Foster (1997)

This movie features the story of a gifted, resilient young girl who is left alone following the death of her mother. She draws inner strength from her loving memories of her mother as she is forced to move from relative to relative in search of a family to replace her mother and abusive father. Her wealthy and bitter grandmother eventually takes her in, although Ellen's life in her grandmother's house becomes more emotionally desolate than ever. This intelligent young girl takes her situation into her own hands, designing a plan that she hopes will provide her happiness. In the end, Ellen's remarkable inner strength and determination enables her to free herself of her dysfunctional relatives and the emotionally traumatic events of her childhood.

Audience: Elementary/Middle School   MPAA Rating: PG-13
Key Issues for Discussion: developing resilience to overcome adversity; influence of a significant mentor; creativity and problem solving in young gifted females

The Emperor's Club (2002)

William Hundert is a revered teacher of Western Civilization at St. Benedict's Academy, an all-boys private school. Each year St. Benedict's holds a contest in which the top three students answer questions about Roman history in a public tournament. The winner is crowned Mr. Julius

Caesar. In his work with the group of highly intelligent young men, Mr. Hundert meets a challenge, Sedgwick Bell, the rebellious son of an influential state senator. Mr. Hundert succeeds in motivating Sedgewick to study for the Mr. Julius Caesar contest but when the contest takes place, he realizes that Sedgewick is cheating. Bell loses the contest, and returns to his rebellious ways. Twenty-five years later, Bell, a wealthy business tycoon, wants to reclaim his intellectual honor by sponsoring a rematch of the Julius Caesar contest and Mr. Hundert learns a difficult lesson regarding character development in men.

Audience: High School   MPAA Rating: PG-13
Key Issues for Discussion: identity development in gifted males; influence of competition in academic settings; moral development in gifted individuals

The Ernest Green Story (1993)

This biographical film depicts the true story of one young man's battle to overcome racial intolerance in the segregated South of the 1950s. Ernest Green, along with eight other gifted African American high school students, comprised a group of the first students to integrate Little Rock's Central High School. Ernest and his peers face racial epithets, abusive mobs, biased teachers, and an uncooperative state government. With the help of mentoring from his grandfather, Ernest emerges as the leader and offers inspiration and encouragement to his friends. The courage and resilience of these nine teenagers allow them to cope with the adversity and overcome the inhumane treatment that they have experienced.

Audience: High School   MPAA Rating: Not Rated
Key Issues for Discussion: developing resilience to overcome adversity; developing a racial identity; influence of a significant mentor; setting high aspirations

Finding Forrester (2000)

Jamal Wallace, an African American teenager living in the Bronx, is given a unique opportunity to attend one of New York's finest prep schools when he performs extremely well on a statewide standardized exam. Upon arriving at the new school, however, he discovers that his test scores were just as important to the administration as his skills on the basketball court. Distraught by the entire incident, Jamal has a chance encounter with William Forrester, a Pulitzer Prize winning author, who helps Jamal to pursue writing, his off-the-court passion. With Forrester's help, Jamal is able to overcome a number of challenges in his new environment, while having a powerful effect on his new mentor in the process.

Audience: High School   MPAA Rating: PG-13
Key Issues for Discussion: influence of a significant mentor; parental expectations for gifted culturally diverse males; influence of peer group; pursuing one's passion

Fly Away Home (1996)
After her mother's tragic death, 13 year-old Amy moves from New Zealand to Canada to live with her father. While struggling to adjust to her new surroundings, Amy discovers a nest of abandoned goose eggs. After they have hatched, she takes care of the goslings, raising them with the care that one would expect from a new mother. When the authorities inform her that it is illegal to raise wild geese without clipping their wings Amy decides that she would rather teach them to fly with the help of her father and a pair of hang gliders.

Audience: Middle School   MPAA Rating: PG
Key Issues for Discussion: dealing with the loss of a loved one; creativity and problem solving; paternal influence on gifted females; finding friends in a new environment

Frankie & Hazel (2000)
Francesca "Frankie" Humphreys and her best friend Hazel Perez are two multitalented middle school girls growing up in a small New Jersey town. Frankie is an accomplished ballerina who wants to pursue playing baseball. Frankie's grandmother and guardian has definite plans for her granddaughter's future in ballet, however. Frankie is torn emotionally as she attempts to please her grandmother while also following her own interests. Meanwhile, the charismatic Hazel has aspirations of becoming the first teenager elected mayor of her community. She dives into her role as a community activist and gains community support for her campaign to improve the town.

Audience: Middle School   MPAA Rating: Not Rated
Key Issues for Discussion: gifted girls supporting each other; gender expectations for gifted young women; coping with familial expectations; leadership talent in young women

Freedom Writers (2007)

Erin Gruwell is a new English teacher who leaves her comfortable California suburb to teach in a tough, highly diverse Long Beach high school. Faced with serious racial tensions, Erin succeeds in building trust with her students when she incorporates innovative methods to teach the Holocaust and helps them to write about challenges from their own lives. Although she faces unsupportive colleagues, she enjoys the success of her students as they graduate and move on to college.

Audience: High School   MPAA Rating: PG-13
Key Issues for Discussion: developing resilience to overcome adversity; influence of a significant teacher as mentor; social injustice and discrimination; setting high aspirations

The Great Debaters (2007)

In the 1930s, the historically black Wiley College in Marshall, TX, celebrated the efforts of its debate coach Melvin B. Tolson. During a time when Jim Crow laws were common and lynch mobs were a pervasive fear for African Americans, Tolson coached his team to a nearly undefeated season and experienced the first interracial collegiate debates in our country. The Wiley debaters, a team of four including a female student and a 14-year-old, received an invitation to compete against Harvard University's national championship team.

Audience: High School   MPAA Rating: PG-13
Key Issues for Discussion: belief in self; developing resilience to overcome adversity; influence of a significant mentor; setting high aspirations

Gross Anatomy (1989)

Joe Slovak is a brilliant first-year medical school student whose casual, nonconforming approach to life becomes tested by a challenging anatomy course. Joe's free-spirited, independent style puts him at odds with Dr. Rachel Woodruff, a demanding professor who questions whether or not this gifted underachiever has what it takes to be a doctor. As Joe approaches the challenges of medical school in his own way, Dr. Woodruff begins to appreciate his brilliant mind and challenges him with a complex medical case study. As he works through the case, he struggles with existential questions regarding medicine and whether it is the right career path for him.

Audience: High School   MPAA Rating: PG-13
Key Issues for Discussion: identity and moral development in gifted males; selective achievement in gifted individuals; alignment of one's value system with life goals

I'll Remember April (1999)

This movie follows the lives of Pee Wee, Duke, Tyler, and Willy, a group of 10-year-old boys growing up on the coast of California during World War II. Duke has an older brother serving in the Marines, and much of what his brother shares with him in his wartime letters becomes part of the daily military reenactments of the four young boys. Willy is a Japanese American whose family is being sent to an internment camp. When he and his family experience racism directed at Japanese Americans, his friends come to his support. After hearing of Japanese submarines off the Pacific coast, the boys enjoy fantasizing about being Marines in search of the enemy. While patrolling the beach, they discover a Japanese sailor who is stranded and wounded. Determined to become heroes, they take him prisoner and keep him a secret from their parents. When the sailor rescues Duke from drowning, the boys befriend their prisoner and struggle with a pact that could betray their country.

Audience: Elementary School   MPAA Rating: G
Key Issues for Discussion: moral development in young gifted males; influence of peer groups; children coping with social injustice and bigotry

The Journey of Natty Gann (1985)

America is mired in the Great Depression, a time when families were often forced to live apart when jobs were available in another part of the country. In this setting, an intelligent and courageous young girl confronts overwhelming odds when she embarks on a cross-country journey in search of her father. During her quest, she forms a close bond with two traveling companions: a protective wolf and a hardened drifter. This film offers a moving story of courage, perseverance, and applying one's intelligence to solve life's problems.

Audience: Elementary School   MPAA Rating: PG
Key Issues for Discussion: creative problem solving in gifted young women; development of resilience to overcome adversity

Little Man Tate (1991)

Fred is a 7-year-old genius being raised by a single mother in New York City. Having trouble fitting in with other children and struggling to make friends, Fred garners the attention of Dr. Jane Grierson, a psychologist who runs a program that addresses the needs of gifted children. Fred's mother Dede agrees, but has second thoughts as she becomes further and further removed from Fred's upbringing. As he is pushed through Dr. Grierson's program, Dede fears that he is missing out on a normal childhood, and must learn to be the mother that Fred has needed all along.

Audience: Elementary-Middle School   MPAA Rating: PG
Key Issues for Discussion: asynchronous development; importance of friendship for gifted children; importance of parental support for talent development

Lucas (1986)

Lucas is an awkward, eccentric high school freshman who has always struggled with his desire to be popular while paying less and less attention to the students who have always considered him a friend. Upon befriending Maggie, a pretty cheerleader who is new to the town, Lucas decides to stand up to those who have always bullied him by trying out for the school football team. With Maggie and big man on campus Cappie at his side, Lucas embarks on a journey of friendship, self-discovery, and football that earns him the respect and admiration of his peers.

Audience: Middle School   MPAA Rating: PG-13
Key Issues for Discussion: importance of friendship for gifted males; examination of stereotypes; value of intellectual and athletic pursuits

Mad Hot Ballroom (2005)

A group of 11-year-old New York City public school students explore the world of ballroom dancing and learn a lot about themselves in the process. Told from the children's perspectives, this documentary presents their experiences as they engage in 10 weeks of lessons in tango, foxtrot, swing, rumba, and merengue and prepare for the culminating citywide competition. Interspersed throughout the film are the students' candid reflections on their lives and the complexity of childhood in a big city. The students triumph in the competition and their teachers celebrate the accomplishment of these new young "ladies and gentlemen."

Audience: Elementary School   MPAA Rating: PG
Key Issues for Discussion: pursuit of one's passion; importance of healthy competition; setting high aspirations

Matilda (1996)

Matilda Wormwood is a bright, sweet young girl whose desire to read books and learn about the world around her is virtually the only thing she cares about. Unfortunately for her, she faces obstacles in almost every direction, from her bratty brother to her evil parents to quite possibly the meanest school principal in history. While at school, Matilda befriends a teacher named Miss Honey, whom she later learns was also terrorized by the principal. Using her remarkable intelligence and a gift for telekinesis, Matilda vows to set things right for Miss Honey and outwit the evil adults in her life.

Audience: Elementary School   MPAA Rating: PG
Key Issues for Discussion: need for acceptance; influence of a teacher as mentor; family issues for gifted children

The Mighty (1998)

The Mighty is a story of two young men who come together as outcasts. Kevin Dillon, a highly gifted yet physically challenged youngster, develops a close friendship with his neighbor Max Cain when he becomes his reading tutor. In return, Max protects him from adversaries in their middle school. Although they both have problems that label them as pariahs, Kevin and Max realize that by combining their strengths and remaining united, they can overcome their individual limitations.

Audience: Middle School   MPAA Rating: PG-13
Key Issues for Discussion: importance of friendship for gifted males; development of resilience to overcome adversity; creative problem solving in gifted young men

Mona Lisa Smile (2003)

Katherine Watson, a first-year art history professor arrives at the prestigious and conservative Wellesley College in the 1950s. She soon discovers that the young women in her classes may be exceptional in their memorization of art history but have much to learn about becoming critical consumers of art. She works diligently to challenge her students and to convince the college's administrators that her unconventional teaching practices require her students to think critically. As she struggles with her own romantic relationships, she mentors the young women as several of them question the traditional societal expectations for females. When the school's administrators hesitate to renew her contract, she decides to leave for Europe and realizes that her young protégés have learned to appreciate her as a teacher, friend, and role model.

Audience: High School   MPAA Rating: PG-13
Key Issues for Discussion: gender issues for gifted females; cultural, community, and familial expectations for gifted females; influence of a significant mentor

Mr. Holland's Opus (1995)
Glenn Holland possesses one lifelong dream—to compose a piece of music that will leave a lasting impression on the world. While struggling to come up with that one perfect piece, Mr. Holland takes a job teaching music at a local school. In dealing with a number of issues, including his wife's pregnancy and a deaf son who will be unable to hear the music on which he works so hard, he discovers that success is not necessarily about that one perfect piece of music. Instead, he finds that sharing something that gives you so much joy with the rest of the world can be just as rewarding.

Audience: High School   MPAA Rating: PG
Key Issues for Discussion: influence of a significant mentor; setting high aspirations; pursuit of one's passion

My Girl (1991)
This film presents the story of one summer in the life of Vada Sultenfuss, a gifted 11-year-old girl growing up in the 1970s. Vada lives with her widowed father and elderly grandmother in their home, which is attached to her father's funeral parlor. Vada, a creative writer, is delighted when she learns her heartthrob, a fourth-grade teacher, is offering a summer poetry class. She enrolls in the adult class and spends her summer struggling with her schoolgirl crush on her teacher. When her father announces his engagement. Vada struggles to accept a replacement for her mother. Moreover, she must overcome the tragic loss of her friend Thomas when he dies from an allergic response to being stung by a hive of bees. With emotional support from family and friends, Vada ends her summer by writing a memorial poem in honor of her beloved friend, enabling her to apply her creativity and deal with her grief.

Audience: Elementary School   MPAA Rating: PG
Key Issues for Discussion: appreciating intelligence in young girls; importance of close friendships; nurturing one's imagination and creativity; dealing with the tragic loss of a loved one; father-daughter relationships

October Sky (1999)

Homer Hickam has no reason to think that he will be any different from other boys growing up in Coalwood, WV, where all young men are expected to become coal miners like their fathers. Homer has no way out of his predetermined life, until 1957 when Sputnik flies over his community. Homer begins a mission to build and launch his own homemade rockets with a group of his loyal friends. Although their frequent mishaps get the "Rocket Boys" in trouble, the small mining community becomes more intrigued with their scientific endeavors, offering resources and support. The efforts of the four aspiring scientists are supported by their science teacher who encourages them to enter the state science fair competition with hopes of securing college scholarships. When the Rocket Boys win the national science fair, earning themselves college scholarships, Homer's father begins to appreciate his son's determination and passion for science.

Audience: Middle/High School   MPAA Rating: PG
Key Issues for Discussion: peer group influence; parental expectations for gifted males; athletic pursuits versus intellectual pursuits; influence of a significant mentor

A Painted House (2003)

During the long hot summer of 1952, 10-year-old Luke Chandler experiences a chapter in his life that will shape him as an adult. As the grandson of a cotton farmer in the Arkansas Delta, Luke observes two groups of migrant workers and two very dangerous men working on his family's farm. Several horrific events take place, and Luke must shelter dark secrets that could shatter lives. As the young boy experiences this complex summer, someone is furtively painting the bare clapboards of the Chandler farmhouse, slowly bathing the dilapidated farmhouse in gleaming white.

Audience: Elementary/Middle School   MPAA Rating: G
Key Issues for Discussion: being true to self; moral development in gifted boys; importance of emotional support from family

Pictures of Hollis Woods (2007)

Hollis Woods is an artistically talented 12-year-old girl who has spent most of her life in foster homes. To her social worker she is trouble because she skips school and runs away, even from the Regans, the one family who wants to give her a real home. When she is placed with Josie Cahill, a quirky retired art teacher, she wants to stay; however, she sees that the loving elderly woman is growing more forgetful every day. Hollis knows that if her social worker discovers this she will be removed from Josie's care, so she plans their winter escape. Through her art and her care of Josie, Hollis ultimately finds her family.

Audience: Elementary School   MPAA Rating: G

Key Issues for Discussion: emotional support from families; art as therapy; emotional sensitivity in gifted girls; developing resilience to overcome adversity

Pride (2007)

Jim Ellis is an aspiring teacher with a lifelong passion for competitive swimming. When he takes a position supervising a deserted recreation center in one of the toughest neighborhoods in Philadelphia, he becomes determined to recruit disenchanted teenagers and transform them into championship swimmers. Despite his challenges with racism, violence, and unsupportive city officials, Ellis takes his team to the state swimming championships where his protégés who represent the Philadelphia Department of Recreation (PDR) exhibit the pride, determination, and resilience he has instilled in them.

Audience: High School   MPAA Rating: PG-13

Key Issues for Discussion: belief in self; developing resilience to overcome adversity; mentors for talent development; social injustice and discrimination

The Red Sneakers (2002)

Reggie Reynolds is the dedicated manager of his urban high school basketball team. His problem is that he wants to be a basketball superstar but his dreams of becoming a college player seem impossible because Reggie is intellectually gifted, but not athletically talented. When the neighborhood junkman sells him a magical pair of red sneakers, he becomes an overnight sensation who leads his team to the New York City high school finals. As Reggie enjoys his instant success, he struggles with the jealousy of his teammates, his mother's changing views of his intellectual abilities, the high scholarly expectations of his math teacher, and a new set of adoring female admirers. In addition, sport scouts descend upon Reggie to offer him a golden future. In the end, Reggie acknowledges his true gifts and remains true to himself and those he loves.

Audience: Elementary School   MPAA Rating: G
Key Issues for Discussion: talent development in urban youth; anti-intellectualism; influence of peer group; societal pressure to be athletic

Ruby Bridges (1998)

This movie presents the inspirational story of Ruby Bridges, a gifted 6-year-old girl chosen to be the first African American child to integrate the New Orleans public schools in the 1960s. Although she is subjected to traumatizing racism for the first time, the love and emotional support of her devoted parents combined with the deep religious faith of her family enables her to develop the resilience she needs to cope with the stress she undergoes each day. This little girl's story of her heroic struggle for a better education is a story of a gifted child displaying exquisite dignity and courage as she continues to believe in herself, her family, and the important mission for which she was chosen.

Audience: Elementary School   MPAA Rating: Not Rated
Key Issues for Discussion: developing resilience to overcome adversity; internal strength and courage in gifted young children; importance of family support

Rudy (1993)

For as long as Rudy Ruettiger has dreamed about playing football at The University of Notre Dame, there has been a friend, family member, teacher, or classmate at his side to tell him that it will never happen. With only his best friend Pete to support him, Rudy keeps the dream alive while working in a factory in suburban Chicago. After Pete's tragic death, Rudy decides that the time to fulfill his dream has come, and heads to Notre Dame to take his shot. With the help of an unlikely mentor, Rudy will attempt to succeed in that which almost no one would ever have thought possible.

Audience: Middle/High School   MPAA Rating: PG
Key Issues for Discussion: familial expectations; importance of friendship; setting high aspirations; importance of a significant mentor

The Sandy Bottom Orchestra (2000)

Norman and Ingrid Green and their 14-year-old daughter Rachel are considered an eccentric family in Sandy Bottom, WI. Ingrid is a sophisticated woman who has abandoned her promising career as a classical pianist to follow her dairy farmer husband to the rural community. As the head of the local church choir, she spends her days trying to introduce new selections of music to the congregation and challenge the community's rural mentality. Norman dreams of being an orchestra conductor. Rachel, a gifted high school freshman, struggles to find friends who appreciate her. As she excels academically, she also outgrows her private violin lessons and her parents struggle with whether to have their daughter audition for a private arts academy. When her father decides to produce a classical concert for the community, both Rachel and Ingrid become members of the orchestra. With the overwhelming success of the concert, the Greens celebrate their community's acceptance and realize that Sandy Bottom is the town where they belong.

Audience: Middle/High School   MPAA Rating: Not Rated
Key Issues for Discussion: being true to self; finding a place where you are appreciated; influence of a significant mentor; women's choices between career and family

The Sandlot (1993)

Fifth grader Scott Smalls is finding it difficult to make new friends after he moves to California with his mother and his athletic stepfather. He idolizes a group of baseball-playing kids in the neighborhood, but fears that he may be too awkward and nonathletic to play with them. After the group's best player takes Scott under his wing, Scott learns valuable lessons about friendship, honesty, and being a 10-year-old.

Audience: Elementary/Middle School   MPAA Rating: PG
Key Issues for Discussion: importance of friendship; creative problem solving in gifted males; balancing academics and athletics; parental influence on gifted males

Searching for Bobby Fischer (1993)

The story of the world champion chess player, Bobby Fischer, serves as a backdrop for this movie. In this story, 7-year-old Josh Waitzkin becomes intrigued with men playing chess in a New York City neighborhood park. When his parents recognize his fascination for the game and his natural talent for chess, his father finds a chess teacher for his son. Under his guidance, Josh brings home impressive trophies from multiple competitions. Josh's father, a sports journalist, becomes overly enthusiastic about his son's abilities as a competitor while his mother, recognizing Josh's sensitivities, points out to her son what is most important in life. Josh's mentor begins to build the competitive edge in his young protégé, insisting that he have contempt for his opponents; however, Josh resists. The tensions between his parents mount and Josh fears disappointing his father.

Audience: Elementary/Middle School   MPAA Rating: PG
Key Issues for Discussion: influence of a significant mentor; importance of healthy competition; dealing with parental expectations

School of Life (2005)
When Michael D'Angelo, a new social studies teacher, arrives at Fallbrook Middle School, he brings a much different approach to teaching. As his students engage in lively discussions and historical reenactments, they realize that Mr. D does not just teach history, he lives it. His passion for the subject becomes infectious yet one frustrated teacher is threatened by the students' enthusiastic response to the dynamic newcomer. When he attempts to learn more about Mr. D's background, he discovers why the inspirational teacher approaches everything he does with so much passion. From Mr. D, the students and teachers at Fallbrook Middle School learn important life lessons not taught in textbooks.

Audience: Elementary/Middle School   MPAA Rating: PG
Key Issues for Discussion: appreciating individual differences; belief in self; facing life's challenges; influence of a teacher as mentor

Selma, Lord, Selma (1999)
This uplifting true story presents the childhood of Sheyann Webb, a charismatic young African American girl living in Selma, AL, during the turbulent Civil Rights Movement. Sheyann sneaks off from her fifth-grade friends before school begins and meets Dr. Martin Luther King, Jr., who is visiting her community. Inspired by Dr. King, she becomes involved in the marches for freedom. Sheyann finds herself the only elementary school student involved in the movement and remains committed to the cause despite the admonitions of her parents and teachers. She finds support in the friendship of a young White seminarian, a Freedom Fighter from the North struggling to get the Black community members registered to

vote. Eventually, Sheyann's passion for the cause convinces her teachers to become active in the movement.

Audience: Elementary/Middle School   MPAA Rating: G
Key Issues for Discussion: developing resilience to overcome adversity in life; importance of courage in pursuit of a goal

Shrek (2001)

Shrek is an ogre who inspires fear in the hearts of the residents of nearby Dulac. Shrek doesn't seem to mind, however, as he has always enjoyed living alone just outside the town and appreciates the peace and quiet. After Shrek's home is taken from him and the beautiful Princess Fiona is kidnapped by the evil Lord Farquaad, Shrek is forced to abandon his life of solitude in order to save them both. Along with his dear friend Donkey, they discover the value of persistence and learn an important lesson about appearances in the midst of their quest.

Audience: Elementary/Middle School   MPAA Rating: PG
Key Issues for Discussion: importance of friendship; acceptance of individual differences; importance of courage in pursuit of a goal

Smoke Signals (1998)

Victor Joseph and Thomas Builds the Fire are two Native American teenagers living on a reservation. Victor is tall, athletic, handsome, and angry; Thomas is gifted, awkward, wears thick glasses, and constantly shares colorful stories. Although they are very different from each other, the budding relationship between Thomas and Victor provides both young men with the support they need to cope with the adversity in their lives. Victor's father, an abusive man, abandoned his family when Victor was a child. When Victor learns of his father's death, he and Thomas travel to Arizona to recover his father's ashes. The journey and subsequent adventure allow Victor to begin to come to terms with his father's life and death.

Audience: High School   MPAA Rating: PG-13
Key Issues for Discussion: developing resilience to overcome adversity; father-son relationships; friendships between gifted males; coping with anger toward missing parents

Spellbound (2002)

This powerful documentary follows eight highly intelligent young people as they compete in the national spelling bee sponsored every spring by Scripps-Howard newspapers. Through vignettes of their daily preparation, family life, and local and regional competitions, viewers gain an insider's look into the culture surrounding such a competition and enjoy the diversity of the eight unique personalities. Viewers also listen to their reflections on studying, competition, victory, and defeat. Once at the national bee in Washington, DC, we observe the competition, celebrate with the final champion, and empathize with those who have come so close.

Audience: Middle/High School   MPAA Rating: G
Key Issues for Discussion: value of persistence; keeping competition in perspective; parental expectations; celebrating diversity in gifted youth

Stand and Deliver (1988)

This film features the biographical story of Jaime Escalante, a math teacher in a tough East Los Angeles high school. He draws upon his own cultural heritage and forms a bond with his largely Hispanic student body. Mr. Escalante dedicates countless hours motivating his students and preparing them for the Advanced Placement (AP) examination. With Escalante as their teacher, the students' academic achievements greatly improve and they excel on the exam. Regardless of their outstanding performance, the AP test administrators do not believe that a group of culturally diverse students from an urban high school are capable of such success. Accusations of cheating take place and Escalante and his students must prove the authorities are wrong.

Audience: High School   MPAA Rating: PG
Key Issues for Discussion: developing resilience to overcome adversity; pursuing one's passion; social injustice and discrimination

Up (2009)

Carl Frederickson, a quiet and shy boy, befriends an outgoing tomboy named Ellie. When Ellie tells Carl of her dreams of moving her clubhouse to Paradise Falls, a majestic waterfall cliff in South America, Carl promises to help her. Carl and Ellie are married, enjoy life, and grow old together. When Ellie dies, she leaves Carl a lonely widower. Rather than be forced into a retirement home, he is determined to fulfill his promise to his wife. He turns their house into a makeshift airship using thousands of helium balloons to lift it off the ground. Russell, a young Wilderness Explorer trying to earn his final merit badge for assisting the elderly, becomes a stowaway on Carl's flying house and joins him on his adventure. With his young friend's help Carl discovers that the real adventures of life that should never be overlooked are the important relationships we have with people around us.

Audience: Elementary School–Adult   MPAA Rating: PG
Key Issues for Discussion: celebrating lifespan changes; pursuing one's dream; managing grief and loneliness; importance of friendships; developing resilience to overcome adversity; heroes as flawed individuals

The War (1994)
During the summer of 1970, Stu and Lidia Simmons watch their father, a Vietnam veteran, return home to Mississippi from the war with high hopes of rebuilding his life and buying a home for his family. Wounded physically and psychologically, he is unable to keep a job. As their father struggles with his scars from the war, he shares his pacifist philosophy about violence with his children. Both Stu and Lidia gain a new appreciation for their father's beliefs about getting along with others. As they face adolescent challenges, they remain inspired by their father's example and succeed in strengthening their close-knit family.

Audience: Middle School   MPAA Rating: PG-13
Key Issues for Discussion: developing resilience to overcome adversity; important relationships between father and children

Wide Awake (1998)
Joshua Beal, a highly sensitive, intelligent fifth grader, attends an all-boys Catholic school. Following the death of Joshua's grandfather, who was also his best friend and role model, Joshua feels lost, despite the fact that his family and friends offer emotional support. This poignant film examines the young boy's struggle to understand mortality, and his preoccupation with knowing whether or not his grandfather is in heaven. Throughout the movie, Joshua faces typical adolescent issues such as coping with a school-yard bully, discovering girls, and developing empathy for boys who are not appreciated by their peer group. Through these experiences, Joshua confronts his issues and realizes that he is "wide awake" with a new awareness of life.

Audience: Elementary School   MPAA Rating: PG
Key Issues for Discussion: dealing with the loss of a loved one; sensitivity in gifted young males; importance of friendship

Wild Hearts Can't Be Broken (1991)
Living in the 1930s, young Sonora Webster dreams of becoming a "diving girl," riding a horse as it dives into the pool below. After leaving her home in Georgia to pursue this dream, a tragic accident leaves Sonora blind, forcing her to question the possibility of making her dream a reality. Overcoming her disability and a striking lack of support from the other individuals involved with the diving horse act, Sonora proves that persistence and dedication can go a very long way.

Audience: Elementary/Middle School   MPAA Rating: G
Key Issues for Discussion: Overcoming a disability; gender issues for gifted females; creative problem solving; developing resilience in the face of adversity

With Honors (1994)
Montgomery Kessler, a Harvard University senior, is determined to graduate summa cum laude. His computer crashes as he is completing his senior thesis. On the way to the library to photocopy a backup version of his printed work, his only copy of the thesis falls into the hands of Simon Wilder, a homeless man living in the basement of Harvard's library. The homeless gentleman who survives by his applied intelligence drives a hard bargain with Monty as he agrees to return the thesis for food, shelter, and favors for each individual page. As Monty and Simon develop a life-changing friendship, Monty views life through Simon's perspective, leading him to question his values and restructure his philosophical world view.

Audience: High School   MPAA Rating: PG-13
Key Issues for Discussion: being true to self; sensitivity and empathy in gifted males; gifted students developing a personal code of ethics

About the Author

Thomas P. Hébert is a professor of educational psychology at the University of Georgia in Athens, where he teaches graduate courses in gifted and creative education and qualitative research methods. He has been a teacher for 13 years, 10 of which were spent working with gifted students at the elementary, middle, and high school levels. He served on the board of directors of the National Association for Gifted Children (NAGC). His work has been recognized by various professional organizations. He was the inaugural recipient of the Mary M. Frasier Equity and Excellence Award from the Georgia Association for Gifted Children (2008) for his research contributions on diverse students. He received the 2008 Neag School of Education Outstanding Alumnus Research Award from The University of Connecticut. The University of Georgia College of Education awarded him a Faculty Research Leave Award in 2008 during which time he traveled throughout the country conducting research on high-achieving men who have overcome serious adversity. In 2000, NAGC named Dr. Hébert an Early Scholar. He conducts workshops nationally and internationally on topics related to gifted education. His areas of research interest include social and emotional development of gifted children, underachievement, culturally diverse gifted students, and problems faced by gifted young men.

Name Index

Jamison, W., 147–148, 150–151, 158, 162, 164–166, 179
Janos, P., 201–202
Janus, S. S., 100
Jenner, B., 274
Johnson, R., 359
Jones, D. J., 157–158
Josselson, R., 155–157, 163, 165–166

Kamprad, I., 274
Kanevsky, L., 244–245
Karinch, M., 269
Karnes, F. A., 98
Kearney, K., 21
Keel, P., 224
Keighley, T., 244–245
Kelly, V., 25–26
Kennedy, D. M., 344, 346
Kerr, F., 258
Kerry, J., 233, 246–255, 268
Keyes, R., 188–189
King, D. S., 274
King, M. L., Jr., 17, 39, 48, 70, 136–137
Kluger, J., 194
Knight, H. V., 98
Koehler, J. L., 71–72
Kranz, L., 224
Kuninsky, S., 362

Labonte, R., 45
Ladson-Billings, G. J., 328–329, 339
Lael, S., 222
Lafrenz, N., 307
Lansford, J. E., 183
Larke, J., 329–330
Lauren, J., 299
Lavoie, R., 304

Leno, J., 101–102, 116, 274
Leppien, J., 177–179
Lewis, B., 81–82, 87, 96, 98, 116
Lim, K., 84–85
Linn, K.-H., 357–358
Locke, D. C., 325
Lorig, S., 224
Louganis, G., 274, 299
Lovecky, D., 65, 97
Lundsteen, S., 73

Mabry, M., 315–316, 322, 331, 338
Maccoby, E. E., 192
Malikow, M., 114
Mandela, N., 39, 48
Mankiller, W., 313–314, 326, 331, 339
Manning, M. L., 337
Marcia, J., 163, 165–166
Marcus, J., 82
Marshall, K., 281, 290–291, 296
Marwood, K. A., 202
Maslow, A., 97–98
Mayer, J., 10–11, 34–38
McBee, M., 134, 209, 212, 223
McCoach, D. B., 233–234, 239, 245–246, 266–267, 269, 275–276
McEwen, M. K., 157
McGinnis, J. C., 98
McKay, H., 74
McLaughlin, S. C., 114
McNair, L., 352
Mendaglio, S., 14, 27–28, 275, 285–286
Michener, J., 121
Midler, B., 117–122, 127–128, 141, 143, 189, 223
Milner, H. R., 239

Subject Index